Praise for *The Little Book of the Autism Spectrum*

As head teacher of a specialist support primary school which has amongst its numbers over 50 pupils with autism I can see a place for this book on the shelves of our resource library. It would be a useful addition to support both parents and practitioners. Easy to read, with bite size nuggets of useful information, the book flows logically, touching on the key areas involved in supporting children with autism. The book provides a basic introduction to the subject of autism, an overview and some manageable strategies and tips to implement.

Dr Samantha Todd has set out in an easily accessible and undaunting way a useful guide book or check list for the teacher wishing to know they have 'got it right.' The book details the key areas that need to be in place to maximise the potential for pupils to make progress and goes on to tell you what you can do to support those learning areas.

Andy Pitts M.Ed autism, Head Teacher,
The Birches Specialist Support Primary School, Manchester

This is a very nice, concisely written work that will be especially helpful for parents trying to get 'up to speed' when their children are newly diagnosed. The book covers a wealth of material quickly without over simplifying. Highly recommended both for finding practical solutions and for better understanding the 'big picture' of what an individual on the spectrum may be experiencing.

Lars Perner, PhD Assistant Professor of Clinical Marketing,
Marshall School of Business, University of Southern California

This excellent little book, cogently written by Dr Samantha Todd fills a useful gap in the literature about autism spectrum disorder. The author, a clinical psychologist working in Manchester, has written a very accessible book which will be appreciated equally by parents and carers as well as by professionals working in children's services. The many themes covered in the book will be particularly relevant to those working in schools and early years settings responsible for autistic children, especially teachers and support staff.

The book is helpfully divided into three sections namely:

1. Understanding the autism spectrum

2. Developing skills and promoting well-being in children and young people with autism.

3. Working with behaviour

Beginning with the assessment process and covering the many questions facing anxious parents at the time of diagnosis, the author helpfully demystifies much of the jargon and the plethora of medical labels which cause confusion for families and also many professionals.

There follows a thoughtful account of the benefits to society of neurodiversity and the positive contribution made by people who are thought to be unusual or different.

For me, however, the key section is found in Chapter 4 where the author introduces the concept of 'the autism lens', a theme which involves the reader viewing aspects of home and school life specifically from the viewpoint of the youngster with autism. This metaphor is developed throughout the remainder of the book and enables the reader to appreciate the subtle differences which impact the lives of children and young people with autism.

The third section of the book focuses on working with aspects of behaviour and will be helpful to everyone attempting to understand, analyse and manage behaviour that is considered challenging in the home and the wider community including educational settings.

The Little Book also contains humorous illustrations of real-life situations and key learning points are provided as a helpful summary to each chapter. Furthermore, the glossary and references are useful aides for follow-up.

Personally I found *The Little Book of the Autistic Spectrum* a fascinating read and as a practitioner educational psychologist I will be recommending it to parents, school staff and colleagues as I believe it gives illuminating insight and plenty of sound practical advice which will be helpful to those who support children with ASD.

Eric Taylor, Educational Psychologist, Persona EPS Ltd

This book is a must-read for parents, professionals and young people with an interest in autism. It is a welcome addition to the existing literature on autism providing a clear, concise, and very readable overview of many of the key aspects to aid the reader in a broad understanding of autism. Through clear text, simple and effective illustrations, and regular key summaries this book guides the reader sensitively and thoughtfully through the facts, the impact, and solutions for working with young people with autism. The author places the young person at the centre of all the chapters focusing on the importance of parents and professionals trying to place themselves in the world of the young person. The later chapters on intervention illustrate this beautifully with multiple real-life examples to guide readers through many of the key issues faced by young people with ASD. There is a strong ethos of inclusion and acceptance throughout the book allowing the reader to place the young person at the centre of their thinking. This non-expert, non-judgemental approach is again a welcome break from the plethora of scientific writing on autism which may not always aid a broader audience in their understanding of autism. The book ends with a clear, practical glossary of terms, well-selected references, and helpful web-links, to guide readers towards further information and support.

Dr Paul Wallis, Director of Psychological Services, CAMHS Directorate, Central Manchester University Hospitals NHS Foundation Trust

This is a great book for people who want to know about autism. It is packed full of facts and information and signposts readers to other books, research, and organisations who can provide further help. The key point reiterated throughout this book is that people with autism are individuals with different personalities, likes and dislikes and that there is no 'one size fits all' approach that will magically work for every autistic person. The focus upon the different ways in which individuals with autism may think about and experience the world really encourages the reader to respond creatively. By using statements from autistic individuals to explain their perspective the author helps readers to gain insight into situations and behaviours which may appear baffling or unusual from the outside but make much more sense when viewed through an 'autism lens'.

The book contains information on most key areas that can be challenging for people with autism from communication difficulties, 'mindblindness', problems with eating, sleeping and tolerating situations due to sensory overload to self-injurious behaviour, psychiatric vulnerabilities, and repetitive behaviours. Each section gives good, sound, practical advice on ways of approaching or managing the difficulties and offers sources of further information and advice. This is no mean feat for such a comprehensive book and is to be applauded.

The book is written in simple language without jargon which makes it easy to read and the key points at the end of each chapter help to pull everything together. The tone is just right and is informative, factual, and interesting. The glossary is excellent and the references are extensive and wide ranging. My only surprises were the omission of Division TEACCH (although visual schedules are well covered) and that the National Autistic Society was not mentioned as a resource for training, publications, and parental support; notably their helpline and Early Bird/ Early Bird Plus parent training schemes.

As a parent of a young man with Aspergers I would have welcomed this book wholeheartedly when he was younger and it probably would have helped me through many anxious times. As a teacher who has worked for many years with children and adolescents with autism I loved the warmth and empathy with which the author talks about the people with whom she works and her complete and utter dedication to these very special individuals.

Pam Smith MBPsS, BMus(Hons), BSc(Hons), PGCE,
Postgraduate Certificate in Professional Studies in Education
(Autism). Special School Teacher, Surrey

THE LITTLE BOOK OF
THE AUTISM
SPECTRUM

TAKE A LOOK THROUGH AN AUTISM LENS ... TAKE A LOOK THROUGH AN AUTISM LENS ... TAKE A LOOK THROUGH AN AUTISM LENS ... TAKE A LOOK THROUGH AN AUTISM LENS ...

Dr Samantha Todd
Edited by Ian Gilbert

 Independent Thinking Press

First published by
Independent Thinking Press
Crown Buildings, Bancyfelin, Carmarthen, Wales, SA33 5ND, UK
www.independentthinkingpress.com

Independent Thinking Press is an imprint of Crown House Publishing Ltd.

First published 2013.

British Library Cataloguing-in-Publication Data
A catalogue entry for this book is available
from the British Library.

Print ISBN 978-1-78135-089-8
Mobi ISBN 978-1-78135-097-3
ePub ISBN 978-1-78135-098-0

Printed and bound in the UK by
Gomer Press, Llandysul, Ceredigion

To J, S, and D, for the confidence

Contents

Acknowledgements .... *iii*

Foreword .... *v*

Preface .... *ix*

Part One: Understanding the Autism Spectrum 1

  1. Introduction to the Autism Spectrum 3

  2. The Diagnosis of Autism 13

  3. A Different Perspective on Autism:
     Neurodiversity 25

  4. Developing Your Autism Lens 31

  5. Talking with Children and Young People
     about Autism 65

**Part Two: Developing Skills and Promoting Well-Being
       in Children and Young People with Autism** 71

  6. What Works and Who Can Help? 73

  7. Autism-Friendly Educational Settings 79

  8. Developing Social Skills 89

  9. Developing Communication and Understanding .. 99

  10. Emotional Well-Being and Mental Health 115

Part Three: Working with Behaviour **125**

   11. Understanding and Managing Challenging
       Behaviours 127

   12. Feeding and Eating Issues 141

   13. Sleep Difficulties 151

   14. Aggression and Self-Injury 159

   15. Managing Repetitive and Restricted Behaviours
       and Routines 167

   16. Managing Sensory Issues 175

Final Remarks 181

Glossary 183

References 189

Further Reading and Resources 195

Index 201

Acknowledgements

Many thanks to my colleagues who have shared their expertise with me and provided feedback for this book. Particular thanks to Jo Bromley and Latha Hackett, and also Frank Bowman, Sarah Rawsthorn, Katy Schatzberger, and Alison Hunter.

Thank you to the children and parents who educate us about autism.

Foreword

It's a trivial thing I know, but it's the closest I can get to understanding what it's like.

I'm fortunate enough to be able to go the gym several times a week once the three girls in my life have gone off to school (that's two students and a vice principal in case you're trying to do the maths). I have a set routine that takes me exactly an hour. Treadmill. Weights. Floor mat. Treadmill. There's a music system there that I can link via Bluetooth to my iPhone and listen on Spotify to the sort of 'work out' music men half my age would turn their noses up at all bass and shouting. All in all, as routines go, it's doing the trick – helping me stay fit, helping me justify the expense of the various technologies I've invested in, and helping me fight at least some of the signs of aging that a decent moisturiser can't reach.

I go there on Mondays, Wednesdays, and Fridays. Just after seven. Usually I'm the only person there. But …

Sometimes I'm not. Sometimes there is someone there before me. And they are on *my* treadmill. And they are listening to *their* music. Or have the television on. Breakfast TV. In *Cantonese*.

And I know it's irrational. I know it's unreasonable. I know I shouldn't feel that way. After all, share and share alike. But I get very angry and I what I want more than anything else is for that person on *my* machine to trip up unexpectedly and allow me to step over their prostrate body as it spins off the treadmill so I can take my rightful place.

You think that's bad? I know someone who has to have her boxed set of coloured pens with each pen in exactly the right order at all times. If she mislays one, she is unable to concentrate until it is found again. If someone asks to borrow one she has an anxiety attack. You can even freak her out by shuffling her pens around *in your mind!*

That apparently irrational way of looking at everyday things is the merest hint at what life seen through the lens of someone on the autism spectrum is like. It's not an illness. It's not a disease. It's a way of looking and thinking and responding that is different from 'the norm' (whatever that is – in many ways we are all somewhere on that spectrum) but that is valid and makes complete sense to the boy or girl experiencing it.

Three things are striking when you start to try and find out how many people are on the autism spectrum. The first is that no one knows. The second is that it affects boys much more than it affects girls. Thirdly, it is a great deal more common than was first thought, especially when recent understanding helps move us away from the 'Is he; isn't he?' black and white term 'autistic' and towards the more nuanced approach behind the 'spectrum' concept.

Foreword

This book is Independent Thinking's first foray into the world of special educational needs, something that we feel is long overdue. With the expert guidance of Dr Samantha Todd, the reader will not only get a feel for life through the 'autism lens' as she calls it but a better understanding of how to work to bring the best out of all children who find themselves on that spectrum.

And, who knows, it may just help with everyone who finds themselves somewhere along that spectrum and wants their treadmill, green pen, or life back.

Ian Gilbert, Hong Kong

Preface

To start making a difference to a child or young person with autism, the most useful step is to understand the condition. Learn about it and make sure everyone working with that child learns about it too. This can reduce stigma and misunderstanding, and increase understanding of that child's individual needs and perspective. This can go a long way towards making the social world more manageable and accessible for children and young people with autism and their families. This understanding is what this book is for.

Developing your autism lens

One of the most positive and productive steps you can take is to try to see the social world from the *same angle* as the child or young person with autism. Once you can do this it is easier to develop useful strategies to support them with the challenges they face. Knowing *why* a situation is proving problematic is a big help in working out what to do, whether that means changing the environment or teaching your child new skills. One size does not fit all when it comes to autism, or people in general for that matter, so we need to take an individual approach.

I call this process *looking through a child's autism lens*. Every child's lens will be different, according to their strengths and difficulties – every child has skills and problem areas with their social interaction, communication, and behaviour. Their temperament, past experience, and the 'fit' between themselves and their environment are also unique. So to look through their lens, you need to know about autism and the unique qualities of the child.

The children mentioned in this book are drawn from my clinical experience, but I do not directly describe individual children I know, in order to protect confidentiality and anonymity.

Looking through an Autism Lens

Social interaction • Communication • Thoughts and feelings • Routines and special interests • Change • Sensory experience • Seeing the big picture...

Part One

Understanding the
Autism Spectrum

Chapter 1

Introduction to the Autism Spectrum

The amount of information available about autism can be overwhelming and it can be hard to know where to begin. This section provides a brief overview of the condition.

- What is autism?
- What is the spectrum of autism?
- What causes autism?
- How many people have autism?
- What helps?

What is autism?

Autism is often described as a *developmental disability*. This means that it is usually first noticed during childhood. People with autism have a disability in terms of the way they understand and interact with other people, and this creates challenges when living in a very social world. However, some people do not think of autism as a disability, but simply as a different way of processing information and understanding the world.

Autism is a lifelong condition. This means that someone with an autism diagnosis will always have the condition, but it doesn't mean they will always be the same. All children change, learn, and develop, so children with autism will also change – they won't be the same at 15 or 40 as they were at 3. However, it is important to keep in mind that they will experience ongoing challenges with their social interactions, communication, and behaviour.

What is the spectrum of autism?

Throughout this book I use the term 'autism' as shorthand for the whole autism spectrum. Autism spectrum diagnoses (also known as autistic spectrum disorders or autistic spectrum conditions) are given to a broad range of children who display significant difficulties in these two areas:

1. Social interaction and communication

2. Social imagination, along with restricted, repetitive behaviour and interests

Wing's triad of impairment

Dr Lorna Wing is a psychiatric consultant for the National Autistic Society, the parent of a child with autism, and high profile researcher and writer regarding the condition. In the 1970s she was instrumental in identifying the core difficulties of autism. She described three key 'impairments' shared by all children who have an autism spectrum condition: impairments in social interaction, social communication, and social imagination, including restricted and repetitive behaviours and interests. This is called the 'triad of impairment' or 'Wing's triad' (Wing and Gould, 1979).

The latest *Diagnostic and Statistical Manual of Mental Disorders* (DSM-V; APA, 2013) reduces the triad to two.

The spectrum of autism has broadened considerably over time. Going back a half century, autism used to refer only to children who seemed to be 'in their own world'. These children show highly repetitive behaviours and routines, with very little interest in other people. This is sometimes referred to as 'childhood autism' or 'Kanner's autism', after the psychiatrist who first described the condition in 1943. These children often have severe delays in language and very unusual speech, or no speech at all.

As the 20th century went on, the spectrum of autism started to widen. In 1944, the Viennese paediatrician Hans Asperger provided the first description of boys with a particular style of thinking and interacting. He described young people with average or above average intellectual ability, and no delay in language, but who showed specific difficulties in social interaction and imagination. The term 'Asperger syndrome' was coined to describe this condition.

So, whilst one person within the autism spectrum may have no spoken language and very little interest in other people, another person within the spectrum may have well-developed language and be keen to make friends, but struggles to do so effectively. What the two individuals share are significant difficulties in their social interaction, communication, and imagination. Both will also have restricted and repetitive interests and behaviour.

The number of terms used to describe children on the autism spectrum can cause confusion. It is important to remember that they are all part of the same 'family' of diagnoses, with the same essential difficulties but with differences in terms of intellectual ability and language development.

Diagnostic terms

DSM-V (APA, 2013) uses the term 'autism spectrum disorder' to include everyone on the autism spectrum. This sits alongside a description of how much the condition affects the individual and each person's individual profile of difficulties.

Children and young people who have already been diagnosed, or are diagnosed using different criteria, may receive one of these alternative diagnoses, all of which fall within the autism spectrum:

- *Childhood autism*: Language development is delayed. Difficulties are usually noticed early, often before the age of 3. There may be an additional learning disability but not necessarily.
- *Asperger syndrome*: Children and young people who receive this diagnosis typically have had no delay in their language development and should have at least average intellectual ability.
- *Atypical autism or pervasive developmental disorder – not otherwise specified*: This diagnosis may be given when children and young people show some or most of the features of autism but do not exactly meet the full criteria. It is important to remember that these are still autism spectrum diagnoses and difficulties may be severe.

■ *High functioning autism*: This term is sometimes used for children and young people whose language development is delayed but who have at least average intellectual ability. There is an ongoing debate about whether Asperger syndrome and high functioning autism are two separate conditions or not. One argument is that high functioning autism is more likely to be picked up before the child starts school, whereas Asperger syndrome may not be noticed until school age. Does it make any difference in real life which diagnosis is made? Approaches to support the young person are broadly the same. However, responses by wider society to the two terms can be very different, with suggestions that Asperger syndrome carries less social stigma.

Is there such as thing as mild or severe autism?

There is a common misconception that people with childhood autism are at the 'severe' end of the spectrum and people with Asperger syndrome or high functioning autism are at the 'mild' end. Children with childhood autism who have limited language and an additional learning disability can certainly appear to have more severe difficulties in that their independence will be limited and their educational and social abilities greatly affected.

However, children without language delay or learning disabilities can also experience severe difficulties as a result of their autism. These difficulties may relate directly to the core areas of social communication, interaction, and repetitive behaviours. They may experience challenges in the following related areas:

- Rigidity – strict rules about how things should be
- Anxiety, particularly social anxiety
- Awareness of difference between themselves and their peers

It is therefore vital not to underestimate the impact of Asperger syndrome or any autism spectrum condition on an individual's life.

What causes autism?

There is very strong evidence that autism has a biological rather than an environmental cause. There is also a strong indication that this is likely to be genetic: if one identical twin has autism, there is a 60–90% chance that their twin will also have the condition. Compare this to non-identical twins or siblings, where if one has autism the other sibling has a 5–10% chance of meeting the criteria for diagnosis. We also know that there are a number of biological differences associated with autism, including some genetic and neurological differences.

We still don't know exactly how autism is caused – for most people there is not yet a clear answer for why *they* developed the condition. It seems likely to be a complex interaction between genes and some other factor(s) in brain development.

How many people have autism?

Current thinking is that about 1–1.5% of children have autism (Baron-Cohen et al., 2009). This number has risen steadily over the past few decades but this does not necessarily mean that autism itself is on the rise. Rather, it may be that the diagnostic criteria have broadened to include autistic spectrum conditions/disorders and Asperger syndrome, and professionals and parents are better educated about autism, so children are more likely to be given a diagnosis.

True or false?

■ *Autism affects more boys than girls*

True. Most studies have found that more boys than girls meet the criteria for autism spectrum conditions, with boys at least three times as likely to have the condition as girls (Nicholas et al., 2008).

■ *Autism is caused by poor parenting*

False. Early theories on the causes of autism included the hypothesis that it was caused by parental 'coldness', particularly on the part of the mother. This hypothesis has been rejected for many years, and the cause of autism is widely accepted as biological.

■ *Autism is caused by the MMR vaccine*

False. There is no good evidence of a link between the MMR (measles, mumps and rubella) vaccination and autism following controversial claims made during the late 1990s.

■ *People with autism have special talents, like in the film* Rain Man

Partly true. A very small percentage of people with autism show an extraordinary talent, such as being able to play complicated tunes after hearing it just once. This is sometimes known as 'savant syndrome'. The vast majority of people with autism do not have one of these profound abilities but have strengths and difficulties just like the rest of the population.

■ *Children can grow out of autism*

False. Children with autism grow up to be adults with autism. With the appropriate support and education they can develop skills and progress, but they will still have the core features of autism as part of who they are.

Chapter 2

The Diagnosis of Autism

Diagnosis can be a necessary step towards children receiving the appropriate support. This chapter explains when and how autism is diagnosed.

- When to seek further assessment
- Who can diagnose autism
- How the diagnosis is made
- What happens next
- Weighing up whether to seek a diagnosis
- Alternative or additional diagnoses

When to seek further assessment

Concerns that a person may have autism can be raised at any stage in their development, from a few months old to adulthood.

The first five years

Sometimes parents or professionals notice potential difficulties very early on. This may be particularly true for children with childhood autism or those with delayed language development.

In the first year of life, some parents notice that their child is not babbling or reaching other expected milestones. This is not a reliable sign of autism but can raise concerns about development. As the baby becomes a toddler, parents may become aware that they do not seem very interested in other people. Communication is not developing as expected – for example, the child may not respond to their own name being called or may spend a lot of time playing in a repetitive way, perhaps lining toys up or flapping their hands repetitively. Some children initially seem to develop in a typical way but then regress, losing speech or other skills; this should always be assessed further.

Health visitors and family doctors can listen to early concerns and refer children on for more specialist assessment when this is appropriate. Even if a diagnosis of autism is not made at this early stage, interventions to help the child's communication and understanding can still help. Diagnosis can usually be reliably made from the age of 3, and sometimes clinicians are able to make a diagnosis before this. However, diagnosis sometimes comes much later for a variety of reasons.

Children from 5 to 10 years

For children with difficulties across the autism spectrum, differences may only become more apparent as the child starts and moves through primary school. They may show differences in the way they interact; perhaps they seem less interested in other kids or less likely to understand and join in with imaginary or group games. They may struggle with change, be very focussed on their own agenda, or seem unable to make or keep friends. Teachers and parents may also notice sensory sensitivities, such as a dislike of noisy playgrounds, assemblies, or the dinner hall, or a reluctance to wear certain fabrics or aspects of uniform.

Some children have quite subtle difficulties which only become clear as the gap with their classmates widens. For example, most young children have trouble sharing toys or taking turns and many can be shy and unwilling to join in. As children progress through school, however, most will develop their social skills and will have fewer problems in these areas. Children with autism may then start to stand out more as their social skills are not developing at the same rate.

Concerns in adolescence

Sometimes it is not until secondary school that difficulties in social interaction are fully recognised, and parents and young people themselves question whether to seek further assessment. The extra social demands of secondary education may highlight difficulties that were always 'managed' up till now.

In primary school, children have the same teacher all day and stay with the same classmates. This can help children to feel settled, and adults can get to know them and their needs. Secondary school usually means more movement around the school and interactions with many more teachers. The young person may struggle to cope with this transition. They may be getting into more trouble at school, refusing to go, or becoming more isolated socially. Their parents and teachers may be really worried about their ability to cope with exams and college if they don't get additional support.

For a diagnosis of autism to be made, difficulties can't simply have started in the teenage years – differences in development must have been evident from the early years, even if these were not a cause for concern at the time.

Who can make a diagnosis of autism?

Anyone making an autism diagnosis should be specially trained to identify the condition. They also need to be able to rule out other diagnoses which can be confused with autism. A diagnosis may be made by a psychiatrist, paediatrician, psychologist, or speech and language therapist. These are specialists who have had additional training in the assessment and diagnosis of autism. Often this help is accessed by referral from the family doctor or another healthcare professional such as a school nurse.

How is the diagnosis made?

Diagnosis may be made by one person or ideally by a team of different professionals. There is no blood test, X-ray, or scan for autism. A diagnosis can only be reached by asking the right questions and observing specific aspects of communication and social behaviour. Guidelines are available that set down standards for the assessment process, such as the National Autism Plan for Children or the National Institute for Health and Care Excellence.

What happens next?

At the end of the assessment process, the clinician or team decides whether a diagnosis is appropriate. The exact diagnosis will depend on the criteria used by the person or team making the judgement. This will usually be the latest criteria from either the American Psychiatric Association's *Diagnostic and Statistical Manual of Mental Disorders* (APA, 2013) or the World Health Organisation's *International Statistical Classification of Diseases and Related Health Problems* (WHO, 1992). Terms commonly used include:

- Autism spectrum disorder
- Childhood autism
- Asperger syndrome
- Autistic spectrum disorder/condition
- Atypical autism or pervasive developmental disorder – not otherwise specified
- High functioning autism

Chapter 1 describes each of these terms in more detail.

Parents should be told first-hand about the diagnosis and have an opportunity to ask questions. They should receive a written report and be provided with more information about autism. Parents may find it helpful to contact useful organisations such as the National Autistic Society in the UK or equivalent organisations in other countries.

Families experience a huge range of different emotions when given a diagnosis of autism for their child. Many experience grief as they understand the impact of the condition on their child, family, and their future. Other parents have had concerns for a long time and the diagnosis comes as something of a relief as it lights the path for more appropriate support.

Parental stress and autism

Research consistently finds higher rates of stress in parents of children with autism (Bromley et al., 2004). Challenging behaviour, concerns about their child's social skills, and worries about the future and appropriate support all contribute to high levels of anxiety. Stress can be reduced by:

- Using formal support groups
- Using informal social support from friends and family
- Interventions that help to reduce challenging behaviours
- Interventions that include a cognitive-behavioural component, enabling parents to understand how their own thoughts and behaviours can increase stress
- Having access to effective multi-agency support, including respite and short breaks (Hastings and Beck, 2004)

Young people who are told about their diagnosis will also experience a range of emotions. Some are relieved as it explains why they feel different or why they have particular strengths and difficulties, and it signposts them to a community of other young people who experience the social world in a similar way. Others feel very angry or sad about the diagnosis or reject it all together. Chapter 5 explores when and how to talk to young people about their diagnosis.

Weighing up whether to seek a diagnosis

Deciding whether to go ahead with an assessment can be a difficult step for many parents. Sometimes parents and carers are worried about 'labelling' their child. They are conscious that their child might feel stigmatised or that other people may look at them differently once they have a diagnosis. They may be worried about being blamed for the child's difficulties or that they will not be taken seriously.

In some cases, parents may already believe that their child has autism, but things are going well in school and at home and they do not feel there is a pressing need. However, there are very clear benefits to seeking a diagnosis in most cases:

- It helps the adults around the child to understand their difficulties and needs more clearly
- Helpful interventions and strategies can be put into place to improve communication, behaviour, and ability to learn
- This can also make the social world more accessible and manageable for children with autism
- It can lead to increased educational support or social support, such as specialised activities

- It reduces the risk of the child or their parents being unfairly blamed for the child's behaviour
- All this should help support children's self-esteem
- It can help adults to anticipate difficulties (e.g. the transition to secondary school) and get support to prevent problems arising
- Children and families can contact autism-specific organisations and support groups, thereby reducing their sense of isolation

Alternative or additional diagnoses

One of the reasons that autism is usually only diagnosed from the age of 3, and by a specialist, is that the person making the diagnosis must have sufficient knowledge to distinguish between autism and conditions that may *look like* autism. Also, some children and young people may have autism in addition to one or more of these other conditions. These may be assessed at the same time. Other diagnoses that are considered include the following.

Attention deficit hyperactivity disorder (ADHD)

ADHD is another developmental condition that is common in children with autism. Children and young people have significant problems with attention, activity levels (being more active than most children), and impulsivity (acting before thinking). Stimulant medication is often prescribed for ADHD, along with the use of behaviour management strategies.

Learning disabilities

Children and young people with learning disabilities are at a greatly increased risk of also having autism. Having a learning disability means that the person has problems understanding new or complex information, managing in everyday life (for their age), and learning new skills. It is important to know if a child has a learning disability or not because:

1. It is vital for guiding their educational needs

2. It is important to know whether their difficulties can be fully explained by their learning problems or whether they have a dual diagnosis

Dyspraxia/developmental coordination disorder (DCD)

Dyspraxia or DCD is another developmental condition that affects a person's motor coordination as well their ability to plan actions. Difficulties in language and perception are also common. Fine motor skills, such as handwriting, and gross motor skills, like riding a bike or walking downstairs, may be affected.

Other syndromes or medical conditions

A number of syndromes or medical conditions are also associated with autism, and the person or team undertaking the assessment will have these in mind. For example, epilepsy and seizures are more common in people with autism. Children with other conditions such as fragile X syndrome, tuberous sclerosis, and Timothy syndrome have a higher rate of autism. However, most children with autism do not have these conditions.

Psychiatric diagnoses

Mental health difficulties such as depression and anxiety can either be confused with or occur at the same time as autism. These will benefit from specialist intervention so it is important that they are considered.

Key learning points

Diagnosis can be made from the early years until adulthood

Diagnosis can only be made by specially trained professionals

Assessment involves observations of the child, asking parents and teachers about their behaviour, and using standardised assessments

Other diagnoses must also be considered so that the appropriate support is offered

The decision to seek a diagnosis can be a difficult one, but receiving a diagnosis can be beneficial for children with autism and their families.

Chapter 3

A Different Perspective on Autism: Neurodiversity

People with autism, their families, and professionals under-stand the autism spectrum from a range of viewpoints. The two most common perspectives on autism are as:

■ A condition made up of *deficits* or impairments – a disability potentially in need of treatment.

■ A *different* way of understanding the world – a natural human variation which should be accepted and respected

The neurodiversity movement takes this second viewpoint, valuing some of the differences found in the ways people with autism think, learn, and experience the social world. The terms 'neurotypical' (people without autism spectrum or other neuro-developmental conditions) and 'neurodiversity' are used to show respect for people's differences.

Stigma and autism

A significant proportion of parents report a sense of stigma or social exclusion in association with their child's autism (Gray, 2002). Equally, children may experience a sense of social isolation and exclusion. Children and young people who show aggressive behaviours may, along with their parents, feel or experience higher levels of stigma. This includes being avoided by others, criticised, stared at, or excluded (not invited to social events or accepted in the wider community). Autism is sometimes described as 'invisible' as it has no physical features, and other people make their judgements based on the behaviours or unusual social responses they can see.

Stigma adds an additional layer of stress to people with autism and their families, and may be particularly potent in communities where little is known about autism, or disability and difference in general. Finding others with similar experiences can provide a buffer against this sense of stigma.

Reducing stigma is everyone's responsibility. Extrapolating findings from research into reducing stigma around mental health (Corrigan et al., 2012) we can predict that the two key strategies are:

- education

- positive contact between people with autism and the general population

The more the general public know and understand, the greater the chance of social inclusion for people with autism. At the ground level, adults around the child can educate others directly; organisations such as the National Autistic Society campaign to a more global audience, with social networking and the internet expanding its reach.

Whilst ethnic diversity is about accepting and celebrating the contribution of different cultural or religious backgrounds, neurodiversity is about taking a similar approach to the differences associated with intellectual functioning. The emphasis is not on looking for a cure for autism or reducing or eliminating its core features. Instead, the focus is on striving for the acceptance of people with autism in society and respecting them as individuals who may think and behave outside the social 'norms' at times. The movement does not deny the challenges faced by people with autism, but it does call on the neurotypical world to make adjustments so that people with autism can navigate and potentially flourish in society.

There is a great deal of value in this point of view. Firstly, it also enables us to identify *strengths* in the way people with autism think, rather than focusing entirely on deficits or impairments. One theory of autism, the empathizing-system-izing theory (Baron-Cohen et al., 2009) highlights these different ways of thinking. The model describes how people with autism frequently show intact or even superior skills in understanding or constructing systems – for example, grasping how a machine works, collecting similar objects, learning a huge range of facts about a topic, or trying repeated movements to see how they work. This contrasts with usually below-average ability to understand other's thoughts and perspectives. There are many situations in which skills at systemising are important and, along with an ability to pay attention to detail, these can be seen as specific strengths of autism. There are a number of well-known, high-achieving people with autism and Asperger syndrome diagnoses. For example, Dr Temple Grandin is an American professor, published author, and autism advocate. Her ability to attend to detail and use her visual memory has been a tremendous benefit to her career.

Secondly, for young people with autism, especially those who are aware of their diagnosis, the neurodiversity perspective encourages a more positive self-image or identity. There is a large community, especially online, of young people and adults who have autism. Together with their families, they describe and at times embrace the differences of autism whilst providing advice and support for managing the challenges of a largely neurotypical world. This can reduce the sense of social isolation for young people who may previously have felt alone or the odd one out. This community also has the potential to change the opinions and behaviour of the neurotypical world for the better. People with autism may experience stigma or discrimination, and a strong community campaigning and educating others can only be a good thing.

Neurodiversity ideas can be readily applied to people with autism who are high functioning, that is, academically fairly able, with a high likelihood of accessing college or employment. It can be more problematic to apply this perspective to people with autism who have severe intellectual disabilities, little or no speech, and limited educational or occupational options. However, many parents and professionals are nevertheless able to identify and value their child's neurodiversity – for example, their climbing skills, their ability to put things in exactly the same order from memory, or learning every route around town.

A third implication of taking a neurodiversity perspective is that it encourages understanding and acceptance of features associated with autism, rather than engaging in a constant battle to try to eliminate these features. For example, many people with autism experience pleasure and enjoyment or stress reduction as a result of 'stimulatory' behaviours, such as spinning, jumping, flapping their hands, tapping, or twiddling something. Parents and teachers are often keen to reduce these activities as they can make the child stand out as 'different', with all the social consequences that can entail. An alternative stance is to accept the need and value for the individual in engaging in these behaviours, understanding why and when they happen, and enabling the person to act out the behaviour so that their needs are met, providing they are not put at any risk.

It is vital to stress that acknowledging and valuing neurodiversity does *not* mean ignoring the very real challenges faced by people with autism.

Key learning points

Autism can be viewed as a *variation* in the way humans think and experience the social world

These differences can be a strength, depending on the skills required in the situation

The social or neurotypical world can be very challenging for people with autism. It is our responsibility to make adjustments and support people with autism to manage these challenges

---

Chapter 4

Developing Your Autism Lens

Looking through a child's 'autism lens' will enable you to provide tailored support. To do this, you need to understand the eight key principles of an autism lens:

1. *Social interactions can be challenging for me*

2. *I may need support to communicate and to understand other people's communication*

3. *I can't always tell what other people are thinking or feeling*

4. *I may have routines I need to stick to, behaviours I need to do over and over again, or special interests that are very important to me*

5. *I may need additional support to manage change*

6. *I may have different sensory experiences to you*

7. *I may be really good at seeing detail but I don't always see the 'bigger picture'*

8. *I am a child or young person first, with my own personal story and my own likes and dislikes*

I will describe each of these principles in detail, so you can begin to put together your individual autism lens for the children you know.

1. Social interactions can be challenging for me

Most social behaviours adhere to unwritten rules. Typically, people understand that conversations and friendships are a *two-way process*. They understand the give and take of relationships. They have developed insight into the social behaviours that help interactions to go smoothly: compliments, showing an interest in the other person, and enjoying shared activities.

Social interaction and autism

These unwritten rules are not obvious for people with autism. Levels of interest in interacting with others varies: some individuals may show almost zero awareness, whilst others are very keen but do not have the necessary skills for the interaction to run smoothly.

Children with autism display social interaction difficulties in different ways. Some may seem absorbed in their own interests and generally unresponsive to the social approaches of other people. Others may respond to another person's approaches but rarely start interactions of their own. Some children and young people with autism are excessively formal and polite, whilst others may talk 'at' their listeners in a way that can be unremitting and one-sided.

Parents and professionals who are just starting to learn about autism are sometimes baffled by the contrasting presentations of the children they know. It can be helpful to understand that, whilst one child may appear 'in their own world' and another may constantly approach others for one-sided interactions, each child is displaying a significant difficulty in social interaction. This obstacle is the challenge they share.

Key learning points for your autism lens

Autism affects the give and take of social interaction

Some children have only a limited interest in interacting with other people

Others are interested in other people but struggle with the skills needed to start and maintain friendships

---

2. I may need support to communicate and to understand other people's communication

If social interaction is the way in which we relate to other people, communication is the tool we use to achieve this. We may use verbal skills (e.g. language and tone of voice) and non-verbal skills (e.g. facial expressions, body language, and gesture). Both verbal and non-verbal methods of communication are affected by autism.

Autism and language

Speech difficulties can be seen across the autism spectrum. For children with classic autism, speech may not develop at all or may be limited to single words or a few phrases. This can be particularly distressing for parents, who recognise how essential speech is for developing relationships, communicating needs, and expressing emotions.

For many children on the autism spectrum, speech is significantly delayed, often developing a couple of years later than expected. After this point, adults around the child still notice unusual features in their speech, such as confusing pronouns (e.g. saying 'he' instead of 'I'). The child or young person may struggle to use speech pragmatically, that is, using it effectively for the purposes of communication. For example, they may be able to talk about dinosaurs in great detail but seem unable to ask to go to the toilet or to join in a game.

Even those young people who haven't had any speech delay may not use their speech logically to communicate their needs or to enjoy a conversation. One mother described to me how her daughter, Isabelle, who had fluent speech, never asked for help. She was often found crying in her bedroom, upset from losing her purse or needing money for lunch at school, but without the skills to push the words from her mouth to ask her mother for assistance. Another feature that can occur is an unusual tone or pitch – speech that is noticeably different for being too loud, too quiet, too flat, too jerky, and so on.

Echolalia – repeating words or phrases the child has heard, either as soon as they hear it or later on – can occur across the autism spectrum. Sometimes this echoed speech can sound empty or lacking in meaning, particularly as it is often repeated in the same manner as the original source. For example, children may repeat a phrase their teacher or parent has used in the same tone: 'Sit down now Christian!', or a line from a film: 'Luke, I am your father!' There is some evidence that echoed speech simply reflects heard fragments or phrases, with no meaning attached to them. However, echoing may sometimes meet some of the child's needs.

- Stimulation (*I enjoy the sounds the words make*)
- Asking for something (*mum understands I say this when I am hungry*)
- Reducing anxiety (*the words make me feel safe*)

Understanding speech

Children with autism have an increased likelihood of having difficulties in their understanding of other's speech. At one end of the spectrum, children may not respond to their own name being called or may understand only very basic instructions, such as 'Shoes off' or 'Eat biscuit'. As we move through the spectrum, comprehension may be more sophisticated but there can still be difficulties in specific areas.

A common problem is the literal understanding of language. Social conversations are peppered with metaphors, sayings, and irony, all of which require the listener to hear beyond the immediate meaning of the words:

- It's raining cats and dogs out there!
- I nearly died when I saw that bill.
- Thank you for saying I looked fat – you make me feel so good.

People with autism do not always understand the 'implied message' in statements such as these, and take the comments at face value. Young people eventually learn the meaning of sayings such as 'Pull your socks up' or 'It's raining cats and dogs', but this does not come naturally. What the speaker *meant* is not understood.

My mum told me to go to my grandma's house round the corner. I went to grandma's front door and then turned back and walked home. Mum said 'What are you doing, you are supposed to be having lunch with grandma?' She didn't tell me that though ...

Non-verbal communication

Children with autism display difficulties in their use and understanding of non-verbal communication, such as eye contact, facial expressions, and gestures.

A common misconception is that people with autism do not make eye contact. This is true for some but it is more often the case that eye contact is *unusual* in some way – staring, looking at a point just beside the other person's eyes, or looking at the 'wrong times'. Eye gaze is an important part of indicating turn-taking in conversation and showing interest. The mistiming of this can make social interactions feel stilted or one-sided.

Facial expressions may seem fixed or lacking in variety. For example, James maintained a passive, blank expression at all times, never giving away his emotions or level of agitation. This meant that his parents found it hard to understand when situations were becoming overwhelming for him and only realised this was the case when his behaviour escalated and he became aggressive. They had to learn to 'read' his emotions from other signs, such as a rise in the volume of his voice or increased flapping of his hands.

People often use gestures to illustrate or emphasise what they are trying to say. However, children with autism may show minimal gestures, sometimes limited to nods and shakes of the head. Equally, people with autism may experience difficulties interpreting the non-verbal communication of others. Subtle changes in facial expression are not recognised and the connection between emotion and appearance is not made, so children may not quickly pick up on parents' frustration or be able to tell when they are pleased.

Take a look at communication through Kaseem's autism lens, as his dad tries to get him to leave the house to go to school:

My dad keeps talking. He is walking up and down and saying lots of words and I am trying to listen but there are too many and I don't know which ones are the important ones. My ears are starting to hurt. He said, 'It's OK, Kaseem, take your time, we've got all day.' So I went off to play my game again and then he came in with my shoes and his voice was even louder this time. He said, 'What's the problem?' and I started to tell him about the game and that I was stuck on level 35 and he said 'Hurry up.' So I played the game really fast.

We can see that Kaseem's dad is probably getting frustrated with his son's lack of progress in leaving the house. Kaseem is missing the subtleties of his father's communication: the irony, tone of voice, and facial expressions. He is failing to understand the implication of his dad's question and request. We will explore later the communication supports that can help in instances like these, but you may already be thinking about how Kaseem's dad can make some changes. Fewer words and saying what you mean are a good place to start.

Key learning points for your autism lens

All children with autism have difficulties in social communication at some level

Some have very little speech

Others can use speech but still struggle to use it for effective social communication

Verbal and non-verbal communication skills are affected

Most children with autism have some problems in their understanding of other's communication

This includes facial expressions, gestures, and language, especially non-literal language

---

3. I can't always tell what other people are thinking or feeling

People with autism all experience some difficulties with their *social imagination*; that is, their ability to understand and predict other people's thoughts, feelings, and actions. Understandably this makes the social world a huge challenge at times.

In fact, one of the major psychological theories of autism, the 'theory of mind', places social imagination at its centre (see Baron-Cohen, 1997 for a detailed description). Essentially, the idea is that the central difficulty in autism is the problem of putting yourself in someone else's shoes.

This ability requires insight into both the other person's cognitive perspective (what they are thinking) and their emotions (what they are feeling). This develops for most people from infancy onward. Babies and toddlers learn to follow their parents' pointing or gaze, demonstrating that they understand where their parent wants them to look. They then go on to develop imaginary play with other children. Both of these behaviours require an ability to understand the other person's intentions. Both are seen less frequently in children with autism.

In typical development, pre-schoolers develop the capacity to understand that two people may have different points of view, depending on the information available to them. They understand that someone may hold a 'false belief' (i.e. believe something that is factually wrong) because they have been given incorrect or insufficient information. Children with autism are delayed in developing this understanding.

For example, I worked with a young man, Tim, who lived in a shared house. I arrived at his home for an appointment but he wasn't there. His housemate rang him to see where he was. He told her that he was at the local fast food place and was surprised that I hadn't realised. Quite simply, because *he* knew where he was, he assumed *I* would know. He had no insight into our different perspectives. Looking at this situation through Tim's autism lens, the situation would look something like this:

I wanted some fried chicken, I was hungry, and so I came here to the fried chicken place. Then Marianne rang me and said Sam was there to see me. Why didn't she come here to meet me, or come earlier or later?

Sometimes this difficulty is referred to as 'mindblindness', which seems like a good way to describe the barrier to 'reading' other people's points of view, emotions, or intentions. It can be really helpful to keep this in mind when trying to understand the behaviour of children with autism. Look at the situation through their lens: what do they understand of your intentions or feelings? Does this change how you handle the situation?

Let's look through Yasmina's autism lens. Yasmina was a young child with no verbal language and intellectual disabilities and who screamed a lot. She particularly screamed when she was hungry. Her parents wanted to teach her to be more patient whilst they were preparing her food. We looked together at the situation through Yasmina's lens:

I'm hungry. I scream. When I scream, my mum and dad get up and leave me. They go in the kitchen and they don't come back for ages. I don't know what they are doing. I don't know when they are going to come back.

We realised that Yasmina probably couldn't read her parents' intentions at all. All she saw was their retreating backs; she didn't know if they were going to make food, wash the dishes, or load the washing machine. To help her understand this, they started giving her clear visual signs of what they were doing: preparing her chair and table, and putting a photo of her cup and plate there for her. She learnt that when these preparations happened, food was being prepared and would arrive soon. The screaming reduced dramatically.

Both of these examples relate to understanding other people's thoughts and intentions, but understanding of other's feelings is also affected by autism. We know that children with autism find facial expressions or emotions hard to interpret, but it goes further than that: they find it very difficult to put themselves in another person's shoes and imagine what they are feeling. Look through Jeanie's Lens:

My baby brother is OK when he is asleep. When he is awake he screams and cries and it hurts my ears. I put my hand on his mouth to stop him screaming and shouted at him to stop. Then my mum shouted at me and pulled my hand away really hard.

Jeannie's problems with social imagination are affecting her in several ways:

- She doesn't show understanding that babies cry because they are hungry or have another need
- She doesn't empathise that he may feel frightened by her actions

■ She doesn't predict that her mum will feel upset or angry as a result of her actions

Although children with autism can't be taught 'social imagination' in a global way, they can learn specific information about feelings or behaviours that will help them to understand other people more. For example, Jeannie could be taught that babies cry because they are hungry or need changing, and that she can help by going to her mum or dad when this happens.

Key learning points for your autism lens

Autism affects social imagination: the ability to understand other people's thoughts, feelings, and intentions

This is sometimes known as 'mindblindness' or a lack of 'theory of mind'

Other people can seem highly unpredictable

The individual may not understand the impact of their behaviour on other people

---

4. I may have routines I need to stick to, behaviours I need to do over and over again, or special interests that are very important to me

Think about the repetitive behaviours or routines which help you feel safe and calm, for example:

- Getting ready to go out by doing tasks in a certain order
- Checking the doors are locked before you go out/go to bed
- Keeping your clothes in certain drawers or cupboards

Take one area of your life where you always do things in a particular order or organise things in a certain way, and imagine what it would be like if this was severely disrupted: socks in the cutlery drawer, underwear in the bathroom cabinet, trousers in a pile under the table. Most of us feel anxious, unsettled, or confused when our routines are broken. For children with autism, these habits are likely to be more rigid and the effect of change more amplified. Toys may always need to be positioned in a certain way or hands washed repetitively.

The problem is not always with the routine itself but with the extent that it interferes with the conflicting needs of the child's family or school. Repetitive behaviour may prevent the child engaging in other activities or learning. Attempts to stop the behaviour can trigger outbursts of more challenging behaviour.

Repetitive behaviour can also include actions like spinning or twiddling an object, turning lights on and off, or watching the same short section of a movie over and over again. Alternatively, children with autism may show more elaborate repetitive behaviours: acting out scenes from a film with characters in the same way each time or insisting on going the same route to the shops every single time.

Any of these repetitive behaviours may provide the child or young person with stimulation or a sense of well-being because the world appears predictable. We have already seen how challenging the social world can seem to a child with autism; repetitive behaviours often provide a focus, structure, and consistency. This isn't very different from people without autism.

Some rigid or repetitive behaviours seem much more closely related to anxiety than to enjoyment. Routines can become embedded and the person with autism becomes highly anxious, or even angry, when asked to make a change. Adults working with these individuals will often need to be highly perceptive to the development of these patterns, so that they can gently make alterations which prevent the habit becoming too established. This may also apply to 'rules' which the young person develops. These rules may provide short-term comfort, as they make life more predictable, but may cause problems elsewhere and ultimately make life difficult or distressing.

Here are some examples from the young person's perspective:

- *My family should never put their feet on furniture*
- *I don't eat anything green, brown, or red*
- *No one is allowed to touch my toys except me*
- *I go to bed at 8 p.m. exactly*
- *All teachers should be female*

Such constraints can be highly restrictive for children and their families. Children will need careful support to understand why these rules need to be more flexible and to feel safe enough to tolerate letting them go.

Special interests

Children and young people with autism are likely to develop special interests or preoccupations that are unusual either because they are so intense or because the topic is not usually appealing to children of their age. Dinosaurs and trains are common interests for young boys; autism will raise the level of importance so that it is much more consuming – often to the exclusion of other activities or topics of conversation. Vacuum cleaners or washing machines are not typical obsessions for young boys either but I have met some individuals who are endlessly fascinated by their inner workings and varieties, with posters of famous vacuum brands on their bedroom wall.

Routines are very important to me...

① I get up at 7am

② I eat three toast triangles and two tomatoes

③ I only wear white trainers

④ This is my seat on the bus

⑤ I have to be at the front of the line

... or the day is WRONG!

Clearly there may be benefits to the young person in having a special interest: comfort, stimulation, direction into careers, extra studies, or out-of-school activities. Difficulties can occur if the fixation leads to socially unacceptable behaviour (e.g. looking into a stranger's kitchen to see what type of washing machine they own) or is too all-consuming and gets in the way of other important aspects of daily living.

As a general rule, it is infinitely better to try to work *with* the special interest, using it as an incentive or a way to relax, than to work *against* it.

Key learning points for your autism lens

Children with autism show repetitive routines or behaviours

They often develop special interests

These may provide stimulation or enjoyment or help reduce anxiety

Problems can occur if the repetitive behaviours or special interests stop the young person or their family carrying out other activities

Difficulties also occur if the young person feels very anxious or upset when they can't carry out the behaviour or access their special interest

---

5. I may need additional support to manage change

Alongside the love of routines often seen in children with autism can come uncertainty or anxiety when faced with change. This varies from individual to individual, but parents and teachers commonly report that the children they know seem to need additional support when faced with disruptions. This can be from the seemingly minor (a change in class-room display) to the major (the end of the summer holidays and returning to a new teacher and classroom). For the child this can feel like having the rug pulled from under their feet.

Take a look through Sonia's lens:

I had just got used to the bus route going to school. I could look out the window and count off the places I like on the way: the video store, the pizza place, the library, the cake shop, and the park. The journey took between 17 and 19 minutes. It made me feel confident going to school. Now there are roadworks and we can't go that way any more. I don't see the places I like. I don't know which way we are going each day or how long it is going to take. I feel sick. I don't think I can take the bus to school any more.

We can help children with autism develop their ability to cope with change. It is important to have some routine and structure in place, whether at school or home. If life generally feels safe and predictable it can help reduce anxiety so that children are more resilient to disruption.

That said, some children continue to have very strong responses to change. Quite often, they do not express this directly and this is when you need to look through the child's autism lens to work out why they are finding a situation difficult. Strategies that can help children with autism cope with disruption include:

■ Preparation for expected changes – for example, showing children their new classroom for the next academic year in advance, perhaps taking photographs of it for them to look at in the holidays

■ Using visual schedules or written supports to show them when changes will be happening (see Chapter 9)

■ Allowing time for the young person to calm down and express their feelings during unexpected changes

---

Key learning points for your autism lens

Children and young people with autism often have more difficulty adjusting to change in their environment

Changes may lead to anxiety, anger, and then changes in behaviour

You can help by:
• Anticipating changes in advance
• Preparing them whenever possible for change
• Using visual supports to explain when and how changes will occur

---

6. *I may have different sensory experiences to you*

We live in a sensory world of sounds, sights, smells, tastes, and touch. Many people with autism experience this sensory world somewhat differently to neurotypical people. This has a significant impact on people with autism and their families and deserves special mention. You should always consider sensory differences when trying to view a situation through a child's autism lens.

If children are sensitive in one of their senses, they are highly likely to be sensitive in others.

'I MIGHT HAVE DIFFERENT SENSORY
EXPERIENCES TO YOU'

Sound sensitivity

Sound can be the most common area of sensitivity. Whilst children may seem unresponsive to some noises (such as their name being called!), they can be highly sensitive to others. Sudden noises or a clash of sounds can be particularly distressing. This is Hamza's story:

I went to the toilet at school. When I was in the toilet the school bell went off right by the door. It was so loud it made me jump and feel scared for a long time. I won't go in that toilet again now. I'll wait till I get home.

Noises that neurotypical people can barely hear may seem much louder for people with autism, and they may not be able to 'tune out' irrelevant noise which can make classrooms and shops much more challenging. Sound sensitivity can be helpful sometimes but at others it can cause anxiety, distress, or anger. All these can effect concentration and behaviour.

Touch sensitivity

Another common characteristic of autism is tactile sensitivity. Often this means a particular enjoyment of touching certain materials. At other times it results in finding the feeling of fabrics or objects almost unbearable. Children may say they find their clothes painful (and so want to be out of them!), that labels are highly irritating, or the slightest unexpected touch from another person is perceived as hurting. Take a look through Michael's lens:

I can't bear the feeling of having my hair cut or my nails trimmed. It feels like my hair is being torn off. My mum has to cut my hair because I know she will be very gentle and stop if I can't stand it.

Sight sensitivity

We all have things we like to observe and things we don't; many people find sunsets and kittens pleasant to look at, and very bright lights or grey skies less appealing. It is all in the eye of the beholder. Children and young people with autism often have visual likes and dislikes but these may be more intense or socially unusual.

Some children experience a high level of enjoyment or comfort from patterns or in the repetitive movement of an object. An interest in a specific part of a DVD, such as the rolling credits at the end, is quite common. Equally, children and young people with autism may find particular visual stimuli unsettling or distressing. They may experience 'visual noise' which can't be tuned out easily: busy wallpaper, leaves blowing in the wind, or a classroom covered in children's artwork can all prove distracting or disturbing. Take a look through Michael's lens:

My mum takes me to the big store in town. It has green everywhere. Green signs, green lights, green bags. The people who work there wear green too. It is too much and it hurts my eyes. I don't like going to the green store. I like the blue store. The lights aren't as bright there either.

Smell sensitivity

Heightened responses to smell can also occur. Children with autism may find some aromas particularly repugnant and this can impact upon daily tasks such as using the toilet or eating dinner. One young boy I worked with was so sensitive to the smell of crisps that he could tell his parents if there was a packet open within ten feet, even if he couldn't see it. The odour made him feel sick and he wanted to avoid places where he might smell crisps.

Sensitivity to pain and temperature

Anecdotally, children and young people with autism can appear over- or under-sensitive to pain and changes in temperature. Whilst parents often describe their child as having a high pain threshold, the same child may yelp if someone touches them lightly.

Children with autism may not tell you when they are in pain. This may be because they can't feel the pain or because they don't understand that you will have knowledge which might mean you can help them reduce the pain (mindblindness again). Parents and professionals need to be aware of their child's signs of pain or injury – for example, a change in behaviour or sleep patterns or becoming more irritable.

Some children and young people do not seem to feel cold and heat as readily and so may not dress appropriately for the weather. This may also be due to a lack of interest in the social rules around dress.

Taste sensitivity

Some children with autism are remarkably sensitive in their tastes. For example, they can tell the difference between different brands of the same kind of rice or detect if the ingredients of a favoured food change slightly.

Other children have a sensory interest in putting objects into their mouths. Sometimes these are unsafe objects, such as cotton wool, leaves, or mud. Feeding difficulties are discussed in greater detail in Chapter 12 along with strategies for change.

Key learning points for your autism lens

People with autism often experience heightened sensory experiences in sight, hearing, smell, taste, and touch

Sometimes people with autism are less sensitive than neurotypical people in some of these areas

This over- or under-sensitivity means that children with autism may experience environments in a very different way to other children

This can affect concentration, stress, and behaviour

---

7. I may be really good at seeing detail but I don't always see the 'bigger picture'

There is quite a lot of evidence that children and young people with autism struggle to see the 'bigger picture', that is, put lots of pieces of information together to draw conclusions. For example, whilst walking down the street you might see a man running holding a woman's handbag. A group of people are chasing him and shouting. A woman is standing further away holding her hand to her head and crying. What conclusions do you draw? The bigger picture is of a woman who has been robbed, and possibly hurt, with bystanders in pursuit of the thief.

Someone who struggles to see the bigger picture may focus on extraneous details, such as the colour and shape of the handbag, the sound of footsteps as they fall on the pavement, or even the goods in the shop window to the left. This is known as 'weak central coherence', described extensively by Uta Frith, Emeritus Professor of Cognitive Development at University College London (see Frith, 2003). The basic premise is that autism stops the child from putting information together to make a coherent 'whole'.

The robbery example is quite an extreme one, and more able children would of course be able to draw the appropriate conclusions from the situation. However, in everyday situations, children with autism are more likely to see the detail than the bigger picture. Sometimes this is a real strength; they may be really skilled at working out detailed plans, seeing how parts of a machine connect together, or spotting slight changes in the environment. One young man walked into my clinic room and immediately told me where all the fire alarm points were along the corridor. If we needed to find a fire alarm quickly, he would be the more able of the two of us.

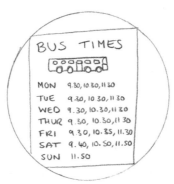

I MAY BE REALLY GOOD AT SEEING DETAIL...
BUT I DON'T ALWAYS SEE THE 'BIGGER PICTURE'

At other times, not being able to see the bigger picture causes stress for children with autism. Remember Yasmina, who thought her parents were simply walking away from her when they went to the kitchen to prepare food? Thinking about this in terms of the bigger picture, Yasmina was not able to put these pieces of information together effectively:

I am hungry. It is lunchtime. My mum has walked into the kitchen. She is getting some pans from the cupboard.

For more able children, problems in seeing the bigger picture can cause difficulties in certain areas of schoolwork – for example, drawing conclusions from a story or predicting characters' behaviour based on their past actions.

Generalising

Putting information together to make a coherent whole also enables us to form generalisations from one situation to the next. We apply the information we have learnt in one situation to a different scenario. This problem with generalising knowledge or skills can often trip up our attempts to change the behaviour of children with autism. They may be able to learn how to manage anger in the clinic, eat green and red food at grandma's, or travel on the number 78 bus, but these new skills are not easily transferred to other situations. This can be frustrating for everyone, but it is important to keep this problem with generalisation in mind rather than seeing the young person as stubborn or unwilling. Children may need extra explanations, practice, and encouragement to try new skills in a variety of settings.

Key learning points for your autism lens

Children with autism may be really skilled in seeing the detail in a situation

They may have more difficulty putting together lots of pieces of information to make sense of a situation

This affects understanding of social scenarios and the ability to draw appropriate conclusions

This also affects generalisation: transferring learning from one situation to another

---

8. I am a child or young person first, with my own personal story and my own likes and dislikes

It should go without saying that there is much more to a child or young person with autism than just their condition. To really be able to look through a child's autism lens some knowledge of that person is essential. Like everyone else, they will have an individual temperament and likes or dislikes shaped by their own experience. They will have strengths or difficulties as well as cultural identities formed in their family or community. This is why one size doesn't fit all when working with children with autism – strategies need to be fine-tuned to meet individual needs.

Children with autism are of course first and foremost children. They have needs for security, comfort, love, stimulation, and fun. They experience the same developmental stages that other children go through, although these may occur slightly earlier or later than average. The 'terrible twos' (which last much longer for most children, with or without autism!), the fears of middle childhood, and the boundary-testing and mood swings of adolescence will all be experienced by children with autism. So, it is important to take developmental stage into account when developing your child's autism lens.

A 'passport' or quick pen picture (as in the example on page 62) can be a good way to start in summarising essential pieces of information about an individual with autism. These are the key points that will be helpful to anyone working with that child. Parents usually have the most knowledge but previous teachers, formal assessment reports, and of course the young person will also be able to enrich the passport with valuable information. A typical pen picture includes information about strengths and interests, alongside the child's individual difficulties and situations in which they may need additional support. Strategies that help can also be included. This can then be shared with the various adults that the child comes into contact with, such as teachers and extended family members.

Key learning points for your autism lens

Every child and young person with autism is different

An individual, person-centred approach is needed

Take into account individual strengths and difficulties, likes and dislikes

One size does not fit all

Chapter 5

Talking with Children and Young People about Autism

At some point, most parents and professionals consider discussing autism with a child or young person, whether that is the individual with an autism diagnosis, their siblings, or classmates. The questions adults often ask themselves are:

- When should I tell the child/other children about the diagnosis?
- What are the pros and cons of talking about autism?
- How should I tell them?
- Who else needs to know?
- Are there written materials or stories I can use to help me?

When should I talk with the child/other children about autism?

There really isn't a right or wrong answer to this question – it depends on several factors. Useful points to consider are: What is the child likely to understand? Have they noticed and commented on any differences between themselves and other children they know? Do the parents or carers understand the diagnosis well enough to answer any questions?

Some children may not have developed the language or understanding to be able to discuss their diagnosis. Others develop this as they grow and become teenagers. As a general guide, if young people are asking direct questions about their differences or difficulties, it may be the right time to answer these questions honestly but sensitively.

What are the pros and cons of talking about autism?

Everyone has their own ideas about the advantages and disadvantages of opening up. It is hard to know how each young person will receive the news that they have an autism spectrum diagnosis. Individual circumstances will dictate the balance of positives and negatives, which may include the following:

Pros

■ Gives young people an accurate explanation of their differences from other children/young people

■ Allows open and honest discussion about their difficulties

■ Provides them with a community of other people with a similar way of seeing the world, potentially reducing any sense of isolation

■ Talking about autism proactively stops young people hearing the information second-hand or by mistake

Cons

■ Autism is a complex condition which may be very hard to understand

■ Young people may resent the diagnosis and worry about its impact on their future life

■ Adults talking about autism may not feel ready to answer questions or manage emotional reactions

Sometimes parents worry that their child will 'use' the diagnosis to excuse their behaviour or opt out of situations they struggle with. Whilst this may be a realistic concern, it is still possible to talk about autism in such a way that young people understand that adults still have positive expectations of them.

How should I talk with a child or young person about autism?

The level at which you talk to a young person about autism will depend on the individual's communication style, but there are some general principles to bear in mind.

Firstly, the person who begins the conversation about autism should be a trusted adult who will be able to answer any questions as they arise. Often this is a parent, but in some circumstances another adult could fulfil this role.

Secondly, the idea of autism should be communicated in a constructive way. As a lifelong diagnosis, it is important that young people receiving this news are not left thinking that they have a 'disease', that the future is hopeless, or that they are alone with the condition. Adults sometimes find it useful to lay the foundations of a discussion about autism, high-lighting the following ideas:

- We are all different and we all have individual strengths and difficulties
- Difference can be affirmative
- Adults have positive aspirations and expectations of the child in question

Positive role models can also be introduced alongside the idea that we all see the world differently. Honest, straightforward answers may be required. Any conversation about autism is very unlikely to be a one-off. Young people may need to return to it at different times, so the first conversation is usually just the starting point.

Siblings, grandparents, and other extended family members do not always find out straightaway that a child in the family has received a diagnosis of autism. It is usually up to parents and the young person to decide when is the appropriate time to share the news.

Talking to other family members about autism gives them the opportunity to understand the child's needs and educate themselves about autism. However, they may need additional written or DVD material to support this. There are a number of useful books for siblings of children with autism (see the Further Reading and Resources section) and some areas have courses or clubs for brothers and sisters to help them understand their sibling better. These clubs can also help siblings feel that there are other kids out there having similar experiences to them.

In mainstream schools, classmates are sometimes told about a child's autism. This can only happen with the explicit consent of the family and after a careful weighing up of potential pitfalls and benefits. If teaching staff and parents, and potentially the child themselves, agree that it would be helpful to share the information, then this may help to increase acceptance of children with autism.

Are there written materials that can support this discussion?

There is a wealth of information, from websites to books, which can support conversations about autism. Many of these feature firsthand accounts by individuals with autism, including positive role models. The Further Reading and Resources section at the end of this book lists a sample of these.

Part Two

Developing Skills and Promoting Well-Being in Children and Young People with Autism

Chapter 6

What Works and Who Can Help?

There is no 'cure' for autism, but intervention can help with communication, interaction, and behaviour, as well as associated problems such as anxiety. Children and young people with autism need additional support in order to reach their potential and manage the social demands of school and the wider world. With the appropriate help, children and young people with autism *can* reach their potential.

The quality of evidence for the various approaches that claim to help varies greatly. There are websites that offer advice to parents and professionals in their evaluation of different methodologies or provide guidelines for evidence-based interventions (e.g. www.researchautism.net and www.nice.org.uk). This guidance can be useful because there are an overwhelming number of interventions – from diet and dolphin therapy to more mainstream approaches such as social skills groups. Some do nothing at all (other than cost parents a lot of money), some are potentially harmful (e.g. chelation, a medical procedure designed to remove toxins from the body using chemicals which can cause kidney or liver damage), and some are at the very early stages of evaluation.

Research suggests the following strategies offer the most benefit:

- Creating educational environments that work *with* autism and thereby enable the young person to learn effectively and optimise their chances for an adult life that is as independent and fulfilling as possible (see Chapter 7)
- Approaches aimed at developing social skills and understanding emotions (see Chapter 8)
- Communication methods that enhance children's ability to interact with the people around them (see Chapter 9)
- Intervening to address associated emotional or mental health difficulties (see Chapter 10)
- Approaches that seek to understand behaviour and teach children alternative ways to behave (see Chapter 11)

There are also general 'well-being' approaches, many of which may not necessarily have been rigorously researched, but most people find to be beneficial. For example, supported social activities, befriending, and support in employment or education choices should all be useful. It is also vital to keep in mind that children with autism have the same basic needs as other children, so they need time to play, relax, and learn as well as secure relationships with other people and caregivers.

Who can help?

Services and agencies specialising in autism vary greatly across geographical areas, with some regions having effective multidisciplinary teams and others experiencing a shortage of appropriate services. Ideally children and young people will have access to the professionals listed below, should they need them. These are the experts in working with children with autism but they may also be involved in training other professionals and parents, and contributing to ongoing support and planning for children and young people.

Teacher/school special needs or inclusion team

All school-age children with autism should be in full-time education. Along with parents or carers, teachers have the most frequent input into children's lives. All teaching staff working with children with autism should have received training so they can understand the condition and provide ways to support children in their class with a diagnosis. Of course, this varies greatly between schools and regions but most educational settings will be able to access or buy in the appropriate training. It is also important that new staff receive the necessary training and it is regularly updated.

Teachers from specialist schools sometimes provide outreach advice to mainstream schools. There are also education consultants from a teaching background who can assess children's educational needs and offer advice to schools.

Speech and language therapists

Speech and language therapists assess children's ability to communicate, including their understanding and expression. They can design interventions based on children's individual communication needs. Sometimes speech and language therapists work directly with children but they also provide teaching programmes for parents and/or staff to implement.

Paediatricians or child/adolescent psychiatrists

Many diagnoses are made by paediatricians or child and adolescent psychiatrists. As medically qualified doctors, these professionals are well placed to distinguish autism from other similar medical conditions. Paediatricians can also assess and treat physical health problems that cause additional challenges for children with autism (e.g. constipation). Psychiatrists can assess and treat any other mental health or behaviour problems or difficulties with medication.

Clinical and educational psychologists

Some psychologists make diagnoses of autism and many also contribute to the assessment process. Roles vary in different areas but generally educational psychologists provide assessment and intervention in schools, and clinical psychologists work with children and parents outside of school. Naturally there is some crossover. Psychologists and related mental health professionals can provide assessments and interventions around skills development, behaviour, and mental health.

Social workers or support workers

Social workers can support families to receive appropriate services and benefits, including care and short breaks for children and their families. Social workers sometimes become involved when there are concerns about a child or their family, yet however their involvement begins, their goal is usually to support families to manage as best they can. In some areas, support workers take on some of this role or act as key workers to coordinate services for families.

Early intervention workers

Some regions employ early intervention workers under a variety of job titles. Their role is to implement communication and behaviour approaches with young children and their families to try to develop children's communication and functioning as early as possible.

Occupational therapists

Occupational therapy with children with autism often focuses on motor skills, sensory issues, and interventions to maximise learning and engagement in activities. They may work directly with the child or young person or provide programmes for teachers and parents to implement.

Residential workers

Some young people access short breaks in residential settings; some young adults move into these settings on a full-time basis. Residential staff should be trained in autism and approaches to support their clients.

The key message is that everyone needs to work together to support children and young people with autism. Not all of these professionals may be involved, and some may only be involved for limited time periods, but it is vital that support is coordinated and communicated between agencies. Parents and professionals working productively together increase positive outcomes for children.

Key learning points

Autism cannot be 'cured' but the appropriate support can improve the communication, behaviour, social skills, and well-being of people with autism

A range of professionals work with children and young people with autism, offering different skills and roles

---

Chapter 7

Autism-Friendly Educational Settings

Children and young people with autism attend all types of schools, from autism-specific schools, to specialist schools for children with disabilities, to mainstream, selective, or private schools. Whichever type of provision is on offer, the school should adopt principles of good practice. These include:

- A positive school ethos about autism
- Staff training and awareness
- Classrooms and whole schools that are accessible to children with autism
- Working together with parents and other agencies
- A broad curriculum that includes social skills
- Effective progress monitoring
- Adapting teaching to meet the needs of children and young people with autism
- Support through transitions

According to the Autism Education Trust (2011), these are the features of schools identified as helpful by teachers and parents, many of which have some research evidence to support them. For example, we know that there is a rationale for teaching in ways that suit the learning styles of many people with autism. There is a lot of research yet to be undertaken to establishing people in education, but these principles are undoubtedly a good framework.

Positive school ethos about autism

A positive ethos means valuing children and young people with autism within the school environment. It usually involves a combination of the following aims:

- Understanding the needs of students with autism and making reasonable adjustments
- Working to include students with autism and to ensure they participate in activities, enjoy school life, and achieve their potential
- High aspirations for students with autism

Staff training and awareness

It is vital that staff working directly with students with autism have attended training to increase their knowledge. It is highly beneficial if *all* staff receive this training, including those with supervisory responsibilities at less structured times of the school day, such as midday assistants/lunchtime staff and new starters.

Classrooms and whole schools that are accessible to children with autism

Careful thought should be put into the built environment and the school routine so that young people with autism can manage any demands and focus on developing their skills.

In the classroom

Quiet working areas for young people who have sensory issues or whose learning is impeded by social demands should be available. The option of a work station with reduced stimulation or distraction can aid learning for some young people with autism.

Another example of an autism-friendly classroom is to put knowledge about visual learning and supports into daily practice. A visual display in the classroom of class rules, sanctions, and rewards will benefit all children, including those with autism, as long as it is used effectively.

In the playground

Breaktimes can present real challenges, given both the social demands and the usually increased level of sensory stimulation. Schools that offer quieter areas or structured activities at every breaktime make these times more manageable and enjoyable.

Individual children may need some adjustments to their school routine or classroom environment. Look through Pete's autism lens for an example:

I used to find it really difficult at the start and end of the day when everyone is going into school or going home. It was so busy and everyone was pushing and shoving. My teacher made a plan so I could go into and out of school by a different door and my mum would meet me there.

Working together with parents and other agencies

There are a number of agencies and professional groups with particular expertise to offer (see Chapter 6). The availability of these services varies greatly between geographical areas, but most schools should have some access to specialist autism support teachers, speech and language therapists, and educational psychologists. Other services often work in partnership with schools – for example, occupational therapists, child health, and child and adolescent mental health services.

This can provide a much more comprehensive and effective way of meeting children's needs and enabling their successful engagement with school.

Schools working together with parents will be at the individual level, with planning focusing on a single child's targets. However, there may be a broader level of parental involvement. Support groups for parents of children with autism and teaching sessions for parents on approaches used within the school are two common and generally well-received ideas. These help parents to feel supported and can also encourage them to put in place learning and behaviour strategies at home, to the benefit of both settings.

A broad curriculum that includes social skills

Including children's emotional and social development as part of the curriculum is not a new concept, and nor is it limited to children with additional needs in the social and emotional aspects of learning. For students with autism, extra attention to their communication, social functioning, emotional well-being, and behaviour is vital. Ideas about addressing these areas are covered throughout this book. There should be an expectation that the young person will be enabled to meet their potential.

With this in mind, independence skills may become a focus during the teenage years. Independent travel, self-care, and managing the demands of the wider world may all be addressed, where appropriate, in order to widen the life choices of young people with autism. This can be facilitated through experiential learning opportunities (e.g. taking pupils shopping to practise using money or going by bus to teach travel skills).

Effective progress monitoring

Setting targets, and monitoring progress in relation to these goals, is a way of keeping aspirations high and picking up difficulties early. It is also a useful tool for communicating with parents and young people about the work the school is doing. Schools may have different ways of measuring progress, but keeping the concept of the broad curriculum in mind is essential.

Standardised assessment tools such as PIVATS can support pupil monitoring and enable teachers to establish individual objectives for the child across the curriculum. This includes the social and emotional aspects of learning. The objectives, and progress made in relation to these objectives, can be shared with everyone working with the child (including their parents). This will be helpful in demonstrating achievement over time and reinforces the message of holding high aspirations for the child in reaching their potential.

Performance Indicators for Value Added Target Setting (PIVATS)

PIVATS is a tool developed by Lancashire County Council in the UK to break down educational progress into small steps. This enables teachers to evidence pupils' strengths, and describe and monitor progress. A standardised approach means that different teachers can describe progress in a consistent way.

Adapting teaching to meet the needs of children and young people with autism

Looking through the child's autism lens can help teachers consider the sorts of adaptations that may be required. Take these three aspects of the lens:

I may need support to communicate and to understand other people's communication

Communicating ideas through talking alone may not give children with autism the best chance of understanding and applying new concepts. Depending on the child's abilities, visual supports – like objects, photographs, graphs, pictures, or key points written down – may all be useful. Practising or role-playing new skills will help to embed them.

I may have different sensory experiences to you

Children with autism may find their sensory experiences get in the way of their learning. For example, very busy wall displays, large group activities, or lots of students sitting very close together in a classroom, dining hall, or PE lesson may cause some children difficulties. Adaptations will depend very much on the needs of the child concerned.

I may be really good at seeing detail, but I don't always see the 'bigger picture'

Young people may need extra support to understand the 'point' of educational tasks. This relates to both the reason for the task and what is expected from the student. Take a look through James's lens:

I don't see the point of English Literature. I can't understand why the characters in a book think a certain way or do the things they do. And I can't see why this is going to help me in my life – I want to be a games designer, I don't need stories.

Explicitly explaining the point of a task, and providing some sort of outcome or goal, can help motivate students who are struggling in this area. Breaking down an assignment into small, achievable steps can also encourage students to persist with an assignment they are finding challenging. For example, if the task is to write a story, it may help if the young person is given a story planner in which they can work out the different parts of the narrative in advance, rather than having to see it as a 'whole' from the start.

Support through transitions

Moving from nursery to school, from one year to the next, from primary to secondary school and to college all require preparation and forethought. (Remember the autism lens: *I may need additional support to manage change.*) Most children with autism will need to start preparing for these transitions early and carefully. Becoming familiar with new teachers, classrooms, schools, or colleges well before the change occurs – through photographs and visits – can make transitions smoother and less stressful. For the move to secondary school, planning should commence at least a year before the move happens, and additional visits are often required to make the transition as successful as possible.

Some transitions are not just about a new environment. A whole new skill set may be required for activities such as moving from one classroom to another for lessons, organising a range of equipment, and homework tasks. Some schools provide extra support in acquiring and practising these skills through summer workshops or small group activities. A nominated transition coordinator can provide an essential link – they will liaise with the receiving school, year teacher, and parents to develop an individual transition plan.

Key learning points

Children with autism are educated in a huge variety of settings but the principle of good autism practice should apply across all of these

Staff training and awareness, as well as working with parents and other professionals, are essential to good practice

Education is about social and emotional development as well as academic attainment

Teaching and the school environment can be adapted to meet the needs of children and young people with autism

Transition times need careful planning and additional support

Chapter 8
Developing Social Skills

Parents and teachers are understandably keen to develop young people's social skills. They know this will help in the development of relationships, the prevention of bullying or the young person feeling isolated, and may eventually help with college or employment. If parents can see their child's social skills developing they may feel more confident about taking their children to see other people or visit different places.

What social skills can children with autism learn?

Research into the area of social skills has produced mixed results (Rao et al., 2008). Social behaviours such as appropriate eye contact, greeting other people, sharing, and turn-taking may all increase as a result of directly teaching these skills. More advanced abilities such as listening to others and knowing when to stop talking can also be improved with guidance. However, the research base is not solid: the results are mixed.

Some studies have found no positive impact at all of pro-grammes to increase positive social behaviours. Others have found changes in only one or two social skills, or that skills practised in groups are not generalised to school or other places. Overall, the evidence suggests that specific teaching of social skills is likely to produce some positive results, but we shouldn't expect to see major changes across the board. So, it is realistic to hope for specific improvements in some social behaviour, but to remain mindful that there is no evidence we can 'cure' core difficulties in social interaction through teaching or training.

However, there is fairly good evidence that children and young people with autism can learn to recognise emotions through taught programmes. In some cases this has involved computer programs or DVDs (e.g. *The Transporters*). Other researchers have used group settings so that children are dealing with real and unpredictable facial expressions. Christian Ryan and Caitriona Charragain of the COPE Foundation in Northern Ireland describe a programme that explicitly teaches the individual elements of facial expressions (Ryan and Charragain, 2010). For example, when we are surprised we raise our eyebrows, open our eyes wide, and our jaw may drop. Children aged between 6 and 14 learnt to recognise emotional expressions through direct teaching, role-play, and games. They completed homework so that the skills were practised, and hopefully generalised, to school and home. Parents were involved to support this approach. After taking part in the four-session course, children were better able to identify emotions. However, the research does not yet tell us whether we can move children on from being able to identify emotions to responding appropriately and empathically.

How can children with autism learn social skills?

Children without autism develop social skills from 'social learning', that is, watching how others behave and receiving praise and approval for some behaviours and disapproval for others. Their behaviour is shaped by other people's actions and responses. This means they can learn antisocial behaviours as well as more positive ones!

We would expect children with autism to learn social skills in a different way. Firstly, they may not have the 'theory of mind' to understand or be influenced by other people's approval. Secondly, they may have difficulties in transferring skills between situations; learning to say hello to the assistant in the supermarket does not mean the woman in the post office will be treated the same way. So, children with autism are likely to need more scaffolding and support in order to develop their skills.

There are two main ways in which social skills may develop: continuous, day-to-day experience in school and the community, and time-limited, specific programmes aimed at teaching social skills in a set of dedicated sessions.

Continuous social skills training – whole class approaches

This is an example of where good autism practice is pretty much the same thing as good practice. We can't necessarily expect children with autism to simply pick up social skills from their peers; for a start, children who develop in a typical way do not always behave in a socially appropriate way. Whole class approaches aim to teach and develop social skills for all children in the class or school.

The explicit teaching of skills – such as greeting, sharing, and starting conversations – in regular 10-minute bursts has been shown to increase these skills for children with autism who have at least average intellectual ability (Kamps et al., 1992).

There are clear benefits to teachers building social skills training into their ongoing schedules. Firstly, this does not rely on bringing in other professionals, so it is more efficient. Secondly, the training is likely to occur over a longer period of time, so we would hope it would generalise more effectively. Thirdly, it provides opportunities for young people with autism to build relationships with the students they see every day.

The principles for teaching social skills are likely to be the same whether this is through a brief, targeted programme or ongoing classroom-based learning. Effective programmes tend to have the following features:

- They use live learning techniques such as role-play and practice
- They explain *why* as well as *how* different social skills are used
- They teach skills explicitly, making clear the 'unwritten rules' of social interaction
- They use specific concrete targets such as giving compliments or taking turns
- They involve parents who can support social skills practice outside the school or clinic

Moving up a gear from whole class approaches, the 'circle of friends' (Whitaker et al., 1998; Kalyva and Avramidis, 2005) aims to help young people with autism integrate with their classmates using a specially selected group who teachers can confidently predict will be supportive of that child. The approach requires that the social difficulties of the young person with autism are discussed within the friendship group. It follows that the 'target' child should consent to this and have some insight into their own difficulties. Research evidence is again mixed, but some positive results have been reported in terms of social interactions and acceptance. Teachers who feel that their student with autism would benefit from a 'circle of friends' need to think carefully about who is in the group and how it will be structured.

Teaching Social Skills

Pick a concrete skill to work on...

Explain <u>why</u> and <u>how</u> the skill is used

> Turn-taking is a good skill because....
> The way to take turns is to...

Practise the skill in different situations

SCHOOL   HOME   COMMUNITY

  ... Reward/reinforce attempts & success

Time-limited social skills programmes

Some children will need a more targeted programme. Most of the research in this area has focussed on short-term, specific programmes aimed at teaching social skills in a very direct, controlled, and measurable way. The emphasis has usually been on young people of at least average intellectual ability rather than those with severe learning disabilities.

These programmes often involve groups of children with similar difficulties, typically those with mainstream intellectual ability but who are experiencing major social interaction problems as a result of their autism. This enables the programme to be as targeted as possible and, anecdotally, young people feel reassured by meeting others with similar needs. This means friendships develop and can flourish with support from parents. The downside is that the positive social skills learnt in the programme may not be generalised to other situations, so this needs to be addressed. Encouraging young people to practise skills outside of sessions in a monitored way may help.

One example of such a programme is described by Christopher Lopata and colleagues at the State University of New York at Buffalo (Lopata et al., 2010). They studied an approach aimed at improving skills, such as recognition of other's emotions, and talking about topics other than the child's own special interest. Skills were taught in a clear and concrete way, with 'unwritten rules' explained. Children worked together on tasks along with a therapist. They learnt through practice, direct instruction, and being given feedback on their use of social skills. They also talked about applying the skills they had learnt in real-life situations. A points reward system was used to reinforce positive social behaviours, with points taken away if the young person invaded someone else's personal space or shared irrelevant information. Parents were also taught how to help their child generalise these social skills in other settings. As a result, children's social skills improved after the programme, particularly their understanding of non-literal language such as common sayings. Parents also thought that their children's social skills had improved more generally. How long these effects lasted is not known, but the early results are promising.

Lopata's study has not been the only one to report positive results from social skills training (e.g. Bauminger, 2002; Webb et al., 2004). Depending on where you live it is possible to buy in packages or access them from local providers such as educational psychologists or speech and language therapists. Off-the-shelf programmes can also be bought, but it is essential to take an individualised look at any approach on offer. We need to think about the young people we know and what social skills difficulties they are experiencing. Use your individual autism lens to do this:

Take a look through Daisy's lens:

I don't think anyone really wants to be my friend. There are two girls in my class I like. I tell them they are my friends all the time. Sometimes they tell me to shut up and say I am going to get them into trouble. They sometimes want to talk about boring things like who is going out with boys in our year. I am not interested in boys.

Take a look through Ryan's lens:

I don't like the other kids in my class. They get too close to me and sometimes they want to play with the toys I am playing with. If I shout really loudly at them they go away. I build really good models in school and sometimes the other kids want to touch them, but I think they will break them so I don't let anyone near them.

We can see that Daisy and Ryan have very different needs in terms of social skill development. Daisy wants to make friends but is probably making social approaches at inappropriate times and is unable to find shared interests. She may benefit from a programme that targets showing interest in other people's preferred topics of conversation and knowing when to start and stop talking. Ryan would rather play by himself and is highly involved in his interests, rejecting the social approaches made by other children. He may need a programme that uses incentives and positive social experiences to enable him to join in activities with other children.

Key learning points

Children and young people with autism need extra support to develop social skills

Social skills interventions are likely to have some positive effects on specific behaviours but will not 'cure' the young person of their social interaction difficulties

Interventions can be offered at different levels: whole class, small class group, or a group of children with similar needs

An individualised approach should be adopted that takes into account the child's individual autism lens

Interventions should explain why, as well as how, we use social skills

Interventions should describe and practise social skills in a meaningful and visual way

Chapter 9

Developing Communication and Understanding

We know that social communication is one of the core areas of difficulty for children on the autistic spectrum. Children's communication has a direct impact on their ability to socialise and express needs or emotions. Individuals who cannot use their language to communicate may resort to challenging behaviour to inform other people about their needs. Equally, if children do not understand other people's communication or comprehend what is happening, this can be a huge obstacle to their learning, behaviour, and emotional well-being. Helping children with autism to develop their communication skills and understanding is therefore a top priority for parents and teachers. Speech and language therapists can offer specialist assessment, advice, and intervention to support this.

The support you need to offer the child will depend on their individual requirements – each child will have specific strengths and difficulties. Understanding other's communication is often seen as the foundation, or seed, for the child's own communication skills. With this seed planted and growing, children are better placed to express themselves through the use of words, pictures, or gestures. The correct use of words, sentences, and grammar follows on from here in typically developing children, but these processes may be disrupted for children with autism.

Some children do not develop speech at all or use just a few words or phrases. Others who can use speech do so only to meet their needs, and not for social enjoyment. Some children have well-developed speech but particular difficulties in specific areas such as understanding non-literal language or expressing their emotions verbally. So, any of these areas may be the target for intervention, depending on how the individual is developing.

Evidence-based communication interventions

■ **Picture Exchange Communication System (PECS)**

A communication approach developed and manualised by Lori Frost and Andy Bondy. Children learn to exchange pictures for items or activities they want as a starting point for developing social communication.

■ **Hanen Programs™, such as More than Words**

A course for parents and carers which teaches them how to help their children reach their communication potential. This is achieved through play, use of visual supports, understanding behaviour, and improving the quality of parent–child interactions.

■ **Social Stories™**

An approach developed by Carol Gray in which short 'stories' are written specifically for individual people with autism to increase their understanding of situations or social behaviours.

■ **Interventions which promote joint (shared) attention and communication**

One example of this is pivotal response training (PRT). PRT targets critical elements of social development, including initiating social interactions and responding to social cues. Children are supported to develop skills in these areas using positive reinforcement and other motivational strategies.

Intensive Interaction

A one-to-one approach developed by practitioners including Phoebe Caldwell and David Hewitt. Intensive Interaction aims to increase the 'social engagement' (e.g. eye contact, turning towards the other person) of people with autism, especially those who have little or no spoken language. Interactions are developed in a relaxed and enjoyable way, often following the sounds, actions, and interests of the person with autism. Research indicates that this approach can increase social engagement (Zeedyk et al., 2009) and clinical experience shows that it can provide a way of 'connecting' with children who otherwise do not engage with the adults around them.

Whatever stage children have reached, there are some key principles in helping them to develop their communication skills:

- We need to look at our own communication first
- Visual supports can assist children to understand others and express themselves

■ We can use children's special interests to develop their communication

We need to look at our own communication first

The way we communicate with children naturally has a significant effect on how they respond. Parents, teachers, and other adults may need to adjust their communication style for children with autism. Making alterations to everyday interactions can provide positive conditions for developing children's ability to understand, respond, and express themselves.

Children without communication difficulties will usually seek out interactions with other people, both for social enjoyment and to get their practical needs met. Children with autism are much less likely to do this, so the adults around them may need to pay special attention to creating opportunities for children to communicate, whatever their ability.

This might include having regular play sessions with the child where you join them in activities that they find particularly enjoyable. This may involve more unusual games like jumping or twirling ribbons or it may mean playing with building blocks or trains. The key point is to find an activity the child is motivated by and gently join them by commenting on or imitating what they are doing. This helps children to share their enjoyment in an activity, as well as giving them opportunities to hear new words or start turn-taking.

Another way of creating communication opportunities is to give children chances to make requests or choices. This means standing back slightly – perhaps keeping hold of a few building blocks to encourage the child to make a request or offering them a choice of two types of biscuit.

Listening to your own language

Our own speech and language may work well with typically developing children, but often needs to be adjusted to meet the needs of children with autism, such as:

- Reducing the number of words you use in each sentence
- Trying not to ask more than one question at once
- Giving children more time to process what you have said – wait and pause before you say anything else

Take a look through Paul's lens.

> My parents ask me loads of questions and talk and talk. Sometimes I can't understand the words because they are saying them too quickly and there are too many of them. I have to put my hands over my ears when they do this.

Another communication trap that most of us fall into at some point is forgetting that children with autism often have a very literal understanding of language. Watch out for using too many metaphors or sayings, or deploying irony and sarcasm. Try to say what you mean in the most straightforward way possible. More able children can learn to understand irony or proverbs, but it may not come naturally to children with autism.

Take a look through Danny's lens.

When I need my dad to help me with my homework, he says 'in a minute'. I time a minute on the computer and he still doesn't come. Then he says 'in a minute' again, even though that means he is going to be at least two minutes. This makes me angry. If I shout really loud he comes in to help.

We can see that Danny has resorted to shouting because he has not understood the implicit message his dad is giving him. A small adjustment on his dad's part may help – for example, saying he will come when he has finished the task he is doing.

Visual supports can help children to understand others and express themselves

Most of us can probably think of times when we find visual information more accessible than words, for example:

- Writing down someone's address or printing out a map instead of trying to remember it
- Keeping a diary or calendar
- Toilet signs in a country where you do not speak the language
- Signalling to a friend who is across a crowded room rather than shouting

Most of us use visual information to help our memories, understanding, and expression. Visual information has some advantages over spoken words: it doesn't disappear immediately so we can look at it repeatedly, it doesn't require us to rely on our recall ability, and it takes out 'social interference' – the added demands of understanding someone's speech.

There are several reasons why visual supports may be particularly beneficial for children with autism. Firstly, a significant proportion of people with autism process visual information more effectively than verbal information (Planche and Lemonnier, 2012). We also know that many people with autism have specific language difficulties, so relying entirely on the spoken word does not give them the best chance of developing their skills. Finally, children with autism are more likely to have difficulties remembering complex information (Williams et al., 2006) and visual supports have the added benefit of providing a permanent reminder. As a result, a number of communication approaches use a visual approach to support children's understanding and development.

Sometimes adults are concerned that using visual information to support children with autism means taking a backward step or that it may delay their speech development. However, using visual supports alongside spoken words in the correct way can improve the development of both understanding and expression.

Visual supports are used across the autism spectrum. The type of intervention appropriate for the child you know will depend on their individual needs. Input is often required from a speech and language therapist or another professional trained in communication approaches. Strategies should be consistent between home and school to make them as effective as possible. Here are some examples of visual supports, moving through the autism spectrum.

Objects of reference

For children with no speech and very early levels of understanding, objects of reference may be used. This means showing the child a single object consistently, usually to communicate the next activity. If their nappy needs changing, they are shown the nappy first to indicate that this is about to happen. A shoe can be held up to indicate it is time to go out. Consistency is key – the same item is used for the same activity, so a small range of familiar objects should be used that the child is able to recognise by sight, touch, or smell. Objects of reference can help anxious or preoccupied children to prepare for what is happening next, thereby making the social world a more predictable place. Children may then learn to use objects of reference for themselves to communicate their own needs.

Picture Exchange Communication System

Whilst objects of reference are used to help develop children's understanding, other approaches aim to develop children's ability to express themselves. The Picture Exchange Communication System (PECS – Frost and Bondy, 2002) mentioned above allows children with very limited verbal communication to express their needs and wishes through simple pictures. The autistic child has access to photographs or pictures depicting items or activities they are motivated by. They hand the relevant picture to an adult when they need something or want to start an activity. Parents, carers, and teachers should respond consistently and positively to such requests – everyone using PECS should be trained to do so. Research shows that for children and adults with very little speech, PECS provides a means of getting their needs met and making some choices. It is not yet clear whether PECS has an impact on speech development, but the system certainly helps some children and young people to communicate more effectively. Without this opportunity, children are more likely to use their behaviour to communicate – and the result may be challenging behaviour.

Visual schedules or timetables

Visual schedules or timetables are a series of photographs or pictures which let the child or young person know what is going to happen next. This may be as straightforward as a 'now and next' board that shows the current activity followed by whatever is coming up. Extended schedules may show what is going to happen at school for that session or even for the whole day. Alternatively, timetables can be used for specific events such as visits to the hospital or shops. This is useful because anxiety or unhappiness about transitions between activities can lead to stress and behaviours like aggression or the refusal to move on.

Preliminary research suggests that visual schedules can help children and young people with autism transfer more easily between activities (Dettmer et al., 2000). Hopefully this means the young person then feels less anxious about any changes.

Visual schedules are cheap to put into place and many children, with or without autism, benefit from having an overview of the session or school day. Even children with well-developed verbal skills can benefit – they may have understood their teacher telling them what will happen that day, but a visual reminder is permanent and easily accessible.

Take a look through Thomas's lens:

I like my schedule at school. Sometimes I am doing something I don't like, like circle time, and then I look at the schedule and see I am doing something good like the computer next. This makes me feel better because I know it's not long till I can go on the computer. I don't always want to come off the computer but then I can see I am going back on later that day and I feel OK about it. If my teacher talks to me too much about coming off the computer I get wound up.

Take a look through Kirsty's lens:

I was scared about going to the dentist so my mum took the schedule with us. It showed what was going to happen. First sit in the waiting room and read a magazine. Then go into the dentist's room and sit in the chair. The dentist will look in my mouth. Then we go home in the car.

Social Stories

Social Stories were developed by Carol Gray in the United States and provide a method to expand children's *understanding* (Gray and White, 2002). The stories are written from the specific point of view of the child or young person, at an appropriate language level, and supported with pictures or photographs. The stories can be used in a huge variety of situations, from understanding why it is a good thing to wash your hands after using the toilet, to why and when people shake hands to say hello. The key principle is that they explain *why* and *how* the world works in a certain way

– they are not simply a list of statements on how children should behave in a given situation. They explain the unwritten rules of social scenarios.

Most of the research into Social Stories shows positive results, although more rigorous studies are needed (Karkhaneh et al., 2010; Nichols et al., 2005). I have seen some real benefits of these stories in clinical practice, covering a wide variety of issues including: why it is good to drink water, why my milk teeth are falling out, and why my parents need to know where I am after school. Stories often need to be read several times to be effective, and it helps if home and school back each other up with the reading of stories.

Take a look through Cathy's lens:

I don't like brushing my teeth. I hate the feeling of the toothbrush and I didn't know why I had to do it every day. My mum and teacher started reading me a story about why it is good to brush my teeth. It says things like my teeth will stay strong and my breath will smell nice. I may not need fillings if I brush my teeth and this is good because I am scared of the dentist.

These are some examples of how visual supports can help children and young people with autism to understand the social world and develop their understanding of language. There are a wide range of ways in which visual supports can be used, depending on the needs of the individual child.

We can use children's special interests to develop their communication

Children with autism may not be as motivated to use communication for social purposes or may find communicating with other people stressful or unpleasant. Other children may talk *at* people about their special interests or be unable to express their emotions or take turns in conversation. Children may need extra incentives to work on their communication in the face of these obstacles. Using their special interests is a great place to start. Here are some examples of this in action:

▧ Involve favourite activities in play

▧ When teaching children to make requests with gestures, words, or pictures, start with something they really like to get them motivated

▧ Include time for their special interests on visual schedules

▧ If you are trying to help a child develop their conversation skills, talk with them about their special interest and directly encourage them to ask you questions

Key learning points

Children with autism have difficulties in communication and understanding across the autism spectrum

We often need to adjust our own speech

Visual supports are often helpful

Children's special interests can be included in developing communication skills

Specialist assessment and advice is often required from speech and language therapists or other professionals with training in specific communication approaches

Chapter 10

Emotional Well-Being and Mental Health

Like anyone else, children with autism experience the full range of emotions, from happiness and excitement through to sadness, anxiety, and anger. Having difficulties understanding emotions in yourself and others does not stop you feeling those emotions. Unfortunately, children across the autism spectrum are more likely to experience anxiety in their everyday lives than other children, and around 80% of parents also describe their child with a diagnosis as being more 'irritable' than most children (Dickerson Mayes et al., 2011). This is probably due at least partly to the extra challenges that children and young people with autism face on a daily basis.

The social world is often not ready to meet the needs of young people with social understanding, communication, or sensory issues. We have to work hard to support the emotional well-being of children with autism. Teenagers and adults with autism are at higher risk of developing mental health difficulties such as depression and severe anxiety (Kim et al., 2000). It is important to take steps early to prevent, observe, and respond to these problems. We can:

- Promote emotional well-being
- Support children to understand their emotions and ways of coping
- Identify and respond to more severe needs

Promoting emotional well-being

Children with autism have the same basic needs as all children when it comes to emotional well-being. Feeling loved by a parent or carer, having time to play and learn, having a secure home and feeling safe – all of these are as important for children with autism as anyone else.

However, extra support is often required beyond these basic requirements to help children with autism to feel relaxed and happy enough to be able to play, learn, and take part in the social world. Take a look through these children's autism lenses and see the obstacles to their emotional happiness:

Taylor's lens: *Social interactions can be challenging for me*

I haven't got any proper friends at school. I don't play with anyone at breaktime and I don't go to any parties. I want to have some friends but I don't know how.

Steven's lens: *I may have different sensory experiences to you*

The worst thing about going to school is waiting in the playground in the morning. It is so noisy and everyone is shouting, and the teacher blows the whistle really loud. It happens at breaktime and lunchtime too and at the end of the day. It stresses me out all day.

Jenny's lens: *I may need additional support to manage change*

I have a new teacher this year and I don't want to go back to school. I liked my old teacher Mr Bridges. The new teacher Miss Oliver will do everything differently. Mr Bridges knew where I needed to sit and he could tell when I needed help.

These sorts of experiences can add up to a chronic level of stress which may increase challenging behaviour or mood difficulties, or both. Children with autism do not need to be kept away from everything that causes them anxiety. This would not teach them the necessary coping skills and may lead to further isolation. However, adjustments do need to be made to enable children to cope with the challenges they face. The types of adjustment required will depend on what you see through the child's autism lens. Here are some changes made for Taylor, Steven and Jenny.

Taylor's lens: *Social interactions can be challenging for me*

My school has started a lunchtime club where we play games that we all like. One of the teachers sits in with us. There are about six boys in the club. I play a fantasy game with Simon. My mum says he might be able to come to my house to play it sometime.

Steven's lens: *I may have different sensory experiences to you*

My teacher has given me a job to do at the start and end of breaktime. My job is to put the books away and get the pens out for the next lesson. They have also shown me a quiet corner in the playground where there are benches. This is where students go if they want to sit quietly or read.

Jenny's lens: *I may need additional support to manage change*

Miss Oliver and Mr Bridges both took me to see my new class-room. Mr Bridges told Miss Oliver that I like to sit in the same place every day. He said he is giving her a book that will tell her all about me so she will know what I need help with.

For children and young people with little or no spoken language, we need to use our autism lenses to promote their emotional well-being as much as possible. The principles are the same whether children have spoken language or not – they are more likely to achieve well-being if:

- They have a routine that is fairly predictable and gives them a sense of how their day will go – for example, through the regular use of visual schedules
- They have consistent caregivers who provide them with love, are generally sensitive to their needs, and put appropriate boundaries in place
- They have opportunities to learn, play, and take part in activities they enjoy

Supporting children to understand their emotions and ways of coping

Children with autism may have difficulty understanding their own emotions as well as other people's. They may also find it difficult to communicate changes in how they are feeling. Some children are experts at covering up their negative moods at school but let it all out at home. Others become overwhelmed by changes in their emotions and respond by becoming very upset or even aggressive.

For children who use language to communicate, helping them develop an 'emotional vocabulary' gives them a better chance of expressing themselves rather than bottling up negative feelings or exploding with emotion. Labelling feelings clearly and frequently – both the child's and your own – is a starting point. For example:

- I felt happy when you gave me that birthday card
- You look sad because we have to leave the park
- You feel angry when it is time to stop playing on the computer

Many children with verbal abilities will be able to develop their emotional understanding as they grow, and there are resources available to support this. One example is the 'Incredible 5-Point Scale' (Buron and Curtis, 2004) which helps children and young people to learn to distinguish between different intensities of emotion and come up with a shared plan for management if they start to feel too angry or anxious. The scales can also be used to help children monitor their own feelings and behaviour and agree ideas for what they, and other people, can do if things start to escalate.

Another approach is Tony Attwood's 'Emotional Toolbox' (Attwood, 2001, 2004). This teaches young people how to reduce the intensity of emotions such as anger or anxiety using 'tools' or strategies. These can be physical tools (e.g. exercise), thinking tools which change patterns of thinking that are maintaining the negative emotion, or social tools which involve other people, or even pets, in managing emotions. A full range of tools can be explored and young people can develop their own individual toolkit to use when dealing with emotions they would like to change.

Both of these approaches incorporate visual supports. Children and young people can use visual ways to express how they are feeling or ask for help to manage their emotions – for example, pointing to an angry face or using an 'I need a break' card. These types of support can help children with autism to generalise their coping strategies as they remind them what to do in different situations. The extra value of visual supports is that they may be easier for the young person to understand and use in times of stress than verbal advice.

Identifying and responding to more severe needs

There are significantly higher rates of both depression and anxiety in people with autism. Not everyone with autism will experience these mental health difficulties. However, the increased risk means that it is helpful for other people to know what to look out for and what help is available and effective.

The risks are thought to be particularly high for young people who are higher functioning. This is because they develop a more acute awareness of the differences between themselves and their peers, their sense of social isolation, and the impact of not being able to reach their potential in terms of college or employment. However, children and young people who can't speak are also at risk of poor mental health, although they may show it in a different way.

Warning signs that mental health is deteriorating include:

- A change in sleep patterns, with more early waking or problems settling at night
- Loss of appetite
- Withdrawing further from social activities, including refusing to leave the house
- Becoming more obsessive or focussed on a restricted range of activities or topics of conversation than usual
- Specific phobias or constant worry

It is easy to see from the list above why depression and anxiety are easily missed by parents and professionals alike – there is a great degree of overlap with the core difficulties of autism. However, it is always worth seeking a professional opinion if you are concerned that these behaviours are increasing. There are a number of approaches that can help young people with autism who are experiencing these additional mental health difficulties. Cognitive behaviour therapy is commonly used, and with good outcomes. Sometimes this is delivered via a computer package which can be easier for young people with autism to access.

Cognitive behaviour therapy

Cognitive behaviour therapy (or CBT) is a widely used 'talking therapy' which can help people experiencing mental health problems such as anxiety, depression, and psychosis. A therapist works with the client or patient, looking at their thoughts, feelings, and behaviour, and the ways these interact. The client leans to recognise, challenge, and change thought patterns which are maintaining the problem.

The effectiveness of cognitive behaviour therapy for people with autism has been well researched, particularly for anxiety and anger problems (e.g. Sofronoff and Attwood, 2003; Wood et al., 2009). The treatment is usually adapted to better meet the needs of someone with autism.

Medication is also used sometimes to treat symptoms of anxiety or depression. Usually this will be an SSRI (selective serotonin reuptake inhibitor, such as fluoxetine). Whilst there is research evidence to support medication in these circumstances, concerns about side effects mean that they are usually only prescribed with careful consideration and alongside other approaches.

If the young person is self-harming or expressing thoughts of not wanting to be alive then advice should be sought urgently. Local child and adolescent mental health services should be able to offer assessment, advice, and intervention.

Key learning points

Children and young people with autism may need additional support to achieve emotional well-being

We may need to make adjustments to their environment to help them achieve this

With additional support, young people with autism can learn to identify and cope with their own feelings

More significant mental health difficulties, such as anxiety and depression, are more common in young people and adults with autism

Specialist help may be required to assess and manage these additional difficulties

---

Part Three

Working with Behaviour

Chapter 11

Understanding and Managing Challenging Behaviours

Over half of children with autism show challenging behaviours; behaviours so intense or frequent that they affect the emotional or physical well-being of the child or others, or prevent them taking part in activities in school or the community (Murphy et al., 2006).

Common behaviour difficulties occur in these areas:

- Sleep
- Toileting
- Feeding
- Physical aggression to other people or objects
- Self-injury such as slapping, biting, or head-banging
- Repetitive behaviours that get in the way of daily life

Essentially children with autism show the same range of behaviours as typically developing children, but they may persist longer, be more resistant to change, and have a more significant impact on the child and those around them. So, it is not surprising that behaviour is one of the reasons that parents and carers of children with autism often have higher levels of stress than other parents, including those of children with other disabilities (Abbeduto et al., 2004; Tomanik et al., 2004).

There are some general principles to consider if you are working with or caring for a child or young person whose behaviour is causing you concern. It may help to remain 'realistic but optimistic' about changes in behaviour. Realism is required; as many parents of children with autism will testify, managing their child's behaviour is a significant part of daily life. The tantrums and sleep/toileting/feeding trials of pre-school childhood and the limit-testing and turbulence of adolescence are also to be anticipated.

Fluctuations in behaviour depend on a multitude of factors, such as changes to the setting or routine, health problems like constipation or toothache, or wider difficulties in the family. A period of positive change can be followed unexpectedly by a return of the unwanted behaviour, leaving parents and professionals feeling as though they are back at square one. Sometimes the best laid plans do not work out as quickly or effectively as hoped; some behaviours are extremely persistent. Although we know that particular interventions can reduce challenging behaviours, nothing has a 100% guarantee of success.

However, it is essential and reasonable to remain positive about change for the majority of behaviours. These problems can and do reduce. The research demonstrates that the most effective approaches to changing behaviour involve:

1. An understanding of why the behaviour is happening – applying knowledge of the behaviour and autism.

2. Strategies that enable the child to learn alternative and more positive behaviours. This may require making changes to the setting and using communication and behavioural methods to help the child develop new skills. For the most part, this means that it is the adults caring for or working with the child who will be doing things differently in order to kick-start change in the child's behaviour.

Group-based parent-training programmes

The three courses described below have been evaluated as part of a research study by the Social Policy Research Unit at the University of York, with positive results (Beresford et al., 2012). Between 80–90% of parents actively participating in these programmes experience improvements in specific behaviours, which is maintained six months later – further evaluation will show how long the effects last.

■ *Riding the Rapids: Living with Autism or Disability* is a 10-week course for parents and carers of primary or secondary aged children with autism or complex needs around their disability. The focus is on understanding behaviour using psychological theory and changing or managing it through communication, teaching new skills, and parents' own stress management.

- *Cygnet* is a six-session course developed by Barnados UK. It is aimed at parents/carers of young people up to the age of 18 and provides information about the nature of autism spectrum conditions, with the remaining sessions dedicated to communication and behavioural strategies.

- *Autism Spectrum Condition Enhancing and Nurturing Development (ASCEND)* is an 11-week course which aims to share practical and theoretical strategies with parents and carers.

There are many more parent-training packages available. For example, the Australian parenting programme Triple P has a specific programme (Stepping Stones) for parents of children with disabilities, including autism. A region may have bought into a particular package or even developed their own.

Research and theory point us in the direction of four key principles in managing challenging behaviours at both home and school:

1. Understand behaviour using a structured approach

2. Look through your child's autism lens

3. Enable children to meet their needs in a more positive way

4. Prevention is better than cure

1. Understand behaviour using a structured approach

We need to know *why* the behaviour is happening before we can know *how* to change it. Strategies are most successful when they follow on logically from an understanding of the behaviour and the child's needs. Psychologists are interested in understanding, in a systematic way, what triggers the behaviour and what keeps it going for each individual child – the technical term for this approach is 'functional analysis'. The key questions to ask about a challenging behaviour are:

- Seen from the child's point of view, why is the behaviour happening?
- What is happening before the behaviour starts?
- What happens afterwards?

It is useful to look at challenging behaviour in a structured way, by observing, recording, and analysing a number of incidents. Examine what happens before, during, and after the behaviour, using both your observations of the situation and how it might be perceived through your child's autism lens. Looking repeatedly at what was happening before and after the behaviour identifies any patterns and possible areas for change. John Clements and Ewa Zarkowska (2000) suggest recording behaviour in terms of settings, triggers, and results.

Settings:

Where? When? Who was there? What was the child doing before the behaviour? How were they feeling? Sometimes we need to step back even further: was the child feeling generally stressed because of home or school difficulties, medical problems, or low mood? All of these may make challenging behaviour more likely. (Most of us can identify with the idea that our behaviour deteriorates when our tolerance is low because of stress.)

Triggers:

What happened just before the behaviour? The setting and triggers may be external or internal; toothache, hunger, boredom, and tiredness can all set off these behaviours.

Results:

What happened afterwards? What was the function of the behaviour? Sometimes it is what happens after the behaviour that is really keeping it going. So, has the behaviour:

- Helped them to escape or avoid a situation they found difficult?
- Helped them get something they wanted?

The same behaviour can have different
FUNCTIONS
GET ME OUT OF THIS LESSON!
I WANT TO PLAY WITH MY TRAINS
I WANT SOMEONE TO COME AND TALK TO ME
I AM SO STRESSED ... I AM GOING TO STAY HERE ...

■ Provided them with social attention at a time they wanted it?

■ Relieved boredom or been enjoyable?

■ Helped them feel better inside by venting frustration, anger, anxiety, or distress?

In this way, the child's behaviour has been shaped by what happens afterwards. This is known as 'conditioning' or reinforcement, and is how most human behaviour is learnt. If the behaviour achieves a result experienced as positive by the child, even occasionally, it is more likely to happen again. If it helps them to avoid or escape a situation they don't like, the behaviour is more likely to happen again. Behaviour keeps happening because at some point it has achieved something that was experienced as beneficial or helpful. It is important to bear in mind that this might be something external, like being given a computer game to play, or internal, like a reduction in stress.

2. Look through your child's autism lens

By putting together your understanding of the behaviour with your knowledge of the individual child and their autism you will find accurate clues about how to make a positive change.

Katie often hides under the table at school and won't come out. Her teacher has noticed that this is more likely to happen just before carpet time, when the children share their news from the weekend or discuss topics by putting their hands up and speaking about ideas. Take a look through Katie's lens:

I may have different sensory experiences to you

The carpet is so itchy. I like sitting at the side near the wall where I can sit on the lino, but sometimes another kid gets there first.

Social interactions can be challenging for me

I don't know when it is my turn to speak so sometimes I shout out my answer, or I don't say anything. I don't know what to say about my weekend: the bits I think were important don't seem to be the right things to talk about. I don't know how long to talk for. Other people seem to know the right things to talk about. I can't wait for it to be over so I can get back to my desk.

We can see how Katie's particular social and sensory difficulties are a barrier to her accessing carpet time, and how hiding under the table is a means of escape/avoidance. Hopefully, by looking through Katie's lens you have already had some ideas for enabling her to access carpet time. You might be thinking about giving her somewhere consistent to sit or something to sit on that she doesn't find irritating. You might consider developing her understanding of the social rules in carpet time, including ideas for topics to talk about and when (and how long) to talk about them. You might reward her for taking part in carpet time as an incentive for changing her approach to the situation. Broadly, this means changing the environment, using communication, and developing new skills.

Michael has no spoken language. When he goes out to the garden or to playtime he bangs sticks or rocks against the walls and windows, and as a result has broken a pane of glass. Look through Michael's lens (we are making some educated assumptions as he is not able to talk to us about his perspective):

I have routines I need to stick to, behaviours I need to do over and over again, or special interests that are very important to me

I like the sound of the sticks and rocks against the window. It makes a loud sharp sound that blocks out the other noises I can hear. All I can hear is their rat-a-tat. This helps me feel more in control.

I may need additional support to manage change

I hate going out from the classroom into playtime. Sometimes a teacher will come and take me inside to play, which is better than being outside.

If a child has no spoken language we will need to do some detective work to understand the situation through their autism lens, combined with recording what has happened before and after the behaviour. In Michael's case, the adults working with him were able to amalgamate their observations of when the stick banging was at its worst with their knowledge of him and autism. They understood that the banging was Michael's way of coping with his sensory sensitivities and his way of meeting his need for stimulation at playtime. Their task was to enable him meet these requirements in a more positive and less destructive way.

3. Enable children to meet their needs in a more positive way

We know that most behaviour serves a function for the child – not necessarily every time, but often enough for it to persist. Remind yourself of the key functions of behaviour (see page 132–134) and think about the strategies you use to achieve these needs yourself. What do you do if you want some social attention? Perhaps text a friend or start a conversation with a colleague. What do you do if you need to vent some frustration? Maybe you fire off an email, grumble to your partner, or play badminton. It is not usually the need that is inappropriate but the way in which it is expressed through behaviour. For example, it is socially acceptable to let a teacher know you need to leave the classroom to use the toilet by putting your hand up and asking to go, but not so acceptable to scream until someone takes you out of the room.

There are two main obstacles for many children with autism to using these more appropriate strategies. Firstly, they may not have the necessary skills to use these more acceptable approaches: socially acceptable behaviours often involve complex social judgements and skills, such as waiting for the right moment, asking for help using verbal communication, or having an awareness of the impact of inappropriate behaviour on other people. Secondly, they may have learnt through experience that challenging behaviours are the more effective strategy. They may have discovered, for example, that you get out of the classroom more quickly if you throw a chair than if you wait for the teacher to finish talking so you can ask for a break. Both of these obstacles will be greater when the child is experiencing more intense emotions or a higher degree of physiological arousal.

So, if our task is to enable children to meet their own needs in a more positive way, we can move forward with the following questions:

- What needs are met by the behaviour? (e.g. stimulation, avoidance/escape, attention)
- What changes can we make to the environment, or to adult behaviour, to meet the need more appropriately?
- What skills does the child need to develop so they can meet their needs in a more positive way?
- What is achievable for them given their current abilities?
- What are the most effective ways of teaching the child these new skills (using the knowledge from your child's autism lens)?

4. Prevention is better than cure

Attempting to reduce challenging behaviour by changing only the way adults respond to it (i.e. cure) is generally a fruitless and punishing journey for all concerned. Although behaviour is shaped by what happens afterwards, we know that behaviours persist because they are occasionally reinforced in some way – like a small lottery win once every few months. Trying to extinguish behaviour simply by responding to it differently (e.g. ignoring, time out, a loss of privilege) takes a phenomenal degree of consistency. Moreover, this can be a very negative experience for the child and adult. It doesn't teach children new strategies for handling situations or address the need that underlies the behaviour. If this want is not addressed the child will continue to struggle and new behaviours are likely to emerge very quickly.

Preventing unwanted behaviours is not the same as avoiding them. Prevention involves:

- Making reasonable adjustments to the environment
- Teaching the child or young person new skills for managing the situation

Charlie used all the behaviours in his repertoire to get visitors to the house to leave: hitting, spitting, screaming, and fetching their coats and shoes! Here is the situation seen through Charlie's lens:

I don't like visitors. They are loud. I don't like their talking or laughing. It hurts my ears and I can't hear the TV. I never know when they are coming or how long they are going to stay. If I hit or spit they go more quickly. It is quiet again then.

Avoiding the situation would have meant stopping visitors coming to the house, which wasn't practical. Instead, Charlie's mum used her understanding of Charlie and his behaviour to develop strategies. Firstly, she let him know when visitors were coming by putting up photos of them and telling him more about the visit. Adjacent to the photos were pictures of what was going to happen after the visitors left (e.g. bath or dinner). This helped Charlie develop some tolerance of visitors, as he was more prepared for their arrival and felt safe in the knowledge they would not be there forever. Secondly, his mum ensured there was a quiet space he could retreat to if he wished, and was clear with both Charlie and the visitors that this was acceptable. Thirdly, she rewarded Charlie for being kind to visitors with a small treat that she could fit into his routine.

Key learning points

Challenging behaviours are commonly shown by children and young people with autism

These can be reduced and more positive behaviours developed

The first step is to understand the behaviour and why it is happening

Preventative strategies and those that teach children new skills are the most beneficial

---

Chapter 12
Feeding and Eating Issues

Research and personal accounts tell us that children with autism often eat a more restricted range of food than other children (Provost et al., 2010; Nadon et al., 2011). This can be extreme with some children eating only one or two types of food, such as crisps or biscuits. Often foodstuffs are restricted along a few different lines: texture (e.g. soft or crunchy), taste (bland or spicy), colour (e.g. eating only pale foods), and familiarity (eating a good range but never trying anything new). Sometimes children want to eat the same thing at every meal for several weeks before moving onto a new preferred food.

Strong food preferences are part of typical development and children with and without autism gradually show fewer of these restrictions as they mature. However, this can be a stressful issue, especially during a child's early years. The experience of trying to cajole, motivate, or coerce children into eating a broader range of food can be very demoralising.

It is advisable to seek dietary advice from a healthcare professional. It may be that the restricted diet is not going to have as much of a health impact as adults fear or that just small nutritional changes are needed.

The evidence base for changing restricted eating behaviours is fairly limited. However, research shows that modifications can be made and children can learn to tolerate a broader range of food (Nadjowski et al., 2003; Paul et al., 2007). Remember the principles for changing behaviour. We need:

1. An understanding of why the behaviour is happening – applying knowledge of the behaviour and autism

2. Strategies that enable the child to learn alternative and more positive behaviours

Why children with autism may show strong food preferences

Look through the child's autism lens to gain an insight into their eating behaviours. Often the key parts of the lens when it comes to eating are:

I may have routines I need to stick to, behaviours I need to do over and over again, or special interests that are very important to me

I may have different sensory experiences to you

If the first of these is at the root of the issue then it is not the taste of the food that is causing the child difficulties. Rather, they have developed fixed beliefs about food or ways of eating:

I don't like different foods touching each other

I can only eat from my blue plate

I do not eat anything new

Sticking to these beliefs and routines may provide a sense of predictability, control, or pleasure. Being asked to break the routine may lead to anxiety or just feel unacceptable.

Most of us have likes and dislikes when it comes to food, so it can be easy to identify with strong food preferences. Children with autism may find particular smells, tastes, or textures highly unpleasant. They may have found the experience of eating something so aversive that they cannot tolerate being in the same room as that food. Some children with autism have extraordinary abilities in discerning subtle taste differences – for example, being able to distinguish between different brands of basmati rice or fresh orange juice.

Often it is a combination of the two parts of the lens identified above that are contributing to the narrow range of food tolerated by the child. Try looking through Anna's autism lens to see eating from her perspective and how this might lead to ideas for change.

Take a look through Anna's lens:

I eat the same lunch every day. I eat two cheese crackers, a crust of dry bread, and a packet of cheese crisps. I don't like butter on the bread because it tastes slimy. I like the way the food looks all the same colour in my lunchbox, and tastes crunchy and dry. Sometimes my mum and dad put something different in and I hate this. Once I opened my lunchbox at lunchtime and found some cucumber in there – it looked green and slimy. I couldn't eat any of it because I kept thinking about the green slime touching all my other food.

In this way we can understand what Anna values about the food she chooses and the loss of control/predictability she feels when presented with unwanted foods.

Strategies that enable the child to learn alternative behaviours

Changing restricted eating behaviours is not always easy, but it is possible. Sometimes it is a matter of timing – an approach that didn't work a couple of years ago can be worth another go. Looking through a child's autism lens will enable you to understand whether it is a sensory issue or a routine, or both, that are keeping the behaviour going.

There are some 'foundations' you can put in place around mealtime routines that can maximise the chances of success for the strategies you have chosen to implement.

Mealtime routines

Having a consistent mealtime routine has several benefits. Eating in a regular place and at regular times will increase the sense of predictability. It may also help children to develop something of an 'appetite clock' so they are sufficiently hungry at those times and ready to eat. Regular snacks are helpful too, whereas children constantly grazing or snacking on their preferred foods will reduce their motivation to eat when it comes to a 'proper' meal.

Reduce stress around mealtimes

Mealtimes can often be a time of real stress. Sometimes this is because adults are feeling worried about their child's eating habits; at others, the child is upset by the environment, which may be noisy, smelly, or socially demanding. This is a good time to look through your child's autism lens and see if there is anything they are finding particularly challenging. Some small changes, such as talking less to the child whilst they are eating, turning off the TV, or playing calming music may help; this will depend entirely on the child.

With these foundations in place, the following strategies can be effective in changing eating behaviours:

- ▪ Taking small steps to increase the range of food
- ▪ Using communication strategies
- ▪ Introducing rewards

Taking small steps to increase the range of food

Looking through the child's autism lens, what patterns are there to the foods they like to eat? Are they the same texture, colour, taste, or type? Whether this is down to a sensory sensitivity or fixed ideas about food, small steps are often more successful than large ones. Think about expanding the diet in minor ways – starting with foods that are similar to their preferred options. Here are some examples:

- If they seem to prefer dry, pale foods, such as plain crisps, try offering very small amounts (pea-sized to begin with) of similar options like breadsticks or crackers

- If they eat sugary foods try small amounts of fruit or other healthier sweet options

- Try 'taster sessions' where about four or five new foods are on offer, again in pea-sized amounts (Paul et al., 2007). Do this when the child is likely to be hungry, for example, a few hours after lunch

- Alternatively, place very small amounts of new foods on the child's plate

- If children have very strong sensory sensitivities, they may need to start just by smelling, playing with, or touching new foods – with no expectation that they will eat them

Using communication strategies

Looking through the child's autism lens may tell you that they need some support to understand aspects of eating or mealtimes. If children do not seem to have a good understanding of mealtime routines, visual schedules can help them understand where meals and eating fit into the rest of the day (see page 108). Children may need additional support to understand what is expected of them during meals. Again, this can be achieved with visual supports, such as a 'now and next' board (e.g. now – sitting and eating; next – TV).

Children with autism who respond well to the Social Stories we met earlier (see page 110) may find these useful when it comes to food. The story may develop their understanding of the benefits of trying new foods so they are more motivated to try.

Take a look through Finn's lens:

I want to have lots of muscles like wrestlers. Wrestlers are really strong and don't get bullied. Meat makes you strong so I eat lots of sausages and burgers. I don't need vegetables – I don't like them and they don't give you muscles.

Looking through Finn's lens helped his mother and me to appreciate how he understood his diet. With the aid of a Social Story we were able to explain, how different food groups were necessary for strength, health, and fitness. With the school, we were also able to look at any problems with bullying.

Introducing rewards

Think of a food that would be really unacceptable to you – what would persuade you to eat it? Some people find Brussels sprouts, tripe, or jellied eels unpalatable. Lots of other people eat them though, so they might not taste that bad after all. If you haven't tasted them, you don't find out. Offering someone five pence to eat them might not be enough of an incentive, but ten pounds might be more motivating, if the timing is right. It is all about finding the right incentive for the individual.

Occasionally, children with autism will willingly try a large range of new foods for rewards as simple as stickers, praise, or the offer of their preferred food. More often, the approach needs to be a combination of small steps, communication, and rewards. If the strategy doesn't work immediately it might be worth returning to in a few months.

Accessing further support

As with all behaviour issues, further support may be necessary to move things forward. Psychologists and other professionals who focus on behaviour can help to work out what is keeping the problem going and suggest strategies to enable the child to change their eating behaviours. When children are consuming a highly restricted diet that is likely to be affecting their health, this advice should be sought sooner rather than later.

Key learning points

Children and young people with autism are more likely to have strong food preferences or a restricted diet

This may be due to sensory sensitivities or a love of 'sameness' when it comes to food

The range of foodstuffs they will eat can be increased, although this is often challenging and may need to be tried in small steps

Mealtime routines, rewards, and communication aids can all be beneficial

Chapter 13
Sleep Difficulties

Problems in getting to sleep, or staying asleep once in bed, are very common for children with autism. Many children do not appear to feel tired as night approaches; they may need to go to sleep but they are not 'switching off'. Other children can get to sleep reasonably well but wake up in the night or very early in the morning – occasionally as early as 2 a.m. There are also many children with autism who find going to sleep on their own very difficult and insist on a parent sleeping with them. These behaviours leave children and parents feeling drained and irritable and make it hard to concentrate and feel relaxed during the day. Children with sleep difficulties are also more likely to show other behaviour problems such as aggression (Mayes and Calhoun, 2009). This chronic lack of sleep can have a huge impact on the whole family.

Sleep difficulties seem to occur across the autism spectrum. Typically developing children may have sleep problems, but children with autism are twice as likely to experience sleep difficulties. Sleep problems shown by children with autism are also more liable to persist for longer and be more challenging to resolve (Sivertsen et al., 2012), but they do respond to intervention (Vriend et al., 2011).

The two interventions that have received the most research attention are medication and behavioural approaches.

Medication

Many parents seek advice from their child's doctor about the possibility of medication to help with sleep problems. Melatonin is a synthetic hormone often prescribed to help children settle to sleep earlier. Very few side effects are reported but long-term use has not yet been thoroughly researched. On average, children using melatonin go to sleep earlier and for longer than before they started using it. However, it does not seem to change the number of times children wake in the night (Guenole et al., 2011; Rossignol and Frye, 2011).

Doctors prescribing melatonin usually want to be sure that appropriate behavioural approaches have already been tried, and that a good sleep routine is in place. Often melatonin is only prescribed for a fairly short period of time or as a last resort. During this time it is hoped that children will develop a more satisfactory sleep pattern which will continue if the melatonin is stopped.

Behavioural approaches

Behavioural approaches for sleep are fairly well supported by research, which shows that many parents who put a sleep programme into place achieve their goals. Behavioural interventions for sleep return to those two essential principles:

1. An understanding of why the behaviour is happening –
   applying knowledge of the behaviour and autism

2. Strategies that enable the child to learn alternative and
   more positive behaviours

Children who have trouble settling to sleep may have a different body clock to other children, but there can be other reasons for sleep difficulties. Whether the problem is going to sleep, staying asleep, or being able to sleep without a parent, it is important to look through the child's autism lens for clues.

David's lens: *I may have different sensory experiences to you*
I can't get to sleep at night. The bed feels too big and I feel like I am floating. I can see a strip of light coming through the gap in the curtains.

Lily's lens: *I may have routines I need to stick to, behaviours I need to do over and over again, or special interests that are very important to me*
I wake up and I want to watch TV. My favourite programme is Hannah Montana. There is one song that I like to watch as soon as I wake up. My mum says it is too early but when I wake up I want to watch the song, and she usually lets me.

Ahmed's lens: *I may need additional support to manage change*
My mum always stays with me till I go to sleep. I can't go to sleep without her there. It makes me feel scared and that I will never be able to sleep. If I wake up and she isn't there I feel scared so she usually stays with me at night.

Looking through these children's lenses, we can see that there are different reasons for their sleep problems, and these will require strategies based on the child's individual needs. Broad strategies that can be tailored to suit the child and their family include:

- Establishing a consistent sleep routine
- Taking a look at the environment through the child's autism lens and making appropriate alterations
- Teaching sleep skills

Establishing a consistent sleep routine

A good sleep routine requires a regular sequence of events before bedtime and a consistent time for going to bed and waking. Children are more likely to feel relaxed and ready to go to sleep if their evening is predictable and calming. Typically, a good sleep routine may include: supper, bath/wash, nightwear on, brush teeth, bed with story, or calm time with parent. This schedule should be followed every night. Ideally children will learn to fall asleep without their parent present, which will help them to settle back to sleep on their own if they wake in the night. This is no different than sleep routines for typically developing children, but sometimes children's difficulties have been so extreme that their routine has become inconsistent or was never established in the first place. If appropriate, a sleep routine can be supported by a visual schedule or Social Story.

Taking a look at the environment through the child's autism lens and making appropriate alterations

Looking through a child's individual autism lens can be really useful when dealing with sleep problems. There are no hard and fast rules – each child's sensory experience of their bedroom will be different. Remember David's experience:

The bed feels too big and I feel like I am floating. I can see a strip of light coming through the gap in the curtains.

David's parents needed to find ways to meet his sensory needs. They tried heavier blankets and some extra cushions in the bed to help him feel more secure. They also added a blackout blind to the window to stop any light from coming in.

Consider the sights and sounds the child will experience at bedtime, and whether any of these can altered to suit their needs. It can also be helpful to bear in mind the temperature of the room and whether any sensitivity to heat or cold is affecting sleep.

Teaching sleep skills

There are numerous obstacles for children with autism to learning to go to sleep on their own, at the time their parents or carers would like, and staying asleep and in bed for long enough. These include:

- Difficulty settling to sleep
- Anxiety
- Limited or no understanding of the impact of their wakefulness on other people
- Body clock – very disrupted patterns of sleep and waking
- Limited understanding of the need for more sleep

Children can be taught sleep skills using communication and behavioural approaches. Communication aids such as Social Stories can help children who are able to use them to understand why sleep is necessary and the benefits of sticking to a regular routine. I used this approach successfully with Ben, whose sleep pattern changed dramatically in summer when he was required to go to bed whilst it was still light outside; take a look through Ben's lens:

I wanted to stay up because it was still light so I knew it was still day. I thought it was still time to play and I didn't want to go to bed. My mum read me a story which told me about the sun going down later in the summer, and how it goes down earlier in winter. I still need to go to bed at the same time on the clock. This means I have enough energy to play in the day.

Behavioural approaches involve parents or carers teaching new sleep behaviours by responding in a particular way to their child. If a child is very anxious about going to sleep alone, parents may need to support them by gradually moving further away as their child drops off, until they are able to tolerate being alone in the room. Behavioural approaches may also include offering rewards for sleep behaviours, such as following the sleep routine or staying in bed till an agreed time.

Parents and carers also need to consider whether they are reinforcing unwanted sleep behaviours. For example, getting up to watch TV with a child who wakes frequently in the night is likely to be maintaining rather than reducing this behaviour. Often parents get into habits they never planned because sleep problems can be so draining.

Further advice and support is often needed to help parents and children to overcome sleep problems. Clinical psychologists and other professionals working with children with autism will be able to assess children's sleep difficulties and devise a plan to deal with them. Approaches such as the Sleep Scotland programme (www.sleepscotland.org) can also have a positive impact on children with autism with problems in this area.

Key learning points

Sleep problems are common, including getting to sleep and staying asleep

Changes to the bedroom environment and bedtime routine can help

Children and young people can be taught 'sleep skills' using communication and behavioural approaches

Further professional advice may be needed, particularly as sleep problems are associated with other behavioural difficulties in the daytime

Chapter 14

Aggression and Self-Injury

Aggression entails physically threatening or hurting other people; self-injury means hitting, biting, or slapping yourself. I have grouped these behaviours together because they share similar triggers and functions and can often be managed using similar strategies. Both self-injury and aggression can cause a great deal of distress to those caring for the child, with the possibility of serious injury as an additional worry.

A starting point should always be to try to *understand* the behaviour, ideally using the structured approach described in Chapter 11. Once we recognise the settings, triggers, and results of the behaviour we can begin to identify strategies for changing it. For example, Imran slapped his father's face sometimes when he tried to kiss his cheek. It didn't happen every time, but by looking closely at the behaviour, we realised it only happened when his father hadn't shaved – Imran hated the itchy feel of his father's stubble against his face. From then on, his father was careful to either be clean shaven or to show his affection in other ways.

Alternative explanations for self-injury

It is vital to check whether there is a medical or physical explanation for self-injury. Infections, pain, seizure activity, and irritation (e.g. rashes) can all trigger a bout of self-injurious behaviour. Some children seem to suddenly start repeatedly hitting themselves around the head; later they are identified as having an ear or throat infection or dental problems. A check-up by a doctor or dentist should always be considered if children start to injure themselves.

Some people experience a release of opiates internally when they self-injure – this can lead to a pleasant effect or reduce distress and physical pain. In a way, children and young people who are injuring themselves in this way are delivering painkillers to themselves. Of course, this does not resolve the underlying physical problem and is likely to lead to more pain as the result of the injury.

Looking at the situation in which aggression or self-injury occurs through the child's autism lens is an essential part of developing an effective strategy. This will help you to identify any needs the child is communicating though their behaviour. Here are some examples of how looking through your child's autism lens can throw light onto these behaviours.

■ *Social interactions can be challenging for me*

Example: *When visitors come to the house my mum always wants me to speak to them and I hate it. I can't wait for them to leave. If I hit them they leave more quickly.*

■ *I may need support to communicate and to understand other people's communication*

Example: *I can't always find the right words to tell my teachers the work is too hard, and I don't understand when they tell me what to do. When I bite my hand they give me a break from the work and a few minutes later they try again.*

■ *I can't always tell what other people are thinking or feeling*

Example: *The other kids at school were all looking at some pictures on the computer and were laughing. I thought they might be laughing at me and I pushed one of them.*

■ *I may have routines I need to stick to, behaviours I need to do over and over again, or special interests that are very important to me*

Example: *All my Lego is placed in my room in exactly the right way. If anyone in my family goes into my room I think they have messed up my Lego. I get really angry and hit the walls.*

■ *I may need additional support to manage change*

Example: *A befriender comes to take me out each week. Sometimes a new person comes and I feel really scared as I don't know what they will be like. I bite my fingers really hard so I can get out the door.*

■ *I may have different sensory experiences to you*

Example: *When we go to the shopping centre it is so bright and noisy and people are everywhere and too close to me. If I bang my head it helps me feel a bit calmer and my mum might take me out.*

■ *I may be really good at seeing detail but I don't always see the 'bigger picture'*

Example: *We were in a traffic jam with lots of police cars in the road. I wanted to get to the toy shop. I could see the toy shop sign but my mum wouldn't drive the car forward, so I pulled her hair.*

■ *I am a child or young person first, with my own personal story and my own likes and dislikes*

Example: *I was bitten by a dog when I was younger and I hate them now. My granddad tried to get me to stroke his friend's dog. I didn't want to so I kicked him and ran off.*

We can see from these examples that children and young people are demonstrating some clear needs or preferences through their behaviour. A key part of trying to reduce self-injury or aggressive behaviour is to identify:

■ How much do we need to change the environment to make it more manageable?

■ What skills does the child or young person need to develop in order to meet their needs without aggression or self-injury?

Let's look at one of the previous examples to illustrate this through Tim's lens:

When we go to the shopping centre it is so bright and noisy and people are everywhere and too close to me. If I bang my head it helps me feel a bit calmer and my mum might take me out.

We can see that sensory overload is one of the main triggers, with 'escape' a function of the behaviour. The head-banging may also help Tim manage his feelings, but this is in a dangerous way that is not resolving the problem.

The first question to ask is about modifying the environment. We can't change the shopping centre or the number of people in it, but we can choose whether to go there or pick a quieter time to visit. Alternatively, Tim could use some ear defenders or play music through earphones if this is something that works for him.

The second question is to consider what skills Tim needs to learn in order to change his behaviour. These could include:

■ Asking for his ear defenders

■ Requesting a break

■ Learning to gradually tolerate busy environments

Using communication supports, such as a 'break' card, could help. A visual schedule showing that the shopping will come to an end after a certain number of stores might help him tolerate going into a few shops. We could also offer Tim rewards for successfully achieving this.

Responding to aggression and self-injury

Whilst prevention is better than cure, it is not always possible to prevent aggressive behaviour or self-injury. There is no one-size-fits-all strategy that works for all children and young people, although generally a low-key response, including a quiet voice and reduced language, is advised, and safety should be the priority. The type of response adults around the child make will depend on both the individual child, the situation in which the behaviour occurs, and how far into the cycle the behaviour has gone. Extreme behaviours often present as a cycle of four stages: trigger, escalation, crisis (or explosion) and recovery.

In the *trigger* phase, an event happens that leads to the child experiencing an increase in their physical arousal or agitation; this could be something that makes them feel angry, frustrated, anxious, or even excited. They sense an increase in adrenaline which gets the blood pumping around their body. At this stage you can try a calm, low-key response: distraction, simple reassurance, removing the trigger if appropriate (e.g. separating two children), or reminders about potential rewards and consequences.

In the *escalation* phase the child or young person becomes increasingly agitated, and this will be visible to people around them. At this stage you can try continuing with a calm, low-key response, further reminders about rewards and consequences, or removing them to a quieter place to calm down.

By *crisis*, the child may appear to have lost control, with more extreme self-injury or aggression occurring. At this stage, the priority is to keep everyone safe and limit the amount of stimulation the person is experiencing. You may need to ask someone else for help where possible. It may be necessary to remove the child or young person to a safe area or, if this is not possible, move everyone else to a safe distance.

In the *recovery* phase, levels of arousal start to decrease and if recovery is allowed to continue, the child will return to their baseline state of arousal. They may also experience a dip as the adrenaline leaves them and appear depressed or remorseful. At this stage, you need to give the person space to return to a calm state, only talking things through at this stage if appropriate. If consequences need to be put in place, wait till the child is able to hear this without escalating again.

Self-injury and physical aggression are very distressing behaviours which can be hard to change without support. Child and adolescent mental health services, specialist educational staff, and specialist disability nurses can all provide advice and intervention. There are also specialist training packages that schools can buy in (e.g. Team-Teach – www.team-teach.co.uk) and these also provide training in positive handling should this be required. There is very little training available to parents on physical responses to aggressive behaviour, mainly due to the legal and safety implications of implementing these alone or in home settings. Keeping everyone safe at home generally means trying to prevent aggressive incidents from occurring and giving the child or young person adequate space when they do.

Some children and young people are prescribed medication if they are hurting themselves or other people. The drug risperidone can have some short-term impact in reducing these behaviours, but this has to be balanced against its side-effects (Jesner at al., 2007). This type of medication is usually only prescribed alongside behavioural approaches or after they have proven unsuccessful.

Key learning points

Self-injury and aggression are often ways of expressing needs

Our job is to enable children and young people to meet these needs in a more positive way

Medical or dental reasons for self-injury should always be checked out

Different approaches work at different stages of the cycle of behaviour

The priority is to keep everyone safe

These behaviours can be prevented using a combination of environmental changes, communication approaches, and teaching the child new skills

Additional support from specialist services is often needed

Chapter 15

Managing Repetitive and Restricted Behaviours and Routines

We need to work *with* the restricted and repetitive patterns of behaviour shown by children and young people with autism. This is a core difficulty in the condition, however, so we cannot expect to stop these behaviours altogether. In some cases it is not necessary to stop restricted or repetitive behaviours – they may be having little negative impact on the child or family and/or may be a source of pleasure and comfort for the child. However, repetitive behaviours and routines can become an issue when:

- The child or young person is distressed by the routine or behaviour

- Not being able to carry out the routine or behaviour leads to a high level of anxiety or challenging behaviour

- The routine or behaviour is seriously getting in the way of learning and social interaction or impacting on family life

In these circumstances, adults around the child will often look for strategies to help manage the behaviour or reduce its impact.

Understanding repetitive behaviour

In keeping with general principles of behaviour management, the first step is to understand what is triggering the behaviour and what is keeping it going. Repetitive behaviours or routines can serve several functions for children and young people with autism. They may:

■ *Help reduce anxiety or stress*

Example: *I like all the things in the house to be a certain way, in the same place all the time. If they move I feel really stressed. Everything outside my house is all over the place. At least I know how things in the house will be every day.* (Ryan)

■ *Help reduce sensory overload – blocking out overwhelming sights, smells, or sounds*

Example: *I carry wrestling figures in my pockets. When I feel stressed I can get my figures out and play with them. Then I can't hear all the noises and the other kids.* (Christopher)

■ *Provide a sense of enjoyment or stimulation*

Example: *I love bouncing on the sofas or cushions. My parents bought me a trampoline and I can bounce on that for hours.* (Tyler)

Knowing which function the repetitive behaviour is serving will guide adults in how they manage it. Our job is to help children meet these needs in a more positive way. Depending on the purpose of the repetitive behaviour we can make environmental changes or teach new skills. We might look at helping the child develop other ways of managing anxiety or stress, or cope with sensory issues, if these seem to trigger repetitive behaviours.

Those are strategies that may reduce the child's need to engage in repetitive behaviours. However, if the repetitive behaviour persists and a more direct approach is needed, it can be useful to try:

- Setting limits around repetitive behaviours or routines
- Preventing problems from developing
- Providing alternatives

Setting limits around repetitive behaviours or routines

Trying to extinguish the routine or behaviour altogether can be a thankless task, and if the behaviour is fulfilling a need for the child or young person, then preventing it altogether may only increase their distress. There are some dangerous behaviours that cannot be tolerated but most can be managed. This means setting limits around them – enabling the behaviour to happen for a limited time or in particular circumstances.

Take a look through Ryan's lens:

My parents and I have done a deal so all the things in my room can stay the way I like them. If the room needs cleaning then I do most of it. The rest of the things in the house still change a lot. I don't like it but at least my things stay in the right place.

Take a look through Christopher's lens:

I used to carry all my wrestling figures with me in a backpack. I have 67 wrestling figures now. My mum, teachers, and I agreed that I could carry five figures with me. I worked out how many I needed to play properly and we agreed five. When I get home I can play with the other 62 as well.

Another way of limiting a repetitive behaviour is to set a time limit on it. Some behaviours are only a problem because they continue for too long or get in the way of other activities.

Take a look through Tyler's lens:

I used to hate coming off the trampoline to go to bed or to school. I still don't like coming off but I know I can go on for ten minutes before school and ten minutes as soon as I come home. Then I get another ten minutes before bedtime.

Any limits require clear boundaries. Writing these out or using visual supports to show the limits gives them a better chance of working. For example, Christopher had a number 5 on the back of his bedroom door to remind him to pick five wrestling toys. Tyler had a visual schedule which included trampoline time. Ryan had a social story about why things could not stay in the same place in the rest of his house.

Preventing problems from developing

Many parents and teachers become highly skilled in spotting potential problems which can arise from repetitive behaviours or routines. It can help to set some limits early on when parents or teachers see these behaviours developing. Routines can become entrenched, so making timely small alterations can prevent problems escalating further down the line.

Providing alternatives

If a repetitive behaviour or routine is problematic by nature then alternatives may need to be provided and encouraged. Whilst some behaviours are not in themselves a problem, others are. Compare these two behaviours:

- Jason is very interested in fires. He is particularly interested in the best way to light a fire. When he gets bored he thinks about lighting fires. He has lit several fires in the back garden and set fire to his bedroom.
- Tamara bangs things against the window when she feels stressed by the environment. Her favourite is a metal spoon. She has broken a window this way, which could have caused injury.

The risks posed by these behaviours are obvious; the key is to find alternatives that help young people to meet their needs. Jason is interested in the physical process of fires and they provide stimulation. The challenge in his case (apart from keeping everyone safe and preventing access to matches and so on) is to find activities that he finds interesting but do not pose the same risks.

Tamara uses her repetitive behaviour to reduce stress and sensory overload. Safer alternatives can be found using our personal knowledge of Tamara – for example, banging things which will not break or giving her a rest from stressful environments.

Special interests

Many young people with autism develop special interests which are unusual either in their intensity or subject matter. This is not harmful most of the time, and in some cases can be beneficial for learning or employment. We all have hobbies and interests and, for most of us, this adds to our sense of identity and well-being. Children and young people with autism are no different.

Unless the special interest is dangerous for the child or others, it is not usually helpful to try to eradicate it. It can be more useful to include the interest when trying to develop communication, learning, and positive behaviours.

■ *Communication*

Example: *When my mum is trying to have a conversation with me, we can take it in turns to talk about things we are interested in. I talk about dinosaurs for five minutes, and she asks me questions. Then we talk about something she is interested in. Then we talk about dinosaurs again at the end.*

■ *Learning*

Example: *I didn't understand why my teeth were falling out when I was a kid. My teacher wrote me a story to explain that milk teeth fall out and grown-up teeth grow in their place. She included pictures of the Simpsons showing all the Simpsons with different teeth.*

■ *Positive behaviours*

Example: *My parents want me to try more vegetables. Every time I try a new vegetable they give me part of a Spiderman jigsaw. When the jigsaw is finished they are going to buy me a DVD. I only have three more pieces to go.*

Limits can also be set around the special interest is if it getting in the way of other activities.

Key learning points

We need to understand the function of repetitive behaviours or routines for each individual child or young person

It helps to try to work with, rather than against, the behaviour wherever possible

We can do this by setting limits around the behaviour or providing alternatives

Special interests can be beneficial and can be included when developing a child or young person's wider skills

Chapter 16

Managing Sensory Issues

Sensory sensitivities can have a profound impact on the behaviour and well-being of some children and young people with autism. There have been various attempts to develop specialist therapies to counteract this problem, such as sensory integration therapy, but more research into this area is needed. Occupational therapists can provide assessment and ideas for intervention. They can also look at a child's sensory profile and their areas of under- and over-sensitivity to find strategies for managing challenging situations.

Many strategies aimed at reducing or managing sensory issues are derived either from:

- Intuitive and non-harmful approaches which seem to work for some people
- Applying principles from other evidence-based interventions

Intuitive/non-harmful approaches

The most obvious approach to sensory sensitivities is to manage the environment so that the child or young person is not unnecessarily exposed to sights, sounds, tastes, textures, or smells which they find intolerable. Labels in clothes, certain flavours, and the noise made by particular toys are all examples of stimuli which can usually be removed or avoided without causing difficulties for the child or those around them. If children find background noise very difficult to tune out, they may need a quieter working area in which they can concentrate. There is nothing wrong in making reasonable adjustments to the environment or routine to support a child experiencing sensory difficulties. In fact, some autism-specific environments are purposely designed to take account of these needs, incorporating non-fluorescent lighting, fabrics and flooring that reduce noise, and uncluttered walls.

In the case of sound sensitivity, it is often not possible to control the amount or type of sound in the environment, such as waiting for a doctor's appointment or walking down a busy street on the way home from school. Some children and young people seem to benefit from the use of ear defenders or listening to music on headphones at such times, provided their safety is taken into account.

Applying principles from evidence-based approaches

Both Social Stories and behavioural approaches have something to offer when supporting young people with sensory issues. Social Stories can assist the child's understanding of *why* a particular sound, smell, feeling, or sight is happening. Sometimes a misunderstanding or lack of knowledge is adding to the stress of the situation. Remember Hamza, who was frightened by the school bell going off by the toilet door? Here is his account following a Social Story:

> *The story helped me by telling me that the bell goes off to let the teacher and children know that it is time to go to the next lesson or go home. The story also told me the times the bell goes off, so I check on the clock and I don't go to the toilet at those times. I still don't like it when the bell goes, but now I know when it is going to happen.*

A Social Story is not likely to make a child *like* something they dislike, but it may reduce some of the stress or help them understand the reason the challenging stimuli is there.

Behavioural strategies are well supported by research and also give us clues in managing sensory issues. These include graded approaches and positive reinforcement.

Graded approaches to increase tolerance

Expecting children and young people to face their biggest sensory challenge head-on is rarely the most effective way of building up tolerance to these sensory experiences. Many interventions use a graded approach to support people in managing anxiety and increasing acceptance of situations they find difficult. This enables them to build confidence and skills gradually. In the case of sensory sensitivities, this might mean:

- A graded approach to trying new tastes or textures – touching, licking, or smelling new foods before being expected to eat them
- Building up the ability to manage noisy, crowded shopping centres by starting in smaller shops

The key principle is to start at the point a child can tolerate and work up slowly from there. An occupational therapist or psychologist can help with these techniques.

Rewards to reinforce children's efforts

Positive reinforcement can be used to encourage children and young people who are trying to manage their sensory issues. For example, children might be offered their favourite activity after trying a new food or 'points' for going into novel situations they are trying to cope with, like going on the bus. Any reward would need to be tailored to the individual child's level of understanding and preferences.

Under-sensitivity to pain and temperature

Under-sensitivity to pain and temperature can cause significant concerns as the child or young person may injure themselves inadvertently. Management is often a combination of staying safe (e.g. making sure water temperature is kept at a safe level through a thermostat), education (e.g. why wearing a coat or hat is advisable in cold weather), and supervision (e.g. looking out for behavioural signs of pain).

Key learning points

We can make environmental changes to reduce the stress or anxiety caused by sensory sensitivity

Some children and young people use additional support, such as ear defenders, to help them cope with their sensory experiences

Social Stories can help children and young people understand why certain noises, sights, smells, and feelings happen

A graded approach can be used to develop tolerance to challenging stimuli

We cannot change children's sensory experiences completely, so we need to remember these sensitivities when looking at challenging behaviour or anxiety

---

Final Remarks

The aim of this book is to help you develop your understanding of autism. It is a huge topic for a little book, so I have listed some additional reading and resources so that you can develop your knowledge and skills further. You may already be using your autism lens to look at the world from a different perspective and generate strategies for the child in your care. This should help you support the person you know with autism to manage the challenges of the social world and reach their potential.

Glossary

Asperger syndrome: A diagnosis in the family of autism spectrum conditions. People with this condition have the features of autism and have at least average intelligence, along with language development that has not been delayed.

Assault cycle: The phases a person can go through when they show extreme levels of physical aggression, including trigger, escalation, crisis and recovery.

Attention deficit hyperactivity disorder: A condition characterised by attentional problems, impulsivity (doing before thinking), and hyperactivity.

Atypical autism: A diagnosis in the family of autism spectrum conditions. This diagnosis may be given when children and young people show some or most of the features of autism but do not meet the full criteria exactly.

Autism spectrum disorder/condition: A term used to encompass all the different categories of autism.

Behavioural approaches: Interventions primarily aimed at changing behaviour by altering aspects of the environment, including analysing and changing how other people respond to the behaviour.

Central coherence: The drive to understand the gist of a situation or context. The 'weak central coherence' theory of autism proposes that people with the condition see the detail in a situation but are unable to put the details together effectively to make a coherent whole.

Childhood autism: Also known as Kanner's autism. A diagnosis that is given to children with autism and very delayed language development or no spoken language at all.

Circle of friends: An approach used usually in mainstream schools to promote inclusion, reduce social isolation, and increase the support network for children with autism.

Cognitive behaviour therapy (CBT): A psychological therapy often used as an intervention for anxiety and depression. Clients explore how their thoughts, feelings, and behaviour interact, and develop alternative ways of thinking to improve emotional well-being.

Developmental disability: A condition that originated at birth or during childhood, is expected to continue indefinitely, and substantially impacts upon functioning in several major areas of life.

Emotional recognition: The ability to identify and distinguish different emotions and the facial expressions and body language that accompany them.

Functional analysis: A way of recording and analysing challenging behaviour with the aim of understanding its function – how that behaviour is beneficial to the person. Functions include escaping or avoiding an aversive situation, gaining something tangible or social attention, providing stimulation or relieving boredom, or expressing needs and feelings.

High functioning autism: A diagnosis that has been used to describe people with autism who have at least average intelligence but whose language development has been delayed.

Learning disabilities: A disability that affects learning and communication, so the person is less able to understand new or complex information, learn new skills, or cope independently. Learning disabilities can be mild, moderate, or severe.

Mindblindness: A term used to describe one of the core difficulties in autism – the ability to accurately predict other people's thoughts, feelings, and behaviour.

Neurodiversity: A way of thinking about people not as 'normal' or 'abnormal', but as having variations in the way we think, learn, and experience the social world.

Neurotypical: A person who does not have a disability or condition such as autism, attention deficit hyperactivity disorder, learning disabilities, or dyspraxia/developmental coordination disorder.

Picture Exchange Communication System (PECS): A communication approach that allows children with very limited verbal communication to express their needs and wishes through simple pictures. The person with autism has access to photographs or pictures depicting items or activities they are motivated by. They hand the picture to an adult when they want something or wish to start an activity.

Reinforcement: A behavioural term used to describe the way behaviour is shaped by its consequences. If a person demonstrates a particular behaviour, and experiences what they feel is a positive result, their behaviour has been positively reinforced. If the behaviour results in them avoiding or ending something unpleasant, then their behaviour has been negatively reinforced.

Self-injury: Actions such as hitting, biting or slapping oneself, or banging one's head. (See **Functional analysis** for possible functions of this behaviour.)

Sensory sensitivities: Heightened sensitivity levels at which a person receives sensory information. People with autism are often more sensitive than other people to sound, visual information, smells, touch, and tastes, finding some of these sensations intolerable or even painful.

Social skills: The way we communicate and behave to get on with people and develop and maintain friendships. This includes taking turns in conversation, expressing an interest in other people, and making appropriate judgements about how to behave in interactions with others.

Social Stories: An approach developed by Carol Gray. Social Stories consist of simple, individualised, written explanations of situations that people with autism may find confusing or challenging.

Theory of mind: The ability to understand or predict what another person thinks, feels, believes, or intends.

Visual schedule: A communication aide to assist understanding of what will be happening or what is expected of a young person, usually a row of pictures or photographs.

References

Abbeduto, L., Mailick Seltzer, M., Shattuck, P., Wyngaarden Krauss, M. B., Orsmond, G., and Murphy, M. (2004) Psychological Well-Being and Coping in Mothers of Youths With Autism, Down Syndrome, or Fragile X Syndrome. *American Journal on Mental Retardation*, 109(3), 237–254.

American Psychiatric Association (2013) *Diagnostic Statistical Manual of Mental Disorders, Fifth Edition* (DSM-V). Washington, DC: APA.

Attwood, T. (2001) *Exploring Feelings: Cognitive Behaviour Therapy to Manage Anxiety*. Arlington, TX: Future Horizons.

Attwood, T. (2004) *Exploring Feelings: Cognitive Behaviour Therapy to Manage Anger*. Arlington, TX: Future Horizons.

Autism Education Trust (2011). *What is Good Practice in Autism Education?* London: AET.

Baron-Cohen, S. (1997) *Mindblindness: Essay on Autism and the Theory of Mind*. Cambridge, MA: MIT Press/Bradford Books.

Baron-Cohen, S., Scott, F., Williams, J., Bolton, P., Matthews, F. E., and Brayne, C. (2009) Prevalence of Autism-Spectrum Conditions: UK School-Based Population Study. *British Journal of Psychiatry*, 194, 500–509.

Bauminger, N. (2002) The Facilitation of Social-Emotional Understanding and Social Interaction in High-Functioning Children with Autism. *Journal of Autism and Developmental Disorders*, 32(4), 283–298.

Beresford, B., Stuttard, L., Clarke, S., Maddison, J., and Beecham, J. (2012) *Managing Behaviour and Sleep Problems in Disabled Children: An Investigation into the Effectiveness and Costs of Parent-Training Interventions: Summary Report*. London: Department for Education.

Bromley, J., Hare, D., Davison, K., and Emerson, E. (2004) Mothers Supporting Children with Autistic Spectrum Disorders: Social Support, Mental Health Status and Satisfaction with Services. *Autism*, 8(4), 409–423.

Buron, K. and Curtis, M. (2004) *The Incredible 5-Point Scale: Assisting Students with Autism Spectrum Disorders in Understanding Social Interactions and Controlling Their Emotional Responses*. Shawnee Mission, KS: Autism Asperger Publishing Co.

Clements, J. and Zarkowska, E. (2000) *Behavioural Concerns and Autistic Spectrum Disorders: Explanations and Strategies for Change.* London: Jessica Kingsley Publishers.

Corrigan, P. W., Morris, S. B., Michaels, P. J., Rafacz, J., and Rusch, N. (2012) Challenging the Public Stigma of Mental Illness: A Meta-Analysis of Outcome Studies. *Psychiatric Services,* 63(10), 963–973.

Dettmer, S., Simpson, R. L., Myles, B. S., Ganz, J. B. (2000) The Use of Visual Supports to Facilitate Transitions of Students with Autism. *Focus on Autism and Other Developmental Disorders,* 15(3), 163–169.

Dickerson Mayes, S., Calhoun, S., Murray, M., Ahuja, M., and Smith, L. A. (2011) Anxiety, Depression, and Irritability in Children with Autism Relative to Other Neuropsychiatric Disorders and Typical Development. *Research in Autism Spectrum Disorders,* 5(1), 474–485.

Frith, U. (2003) *Autism: Explaining the Enigma.* London: John Wiley and Sons.

Frost, L. and Bondy, A. (2002). *The Picture Exchange Communication System (PECS).* Newark, DE: Pyramid Educational Consultants.

Gray, C. and White, A. L. (2002) *My Social Stories Book.* London: Jessica Kingsley Publishers.

Gray, D. (2002) "Everybody just Freezes. Everybody is Embarrassed": Felt and Enacted Stigma Among Parents of Children with High Functioning Autism. *Sociology of Health and Illness,* 24(6), 734–749.

Guenole, F., Godbout, R., Nicolas, A., Franco, P., Claustrat, B., and Baleyte, J.-M. (2011) Melatonin for Disordered Sleep in Individuals with Autism Spectrum Disorders: Systematic Review and Discussion. *Sleep Medicine Reviews,* 15(6), 397–387.

Hastings, R. P. and Beck, A. (2004) Practitioner Review: Stress Intervention for Parents of Children with Intellectual Disabilities. *Journal of Child Psychology and Psychiatry,* 45(8), 1338–1349.

Jesner, O. S., Aref-Adib, M., and Coren, E. (2007) Risperidone for Autism Spectrum Disorder. *Cochrane Database of Systematic Reviews,* January 24(1): CD005040.

Kalyva, E. and Avramidis, E. (2005) Improving Communication between Children with Autism and Their Peers through the 'Circle of Friends': A Small-Scale Intervention Study. *Journal of Applied Research in Intellectual Disabilities,* 18(3), 253–261.

References

Kamps, D., Leonard, B., Vernon, S., Dugan, E., Delquadri, J., Gershon, B., Wade, L., and Folk, L. (1992) Teaching Social Skills to Students with Autism to Increase Peer Interactions in an Integrated First-Grade Classroom. *Journal of Applied Behaviour Analysis*, 25, 281–288.

Kanner, L. (1943) Autistic Disturbances of Affective Contact. *Nervous Child*, 2, 217–250 (reprinted 1968 in *Acta Paedpsychiatrica*, 35(4), 100–136).

Karkhaneh, M., Clark, B., Ospina, M. B., Seida, J. C., Smith, V., and Hartling, L. (2010) Social Stories to Improve Social Skills in Children with Autism; A Systematic Review. *Autism*, 14(6), 641–662.

Kim, J. A., Szatmari, P., Bryson, S. E., Streiner, D. L., and Wilson, F. J. (2000) The Prevalence of Anxiety and Mood Problems among Children with Autism and Asperger Syndrome. *Autism* 4(2), 117–132.

Lopata, C., Thomeer, M. L., Volker, M. A., Toomey, J. A., Nida, R. E., Lee, G. K., Smerbeck, A. M., Rodgers, J. D. (2010) RCT of a Manualised Social Treatment for High Functioning Autism Spectrum Disorders. *Journal of Autism and Developmental Disorders*, 40, 1297–1310.

Mayes, S. D. and Calhoun, S. L. (2009) Variables Related to Sleep Problems in Children with Autism. *Research in Autism Spectrum Disorders*, 3(4), 931–941.

Murphy, O., Healy, O., and Leader, G. (2006) Risk Factors for Challenging Behaviors among 157 Children with Autism Spectrum Disorder in Ireland. *Research in Autism Spectrum Disorders*, 3(2), 474–482.

Nadon, G., Feldman, D. E., Dunn, W., and Gisel, E. (2011) Mealtime Problems in Children with Autism Spectrum Disorder and their Typically Developing Siblings: A Comparison Study. *Autism*, 15(1), 98–113.

Najdowski, A. C., Wallace, M. D., Doney, J. K., and Ghezzi, P. M. (2003) Parental Assessment and Treatment of Food Selectivity in Natural Settings. *Journal of Applied Behavior Analysis*, 36(3), 383–386.

Nicholas, J. S., Charles, J. M., Carpenter, L., King, L. B., Jenner, W., and Spratt, E. G. (2008) Prevalence and Characteristics of Children with Autism-Spectrum Disorders. *Annals of Epidemiology*, 18(2), 130–136.

Nichols, S., Hupp, S. D. A., Jewell, J. D., and Zeigler, C. S. (2004) Review of Social Story Interventions for Children Diagnosed with Autism Spectrum Disorders. *Journal of Evidence-Based Practices for Schools*, 6(1), 90–120.

Paul, C., Williams, K. E., Riegel, K., and Gibbons, B. (2007) Combining Repeated Taste Exposure and Escape Extinction. *Appetite*, 249, 708-711.

Planche, P. and Lemonnier, E. (2012) Children with High-Functioning Autism and Asperger's Syndrome: Can We Differentiate their Cognitive Profiles? *Research in Autism Spectrum Disorders*, 6(2), 939-948.

Provost, B., Crowe, T. K., Osbourn, P. L., McCalin, C., and Skipper, B. J. (2010) Mealtime Behaviours of Preschool Children: Comparison of Children with Autism Spectrum Disorder and Children with Typical Development. *Physical and Occupational Therapy in Pediatrics*, 30(3), 220-233.

Rao, P. A., Beidel, D. C., and Murray, M. J. (2008) Social Skills Interventions for Children with Asperger's Syndrome or High Functioning Autism: A Review and Recommendations. *Journal of Autism and Developmental Disorders*, 38, 353-361.

Rossignol, D. A. and Frye, R. E. (2011) Melatonin in Autism Spectrum Disorders: A Systematic Review and Meta-Analysis. *Developmental Medicine and Child Neurology*, 53(9), 783-792.

Ryan, C. and Charragain, C. N. (2010) Teaching Emotion Recognition Skills to Children with Autism. *Journal of Autism and Developmental Disorders*, 40, 1505-1511.

Sivertsen, B., Posserud, M. B., Gillberg, C., Lundervold, A. J., and Hysing, M. (2012) Sleep Problems in Children with Autism Spectrum Problems: A Longitudinal Population-Based Study. *Autism*, 16(2), 139-150.

Sofronoff, K. and Attwood, T. (2003). A Cognitive Behaviour Therapy Intervention for Anxiety in Children with Asperger's Syndrome. *Good Autism Practice*, 4(1), 2-8.

Tomanik, S., Harris, G. E., and Hawkins, J. (2004) The Relationship between Behaviours Exhibited by Children with Autism and Maternal Stress. *Journal of Intellectual and Developmental Disability*, 29(1), 16-26.

Vriend, J. L., Corkum, P. V., Moon, E. C., and Smith, I. M (2011) Behavioral Intervention for Sleep Problems in Children with Autism Spectrum Disorders: Current Findings and Future Directions. *Journal of Pediatric Psychology*, 36(9), 1017-1029.

References

Webb, B. J., Miller, S. P., Pierce, T. B., Strawser, S., and Jones, P. (2004) Effects of Social Skill Instruction for High Functioning Adolescents with Autism Spectrum Disorders. *Focus on Autism and Other Developmental Disabilities,* 19(1), 53-62.

Whitaker, P., Barratt, P., Joy, H., Potter, M., and Thomas, G. (1998) Children with Autism and Peer Group Support: Using 'Circles of Friends'. *British Journal of Special Education,* 25(2), 60-64.

Williams, D. L., Goldstein, G., and Minshew, N. J. (2006) The Profile of Memory Function in Children with Autism. *Neuropsychology,* 20(1), 21-29.

Wing, L. and Gould, L. (1979) Severe Impairments of Social Interaction and Associated Abnormalities in Children: Epidemiology and Classification. *Journal of Autism and Childhood Schizophrenia,* 9, 11-29.

Wood, J. J. Drahota, A., Sze, K., Har, K., Chiu, A., Langer, D. A. (2009) Cognitive Behavioral Therapy for Anxiety in Children with Autism Spectrum Disorders: A Randomized, Controlled Trial. *Journal of Child Psychology and Psychiatry,* 50(3), 224-234.

World Health Organization (1992) *International Statistical Classification of Diseases and Related Health Problems, 10th Revision* (ICD-10). Geneva: WHO.

Zeedyk, M. S., Caldwell, P., and Davies, C. E. (2009) How Rapidly Does Intensive Interaction Promote Social Engagement for Adults with Profound Learning Disabilities? *European Journal of Special Needs Education,* 24(2), 119-137.

Further Reading and Resources

Websites

www.autism.org.uk

The National Autistic Society has a wealth of information on all aspects of autism. There is also a link on the site to international autism organisations.

www.autism-society.org

The US-based Autism Society of America.

www.researchautism.net

A UK charity dedicated to research into autism, including a helpful review of interventions.

DVDs

Two really good DVD introductions about autism are:

Beguley, M. (1992) *A is for Autism*. London: BFI.

Hoy, R. (2007) *Autism and Me*. London: Jessica Kingsley Publishers.

Biopic of Temple Grandin:

Jackson, M. (2010) *Temple Grandin*. HBO Home Video

Books

Introduction to the autism spectrum

Attfield, E. and Morgan, H. (2007) *Living with Autistic Spectrum Disorders: Guidance for Parents, Carers and Siblings*. London: Paul Chapman Publishing.

Attwood, T. (2008) *The Complete Guide to Asperger's Syndrome*. London: Jessica Kingsley Publishers.

Baron-Cohen, S. (2008) *Autism and Asperger Syndrome: The Facts*. Oxford: Oxford University Press.

Notbohm, E. (2005) *Ten Things Every Child with Autism Wishes You Knew*. Arlington, TX: Future Horizons.

Tantum, D. (2011) *Autism Spectrum Disorders through the Life Span*. London: Jessica Kingsley Publishers.

Williams, C. and Wright, B. (2004) *How to Live with Autism and Asperger's Syndrome: Practical Strategies for Parents and Professionals*. London: Jessica Kingsley Publishers.

Wing, L. (1996) *The Autistic Spectrum*. London: Constable and Robinson.

Diagnosing autism

American Psychiatric Association (2013) *Diagnostic Statistical Manual of Mental Disorders, Fifth Edition* (DSM-V). Washington, DC: APA.

National Initiative for Autism: Screening and Assessment (2003) *National Autism Plan for Children (NAPC)*. London: National Autistic Society.

National Institute for Health and Clinical Excellence Autism (2011): *Recognition, Referral and Diagnosis of Children and Young People on the Autism Spectrum*. London: NICE.

World Health Organization (1992) *International Statistical Classification of Diseases and Related Health Problems, 10th Revision* (ICD-10). Geneva: WHO.

First-hand accounts of autism

Grandin, T. (2006) *Thinking in Pictures and Other Reports from My Life with Autism*. London: Bloomsbury.

Grandin, T. (2012) *Different – Not Less: Inspiring Stories of Achievement and Successful Employment from Adults with Autism, Asperger's and ADHD*. Arlington, TX: Future Horizons.

Jackson, L. (2002) *Freaks, Geeks and Asperger Syndrome: A User Guide to Adolescence*. London: Jessica Kingsley Publishers.

Love, J. (2007) *How Joshua Learned: Making Sense of the World with Autism*. London: National Autistic Society.

Sainsbury, C. (2000) *Martian in the Playground: Understanding the Schoolchild with Asperger's Syndrome*. Bristol: Lucky Duck Publishing.

Williams, D. (1998) *Nobody Nowhere: The Remarkable Autobiography of an Autistic Girl*. London: Jessica Kingsley Publishers.

Theories of autism

Baron-Cohen, S. (2009) Autism: The Empathizing-Systemizing (E-S) Theory. *Annals of the New York Academy of Sciences*, 1156, 68–80.

Baron-Cohen, S. (1995) *Mindblindness: An Essay on Autism and Theory of Mind*. Cambridge, MA: MIT Press/Bradford Books.

Frith, U. (2003) *Autism: Explaining the Enigma*. London: John Wiley and Sons.

Talking with children and young people about autism (including resources to share)

Adams, S. (2009) *A Book About What Autism Can Be Like*. London: Jessica Kingsley Publishers.

Doherty, K., McNally, P., and Sherrard, E. (2008) *I Have Autism ... What's That?* London: National Autistic Society.

Gerland, G. (2000) *Finding Out about Asperger Syndrome, High Functioning Autism and PDD*. London: Jessica Kingsley Publishers.

Kershaw, P. (2011) *The ASD Workbook: Understanding Your Autism Spectrum Disorder*. London: Jessica Kingsley Publishers.

Pike, R. (2008) *Talking Together about an Autism Diagnosis: A Guide for Parents and Carers of Children with an Autism Spectrum Disorder*. London: National Autistic Society.

Welton, J. (2004) *Can I Tell You About Asperger Syndrome? A Guide for Friends and Family*. London: Jessica Kingsley Publishers.

Books for siblings

Frender, S. and Schiffmiller, R. (2007) *Brotherly Feelings: Me, My Emotions and My Brother with Asperger's Syndrome*. London: Jessica Kingsley Publishers.

Gorrod, L. (1997) *My Brother is Different*. London: National Autistic Society.

Autism-friendly educational settings

Charman, T., Pellicano, L., Peacey, L., Peacey, N., Forward, K., and Dockrell, J. (2011) *What is Good Practice in Autism Education?* London: Centre for Research in Autism and Education; Department of Psychology and Human Development, Institute of Education; University of London.

Costley, D., Keane, E., Clark, T., and Lane, K. (2012) *A Practical Guide for Teachers of Students with an Autism Spectrum Disorder in Secondary Education*. London: Jessica Kingsley Publishers.

www.education.gov.uk

Government resources for education staff.

www.lancashire.gov.uk/education/pivats

PIVATS (Performance Indicators for Value Added Target Setting) is used to monitor students up to Level 4 of the national curriculum.

Developing social skills and understanding emotions

Cotugno, A. J. (2011) *Making Sense of Social Situations: How to Run a Group-Based Intervention Program for Children with Autism Spectrum Disorders.* London: Jessica Kingsley Publishers.

Howlin, P., Baron-Cohen, S., and Hadwin, J. (1998) *Teaching Children with Autism to Mind-Read.* Chichester: John Wiley and Sons.

Perks, S. (2007) *Body Language and Communication: A Guide for People with Autism Spectrum Disorders.* London: National Autistic Society.

Whitaker, P., Barratt, P., Joy, H., Potter, M., and Thomas, G. (1998). Children with Autism and Peer Group Support: Using 'Circles of Friends'. *British Journal of Special Education,* 25(2), 60–64.

www.thetransporters.com

The Transporters is a DVD which teaches emotion recognition to 4 to 8-year-olds and developed by the Autism Research Centre in the UK.

Developing communication and understanding

Barton, M. (2012) *It's Raining Cats and Dogs: An Autism Spectrum Guide to the Confusing World of Idioms, Metaphors and Everyday Expressions.* London: Jessica Kingsley Publishers.

Frost, L. and Bondy, A. (2002) *The Picture Exchange Communication System Training Manual,* 2nd edn. Newark, DE: Pyramid Educational Consultants.

Gray, C. (2010) *The New Social Story Book.* Arlington, TX: Future Horizons.

Gray, C. and White, A. L. (2002) *My Social Stories Book.* London: Jessica Kingsley Publishers.

www.pecs.org.uk

Pyramid Educational Consultants is the official provider of the Picture Exchange Communication System (PECS) in the UK and Ireland.

www.thegraycenter.org

Further information about Social Stories including how to access training.

Intensive interaction

www.do2learn.com

Free download of communication cards and pictures to make visual supports.

www.hanen.org

The Hanen Centre provides workshops and training designed for parents and educators, such as More Than Words.

www.intensiveinteraction.co.uk

An approach to teaching communication skills to children and adults with severe learning difficulties or autism.

www.phoebecaldwell.co.uk

Useful information on the autistic spectrum from an expert practitioner in intensive interaction.

Emotional well-being and mental health

Attwood, T. (2001) *Exploring Feelings: Cognitive Behaviour Therapy to Manage Anxiety.* Arlington, TX: Future Horizons.

Attwood, T. (2004) *Exploring Feelings: Cognitive Behaviour Therapy to Manage Anger.* Arlington, TX: Future Horizons.

Buron, K. and Curtis, M. (2004) *The Incredible 5-Point Scale: Assisting Students with Autism Spectrum Disorders in Understanding Social Interactions and Controlling Their Emotional Responses.* Shawnee Mission, KS: Autism Asperger Publishing Co.

Jaffe, A. V. and Gardner, L. (2006) *My Book Full of Feelings: How to Control and React to the Size of Your Emotions.* Shawnee Mission, KS: Autism Asperger Publishing Co.

Challenging behaviours

Aitken, K. J. (2012) *Sleep Difficulties and Autism Spectrum Disorders: A Guide for Parents and Professionals.* London: Jessica Kingsley Publishers.

Clements, J. (2005) *People with Autism Behaving Badly: Helping People with ASD Move on from Behavioral and Emotional Challenges.* London: Jessica Kingsley Publishers.

Clements, J. and Zarkowska, E. (2000) *Behavioural Concerns and Autistic Spectrum Disorders: Explanations and Strategies for Change.* London: Jessica Kingsley Publishers.

Schopler, E. (1994) *Parent Survival Manual: A Guide to Crisis Resolution in Autism and Related Developmental Disorders*. New York: Kluwer Academic/Plenum.

Whitaker, P. (2008) *Challenging Behaviour and Autism: Making Sense, Making Progress*. London: National Autistic Society.

www.team-teach.co.uk

Training in positive behaviour strategies for professionals.

www.challengingbehaviour.org.uk

Charity specialising in severe learning disabilities and behaviour.

www.sleepscotland.org

Charity providing training and support to parents of children with additional needs.

Parent training courses

Bromley, J., Todd, S., and Mellor, C. (2012) *Riding the Rapids: Living with Autism or Disability. Course Manual*. Central Manchester University Hospitals NHS Foundation Trust – available to facilitators trained in the approach. Visit: **www.encompasspsychology.co.uk**

Wright, B. and Williams, C. (2007) *Intervention and Support for Parents and Carers of Children and Young People in the Autistic Spectrum: A Resource for Trainers*. London: Jessica Kingsley Publishers.

www.barnardos.org.uk/cygnet

Cygnet provides parenting support and practitioner training programmes focussed on autism.

Managing sensory sensitivities

Bogdashina, O. (2003) *Sensory Perceptual Issues in Autism and Asperger Syndrome*. London: Jessica Kingsley Publishers.

Caldwell, P. and Horwood, J. (2008) *Using Intensive Interaction and Sensory Integration: A Handbook for Those Who Support People with Severe Autistic Spectrum Disorder*. London: Jessica Kingsley Publishers.

Index

A

aggression 108, 127, 151, 159–166, 183
anxiety 9, 19, 23, 36, 47, 50, 51, 54, 73, 108, 115, 116, 117, 120, 121, 122, 123, 134, 143, 156, 167, 168, 169, 178, 179, 184, 189, 190, 191, 193, 194, 201
Asperger, Hans 6
Asperger syndrome 6, 7, 8, 9, 10, 17, 28, 183, 191, 192, 193, 196, 197, 198, 202
assault cycle 183
attention deficit hyperactivity disorder (ADHD) 21–22, 197
Attwood, Tony 120, 122, 189, 193, 196, 201
atypical autism 7, 183

B

Baron-Cohen, Simon 10, 28, 42, 189, 196, 197, 199
behavioural approaches 152, 156, 157, 158, 166, 177, 183
Bondy, Andy 101, 107, 190, 200
Buron, Kari Dunn 119, 190, 201

C

Caldwell, Phoebe 102, 194, 200, 202
causes (of autism) 9, 11
central coherence 58, 184
Charragain, Caitriona 90, 193
child and adolescent mental health services 82, 123, 165
childhood autism 5, 7, 8, 14, 17, 184
circle of friends 93, 184, 191

classrooms 54, 79, 81, 87
Clements, John 132, 190, 201
cognitive behaviour therapy 122, 184, 189, 193, 201
communication:
    difficulties 103
    non-verbal 37
    opportunities 104
Curtis, Mitzi 119, 190, 201

D

depression 23, 116, 121–123, 184, 190
developmental coordination disorder (DCD), *see* dyspraxia
developmental disability 3, 184, 193
diagnosis:
    categories of diagnosis 17
    getting a diagnosis 13–18
    terms 7
Diagnostic Statistical Manual of Mental Disorders (DSM-V) 5, 7, 189, 196
dyspraxia 22, 185

E

early intervention workers 77
eating problems 141–149
echolalia 36
emotional recognition 184
emotional well-being 83, 99–123, 184, 201
Emotional Toolbox 120
empathizing-systemizing theory 28
eye contact 37, 89, 102

F

facial expressions, 34, 37, 38, 41, 90, 184
   understanding of 38, 40, 44
feeding issues, *see* eating problems
fluoxetine 123
fragile X syndrome 23, 189
Frith, Uta 58, 190, 197
Frost, Lori 101, 107, 190, 200
functional analysis 131, 184, 186

G

genetics 9
gestures 37, 38, 41, 100, 112
Grandin, Temple 28, 195, 197
Gray, Carol 26, 101, 110, 187, 190, 200

H

Hanen Programs 101, 200
Hewitt, David 102
high functioning autism 8, 18, 185, 190, 191, 192, 198

I

inclusion team(s) 75
Incredible 5-Point Scale 119, 190, 201
Intensive Interaction 102, 194, 200, 202
International Statistical Classification of Diseases and Related Health Problems (ICD-10) 17, 194, 197

K

Kanner, Leo 5, 184, 191

L

language:
   delayed 7, 8, 14, 184, 185
literal understanding of 37, 104

learning disabilities 9, 22, 95, 185, 194, 202
Lopata, Christopher 95, 96, 191

M

mealtimes 145, 147
medication 22, 76, 123, 152, 166
melatonin 152, 190, 193
mindblindness 43, 45, 56, 185, 189, 197
MMR vaccine 11

N

neurodiversity 25–30, 185
neurotypicality 25, 28, 29, 30, 53, 54, 57, 185

O

objects of reference 107
occupational therapist(s) 77, 82, 175, 178, 192

P

paediatrician(s) 6, 16, 76
parental stress 19, 26, 128, 130, 145, 191, 193
passport 63
Performance Indicators for Value Added Target Setting (PIVATS) 85, 199
pervasive developmental disorder – not otherwise specified 7, 17
Picture Exchange Communication System (PECS) 101, 107, 108, 185, 190, 200
playgrounds 15, 82, 117, 118, 197
psychiatrist(s) 5, 16, 76
psychologist(s), educational/ clinical 16, 76, 82, 96, 131, 148, 157, 178

R

reinforcement 102, 134, 177, 178, 186

repetitive behaviour 5, 9, 46, 47, 50, 127, 167–174

residential worker(s)78

respite care 19

restricted behaviour 167–174

rewards, *see* reinforcement

rigidity 9

risperidone 166, 191

routines 5, 31, 46, 47, 50, 51, 136, 142, 143, 144, 145, 147, 149, 153, 154, 161, 167–174

Ryan, Christian 90, 193

S

savant syndrome 12

self-injury 127, 159–166, 186

sensory sensitivities:
  pain 54, 56
  sight 55
  smell 56
  sound 54
  taste 57
  touch 54

sensory integration therapy 175, 202

siblings 9, 65, 68, 69, 192, 196, 198

short break(s) 19, 77, 78

sleep difficulties 151–158, 201

social skills: 15, 19, 73, 74, 78, 79, 83, 89–98, 186, 191, 192, 199
  communication 4, 9, 41, 99, 101
  imagination 4, 5, 6, 41, 42, 45

interaction x, 4, 5, 6, 15, 31, 32, 34, 38, 90, 93, 95, 98, 101, 116, 117, 135, 160, 167, 189, 190, 193, 201

Social Stories 101, 110, 111, 147, 156, 177, 179, 187, 190, 191, 200

social worker(s) 77

special interests 31, 46, 48, 50, 103, 112, 113, 136, 142, 153, 161, 172, 174

speech and language therapist(s) 16, 76, 82, 96, 99, 107, 113

selective serotonin reuptake inhibitors (SSRI) 123

stimulatory behaviours 29

support worker(s) 77

T

theory of mind 42, 45, 91, 187, 189, 197

timetables, *see* visual schedules

Timothy syndrome 23

transition 16, 21, 87, 88

triad of impairment 5

tuberous sclerosis 23

twins 9

V

visual schedules 52, 108, 118, 147

visual supports 52, 85, 101, 102, 105–107, 111, 113, 120, 147, 170, 190, 200

W

weak central coherence theory 58, 184

Wing, Lorna 5, 193, 196

Z

Zarkowska, Ewa 132, 190, 201

978-178135010-2

978-178135102-4

978-178135104-8

i www.independentthinkingpress.com

Before the College Audition

Chelsea Diehl

Table of Contents

About the Author. xiii
About MCA xiv
Introduction. xv
Key Information xvii
Making Your List xxiii
The Interviews xxvii

Note: Featured interviews are listed in italics.

Alabama. **1**
Alabama State University 1
University of Alabama at Tuscaloosa 4
University of Alabama at Birmingham. 6

Arkansas **7**
University of Arkansas—Fort Smith. 7

California **8**
California State University, Fullerton 8
Chapman University 12
Loyola Marymount University 15
University of California, Los Angeles 19
Biola University 24
California State University, East Bay 25
California Institute of the Arts 26
University of La Verne 26
Point Loma Nazarene University 27
University of California, Berkeley 27
University of California, Riverside. 28
University of California, Santa Barbara 29
Vanguard University 30
Whittier College 31

Colorado **32**

Colorado Mesa University 32
University of Northern Colorado 33

Connecticut **34**

University of Connecticut 34
Eastern Connecticut State University 38
Southern Connecticut State University 38
Western Connecticut State University 39

Delaware **40**

University of Delaware 40

Florida **41**

Florida State University 41
University of Central Florida 45
Flagler College 51
Florida International University 51
Florida Southern College 52
Palm Beach Atlantic University 52
Southeastern University 53

Georgia **54**

Shorter University 54
Armstrong Atlantic State University 57
Clark Atlanta University 57
Columbus State University 58
Georgia College 58
Georgia Southwestern State University 59
Reinhardt University 60
Savannah College of Art and Design 60
University of West Georgia 61

Illinois **62**

DePaul University 62
Loyola University Chicago 66
Millikin University 67
Roosevelt University 71
Eureka College 75
Illinois State University 76
Knox College 76
North Central College 77

Northern Illinois University 78
Rockford University 79
Southern Illinois University Edwardsville 80
Southern Illinois University Carbondale 80
University of Chicago 81
University of Illinois at Chicago 81
University of Illinois at Urbana-Champaign 82

Indiana **83**
Ball State University 83
Indiana University 87
Butler University 92
DePauw University 92
Indiana Wesleyan University 93
University of Indianapolis 94

Iowa **95**
Clarke University 95
Luther College 95
St. Ambrose University 96
University of Iowa 96
Waldorf College 97

Kansas **98**
Wichita State University 98
Baker University 101

Kentucky **102**
Campbellsville University 102
Centre College 102
Morehead State University 103
University of Kentucky 104
University of Louisville 104

Louisiana **106**
Tulane University 106

Maryland **107**
Frostburg State University 107
McDaniel College 108
Washington College 109

Massachusetts *110*

Boston University 110
Emerson College 115
Amherst College 119
Fitchburg State University 120
Regis College 120
Salem State University 121
Smith College 122
Wellesley College 122
Worcester State University 123

Michigan *124*

University of Michigan 124
Grand Valley State. 129
Hope College 129
Michigan State University 130
Oakland University 130
University of Detroit Mercy 131
Western Michigan University 131

Minnesota *132*

Bethel University 132
College of Saint Benedict/Saint John's University. 133
Hamline University. 133
Saint Mary's University of Minnesota 134
Winona State University. 135

Mississippi *136*

Jackson State University. 136
Mississippi University for Women 136

Missouri *137*

Webster University 137
Drury University. 141
Lindenwood University. 142
Missouri State University 143
Northwest Missouri State University 144
Stephens College. 144
Truman State University 145
University of Missouri—Kansas City. 145

Montana *147*

Rocky Mountain College 147

Nebraska **148**
Chadron State College 148
Nebraska Wesleyan University 148
University of Nebraska at Kearney 149

Nevada **150**
University of Nevada, Reno 150

New Hampshire **151**
University of New Hampshire 151
Dartmouth College 154

New Jersey **155**
Fairleigh Dickinson University 155
Montclair State University 157
Centenary College 161
Drew University 162
Kean University 162
Ramapo College 163
Rowan University 164
Rutgers University 164
Seton Hall University 165

New Mexico **166**
New Mexico State University 166
Santa Fe University of Art and Design 167

New York **168**
Fordham Theatre Program, Fordham University 168
Hofstra University 172
New York University 177
Pace University 180
Syracuse University 185
Wagner College 189
Brooklyn College, City University of New York 193
City College of New York 193
Hunter College 194
Niagara University 194
Skidmore College 195
St. Lawrence University 196
St. Bonaventure University 196
State University of New York at Binghamton 197
State University of New York at Potsdam 198

North Carolina **199**

East Carolina University 199
Elon University 201
Appalachian State University 203
Fayetteville State University 204
Gardner-Webb University 205
Greensboro College 205
Guilford College 206
Meredith College 207
University of North Carolina—Asheville 207
Western Carolina University 208

North Dakota **209**

Dickinson State University 209
Minot State University 209

Ohio **211**

Baldwin Wallace University 211
University of Cincinnati—College-Conservatory of Music 215
Capital University 223
Franciscan University of Steubenville 224
Heidelberg University 224
Kenyon College 225
Marietta College 225
University of Findlay 226
Wittenberg University 226
Wright State University 227

Oregon **228**

George Fox University 228
Pacific University 229
Southern Oregon University 229

Pennsylvania **231**

Muhlenberg College 231
Temple University 235
University of the Arts 238
Alvernia University 242
Cedar Crest College 242
DeSales University 243
Dickinson College 243
Elizabethtown College 244
Gettysburg College 245
Indiana University of Pennsylvania 245

Lycoming College 246
Messiah College 246
University of Pittsburgh 247

Rhode Island **248**
Providence College 248
Roger Williams University 249

South Carolina **250**
College of Charleston 250
Limestone College 251
Newberry College 251
North Greenville University 252
Winthrop University 252
Wofford College 253

South Dakota **254**
Mount Marty College 254
Northern State University 255
South Dakota State University 255

Tennessee **256**
Bryan College 256
Cumberland University 256
Lipscomb University 257
Middle Tennessee State University 258
Sewanee: The University of the South 258
Trevecca Nazarene University 259

Texas **260**
Baylor University 260
Hardin Simmons University 260
Lamar University 261
McMurry University 262
Midwestern State University 262
Rice University 263
Stephen F. Austin State University 263
Texas A&M University 264
Tarleton State University 265
Texas Christian University 265
Texas Woman's University 266
University of St. Thomas 267
University of Texas at Austin 267
University of Texas at El Paso 268

Utah *270*

Brigham Young University 270

Vermont *275*

Middlebury College 275

Virginia *276*

Eastern Mennonite University 276

George Mason University 276

Hollins University 277

University of Mary Washington 278

Washington *279*

Central Washington University 279

Saint Martin's University 280

Seattle University 280

University of Puget Sound 281

University of Washington 281

Wisconsin *283*

Carthage College 283

Marquette University 284

University of Wisconsin—Parkside 284

University of Wisconsin—Stevens Point 285

University of Wisconsin—Whitewater 285

About the Author

Chelsea Diehl is a Boston-based college audition coach and consultant and is the founder of *My College Audition* (www.mycollegeaudition.com). *My College Audition* (MCA) is a resource for high school students looking to obtain a degree in musical theatre or acting at the collegiate level. MCA provides one-on-one coaching to help students succeed in the competitive college audition process. MCA's students continue to gain acceptances to the top programs throughout the country, and MCA proudly maintains a 100% acceptance rate for full-time students.

Chelsea received her BA in acting and theatre education from Emerson College in Boston, MA. After graduating, Chelsea returned to Emerson to teach for the Emerson Summer Arts Academy for three summers.

Chelsea's first book, *Admit One: Ten Steps to Choosing Your Acting or Musical Theatre College Program,* is a highly regarded college audition guidebook that has been dubbed by students and parents alike as essential in navigating the college audition and selection process. Chelsea's writing has been featured in various blogs and websites, including Acceptd, Samuel French, Smart College Visit, NerdWallet, CollegeXpress, and the Performing Arts Network. She has lectured on the subject at several locations, including Destination Broadway, the Drama Book Shop, the New England Theatre Conference, and other private venues across the United States.

As a firm believer in practicing what she preaches, Chelsea can be found on the stage and screen. Recently, she has been featured in commercials for Staples, Big Y, and Conoco.

Chelsea resides in the North End of Boston with her husband, Andrew, and their Cavalier King Charles, Cooper.

To contact Chelsea, you can reach her at chelsea@mycollegeaudition.com.

About MCA

My College Audition

Founded in 2008 by Chelsea Diehl, *My College Audition* (MCA) provides one-on-one coaching and consulting for the competitive college audition process. MCA's students continue to gain acceptances to the top programs throughout the country, and MCA proudly maintains a 100% acceptance rate for full-time students. MCA prides itself on being in touch with current college audition trends and maintaining strong relationships with college faculty.

MCA coaches work with students to select and prepare monologues and songs, prepare headshots and résumés, practice interview and adjustment techniques, choreograph and film pre-screen videos, run through mock auditions, and so much more. All coaches are working professionals in the field, and you can find them on Broadway and off-Broadway, in regional theatres, and featured in film/television/commercial/voice-over work.

MCA also consults with students during the application process to assist in selecting a desirable, appropriate, and realistic set of schools to apply to and in dealing with all of the other issues that arise during the college audition process. From master classes with distinguished faculty, to deciding on the perfect audition attire, to personalized and in-depth coaching, and culminating with mock auditions, MCA students leave the process feeling prepped, excited, and ready to showcase their best self.

Our students come from all over the world. While we are based in Boston for in-person lessons, more than half of our students work with us via Skype or FaceTime with equal success. Past acceptances include Emerson College; University of Michigan; Ithaca College; The Hartt School of Music, Dance and Theatre; Syracuse University; Shenandoah Conservatory; Baldwin Wallace University Conservatory of Music; Boston Conservatory; Pace University; Montclair State University; Boston University; University of California, Los Angeles; and many, many more! To read a full list of testimonials and acceptances, please visit us at www.mycollegeaudition.com.

To learn more about *My College Audition* or to arrange a consultation to discuss our offerings, please email us at info@mycollegeaudition.com.

Introduction

It's time to begin thinking about putting your college list together! You've taken the right steps: met with your guidance counselor, registered for the SATs, kept your grades up, and even visited some campuses over spring break. Now all you need to do is finalize your college list, submit those apps, and college, here you come!

. . . *Oh, but wait,* you think, as you take a closer look at the guidelines for a musical theatre applicant.

It looks like I'm going to have to audition at this school. Well, now that I'm looking, I'm going to have to audition at all of these schools. How will this work with my fall show schedule? Wait, what are Unifieds? This one wants a 16-bar up-tempo, and this one needs a classical monologue in verse not to exceed two minutes. This one wants a choreographed dance alongside two contrasting 32-bar cuts and two contrasting contemporary monologues. Once I figure out what all of this means, I'll try to begin selecting pieces, I guess . . .

Wait! They only accept 15 kids out of 2,000 who audition?!

It looks like I'll also need a pre-screen video for these three schools, and they all have different deadlines and requirements. I'll start by figuring out what a pre-screen is, and then I guess I'll find someone to record it? My résumé needs updating. My headshot was taken when I was 12. And why do all of these schools have additional performing arts supplement essays?

Why is this so hard?!

And right when you think you should have really listened to your parents and chosen to be a doctor, a lawyer, a scientist, or anything but a performer, you breathe a sigh of relief knowing that *you got this.* You're an actor, and you know nothing worth having comes easy.

It's true: If you decide to pursue an undergraduate degree in musical theatre or acting, you *are* going to have a significantly more arduous and time-consuming application process than many of your friends in high school.

However, here is what I'm not going to do: discourage you. Many people, in regard to theatre, will say (and stop me if you've heard this one before), if you can do anything else with your life and be happy, *do it*! And it's true. If you know you would be equally happy pursuing a different career, by all means, you will save yourself a lot of heartache. But for the rest of you, the eternal artists and dreamers, I firmly believe there is a place in this crazy theatre world for everyone.

Here's what I will encourage you to do: get organized. *Now*. Be realistic with your talent and ability and assess your strengths against the odds of each school. Be honest with yourself. Do you want to pursue a BFA at a conservatory because you have heard that is the *only* path to pursuing your dreams? Or, realistically, do you also like doing stage makeup and would you be thrilled to pursue a BA in acting with a minor in another area? Keep in mind: A school in and of itself does not guarantee *anything*—college is what you make of it. If you look at any playbill on Broadway, there is a mix of performers from highly regarded conservatories right down to never-heard-of-before programs in the middle of Missouri. Talent is talent. Sure, a top-notch school certainly has its perks, connections, and outstanding faculty, but if you attend a top-notch school and don't continually work hard to better yourself and your craft, that $100,000 (or more) education won't be worth much in the end. As one of my students once said to me in response to why he'd be a good fit for a program: "Hard work beats talent when talent doesn't work hard."

Only you know what you need to be happy and fulfilled both as an artist and as a human being. Combine what you know to be true about yourself with the reality of these competitive programs and you should be able to begin formulating a list of schools.

This book has been designed to give you an idea of the multitude of undergraduate musical theatre and theatre options that are available to you. Many are schools within your very own state that you may not have even known had a theatre program! While many of you have a firm idea of what you want ("I am only looking for BFAs that are in New York City"), I encourage all students to keep an open mind while sifting through the interviews in this book. You may discover a few programs that weren't previously on your radar. By no means do I want you to jeopardize what you want and believe you deserve in a training program, but adding a few lesser-known schools as matches and safeties wouldn't be the worst idea for your wallet and sanity come decision time.

Find a school that fits *you*—one that fits into your budget, your needs and abilities as a performer, and your needs as a human being. Most important, find a program that you think will help you be the most well-rounded, polished performer and young adult by the time you graduate. The goal of this book is to help you put together a realistic and desirable set of reach schools, match schools, and safeties.

First, we'll begin by defining some terms that will appear throughout these pages. If you are ready to tackle this crazy process, turn the page. Let's do this.

Key Information

Acceptd

Acceptd is the largest performing and visual arts network in the world. Most schools opt to use Acceptd as a way to accept pre-screen videos. It's easy to upload a video to the network's site and send it to any schools that require a pre-screen or allow you to audition by submitting a DVD. You can also apply to and be discovered by colleges and universities, festivals, scholarship offerings, and competitions directly on the site (www.getacceptd.com).

Actors' Equity Association (AEA)

AEA is the labor union that represents theatre actors and stage managers in the United States. In order to join AEA (or be "Equity" as most members say), you must be employed under an Equity contract, complete the 50 weeks required of an EMC candidate (defined below) or be a member of a sister union for more than a year. The sister unions are SAG-AFTRA, AGMA (American Guild of Musical Artists), AGVA (American Guild of Variety Artists), or GIAA (Guild of Italian-American Actors).

Bachelor of Arts (BA)

The BA degree is awarded for an undergraduate course or program in liberal arts, sciences, or both and is generally awarded after four years. The BA is usually around 30%–40% curriculum in your chosen performing arts major. The remaining 60%–70% is comprised of general education classes and allows for double majoring or pursuing a minor. The BA offers much more flexibility and a greater ability to pick and choose your class schedule.

Bachelor of Fine Arts (BFA)

The BFA is the standard undergraduate degree for students seeking a professional education in the visual or performing arts, and are generally four-year programs. The majority of the course load in the BFA consists of roughly two-thirds or more hours in the major discipline. This is an intense study of your chosen major, and at many programs, it allows little to no room for pursuing another outside interest academically. If you are pursing a BFA at a conservatory or conservatory-like program, you can expect approximately 75% of your classes to be in your performing arts major. Consider each program individually to uncover what your opportunities are surrounding each school's BFA major.

Bachelor of Music (BM)

The BM is a degree awarded by a college, university, or conservatory upon completion of a program of study in music. A bachelor of music in musical theatre is housed in the school of music, and you can expect to take such classes as music theory, applied voice, and music theatre history, on top of acting and dance training. The BM is much like a BFA at many schools: the majority of your course load will be within your chosen major.

Bachelor of Science (BS)

The BS degree is typically awarded for studies in natural science, pure science, or technology. In terms of performing arts, most often a school that offers a BS will offer a BS in theatre arts. This degree is most similar to the BA degree, and many schools offer the BA and BS alongside each other. Much like the BA, the BS is usually around 30%–40% curriculum in your chosen performing arts major. The remaining 60%–70% is comprised of general education classes and allows for double majoring or pursuing a minor.

Classical Monologue

The exact definition of a classical monologue can vary depending on whom you ask. Generally, a classical monologue is considered Elizabethan (such as Shakespeare), Chekhovian, or Greek. Some other authors to consider include Moliére, Euripides, Marlowe, and Sophocles. Each school has its own standard of what it expects in a classical monologue, so make sure to follow each school's specific guidelines.

Conservatory

A conservatory is a school of advanced studies, usually specializing in one of the fine arts. You will take 75% of all credits within your major. This does not mean, however, that you won't take some general education classes—you will still have to meet core requirements.

Conservatory Style (Within a Liberal Arts School)

A conservatory-style program is one at a liberal arts school with training that is nearly as focused as that at a conservatory. Usually, 50%–75% of your credits will be within your major.

Contemporary Monologue

Technically, a contemporary monologue is considered anything written after 1900. However, to me, a contemporary monologue is one written within the past 5–10 years. The language used in the piece should accurately reflect how you speak in real life. Be sure to check out the websites of your chosen schools, as many programs list what monologues they prefer seeing and those that they deem as overdone or inappropriate.

To help ease the process of finding appropriate contemporary monologues, use the following guidelines:

1. **Present tense.** Monologues must be in the present tense. Storytelling monologues or monologues that solely talk about past events are dull and hard for an auditor to connect to. I want to feel like I am a fly on the wall witnessing a conversation between two people.

2. **Scene partner.** Make sure you are talking to one specific person (or sometimes a group of people) in your monologue. Talking to "yourself" or the "audience" simply does not

work in a college audition setting. You should have a clear, defined person that you are speaking with.

3. **Super objective.** A super objective is something that you ultimately want from the person you are talking to by the end of the monologue. Your character should want something, and this desire drives the entire piece. If there is nothing that you are working toward in a monologue, why is your character talking for two minutes straight? If you can't decipher a clear super objective, you may want to consider a different piece.

Cut Program/Juries

Some BFA/BA programs perform cuts at the end of sophomore year, meaning that students must re-audition to remain in their major. However, this is becoming less and less the norm, and many programs that once instituted cuts have now eliminated the practice. Other schools perform "juries" in which the performing arts faculty appraises students' work ethic, commitment to the program, and growth. Juries are most often used for evaluation purposes rather than an opportunity to downsize the program. For example, if students aren't showing up to class or have failing grades, these might be grounds for putting them on probation after their juries.

Equity Membership Candidate (EMC)

This program permits actors and stage managers in training to credit theatrical work in an Equity theatre towards eventual membership in Equity. After securing a position at a participating theatre, you may register as a candidate. You must complete 50 weeks of EMC work at participating theatres in order to join AEA.

Kennedy Center American College Theater Festival (KCACTF)

KCACTF is a national theater program involving 18,000 students from colleges and universities nationwide whose goal is to encourage and recognize the finest work produced by university and college theater programs. Their goal is also to provide opportunities for participants to further develop their theater skills and achieve professionalism. Through state, regional, and national festivals, KCACTF participants celebrate the creative process while getting the chance to witness one another's work. KCACTF honors excellence of overall production and offers students individual recognition through awards and scholarships in playwriting, acting, criticism, directing, and design.

League of Resident Theatres (LORT)

LORT is the largest professional theatre association of its kind in the United States, with 74 member theatres located in every major market in the U.S., including 29 states and the District of Columbia. LORT theatres issue more Equity contracts to actors than Broadway and commercial tours combined. The principle objective of LORT is to promote the general welfare of resident theatres in the United States and its territories.

Liberal Arts

A liberal arts school provides training in all the academic disciplines, such as languages, literature, history, philosophy, mathematics, and science, providing information of general cultural concern. Typically, 50% of your credits are within your major.

Master of Fine Arts (MFA)

The MFA is a graduate degree typically requiring two to three years of postgraduate study in the visual arts, creative writing, graphic design, photography, filmmaking, dance, theatre, or other performing arts, as well as some theatre management and arts administration. Many people pursue an MFA in order to teach at the collegiate level, receive more training, and build connections in the industry.

MidWest Theatre Auditions (MWTA)

Each year, over 600 acting auditionees and 100 design, technical, and stage management interviewees from collegiate institutions participate in a weekend of auditions for invited theatre representatives in the hopes of gaining professional theatrical work. Both Equity and non-Equity are invited and you must be nominated by a college professor or theatre professional to attend.

National Association of Schools of Theatre (NAST)

NAST is an organization of schools, conservatories, colleges and universities that establishes national standards for undergraduate and graduate degrees and other credentials. Institutional membership is gained only through the peer review process of accreditation.

National Unified Auditions (Unifieds)

The National Unified Auditions allow students to audition for a large number of performing arts programs in one central location over the course of a few days. Not every school attends these auditions, but there are certainly quite a few that do. The locations include New York (typically a weekend in late January or beginning of February), Chicago (typically a weekend in the beginning of February), Las Vegas (typically a day in the middle of February), and Los Angeles (typically a weekend in mid-February). There are obvious benefits to attending Unifieds—you are able to knock out the majority of your school choices in one location while saving time and money instead of traveling to each individual school. There are also downfalls—it can be a bit intimidating being surrounded by the vast amount of students auditioning, you don't get to see the school's campus and get a vibe for the school, and you miss the opportunity to meet other faculty and staff.

Instead of the National Unified Auditions, some schools will also hold auditions for their programs on the same dates and in the same locations as Unifieds, but they are not officially connected with them. Alternatively, schools will travel to remote locations and host their own auditions to reach a greater pool of candidates who may not be able to travel to their campuses. In short, each school has its own audition schedule and set of standards.

New England Theatre Conference (NETC)

NETC is a non-profit organization dedicated to providing its members with professional services, career development, and recognition awards in the live theater arts. At the annual auditions, an average of 50 companies are represented and audition actors in a "cattle call"-like setting (auditions in which a large number of performers can be seen over the span of one to two days). The companies represented include summer and year-round theatres (Equity and non-Equity), college-based summer theatres, repertory companies, touring companies, and much more.

Pre-Screen Video (Pre-screen)

A pre-screen is a recorded audition that schools use to screen their applicants before inviting them to a live, in-person audition. This has become a prerequisite for many schools in the past couple of years. If they like what they see in the pre-screen, you will be asked to audition in person at a "callback." Each school's pre-screen requirement varies, but as a musical theatre applicant you can expect to perform contrasting monologues, two different cuts of contrasting songs, and a choreographed dance. As an acting applicant, you will most certainly need two contrasting monologues at minimum. There are usually strict time requirements—make sure to follow them exactly! You don't want to jeopardize your chance of being invited to audition live at your dream school because you neglected to keep your monologue under the one-minute time requirement.

These videos have become quite popular, so it's important to showcase your best self, but they do not need to be shot professionally.

Here are some tips to make the best pre-screen video possible with the resources available to you:

1. Use a quality digital camera. Don't have one? Put up a status on Facebook and see if any of your friends have one you can borrow. Uncle Fred may pull through with a camera you didn't know he had that would probably beat a cell phone video.
2. Use a tripod—or even stack a lot of books to rest your camera on. Even though your dad claims to be a professional, his shaky hands will not be a good look on your pre-screen video.
3. Make sure we can see you *and* hear you. Don't let your accompanist overpower you. Make sure the room is well lit and your little brother remains quiet in the room next to you.
4. Shoot from the waist up or full body against a blank white wall. You should be the main focus of this video—not the art hanging in the background.
5. Dress as if you are going on a first date, not a job interview. Show us your personality but remain polished and neat.
6. Re-film. Take multiple takes. Practice makes perfect!

Screen Actors Guild-American Federation of Television and Radio Artists (SAG-AFTRA)

SAG-AFTRA is the labor union that represents film and television principal and background performers, journalists, and radio personalities worldwide. A performer becomes eligible for SAG-AFTRA membership under one of the following two conditions: 1) proof of SAG or AFTRA employment or 2) employment under an affiliated performers union.

Showcase

Showcase presentations (a mixture of songs, scenes, dance routines, monologues, and more) are used to assist students in their senior-year transition into the professional theatrical world. Most schools host their showcases in New York City, in Los Angeles, or directly on their campuses and invite industry professionals, such as agents and casting directors, to attend. The success of showcases differs dramatically from school to school. Some schools forgo a showcase altogether and simply invite these professionals to their campus throughout the year to audition their students.

Southeastern Theatre Conference (SETC)

The SETC annual convention is a gathering of artists, theatre companies, theatre educators, and more that come together to participate in auditions, lectures and workshops to celebrate theatre. There is also a mass audition that is run like a cattle call where you are able to audition in front of numerous professional companies in one audition. In March of each year, the SETC convention hosts over 100 representatives from undergraduate programs to audition potential students. It's a great chance to get in front of some of your desired programs that you may not be able to travel to and make some connections. Often this won't serve as your final audition for a school, but if a representative shows interest, it might be worthwhile to follow up with that program.

Summer Stock

"Summer stock" is the name given to theatrical productions that are performed by a "stock company," or a group of core resident actors, during the summer. Professional theatres tend to hire college students from large cattle call auditions. Among the most popular are SETC, NETC, and StrawHat. Many colleges actively promote participation in these auditions or will invite summer stock producers/directors to audition their students on campus.

Many summer stock companies provide students with EMC points to be put toward completing the necessary 50 weeks of employment to join AEA. Beyond EMC points, summer stock programs offer a chance to build your résumé and make professional connections throughout your college career.

University/Resident Theatre Association (URTA)

The University/Resident Theatre Association is the nation's oldest and largest consortium of professional, graduate (MFA) theatre training programs, and partnered professional theatre companies. URTA hosts National Unified Auditions each winter with hundreds of candidates auditioning and interviewing for a variety of graduate training programs.

Up-Tempo/Ballad

An up-tempo is a fast-paced, high-spirited song. A ballad is a song in which each stanza, or group of four lines, is followed by the same refrain, or chorus. It is usually a slower song, often about love. Schools may ask you to prepare 16 or 32 bars of both a ballad and an up-tempo, but you should always have the full songs ready to go as well. I suggest having two of each prepared that you are confident and excited about. You never want to have to say no if you are asked, "Do you have anything else?"

United States Institute for Theatre Technology (USITT)

The United States Institute for Theatre Technology is a place to network, exchange ideas, and grow. USITT is made up of professionals and pre-professionals in design, production and technology for the performing arts. USITT hosts events and conferences throughout the year.

Making Your List

Here's the deal: Your list of potential schools is going to be much longer than that of your friend who hopes to go to school for business. Not only do you need to be admitted academically for your school, but you need to audition for the performing arts program as well. You have double the amount of work and double the chance for rejection. I hate to be the one to tell you this (sorry, parents!), but I encourage you to have between **10 and 15 schools** on your list. This will include a healthy mix of reach schools, match schools, and safeties.

Reach School

I recommend having 4–6 reach schools on your list.

Depending on whom you ask, this can mean many things. To your guidance/college counselor, a reach school is any school in which your academic credentials fall short of the standard that the school expects. In terms of performing arts, a reach school is a program that is highly competitive and only accepts a dozen or so students each year. Acceptance to a reach performing arts program is based on your audition, and the number of applicants auditioning greatly exceeds the number ultimately accepted (typically, less than 10% of those who audition are accepted). These two definitions of a reach school must be approached as two separate entities, as you will typically apply to the school and apply separately to the performing arts program. However, in many cases, these two definitions of a reach school are one and the same—many competitive performing arts programs are housed within a rigorous academic setting.

TIP More often than not, reach schools are a student's dream schools. Popular, unique, outstanding programs often become reach schools because everyone and his or her uncle auditions there. But to that I say: Go for it! Don't let fear or rejection deter you. I always encourage students to put reach schools on their list *before* I even hear them perform for the first time. Shoot for the moon! You have matches and safeties to back you up. No matter how talented you are, there are schools that will still be a reach for you. They are for everyone when they only accept 10 students.

Match School

I recommend having 5–7 match schools on your list.

When both academics and odds of getting into the performing arts program align, you have found a match school. For academics, a match school is one where your academic credentials fall well within the school's standards for incoming freshmen. In terms of musical theatre or acting, a match school can be a program that has a higher rate of acceptance from auditions, one where you believe your talent is on par with its current students, a school that specifically looks for a trait/ability/skill you possess, a lesser-known program, or one that has a greater number of starting freshmen.

TIP Clearly, match schools are different for everyone. What might be a reach to one could be a great match for another. For many of my students, a match school is a school in which they have no doubt they will be admitted academically and there is a strong likelihood, based on their skill and ability, that they will be admitted to the musical theatre/acting program. If you fall in love with a school and want to better your odds of acceptance to its performing arts program, and would be equally happy studying BFA/BA acting, musical theatre, or dance, find a school where you can audition for all programs simultaneously.

Safety School

I recommend having 2 safety schools on your list.
A safety school is exactly what it sounds like. There is no doubt you will be admitted academically *and* into the performing arts program. Oftentimes, a safety school for a musical theatre or acting applicant is one in which there is no entrance audition required to be admitted to the theatre program. To me, a safety school is also one that is realistic financially. Not only will you get in academically and for your chosen major, but also you should be absolutely certain you can afford it if no financial aid or scholarships come through.

TIP Many times, safety schools are a student's least favorite option out of all of their schools. When there is no audition involved, students feel like it's not a competitive program and they won't thrive once on campus. However, that is not true! There are amazing programs that are non-audition programs (many featured in this book!) and are academically stimulating and prestigious in their theatrical training. I encourage you to pick some safety schools that you truly like and would be ultimately happy in attending. Find a school where you fall in love with the campus, feel like it's a good fit academically, and can see yourself performing on the stage. If you are still worried about not being pushed artistically, find a school that is located close to a bustling city or one that is close or connected to a regional theatre. You can make your own performance opportunities if you feel like what you are looking for is not available on campus. Never put a school on your list (and pay the application fee) if you wouldn't truly be excited about attending.

To further determine if a school is a reach, match, or safety for you:
Adequately compare your grades and scores against the school's standards, have a coach or your drama teacher assess your talent and ability and give you an idea of where you stand, assess the reality of how many students audition versus how many are accepted each year, decide if you would like to be considered for all performing arts majors to better your odds when auditioning, and determine how much financial aid you will realistically need in order to attend any program (and whether it will be available).

Once you determine what is a reach, match, or safety for you:

You need to come up with what I call your "non-negotiables." These are things you need to be completely content with in your performing arts program. **I encourage you to have five.**

If academics are important to you, don't convince yourself you'd be satisfied at a school that has weak academics but an outstanding performing arts program—you'll ultimately be denying yourself something that makes you happy as a well-rounded human being. If you are a strong dancer and don't want to jeopardize your dance training, don't settle for a school that won't continue to push you in that area.

A word of caution when preparing your non-negotiables: Keep an open mind. If you believe you *only* want to be in a city, but in reality you just don't want to see the same faces every day on a small campus, a large school with more than 30,000 students located just outside a city might work just as well. Be stern in what you need to be fulfilled but open enough to be receptive to new possibilities.

As you sift through the interviews in this book, keep your non-negotiables on hand. It will help in weeding out prospective schools.

Let's put this notion into practice. We'll use a fake student named Daisy. Here are some stats on Daisy:

- Wants a BFA in musical theatre, but is also looking at some BA musical theatre options
- Wants to be able to take classes outside her performing arts major as well
- Overwhelmed by the idea of a big school
- Would like to perform professionally during the summers
- Unable to get to each campus to audition

With that background, here are five hypothetical non-negotiables for Daisy:

1. The school needs to have a liberal arts program and a population no greater than 10,000.
2. The school must offer a degree in musical theatre or a track in musical theatre.
3. The school must offer the ability to minor (in either the performing arts or an outside interest).
4. The program attends Unifieds or accepts video auditions.
5. The program actively promotes summer stock auditions or regularly hosts master classes with professionals on campus.

With these five non-negotiables in mind, Daisy would be able to narrow down her list significantly as she flips through the pages of this book.

If you've taken note of everything, you should have a sheet that looks like this (filled out) on hand before you begin perusing the surveys:

Non-negotiables

Non-negotiable #1:
Non-negotiable #2:
Non-negotiable #3:
Non-negotiable #4:
Non-negotiable #5:

While you read the surveys, also have the following spreadsheet on hand so you can begin to formulate your list. This list will be based on your non-negotiables and must incorporate the previously discussed standards of what classifies as a reach, match, and safety (which will require lots of thought and discussion):

School List

Reach #1:	Match #1:	Safety #1:
Reach #2:	Match #2:	Safety #2:
Reach #3:	Match #3:	
Reach #4:	Match #4:	
(Reach #5):	Match #5:	
(Reach #6):	(Match #6):	
	(Match #7):	

The Interviews

A NOTE ON HOW WE PICKED THE SCHOOLS AND INTERVIEWS

Over the course of a year, I have reached out to more than 1,000 colleges and universities with active theatre programs. Through in-person sit-downs, Skype, emails, and sometimes FaceTime, I have put together a selection of more than 200 interviews containing input from over 300 professors and department heads of theatre programs spanning across 40 states. These surveys were collected throughout the 2013–2014 academic year.

Within most states, I have featured a select number of schools by giving them an extensive interview. My hope was to try to feature one program from every state (or more). These are schools that continually pop up on my students' college lists and are *amongst* the most popular in their state. These are not the "best" schools, and they are not ranked in any way. However, they are certainly *among* the best and are continually well-regarded and sought-after programs. For these schools that regularly top my students' lists, my hope was to give readers the inside scoop on what these schools are truly looking for in an applicant and in an audition. Want to know what your dream school's pet peeve is in the audition room? What the auditors look for in a monologue and a song? The school's best advice for auditioning? Flip to that school's page and check it out.

My other goal in this venture was to give readers the opportunity to gain exposure to programs that may not have previously been on their radar. Let's say you know you want to stay on the East Coast but are having a tough time filling your list with appropriate schools. Simply turn to those states where you know you would like to be and check out some exciting finds—there may be something there that surprises you. If finances are a concern and you know you need to stay in state, you now have some new programs to consider. Finding programs that may be more of a match or safety school can be difficult when you have only heard of the prestigious programs, so I encourage you to read each and every interview. There are lots of tremendous theatre programs that aren't necessarily at the forefront of an applying student's mind but are very worthy of their attention.

If a college isn't in this book, that absolutely does not make its department in any way less credible. There are many programs that are not in this book that I truly hope to feature in future editions. Make sure you do your own research if there is a school missing that you are considering. The best way to succeed in this process is to be as informed as humanly possible.

Get reading, and break legs!

—Chelsea Diehl

■ Alabama State University
Montgomery, AL

Compiled by: Dr. Wendy R. Coleman, Chair, Theatre

Population of School: 5,500+

Conservatory or Liberal Arts: University, liberal arts

Degrees Offered:

BFA in dance
BA in theatre arts (concentrations: performance/tech/generalists)

Population of Department(s): 143 students

Theatre Scholarships Available: Yes

Audition Required for BFA: Yes

Audition Required for BA/BS/BM: No

Pre-screen Video Audition Required: No

Attends Unifieds: Yes

Location of Unifieds: SETC

Number of Students Auditioning Each Year: N/A

Number of Students Accepted Each Year: 20–40

Cut Program or Audition to Remain in Program: Yes

Minors in Musical Theatre/Acting: Theatre arts and dance

Prominent Alumni: Bonita Hamilton (*The Lion King*), J. Bernard Calloway (*Memphis*), Yohance Myles (TV/film credits), Tim Ware (Broadway's *Kinky Boots*)

What do you look for in a potential student?

Confidence, academics, talent, "can-do" attitude, experience.

What are some of the auditors' pet peeves?

Negativity or resistance to requests in the audition. For example, when asked to sing, the auditionee replies, "Oh, I can't sing."

What are your audition requirements?

After acceptance to the university, very early in the first semester as a theatre major, students must audition so that faculty can observe raw talent. All auditionees for theatre must act, sing, and dance. Auditionees for the BFA program must apply for audition slots.

In your eyes, what makes up an excellent college audition monologue? Song?

A monologue that suits the student's age and shows the student at his or her best. A song that fits the student's range and showcases his or her voice at its strongest and best range.

If there were one monologue you never wanted to see again, what would it be?

Anything from *The Vagina Monologues* or any other such monologue that can put the audition panel at dis-ease.

If there were one song you never wanted to hear again, what would it be?

Haven't really heard one yet!

Can you walk me through what I can expect at your on-campus auditions?

Students come in early and register. When called to the stage, they act, sing, and dance—in that order—with a prepared monologue and song and a brief taught dance piece.

What's a memorable audition you can remember?

A shy, quiet, unassuming young lady walked onto the stage, opened her mouth, and *blew us away*.

What is your biggest piece of advice for potential students auditioning?

Be yourself. Be your best. Be genuine and represent your own talent well.

After I audition, is there a good way to follow up?

In this age of technology, send an email saying thank you for the opportunity to audition and that you look forward to hearing from the program soon—just that short, simple, and straightforward.

Would I get a showcase at the end of senior year?

Actually, it would be during the fall semester of your senior year.

Do I have to audition to be accepted into the showcase?

Yes, but we work to help you get ready!

Where are showcases held, and are they successful?

Showcases are held on our mainstage, and we've had success from them, including grad school.

Will I be able to audition/perform as a freshman?

You will be able to audition, but absolutely *no* guarantees are made as to whether you will be able to perform during the freshman year. It is not prohibited though.

In what ways can I be involved with the department aside from performing?

Technical theatre, stage management, costuming, set design, lighting and sound, publicity.

Say I get a BA rather than a BFA. Will I actually get to perform?

Yes.

I love to sing, but I don't consider myself a dancer. Can I still seek a degree in musical theatre at your school?

No, we don't offer a degree in musical theatre.

I want to get a BFA in acting, but I also love to sing. Can BFA/BA acting students take voice lessons with top voice faculty?

Yes.

Do you discourage or encourage students to audition for theatre outside of the department during the academic year?

We discourage outside auditions due to the rigorous schedule we have in the department.

Does your school regularly work in conjunction with any regional theatres?

Not at this time.

What do students typically do during the summers? Do you actively promote participation in summer theatre auditions?

Students typically participate in internships or summer stock programs.

How many musicals versus straight plays do you do in a season?

At least one each year.

What are some of your alumni up to? Do you have an active alumni network?

We are developing a strong alumni network.

What is the portfolio/interview process for a technical theatre student?

We accept students without a portfolio, but those interested in a scholarship in technical theatre must present some form of portfolio.

What do you expect to see on a technical theatre résumé?

A résumé is not required.

I'm interested in lighting, sound design, and stage management. What major should I go for? Can I minor?

Theatre arts with generalist concentration.

Anything else I should know?

We have just launched the only BFA in dance offered at an HBCU (Historically Black College/University) in the nation!

■ University of Alabama at Tuscaloosa

Department of Theatre and Dance
Tuscaloosa, AL

Compiled by: William Teague, Chair, Department of Theatre and Dance

Population of School: 34,000

Conservatory or Liberal Arts: Liberal arts

Degrees Offered:

BA in theatre

BA in dance

Musical theatre track (60 hours)

Population of Department(s): 140 undergrad theatre majors, 160 dance majors, 40 theatre MFA candidates

Theatre Scholarships Available: Yes

Audition Required for BA: Not for general BA in theatre, but yes for musical theatre track

Pre-screen Video Audition Required: No

Attends Unifieds: No

Number of Students Auditioning Each Year: 100 for musical theatre

Number of Students Accepted Each Year: 13

Cut Program or Audition to Remain in Program: Yes—all areas

Minors in Musical Theatre/Acting: No in musical theatre; yes in general theatre

Prominent Alumni: Norbert Leo Butz, Michael Emerson, Stephen Tyrone Williams, Soneqia Martin-Green, Jake Boyd

What do you look for in a potential student?

Smart and talented, but mostly a drive and desire to succeed and willingness to learn.

What are some of the auditors' pet peeves?

Overconfidence.

What are your audition requirements?

A 90-second monologue, a dance routine (taught at audition), and a song.

Can you walk me through what I can expect at your on-campus auditions? A welcome "meet and greet" is held in the lobby before the formal process starts, with current students and faculty, as well as videos and handouts. Then there is a general meeting with parents and students, including faculty and guest introductions, an overview of the day's activities, and a short musical performance by current students. Auditionees are then broken into small groups and attend workshops when not auditioning. The department chair and a member of the university admissions office meet with the parents for an extended Q&A. The entire process usually begins at 10:30 a.m. and runs until 5 p.m.

What is your biggest piece of advice for potential students auditioning?

Be prepared and confident, but not too confident. A little nervousness is a good thing.

If I audition for your BFA musical theatre program, but don't get accepted, do you still consider me for your BFA acting program or your BA program?

Yes.

After I audition, is there a good way to follow up?

Email is best.

Would I get a showcase at the end of senior year?

Yes, in mid March in New York City, usually at Theatre Row.

Do I have to audition to be accepted into the showcase?

Yes.

Where are showcases held, and are they successful?

Theatre Row is on 42nd Street in New York City. We usually have about 15–17 in the showcase. For the last two years, we have had almost 100% agent representation and casting for those in the showcase.

Will I be able to audition/perform as a freshman?

Yes!

If there is a graduate program, will I get the same performance opportunities as an undergraduate?

Yes, we only have seven to nine grad actors and numerous roles—nine fully mounted productions a year, with additional local showcases and one-night shows.

In what ways can I be involved with the department aside from performing?

Our design tech area is just as active as performing.

I love to sing, but I don't consider myself a dancer. Can I still seek a degree in musical theatre at your school?

Singing, dancing, and acting are the three components of the musical track. You must at least be a passable dancer.

I want to get a BFA in acting, but I also love to sing. Can BFA/BA acting students take voice lessons with top voice faculty?

Not usually.

Do you discourage or encourage students to audition for theatre outside of the department during the academic year?

Departmental approval is required.

Does your school regularly work in conjunction with any regional theatres?

Yes.

What do students typically do during the summers? Do you actively promote participation in summer theatre auditions?

Virtually all students work in some type of summer theatre.

How many musicals versus straight plays do you do in a season?

Three musicals and six straight plays.

What are some of your alumni up to? Do you have an active alumni network?

We have alumni working in all areas of theatre—Broadway, regional theatre, national tours, TV, film, management, and so on. Yes, our network is active, particularly in New York City and Chicago.

What is the portfolio/interview process for a technical theatre student?

We interview on the fall and spring "Audition Days," as well as SETC and USITT, and on individual appointments on campus. We are not too strict on the contents of the portfolio, since backgrounds vary significantly. The faculty member in the area (scenery, costume/lighting, etc.) meets individually with the student for the review and interview.

What do you expect to see on a technical theatre résumé?

A listing of shows worked and position on the shows.

I'm interested in lighting, sound design, and stage management. What major should I go for? Can I minor?

We offer courses and actual production experiences in all three areas; however, the degree is a BA in theatre. Yes, you can minor.

Anything else I should know?

We have the best football team in the country and a great college atmosphere here in Tuscaloosa!

■ University of Alabama at Birmingham
Birmingham, AL

Compiled by: Kelly Allison, Chair

Degrees Offered:

BFA in musical theatre (pending for a fall 2014 start)
BA in theatre with general, performance, and design/technology concentrations
BA in film
Minors in theatre and film

Population of Department(s): 90 theatre majors, 16 film majors, 10 theatre minors, 15 full-time faculty, 4 full-time professional production staff, and 2 full-time administrative staff

Audition to Declare a Theatre/Musical Theatre Major? Auditions for musical theatre BFA only; no audition required for theatre BA concentrations.

Three things you would like our readers to know about your performing arts department:

1. Housed in Alys Stephens Center, the premiere performing arts facility in the state of Alabama.

2. Training partnerships with the Alabama Shakespeare Festival and the Alabama Ballet.

3. Successfully place many graduates in the finest advanced training programs in the country.

■ University of Arkansas—Fort Smith

Fort Smith, AR

Compiled by: Bob Stevenson, Associate Professor/Director of Theatre

Degrees Offered:

BA in theatre (acting/directing)
BA in theatre (design/tech)

Minors Offered:

Theatre
Music

Population of Department(s): 50 students

Audition to Declare a Theatre/Musical Theatre Major? Not required

Three things you would like our readers to know about your performing arts department:

1. Six or more productions a year, including comedy/drama, musicals, Shakespeare, original work, and video/film projects.

2. Two nationally selected productions, and four regionally selected/toured productions via the Kennedy Center in Washington, DC, in the last seven years.

3. One of the only schools in the nation that produces original, physically devised pieces using circus/athletic storytelling.

California

■ California State University, Fullerton
Fullerton, CA

Compiled by: Mitchell Hanlon, Professor of Musical Theatre, Musical Theatre BFA Program Coordinator

Population of School: Almost 38,000

Conservatory or Liberal Arts: Both, BFA and BA programs

Degrees Offered:

BFA in musical theatre or acting

BAs in applied (general) studies or specialized studies in theatre (playwriting, design and technical production, directing, teaching)

MFAs in acting, directing, and design and technical production

Population of Department(s): Approximately 650 theatre and dance majors

Theatre Scholarships Available: Yes, for continuing students. Many smaller scholarships with a variety of criteria are available for students in all areas of the department. No scholarships are available for incoming students, although we do have musical theatre freshman scholarships that are auditioned/awarded each September.

Audition Required for BFA: Yes. Acting, singing, and dance (ballet, jazz, and tap) juries at the end of the sophomore year. No auditions for freshman entrance. For transfer students, auditions are required if they hope to enter the sophomore or junior (BFA) level.

Audition Required for BA/BS/BM: No

Pre-screen Video Audition Required: Basically no, since we don't audition freshmen. Transfers hoping to get in to the sophomore level of musical theatre class can send audition videos for fall sophomore-level placement. We also have a "Silver Bullet" video submission for incoming freshmen who don't meet the stricter, out-of-local-area GPA requirements imposed by our campus (and most of the California State University system).

Attends Unifieds: Yes (for grad student recruiting only)

Location of Unifieds: URTA

Number of Students Auditioning Each Year: For the end-of-sophomore-year BFA musical theatre (MT) auditions, there are approximately 30 qualified applicants. That pool is much larger in the freshman year, but many students self-select other majors or degree programs when they realize the competitive rigors of the BFA MT program, while others find they don't assess forward in acting, musical theatre, or dance classes. For the BFA acting program, approximately 60–75 students audition at the end of sophomore year.

Number of Students Accepted Each Year: BFA musical theatre accepts 8–12 (average 10); BFA acting accepts 12–16 (average 14+)

Cut Program or Audition to Remain in Program: Once in the BFA program, there are juries in December and May of the junior year and December of the senior year (for both BFA programs), but not with the intention of cutting. We hope that students progress and stay in the program.

Minors in Musical Theatre/Acting: No

Prominent Alumni:
Broadway: Mara Davi (*A Chorus Line*, *The Drowsy Chaperone*, and recurring guest star on NBC's TV show *Smash*); Dashaun Young (Simba, *The Lion King*); Jennifer Hubilla (Kim in *Miss Saigon*, both U.S. national and the Cameron Mackintosh UK tours); Ryan Sander (dance captain, *Mamma Mia!*)

Television and film: Marc Cherry (creator/producer: *Desperate Housewives*, writer: *Golden Girls*); Linda Emond (film: *Julie & Julia*, TV: *Law & Order: SVU*, *The Good Wife*, *Elementary*); Kirsten Vangsness (*Criminal Minds*)

What do you look for in a potential student?
A relentless work ethic, combined with talent and passion.

What are some of the auditors' pet peeves?
Bad song or scene choices (or bad coaching). Students being unprepared.

What are your audition requirements?
For acting, the jury is a two-person, three-minute scene, and if asked, callbacks of a monologue (approximately one minute). For musical theatre, the same acting jury, plus voice jury (prepare four songs showing variety and acting) and dance juries in tap, ballet, and jazz.

In your eyes, what makes up an excellent college audition monologue? Song?
Wisely chosen material that shows off the performer's strengths and type, and songs that don't rely on simply loud notes or exhibit flaws and vocal limits.

If you require a pre-screen video audition, what do you look for in those submissions?
For musical theatre, sophomore placement (including transfer students) looks for acting choices in the song and a good sense of pitch and rhythm. Highly qualified candidates will show control of tone and dynamics as tools of specific, appropriate acting choices. Acting has no pre-screen video auditions for sophomore placement.

Can you walk me through what I can expect at your on-campus auditions?
Saturday—Vocal auditions (sing at least two songs as requested by the panel from your repertoire list, with shorter cuts ready)
Sunday—Three-hour dance jury: quickly learn (en masse) and perform (four per group) a combination in jazz, ballet, and tap (one hour each)
Monday—Acting jury (prepared three-minute scene) with possible monologue callbacks

What is your biggest piece of advice for potential students auditioning?

Choose material wisely and with outside help. Overprepare, and then relax and do your best. We are not looking for flaws—we want you to be great. Remember, a good audition is akin to an opening night performance: material that is well chosen, that shows both vocal ability and solid acting choices, with a relaxed joy of performing.

If I audition for your BFA musical theatre program, but don't get accepted, do you still consider me for your BFA acting program or your BA program?

Yes. Students who jury for BFA musical theatre are also considered for BFA acting (unless they choose otherwise). It is common for strong BFA acting students to have come from the musical theatre candidates.

All performance students enter the university as "Applied Studies BA," and if unsuccessful at jury have the option to continue as Applied Studies BA or change emphasis (to a Specialized Study in Theatre) or major. It is always the student's choice.

After I audition, is there a good way to follow up?

All students are notified of the jury outcome within a week. A pleasant email is always OK.

Would I get a showcase at the end of senior year?

Both BFA programs do a senior showcase.

Do I have to audition to be accepted into the showcase?

No. It is an integral part of the BFA programs and coursework.

Where are showcases held, and are they successful?

Musical theatre showcases are held in New York City; acting showcases are held in Los Angeles. They are quite successful. As an example, our New York showcase for this year's nine musical theatre seniors garnered representation inquiries for each, and most got multiple inquiries. So far, five of the nine have been called directly by casting agents in consideration for major roles (both Broadway and national tours, as well as television series work [NBC]). We have many industry professionals at our showcases, sometimes multiple people from the important, larger agencies. The high quality of our students and their training is well known and well regarded.

Will I be able to audition/perform as a freshman?

Yes and no. First-semester freshmen are not allowed to audition for the fall portion of the general mainstage season. However, first-semester freshmen *can* audition and do perform for student-directed one-acts, directing class scenes and new play readings, as well as the BA showcase (bi-weekly student-produced performance series). In December of their freshman year, freshmen can begin to audition for the mainstage season.

If there is a graduate program, will I get the same performance opportunities as an undergraduate?

Yes. Once in the BFA acting or BFA musical theatre program, students are guaranteed casting each semester—the same as our MFA actors. BFA students are also guaranteed a substantial role before they graduate. We also try to have them perform in a variety of our venues (both on and off campus), with a variety of directors, and in a variety of genres (musical and straight, comedy and drama, contemporary and period, and so on).

In what ways can I be involved with the department aside from performing?

Students can be involved as part of the technical crew in any/all areas (lighting, sound, wigs, costume, running crew). Also, students can direct, write, stage manage, and design shows, as well as be involved with the BA showcase, extramural clubs, or attend career-building seminars and guest artist master classes.

Say I get a BA rather than a BFA. Will I actually get to perform?

All majors in the department are permitted to audition for the season of plays. However, preference is given to those students in the BFA and MFA programs. That said, many of our BA students are cast each semester. Also we have a specific series of showcase performances on campus each semester only for BA students.

I love to sing, but I don't consider myself a dancer. Can I still seek a degree in musical theatre at your school?

No. Our BFA is strictly a triple-threat program. Having said that, we do have people who have made the BFA program that arrived as freshmen with little or no dance training. They worked hard in the first two years studying ballet, jazz, and tap to catch up. But you need to want to study dance seriously to make this program.

I want to get a BFA in acting, but I also love to sing. Can BFA/BA acting students take voice lessons with top voice faculty?

Possibly privately (at their own expense), but not as part of their curriculum.

Do you discourage or encourage students to audition for theatre outside of the department during the academic year?

If the student is in either of the BFA professional training programs, during the school year the student must request permission from the acting/directing faculty before accepting any role outside of the department. Faculty have granted BFA requests to perform with local professional and semi-professional theatres, and that would supersede the department's obligation to cast them in that semester. Also, seniors near graduation are definitely encouraged to audition for professional work. We even bring professional auditions on campus at times.

BA students are highly encouraged to audition for outside engagements. We freely share audition information with them whenever received.

Does your school regularly work in conjunction with any regional theatres?

Yes.

What do students typically do during the summers? Do you actively promote participation in summer theatre auditions?

Students of all levels can and do find summer regional productions to be in. There are many shows, companies, and auditions in Los Angeles. Many students need to earn money with summer jobs. We encourage auditions for summer theatre, especially seniors.

How many musicals versus straight plays do you do in a season?

Two musicals and six plays (and two dance shows) on campus each year *and* a different two musicals and five to six plays in our smaller off-campus venue.

What are some of your alumni up to? Do you have an active alumni network?

The alumni network is strong both in Southern California and with our many alums working and settled in New York. The network of theatre alums includes professional writers, directors, casting people, actors, stage managers, and designers in New York, Los Angeles, Chicago, and Las Vegas. Several new theatre companies (both in Southern California and elsewhere) have been started by department alums.

What is the portfolio/interview process for a technical theatre student?

Each semester, both grad students and undergrads present their work to the design faculty for review.

What do you expect to see on a technical theatre résumé?

No résumé is expected at the undergrad level.

I'm interested in lighting, sound design, and stage management. What major should I go for? Can I minor?

Mostly our students specialize in two design/tech fields. There are no minors in the theatre program.

Anything else I should know?

While we don't have large scholarship endowments, we are not the price tag of private programs either. Unfortunately, some mistakenly assume that "more expensive" equates to a "better education," and thus overlook our program. However, we are probably the best value for any nationally ranked drama program. Our average tuition is only about $7K per year, and even our out-of-state tuition is less than $20K per year. And still, we do a huge season of plays and musicals that all have fully designed productions with automated sets; professional lighting; full orchestra (for musicals) designed; and custom-built costumes, wigs, and makeup.

Also know that the BFA musical theatre program is highly competitive and draws serious students from all over the United States.

■ Chapman University
Department of Theatre
Orange, CA

Compiled by: Dr. Nina LeNoir, Professor, Chair, Department of Theatre

Population of School: 7,570 total; 5,681 undergrads

Conservatory or Liberal Arts: Liberal arts

Degrees Offered:
BFAs in theatre performance, screen acting
BA in theatre

Population of Department(s): 181

Theatre Scholarships Available: Yes

Audition Required for BFA: Yes

Audition Required for BA/BS/BM: Audition, interview, portfolio

Pre-screen Video Audition Required: Not at this time; check website

Attends Unifieds: No

Number of Students Auditioning Each Year: 470

Number of Students Accepted Each Year: 40–45

Cut Program or Audition to Remain in Program: No

Minors in Musical Theatre/Acting: No

Prominent Alumni: Matthew McCray, Hallock Beals

What do you look for in a potential student?

Potential for growth, commitment, seriousness of purpose, ability in chosen area.

What are some of the auditors' pet peeves?

Inappropriate dress, lack of knowledge about program auditioning/interviewing for.

What are your audition requirements?

For acting BFA programs, two monologues and interview; for BAT program, portfolio review and interview (one monologue optional).

In your eyes, what makes up an excellent college audition monologue?

A piece the student would possibly be cast in; a character that is realistic and not exaggerated or a caricature.

If there were one monologue you never wanted to see again, what would it be?

"Tuna fish" or "jock strap in washing machine" monologue.

Can you walk me through what I can expect at your on-campus auditions?

The student arrives on campus, checks in at registration, and, when called, goes to the audition room. Two faculty serve as auditors. The student will perform monologues if acting or review his/her portfolio with faculty if BA. There will be a short interview. The process takes approximately 10 minutes. This may be changing; always check our website.

What's a memorable audition you can remember?

Have seen too many to have one memorable audition.

What is your biggest piece of advice for potential students auditioning?

Be yourself; be prepared with your work; breathe. We know you are nervous, but keep in mind that we are on your side and want you to do well.

If I audition for your BFA musical theatre program, but don't get accepted, do you still consider me for your BFA acting program or your BA program?

We have no musical theatre program. We ask BFA candidates if they are interested in the BAT program, and we will consider them for the BAT if they are interested and not accepted to the BFA.

After I audition, is there a good way to follow up?

No follow-up is needed. A thank you note is nice, but not necessary.

Would I get a showcase at the end of senior year?

We have a showcase in Los Angeles at this time, but are reconsidering it. We will have an opportunity for BFA seniors to interact with industry professionals, but we are evaluating if the physical showcase is the best way for that to happen, given changes in the industry.

Do I have to audition to be accepted into the showcase?

No, but it is open only to BFA students.

Where are showcases held, and are they successful?

Showcases are held in Los Angeles. Success is a relative term—we have good attendance, and the majority of students in the showcase have been contacted for follow-up meetings by industry professionals who attended. There are no guarantees, and it is up to the student to follow through with contacts made.

Will I be able to audition/perform as a freshman?

Yes, but only for spring shows. Fall shows are cast at the end of the previous spring semester.

In what ways can I be involved with the department aside from performing?

All students have to serve on production crews for shows as part of the curriculum (twice for BFA screen acting; four times for other degrees).

Say I get a BA rather than a BFA. Will I actually get to perform?

Yes. Auditions are open to all, and BAs are frequently cast. There are also several student-produced projects, again open to all majors, and those are also open to non-majors.

I want to get a BFA in acting, but I also love to sing. Can BFA/BA acting students take voice lessons with top voice faculty?

Yes.

Do you discourage or encourage students to audition for theatre outside of the department during the academic year?

We discourage auditions outside the department during school terms. However, it is possible, but requires consultation with the student's advisor to ensure that performance in classes is not affected by outside work.

Does your school regularly work in conjunction with any regional theatres?

No.

What do students typically do during the summers? Do you actively promote participation in summer theatre auditions?

Students are involved in a wide array of summer activities, including summer travel courses, internships, and working at various theatres, including two companies affiliated with faculty members (Shakespeare Orange County, OC-Centric). We do not actively participate in summer stock auditions.

How many musicals versus straight plays do you do in a season?

We will usually do one musical and four non-musical productions.

What are some of your alumni up to? Do you have an active alumni network?

Alumni work in a variety of venues. Technical theatre graduates work with some top entertainment companies; performers usually stay in Los Angeles, though some go to New York. They report working in television, film, stage, commercials, and voice-overs. We have a growing alumni network in Los Angeles and New York.

What is the portfolio/interview process for a technical theatre student?

Students meet with a faculty member to review their portfolio and interview.

What do you expect to see on a technical theatre résumé?

Some technical experience, and a pattern that shows increasing responsibility.

I'm interested in lighting, sound design, and stage management. What major should I go for? Can I minor?

Students interested in design usually follow the theatre technology area of study of the BAT. Students interested in stage management can follow the theatre technology area of study or theatre studies area of study. We do not have a formal "design" program. The emphasis is on theatre technology. Students interested in an area of design may pursue that design area through active mentorship/assistantship opportunities and receive preparation appropriate for grad school studies.

Anything else I should know?

Chapman has no theatre minor. Students interested in majoring in theatre should apply and audition/interview for the major at entrance to the school, even if it is a second major or second-choice major. Otherwise, they will have to audition as a current student at the end of their freshman year.

■ Loyola Marymount University
Department of Theatre Arts and Dance
Los Angeles, CA

Compiled by: Kevin J. Wetmore, Jr., PhD, gent. Chair, Department of Theatre Arts

Population of School: 6,870 undergrad, 9,543 total

Conservatory or Liberal Arts: Liberal arts

Degree Offered:
BA in theatre arts

Population of Department(s): 157 majors, 61 minors

Theatre Scholarships Available: Yes (selected by faculty)

Audition Required for BA/BS/BM: DVD audition is required

Pre-screen Video Audition Required: DVD audition is required

Attends Unifieds: No

Number of Students Auditioning Each Year: We receive about 200 audition DVDs each year

Number of Students Accepted Each Year: Varies

Cut Program or Audition to Remain in Program: No

Minors in Musical Theatre/Acting: No

Prominent Alumni: Linda Cardellini, Gloria Calderon Kellett, Colin Hanks, Amber White

What do you look for in a potential student?

Talent, range, committing to strong choices, performance beyond mere memorization, and pieces that display the student's artistic self. This is our one chance to get to know who you are on stage or in front of a camera. We look for material that shows self-awareness: age, ability, appropriate for the level of experience. Please, no Juliets, no Laura Wingfields, no Durang. We've seen these so many times that unless you make us see the piece in a new, dynamic, unexpected way, you're driving us crazy.

What are some of the auditors' pet peeves?

Material we've seen a dozen times with nothing new. Not making choices. No contrast between pieces. Inappropriate material (we don't mean use of obscene language, which is fine when appropriate, but please don't audition for college with a monologue as King Lear). Emoting rather than emotionally connecting or single-indicator emotions (yelling and pointing is "angry," whining is "sad"). Since we only require DVD auditions, don't turn your audition into a mini film. I'm not interested in how well you edit or can manipulate technology. This is to show me how well you act. Conversely, don't just use the webcam on your computer to capture yourself sitting at your desk saying lines. While I have seen some very effective versions of this, mostly it just comes off as amateur and last minute. Make the effort to do it well, as this is your calling card.

What are your audition requirements?

Two contrasting monologues (one classical, one contemporary) and eight bars of a song.

In your eyes, what makes up an excellent college audition monologue?

A well-performed, emotionally connected piece that displays the student's abilities as well as gives a glimpse of who he or she is as an artist and as a person. Any audition that surprises me in a good way. Positive energy. At your age, you're not an actor—you're an auditioner. Acting is the reward for doing your job well, so you may as well start now.

If there were one monologue you never wanted to see again, what would it be?

Anything from Christopher Durang. Love him as a playwright, but I have seen his pieces done so many times, by so many students. And anything from *Romeo and Juliet.* Again, love the play, but don't need to see it again unless you're going to wow me so much it's like I never read it. You want to do Shakespeare? Give me *Cymbeline, Winter's Tale, Two Noble Kinsmen,* or *Love's Labours Lost*—the stuff I never see. Do it well, and we will pay attention and be more interested.

If there were one song you never wanted to hear again, what would it be?

Varies from year to year. This year we're seeing a lot from *Legally Blonde* and *Les Mis.* Not that these are bad choices or bad pieces—they often do everything an audition song is supposed to. But we see a lot of them. And you don't want to be the tenth person in a row singing the same song. Don't go with the herd or the obvious. Find a song that suits you, and sing it well.

If you require a pre-screen video audition, what do you look for in those submissions?

Since that is the only thing we do (video audition, not live), all of the above.

What's a memorable audition you can remember?

Again, given that we only do DVD auditions, one that stands out in memory is a student spliced herself into real films (like *When Harry Met Sally*), removing the character and playing opposite the other actors in other shots. It was memorable, but it told us nothing about her as an actor.

What is your biggest piece of advice for potential students auditioning?

Be yourself. Pick great material. Know that you are auditioning for professionals who have seen a lot. So do your audition, and do it well.

Would I get a showcase at the end of senior year?

Yes. We have a senior showcase here in Los Angeles.

Do I have to audition to be accepted into the showcase?

Yes.

Where are showcases held, and are they successful?

We rent a theatre in Los Angeles, holding the showcase a week after graduation. On average, 80 or so agents and managers attend. In most years, we have a 65% success rate of students signing with representation within a week of the showcase, although last year we had a 100% success rate. We promise equal opportunity, but we cannot promise equal results.

Will I be able to audition/perform as a freshman?

Yes.

If there is a graduate program, will I get the same performance opportunities as an undergraduate?

We do not have a grad program.

What ways can I be involved with the department aside from performing?

Crew, design, writing, directing. We offer a good deal of opportunities for student writing. Students study with Pulitzer Prize-winning playwright Beth Henley. Almost every year ends with a New Works Festival of student writing, also directed by students. Upper-class students with an interest in design are often offered the opportunity to design for a mainstage or workshop show. We are also strongly committed to Theatre for Social Justice, so our students go into the community to work with disenfranchised and underprivileged groups to create theatre for the community.

I love to sing, but I don't consider myself a dancer. Can I still seek a degree in musical theatre at your school?

We don't have a musical theatre degree, so you're fine. Many of our students are less interested in musicals and more interested in dramatic acting, as well as film and television.

I want to get a BFA in acting, but I also love to sing. Can BFA/BA acting students take voice lessons with top voice faculty?

Yes. Many of our students also train in the music department, performing with our award-winning choruses and opera program. We have had students close a show with us, and then the following week perform with a choir at the Vatican.

Do you discourage or encourage students to audition for theatre outside of the department during the academic year?

Students are welcome to audition outside the department. LMU has one of the top 10 film schools in the nation. The School of Film and Television trains film and production majors, all of whom need actors for their many projects. If you graduate from our program and you don't have a reel, you've done something wrong. We are also in the heart of Los Angeles, so students are free to audition and work off campus, if they can, so long as it does not profoundly affect their coursework.

Does your school regularly work in conjunction with any regional theatres?

We work with local theatres in Los Angeles. All of our faculty are working professionals, so it is not unusual for them to bring students to a local theatre where they are performing, designing, and/or directing in order to demonstrate how things work in the professional world, as well as give students connections for their post-graduation careers.

What do students typically do during the summers? Do you actively promote participation in summer theatre auditions?

Yes. We have had success with KCACTF and URTAs, placing students in summer theatres. Other students remain in Los Angeles and work in the industry or intern for local production companies. Others return home to work in local theatres.

How many musicals versus straight plays do you do in a season?

We do one musical and five straight plays, plus a dozen smaller projects. The campus drama club, the Del Rey Players, have their own state-of-the-art theatre, which they run and select the season, which often (but not always) consists of one musical and three straight plays.

What are some of your alumni up to? Do you have an active alumni network?

Our alum go to grad school, act professionally, work in casting offices, teach, and work in local theatres. Many do go on to careers within the industry. Many choose to remain in Los Angeles, while others depart for New York after graduation. We've seen many alum on television or working off-Broadway within five years of graduating. (See our alumni profiles on our web page).

What is the portfolio/interview process for a technical theatre student?

We ask for a letter from a director or teacher who knows your work and any kind of portfolio you may have. We recognize, however, that many high school students will not necessarily have a huge amount of design work, but will have done a good deal of technical work. Thus, we ask primarily for a résumé.

What do you expect to see on a technical theatre résumé?

Crew work on high school and community shows. Any design or stage management experience always makes us excited.

I'm interested in lighting, sound design, and stage management. What major should I go for? Can I minor?

Major in theatre. You will get much more résumé credits than the actors, as we have a small technical pool and there are many opportunities for work. We also have work-study, so one can get paid to hang and focus lights, learn about being a master electrician or rigger, and not have to wait tables after graduation if one is an actor as well.

Anything else I should know?

Our study abroad program is fairly remarkable. Every other year, 20–25 students go to Bonn, Germany, and Moscow, Russia, for four and a half months to study at the Moscow Art Theatre and then in Bonn. Students perform a play in a professional theatre in Germany, but also take classes in Stanislavski, Brecht, European Theatre history, ballet, voice, and so on. It is a life-changing experience that all who attend regard as the single most important event in their development as performers.

All of our faculty, as noted above, are working professionals. We are not hiding away in an ivory tower somewhere. We practice what we preach and what we teach. You will be learning from folks who are doing it, in Los Angeles, and who can become lifetime mentors.

■ University of California, Los Angeles
School of Theater, Film, and Television
Los Angeles, CA

Compiled by: Natasha Levy, Recruitment and Admissions Coordinator

Population of School: 40,000

Conservatory or Liberal Arts: Liberal arts

Degrees Offered:

BA

MFA

MA

PhD

Population of Department(s):

Theater Department: 319 (267 undergrads and 52 grad students)

Film, Television & Digital Media Department: 350 (71 undergrads and 279 grad students)

Theatre Scholarships Available: UCLA Alumni Arts Scholarships and UCLA Regents Scholarships

Audition Required for BA/BS/BM: An audition and interview are required for the BA in theater for the specializations in musical theater and acting. An in-person interview is required for all other specializations (design/production, directing, playwriting, and general theater studies).

Pre-screen Video Audition Required: No

Attends Unifieds: No

Number of Students Auditioning Each Year: Approximately 1,000 audition

Number of Students Accepted Each Year: 100 freshmen; 20 juniors

Cut Program or Audition to Remain in Program: No

Minors in Musical Theatre/Acting: No. The BA degree is a major in theater. The diploma says "theater" and does not list a specialization. However, all applicants choose a specialization when they apply. All students take the same liberal arts core courses throughout their four years, but each specialization has its own conservatory-style course progression that begins in the sophomore year following a "freshman experience" year. The major is thus like a standard liberal arts BA/conservatory-style "hybrid" of sorts. The specializations are acting, musical theater, design/production, directing, playwriting, and general theater studies (sort of a design-your-own major).

Prominent Alumni: Tim Robbins, Tom Schumacher, Michael Stuhlbarg, Nancy Cartwright, Mariska Hargitay, Beth Behrs, Carol Burnett, James Dean, George Takei

What do you look for in a potential student?

Number one is intellectual curiosity—a hunger for learning about their world. We seek out applicants with a strong interest in things outside of theater and, of course, talent and experience—or raw talent even without much experience.

What are some of the auditors' pet peeves?

- Scenes from a monologue book with its attendant not understanding the play or even the moments leading up to that scene. One cannot "work" with the actor at the audition if he or she can't answer questions about plot, intention, and so on.
- Not knowing anything about the playwright.
- Not knowing lines because it is obvious the scenes were learned a week before at most—easy to spot.
- Doing scenes, accompanied by the blocking, from a show the student was in.
- Applicants who are overly "done up" or applicants who look sloppy, as in I-just-rolled-out-of-bed-and-made-it-over-here.
- Playing accents or playing outside of a believable age range (an old person).

What are your audition requirements?

For theater (acting): An interview and two monologues, one and a half minutes each (classical and contemporary)

For theater (musical theater): An interview; two monologues (classical and contemporary); two songs, 16 bars each (ballad and upbeat); dance audition in a group

For theater (design/production): Interview and portfolio review

For theater (directing, playwriting, and general theater studies): Interview

In your eyes, what makes up an excellent college audition monologue?

First, it should be between one and two minutes in length. There should be a distinct beginning, middle, and end. It needs to be clear who is saying what to whom and why in the speech. The character needs to be striving for something over the course of the speech that is difficult to achieve. It is best if the monologue is directed to one or more characters in the environment with the speaker rather than a soliloquy, in which the character speaking is alone. (Soliloquies can certainly be successful as audition pieces, but they are far more difficult.) The audition piece should be something that the student not only loves, but also can relate to and personalize. (Personalization is of the utmost importance. Students need to make their characters' needs, problems, and actions full and truthful.) The student should have broken the speech down into beats or units of action and tried different actions in an attempt to achieve his or her objective over the course of the monologue.

In your eyes, what makes up an excellent college audition song?

An excellent college audition song is very similar to what would be "excellent" for a professional musical theater singing audition. Some key components:

- Sing a song that plays to your strengths—in the right key and clearly illustrating your vocal range and style. The college audition is not a time to try to stretch far beyond your capabilities or comfort zones. If there are very scary high notes (belting or otherwise) that are not consistently solid when you practice, rest assured there is probably a better song choice or key. Style-wise, sing what feels right. For example, if you have a great flair for pop/rock music, then by all means sing a pop or rock tune (there are now plenty of these in the musical theater canon). If you are more of a classical or "legit" singer, choose a classical or "legit" song. There is no reason to sing something that feels foreign and awkward. A good musical theater program will help you stretch into a variety of vocal styles, but in the meantime, play to your strengths.
- Sing a song that is age appropriate. That means a person close to your age could sing it. You may identify with Tevye in *Fiddler on the Roof* (and may have played the role in high school!), but Tevye is not 17 or 18 years old. Perchik and Motel are closer to that younger age, and their songs from *Fiddler* might be good choices—*if* they play to your strengths (see above).
- Sing a song that you have known for a while, so that it's "in your body." The great Los Angeles musical theater guru, Carol Weiss, says: "It takes about six months for a song to really get into your body"—that is, into your muscle memory. I would add that if you have been working on the song for less than two months, it's probably not in your muscle memory, and there are probably better choices. With all the stresses and distractions of auditioning, the last thing you want to feel is less than solid on your song(s).
- Finally, and probably most important, sing a song that is joyful for you to sing. That doesn't mean it has to be a happy song. It should just feel good to sing. You should feel passionate about singing it and about telling the story the song conveys.

If there were one monologue you never wanted to see again, what would it be?

The "tuna fish" monologue from Christopher Durang's *Laughing Wild.*

If there were one song you never wanted to hear again, what would it be?

I don't think there is one song I never want to hear again. Yes, there are some songs that are in vogue for a time; for example, anything that is currently on Broadway or on a cast album that a lot of people in your peer group are crazy about. You might want to avoid these kinds of songs because "everyone is using them for auditions." On the other hand, if the song plays to your strengths, is age appropriate, is "in your body," and is joyful for you to sing, I generally don't care what it is. Having said that, you must honor the parameters given by any particular school. Some schools have lists of "Please do not sing" songs. Don't sing a song from that list! Otherwise, trust your instincts and your heart, prepare thoroughly, and tell the story of the song as clearly and sincerely as you know how.

Can you walk me through what I can expect at your on-campus auditions?

Below are the five steps for an applicant auditioning for the musical theater specialization:

1. Information session for applicants and parents: At the information session, you will learn about the UCLA Theater Department as well as our undergrad musical theater curriculum. You will also have a chance to ask any questions you may have about the theater program.

2. Dance: Under the direction of a choreographer, students will learn and perform a dance routine.

3. Voice: Students should prepare two musical selections: a ballad and an up-tempo. Music should be comprised of show tunes from published musicals. Please bring the sheet music in your key. You will be asked to sing at least 16 bars, but you should be prepared to sing the entire song.

4. Interview: There will be a short interview during which you will discuss your goals and aspirations as a student studying theater in a college setting.

5. Monologue: You must fully prepare and memorize two 90-second monologues. Be prepared to answer questions and discuss the play and author, if asked. You should prepare one classical monologue (prior to 1800) and one contemporary monologue (after 1800).

What's a memorable audition you can remember?

A young woman did an obscure male monologue from *Cymbeline,* an obscure Shakespeare play. But it wasn't the material or the fact that she took a man's part. It was the specificity of detail, the layers of intention and character choice, the confidence, and above all the sheer *joy* of performing the piece. The monologue was way too long, but I let her go because I loved watching her enjoy the opportunity to act.

What is your biggest piece of advice for potential students auditioning?

In addition to heeding the warnings in the pet peeves above, show that you are pleased to be there. Smile during your dance and singing auditions, and show enthusiasm and charm. Know your material. Who is the playwright? Know who your character is and be able to answer questions about the plot and your character's intentions. Work on your auditions well in advance of the auditions.

After I audition, is there a good way to follow up?

Yes. We give each applicant who auditions (and/or interviews) a card with a follow-up email address—just for him or her. We are glad to answer any questions via email. However, we do not give critiques or reasons for acceptance or denial. The university will notify the applicant either way in mid-March (freshmen) or mid-April (junior transfers).

Would I get a showcase at the end of senior year?

Yes.

Do I have to audition to be accepted into the showcase?

Yes.

Where are showcases held, and are they successful?

Our showcase is held in Hollywood, CA.

Will I be able to audition/perform as a freshman?

Yes, after the first quarter.

If there is a graduate program, will I get the same performance opportunities as an undergraduate?

Grad and undergrad productions have, for the most part, separate and discreet grad or undergrad casting pools. The two rarely, if ever, are mingled in the same cast. The seasons average an equal amount of grad versus undergrad productions.

In what ways can I be involved with the department aside from performing?

There are several student producing organizations within the department as well as on campus. There are some work-study opportunities for students who qualify.

Say I get a BA rather than a BFA. Will I actually get to perform?

All actors at UCLA are in a BA program in theater. The acting classes are *only* for the acting and musical theater specialization students. The actors in the productions are BA students (both theater majors and minors).

I love to sing, but I don't consider myself a dancer. Can I still seek a degree in musical theatre at your school?

Yes, if we determine you have raw potential and that you are trainable in dance at the time of your audition.

I want to get a BFA in acting, but I also love to sing. Can BFA/BA acting students take voice lessons with top voice faculty?

Only musical theater students (all BA students) can take the departmental group singing and the individual voice lessons.

Do you discourage or encourage students to audition for theatre outside of the department during the academic year?

Neither, but we do take roll every day and have severe grading consequences for absences. It is up to each individual student to determine whether or not he or she has the time management skills necessary for outside activities, be it acting, designing, or working.

Does your school regularly work in conjunction with any regional theatres?

No, but UCLA owns the Geffen Theater across the street. It is one of the leading professional theaters (LORT B) in Los Angeles. Our students (design, directing, stage management) regularly intern and assist when the artists are in residence. Acting opportunities are very rare but have occurred from time to time.

What do students typically do during the summers? Do you actively promote participation in summer theatre auditions?

Many take general education classes at junior colleges or other schools in order to have a more open schedule during the year; many go abroad for a summer abroad educational experience; and many perform, design, and so on. We do not actively promote or discourage any summer activity.

How many musicals versus straight plays do you do in a season?

One major musical versus at least six major straight plays. There are more lower-tier plays as well.

What are some of your alumni up to? Do you have an active alumni network?

Alumni run the gamut of post-graduation life activities—grad school, Broadway, regional theater, film, television, waiting tables, designing, playwriting festivals, and so on. We have an active "unofficial" alumni network.

What is the portfolio/interview process for a technical theatre student?

Present a portfolio (if the student has one) or list of experiences at the interview. All is covered in the interview.

What do you expect to see on a technical theatre résumé?

The whole range: Practically nothing (may have some stage crew experience but a real drive, need, and want to do it) to "you name it"—has been a technical director, stage crew head, builds scenery, and so on. We are looking for the desire, as much as the experience.

I'm interested in lighting, sound design, and stage management. What major should I go for? Can I minor?

All our specializations are in the theater major. UCLA allows minors in another department (even film).

Anything else I should know?

Our program is a BA but acts like a BA/BFA hybrid. Its focus is academic (half of a student's units are in general elective courses, like a typical BA), but students specialize at the beginning of the sophomore year (acting, musical theater, design/production, directing, playwriting, general theater studies) like a BFA. We feel that this produces a smarter, better-educated, more well-rounded undergrad.

■ Biola University
La Mirada, CA

Compiled by: Dr. Kate Brandon, PhD, Associate Professor, Theatre & Communication Studies

Degrees Offered:

Theatre and communication studies with a drama concentration

Minors Offered:

None at this time

Population of Department(s): 15 theatre majors, 8 drama concentration students

Audition to Declare a Theatre/Musical Theatre Major? Not currently

Three things you would like our readers to know about your performing arts department:

1. We focus on developing the whole person through an integrated approach where faith and craft are developed together.

2. We have committed Christian faculty dedicated to preparing students for the professional environment.

3. We have a low student-to-faculty ratio, which allows for mentorship and pre-professional growth opportunities.

■ California State University, East Bay
Department of Theatre and Dance
Hayward, CA

Compiled by: Thomas Hird, Chair

Degrees Offered:

Theatre arts
Acting
Dance
Musical theatre
Technology and design
Directing: sharing a creative vision with society
Solo performance
All bodies and abilities
Music

Minors Offered:

Theatre
Dance
Music

Population of Department(s): 65

Audition to Declare a Theatre/Musical Theatre Major? No

Three things you would like our readers to know about your performing arts department:

1. We offer a holistic approach to performance training that encourages students to challenge themselves in every segment of the production process.

2. While we continue to value traditional boundaries and literature, our students often create original work for their senior performances that integrate a variety of performance techniques to tell an intimate story.

3. There are no grad students to compete for roles or production assignments, so performers audition for shows from their first year and students often design full shows.

California Institute of the Arts
Valencia, CA

Compiled by: Nataki Garrett, Associate Dean and Co-Head of BFA Acting

Degrees Offered:

Design and production, which includes scenic (MFA, BFA) with concentrations in video for performance (MFA) and applied design for performance (MFA), costume (MFA, BFA), lighting (MFA, BFA), sound (MFA, BFA), technical direction (MFA, BFA), production management (MFA), producing (MFA), and stage management (MFA, BFA)
Performance, which includes directing (MFA), acting (MFA, BFA), and writing (MFA)

Minors Offered:

None or integrated media

Audition to Declare a Theatre/Musical Theatre Major? An audition is required for acting programs

Three things you would like our readers to know about your performing arts department:

1. California Institute of the Arts School of Theater is a professional training program dedicated to developing new forms and voices. We are a practical-based training program, which means we believe students learn by doing.
2. We train across a broad spectrum of artistic settings and media.
3. We aim to create artists with the agency to sculpt their own careers.

University of La Verne
La Verne, CA

Compiled by: Dr. David Flaten, Chair, Department of Theatre Arts

Degrees Offered:

BA in theatre arts, with emphases including acting, directing, design, management, and technical theatre

Minors Offered:

Theatre arts minor is individual, based only on a number of units taken in the program

Population of Department(s): 40–50 theatre majors, 4 full-time faculty staff, plus adjuncts and guest artists

Audition to Declare a Theatre/Musical Theatre Major? Every student auditions or presents a portfolio for review at the beginning of each semester. A major is declared by end of second year.

Three things you would like our readers to know about your performing arts department:

1. Students receive much individual attention, as class sizes are intentionally small with a rich guest artist program and supportive culture.
2. Production-oriented program: 2012 season produced more than 20 student-directed projects plus *Urinetown* and Shakespeare.
3. Safe community 35 miles from Los Angeles with many contacts.

■ Point Loma Nazarene University
San Diego, CA

Compiled by: Dr. Paul R. Bassett, Chair, Department of Communication & Theatre

Degrees Offered:

Theatre

Minors Offered:

Theatre

Population of Department(s): 12

Audition to Declare a Theatre/Musical Theatre Major? No

Three things you would like our readers to know about your performing arts department:

1. High student–faculty ratio.
2. Internships available at major theatres in San Diego.
3. Fall study abroad program in London each year.

■ University of California, Berkeley
Berkeley, CA

Compiled by: Michael Mansfield, Undergraduate Academic Advisor

Degrees Offered:

BA in dance and performance studies
BA in theater and performance studies

Minors Offered:

Dance and performance studies
Theater and performance studies
Our curriculum is taught within the context of a liberal arts education. Students opt to work with our undergrad academic advisor to craft their own emphasis, drawing from at least one of the following: acting, arts and social justice, arts administration, choreography, dance performance, design (costume, lighting, scenic, sound), dramaturgy, performance, performance studies/critical studies, playwriting, production management

Population of Department(s): 100 theater majors, 20 dance majors, 80 theater minors, 60 dance minors

Audition to Declare a Theatre/Musical Theatre Major? No

Three things you would like our readers to know about your performing arts department:

1. The Department of Theater, Dance, and Performance Studies teaches performance as a mode of critical inquiry, creative expression, and public engagement. Through performance training and research, we create liberal arts graduates with expanded analytical, technical, and imaginative capacities. As a public institution, we make diversity and inclusion a key part of our teaching, art making, and public programming. The fluid cross-training between the dance, theater, technical theater, and performance studies is a hallmark of the program.

2. Our season features four mainstage shows, five workshop productions, and a new play reading series. Undergrads are the focus of our production season, and they receive course credit for participating as student actors, designers, directors, or stage managers.

3. Faculty areas of interest: acting, African studies, American studies, Asian American performance, choreography, classics, dance history, design, directing, disability studies, filmmaking, gender studies, human rights, interdisciplinary performance, Latin American performance and politics, modern dance technique, new media, performance theory, performance and technology, performance culture, performance literature, performance theory, playwriting, rhetoric, theater history, voice and speech.

■ University of California, Riverside
Riverside, CA

Compiled by: Stu Krieger, Professor and Department of Theatre Chair

Degrees Offered:

We are currently in transition to officially become the Department of Theatre, Film & Digital Production. Our undergrad major has four tracks: acting, stage production, writing, and filmmaking.

Minors Offered:

Theatre minors can also focus on any of the four available tracks.

Population of Department(s): An average of 125 students in the major, 9 full-time faculty, 4 production staff

Audition to Declare a Theatre/Musical Theatre Major? No, auditions are not required for admission to our program. Admittance is based on regular University of California academic and personal criteria.

Three things you would like our readers to know about your performing arts department:

1. With the close proximity to Los Angeles, our program strives to interact with the working population of film and stage professionals there. In recent years, guest speakers in our classes have included producer/director Garry Marshall, *Avatar* and *Titanic* producer Jon Landau, *Mad Men* creator Matthew Weiner, and *Homeland* co-creator Howard Gordon, plus actors William Fichtner, Max Adler, Juliet Mills, Eric Stoltz, and numerous others from the world of entertainment.

2. Our faculty members are all working professionals in addition to their academic duties, working in film, television, and theatre. Résumés and credits are available on our website.

3. Our program produces five to seven stage shows, one musical, and one department film per year, starring student actors and produced by student crews.

■ University of California, Santa Barbara
Santa Barbara, CA

Compiled by: Lauren Ward, Undergraduate Advisor

Degrees Offered:

BA theater (design, directing, playwriting, theater and community, or theater studies)
BFA theater (acting)
BA dance
BFA dance

Minors Offered:

Theater (theater studies)
Theater (design and production)

Population of Department(s): About 250 students (minor and major)

Audition to Declare a Theatre/Musical Theatre Major? Auditions are required for dance degrees and BFA theater. Auditions are not required for BA theater.

Three things you would like our readers to know about your performing arts department:

1. Dedicated to the study and practice of theater in all its phases, the Theater Department offers a wide range of classes appropriate for non-majors pursuing a liberal arts education and for majors preparing for a professional or educational career. The department currently awards BFA and BA degrees at the undergrad level and MA and DPhil degrees at the grad level.

2. All degree programs emphasize the study of dramatic literature and history as well as studio courses and participation in the production program. While the general education needs of the university are supported by the department through numerous course

offerings and a very active performance program, the approximately 240 undergrad majors and 25 grad students reap the benefits of a department committed to excellence situated in a large university. The experience of the faculty and their active involvement present the student with excellent mentorship.

3. UCSB Dance is committed to contributing to an artistically and intellectually vibrant global society by offering a rigorous conservatory-style contemporary dance program. This training program, in an enlightened liberal arts setting, provides the environment and resources necessary for faculty and students to achieve excellence in their creative and academic research. Two degree programs, BFA and BA, are offered for students interested in pursuing a career in dance. The curriculum for both BFA and BA degrees is studio centered. The main thrust of the training is directed toward developing performers and creative artists who are technically proficient, aesthetically astute, and historically informed. Central to both programs are daily technique classes in modern dance and ballet. A sound basis in the craft of choreography is provided, as well as a variety of courses in dance history, writing for dance, design, music, stage production, and technical aspects of the theater.

■ Vanguard University
Costa Mesa, CA

Compiled by: Susan Berkompas, Department Chair

Degrees Offered:

BA with concentrations in musical theatre, performance/directing, and design/technical

Minors Offered:

Theatre minor and liberal arts degree with an emphasis in theatre

Population of Department(s): 56 majors and 10 minors are currently enrolled

Audition to Declare a Theatre/Musical Theatre Major? Auditions are highly recommended but not mandatory

Three things you would like our readers to know about your performing arts department:

1. One of two U.S. Christian universities accredited by the NAST.
2. Seven mainstage productions per year.
3. Professional theatre company, American Coast Theater Company, in residence during summer months.

■ Whittier College
Whittier, CA

Compiled by: Brian A. Reed, Theatre Department Chair

Degrees Offered:

Theatre (performance emphasis)
Theatre (design and technology emphasis)

Minors Offered:

Theatre
Film studies

Population of Department(s): 50–60 majors and minors

Audition to Declare a Theatre/Musical Theatre Major? No

Three things you would like our readers to know about your performing arts department:

1. We hold Theatre Talent Scholarship auditions for prospective students in February.
2. We are in a great location for close proximity to the entertainment industry, roughly halfway between Hollywood and Disneyland.
3. We send students to the Region VIII KCACTF each year for the Irene Ryan auditions.

Colorado

■ Colorado Mesa University
Grand Junction, CO

Compiled by: Timothy D. Pinnow, Department Head

Degrees Offered:

BA in theatre arts with concentrations in acting/directing, musical theatre, design/technology, dance

Minors Offered:

Theatre

Dance

Population of Department(s): 120

Audition to Declare a Theatre/Musical Theatre Major? Yes

Three things you would like our readers to know about your performing arts department:

1. Performance season includes two musicals, two plays, two dance concerts, one to three black box productions, and 10–20 one-acts per year.
2. All faculty have significant professional experience.
3. Program is designed as a pre-professional program, preparing students to directly enter the profession.

■ University of Northern Colorado

School of Theatre Arts and Dance
Greeley, CO

Compiled by: David Grapes, School Director and Professor of Theatre

Degrees Offered:

NAST-accredited – Pre-Professional Programs:

BA in musical theatre

BA in theatre education

BA in theatre with concentrations in acting/performance studies, design and technology, theatre studies

MA in theatre education (non-resident summer intensive)

Minors offered:

Theatre studies

Dance

Population of Department(s): 320+ majors, 120 minors, 23 full-time faculty and staff plus adjuncts and guest artists

Audition to Declare a Theatre/Musical Theatre Major? Auditions and/or interviews are required for all incoming students in all degree areas.

Three things you would like our readers to know about your performing arts department:

1. Twenty-one of our alumni have appeared in 45 different Broadway productions. We also have had amazing alumni success in the film and television industry, national tours, regional theatre, and teacher education. Alums and former students include Nick Nolte, Steven Dietz, Greg Germann, and Susan Crabtree. A full alumni list can be found on our website.

2. We have a very active professional guest artist program and bring 10–20 industry professionals and working artists to campus each year.

3. We perform annual showcase productions in both New York City and Los Angeles. Also, we operate the Little Theatre of the Rockies, an 80-year-old professional summer stock theatre company on campus each summer.

Connecticut

■ University of Connecticut
Dramatic Arts Department
Storrs, CT

Compiled by: Vincent J. Cardinal, Head, Department of Dramatic Arts

Population of School: University, 30,256; School of Fine Arts, 555; Drama, 150

Conservatory or Liberal Arts: Both

Degrees Offered:

BFA in light, set, costume, sound design, technical direction, acting, puppetry
BA in theatre studies with focus in stage management, arts administration, dramaturgy, directing

Population of Department(s): 40 acting undergrads, 35 design/technical theatre undergrads, 10 puppetry undergrads, 30 theatre studies undergrads

Theatre Scholarships Available: Merit, academic, and need

Audition Required for BFA: Yes

Audition Required for BA/BS/BM: Interview

Pre-screen Video Audition Required: No

Attends Unifieds: No

Number of Students Auditioning Each Year: Approximately 100

Number of Students Accepted Each Year: 10

Cut Program or Audition to Remain in Program: No

Minors in Musical Theatre/Acting: No

Prominent Alumni: Austin Stowell (*Dolphin Tale, Secret Life of the American Teenager*), Jackie Burns (Elphaba in *Wicked* on Broadway), Bobby Moynihan (*Saturday Night Live*), Jennifer Barnhart (*Avenue Q* on Broadway, Puppetry), Dan Lauria (*Lombardi* on Broadway, TV's *The Wonder Years*)

What do you look for in a potential student?

A set of needs that our program can fulfill, flexibility in taking notes, innate talent, a desire to grow, and enthusiasm for the work.

What are some of the auditors' pet peeves?

Lack of preparation.

What are your audition requirements?

- Two contrasting monologues, memorized and not longer than four minutes total. One should be from a contemporary play, and one should be from a verse piece from a Shakespearean play. In addition to the two monologues, you will be required to sing a song not longer than 30 seconds or 16 bars. Make sure to bring a tape/CD of the music and a battery-powered tape/CD player; check to ensure it is working and cued to the proper place. We are interested in how you handle a lyric and melody, even if you do not consider yourself a singer.
- There will be a 40-minute group warm-up session. Please wear clothes appropriate to warm up. You will have time after the warm-up to change into your audition clothes.
- Please bring a headshot and résumé with you. Include your telephone number and address on the résumé. (If you don't have an 8×10 headshot, a recent photo is acceptable.)
- There will be one chair available for your use. If you need it, place it where you want it prior to your introduction.
- Before you begin performing your pieces, give us the following information only: your name, the character's name, and the title and author of the play from which your monologue is taken.
- The faculty strongly advises that you avoid any regional dialect or foreign accent in your audition, even if the script clearly calls for such accents. We feel that accents too often obscure a student's native acting ability—it is that acting ability we wish to evaluate.

In your eyes, what makes up an excellent college audition monologue? Song?

A piece that has an active goal and is within the range of a role that this actor might play.

If there were one monologue you never wanted to see again, what would it be?

The "tuna fish" monologue from *Laughing Wild* (1987) by Christopher Durang.

If there were one song you never wanted to hear again, what would it be?

"My New Philosophy," from *You're a Good Man, Charlie Brown.*

Can you walk me through what I can expect at your on-campus auditions?

Auditions for the BFA acting program at the University of Connecticut are scheduled at 15-minute intervals beginning at 10:00 a.m. There will be a 40-minute group warm-up session. Please wear clothes appropriate to warm up. You will have time after the warm-up to change into your audition clothes. Two contrasting monologues, memorized and not longer than four minutes total. One should be from a contemporary play, and one should be from a verse piece from a Shakespearean play. In addition to the two monologues, you will be required to sing a song not longer then 30 seconds or 16 bars. Make sure to bring a tape/CD of the music and a battery powered tape/CD player; check to ensure it is working and cued to the proper place. We are interested in how you handle a lyric and melody, even if you do not consider yourself a singer.

What's a memorable audition you can remember?

A student who came from a school with no theatre program. She did Emily from *Our Town*, and it was breathtaking. When I asked her who worked with her on the piece, she replied, "Nobody. You are the first person to ever hear this except for the cows. I would practice in the pasture, and then I would practice in the barn when the weather got bad." Use what you've got to accomplish what you want.

What is your biggest piece of advice for potential students auditioning?

Think of it as the school auditioning for them and have fun.

After I audition, is there a good way to follow up?

Email.

Would I get a showcase at the end of senior year?

Yes.

Do I have to audition to be accepted into the showcase?

No.

Where are showcases held, and are they successful?

Showcases are held in New York City and on campus, and yes.

Will I be able to audition/perform as a freshman?

Auditions, no. Performances as an extension of studio work.

If there is a graduate program, will I get the same performance opportunities as an undergraduate?

Yes, there is a grad program. All undergrad actors have casting opportunities each semester. Mainstage casting earns EMC.

In what ways can I be involved with the department aside from performing?

Participation at all levels of production and operation through work-study or volunteering.

Say I get a BA rather than a BFA. Will I actually get to perform?

Many of our BA students have performed on our mainstage, in our studio, and in our Department Series, although BFA acting students have priority consideration. There are also performance opportunities in our reading series, in our new works series, and through the student drama organization, Dramatic Paws.

Do you discourage or encourage students to audition for theatre outside of the department during the academic year?

Our BFA students rarely have time to work outside of the school during the regular school year.

Does your school regularly work in conjunction with any regional theatres?

We work with TheatreWorks and Hartford Stage, as well as many New York City-based theatres.

What do students typically do during the summers? Do you actively promote participation in summer theatre auditions?

We offer a very active summer season, which employs many of our students, along with top-flight professionals including Terrence Mann, Barrett Foa, Liz Larsen, and Pat Sajak. Other students work around the country in summer stock and festival situations.

How many musicals versus straight plays do you do in a season?

We offer three or four musicals and five or six straight plays to make up a nine-show annual offering.

What are some of your alumni up to? Do you have an active alumni network?

We have a strong and enthusiastic alumni network with strong bases in Los Angeles and New York.

What is the portfolio/interview process for a technical theatre student?

Your first step is to schedule an interview/portfolio review with the head of our design tech program. The actual meeting in person or by Internet connection is a discussion of your work so far and what you hope to accomplish.

What do you expect to see on a technical theatre résumé?

A passion for the theatre, potential, and evidence of commitment through work.

I'm interested in lighting, sound design, and stage management. What major should I go for? Can I minor?

All of the design and technical majors are BFA based with the potential to cross over into complementary design areas. Stage management is a BA degree with plenty of hands-on opportunities.

Anything else I should know?

Connecticut Repertory Theatre (CRT), part of the School of Fine Arts at the University of Connecticut, is the professional producing arm of the Department of Dramatic Arts. CRT stages an array of the best in theatre, from classic plays and musicals to premieres of the latest contemporary work, featuring some of the nation's finest theatre professionals onstage with the department's most promising students. The synergy between professionals and advanced student artists creates extraordinary theatre and a unique learning environment. Recent performing guest artists include Kim Zimmer, Jerry Adler, Barrett Foa, Andrea McArdle, Joyce DeWitt, Kevin Meaney, Pat Sajak, Liz Larsen, and Tina Fabrique. Student performers earn EMC points.

We have a very unique puppetry program that influences all areas of our study (www .drama.uconn.edu/?page_id=124).

Classes in puppetry were first taught at UConn in 1964 by Professor Frank W. Ballard, who had joined the faculty of the Theatre Department as a set designer and technical director eight years earlier. After three years, the demand for these courses had grown so drastically that the department had to limit enrollment in puppetry classes.

Professor Ballard's first full-length puppet production, *The Mikado*, was presented on the stage of the Harriet S. Jorgensen theatre as one of the department's mainstage productions. UConn soon became one of only two (soon to be three) universities in the country offering a BFA degree in puppet arts and the only institution in the country offering master's degrees (both MA and MFA) in the field.

Graduates of the puppetry program perform and design for many theatres around the world. They appear in, build for, and manage internationally recognized television programs (such as *Between the Lions*) and films, write books, design toys, teach children, and direct prominent schools and museums.

In 1990, Bart. P. Roccoberton, Jr., succeeded Frank Ballard as director of the Puppet Arts Program. In addition to the full-stage Puppet Productions that are mounted for the department's Connecticut Repertory Theatre, puppetry majors are encouraged to mount their own productions, which are presented at the university and toured to schools, museums, and theatres. Nearly 500 student puppet productions have been presented since 1964.

■ Eastern Connecticut State University
Willimantic, CT

Compiled by: Ellen Faith Brodie, Director of Theatre

Degrees Offered:

BA in theatre with concentrations in acting and directing; theatre history, theory, and criticism; theatre technology and design

Minors Offered:

Theatre
Costume and fashion design
Film studies

Population of Department(s): Approximately 50 majors, 20 minors

Audition to Declare a Theatre/Musical Theatre Major? No

Three things you would like our readers to know about your performing arts department:

1. Guest artists work with students on campus and in the field via productions and master classes on a regular basis.

2. The weeklong New York City showcase program, Los Angeles spring break program, and month-long summer in London program offer students opportunities to train with professionals in the field as well as explore these cultural meccas of stage and screen.

3. The theatre program includes state-of-the-art training as well as breadth and depth of context, which leads to numerous placements in internships, jobs, and grad degree programs.

■ Southern Connecticut State University
New Haven, CT

Compiled by: John Carver Sullivan, Chair, Theatre Department

Degrees Offered:

BS in theatre

Minors Offered:

Theatre, 18 credits

Population of Department(s): 50

Audition to Declare a Theatre/Musical Theatre Major? No

Three things you would like our readers to know about your performing arts department:

1. You receive a broad four-year degree, which prepares students for grad school.

2. Student can concentrate on acting, dance, and tech.

3. Our alums are in grad school or auditioning and working in New York City, and most recently we have an alum in *Mistresses*, a new cable series. Dan Lauria is also an alum, and we have many fine drama teachers throughout the state of Connecticut.

■ Western Connecticut State University
Danbury, CT

Compiled by: Pam McDaniel, Chair

Degrees Offered:

BA in theatre arts (concentrations in performance, design/tech, arts management, and drama studies)
BA in musical theatre

Minors Offered:

Theatre arts

Population of Department(s): 110 majors/minors

Audition to Declare a Theatre/Musical Theatre Major? An audition is required for a musical theatre degree. No audition is required for theatre arts concentrations.

Three things you would like our readers to know about your performing arts department:

1. Students act as "the company" of our department, training and receiving experience working in sound, lighting, set construction, paint crew, makeup and hair design, box office, performance, marketing, and the many other aspects of the theatrical industry.

2. There are many outside opportunities, including summers in Edinburgh, Scotland; a New York City industry showcase for graduating seniors; an annual production at TBG Theatre in New York City; yearly participation in the USITT, the KCACTF, the Humana Festival of New Plays, and many others.

3. We are excited to report that, beginning in the fall of 2014, the Department of Theatre Arts will move into a state-of-the-art, $98 million School of Visual and Performing Arts facility with technology surpassing that of many Broadway houses.

Delaware

■ University of Delaware
Newark, DE

Compiled by: Allan Carlsen, Assistant Professor of Theatre, Undergraduate Theatre Advisor, and Coordinator, Director, Healthcare Theatre

Degrees Offered:

No majors in theatre, but we do have majors in music (www.music.udel.edu/Pages/home .aspx)

Minors Offered:

Theatre studies
Theatre performance
Theatre production

Population of Department(s): Currently we have 280 theatre minors representing every major, college, school, and department at UD

Audition to Declare a Theatre/Musical Theatre Major? No

Three things you would like our readers to know about your performing arts department:

1. We have a professional resident theatre company at UD, now in its sixth year, the Resident Ensemble Players (www.rep.udel.edu/Pages/default.aspx).
2. We have a grad theatre training program at UD, currently on hiatus due to financial restructuring, the Professional Theatre Training Program.
3. We also have a new program beginning its sixth year, Healthcare Theatre (www.udel.edu/ healthcaretheatre).

Florida

■ Florida State University
Tallahassee, FL

Compiled by: Kate Gelabert, Associate Professor; Director, BFA Music Theatre, and Jean Lickson, Associate Professor, Acting-Directing

Population of School: 31,005 undergrads

Conservatory or Liberal Arts: Liberal arts

Degrees Offered:
BFA in music theatre and acting
BM in music theatre, College of Music
BA in theatre

Population of Department(s): Music theatre program currently has 33 students; acting has 40

Theatre Scholarships Available: Yes, approximately 22 various scholarships; amount varies from year to year

Audition Required for BFA: Yes

Audition Required for BA/BS/BM: For BA theatre, no; must be accepted to the university by GPA

Pre-screen Video Audition Required: Yes, for both acting and music theatre

Attends Unifieds: No

Number of Students Auditioning Each Year: About 200 each for music theatre and acting

Number of Students Accepted Each Year: 10–15 for music theatre; 8–12 for acting

Cut Program or Audition to Remain in Program: No. We do not have a cut system. However, students may be dismissed for academic reasons or not making adequate progress as demonstrated in their yearly juries.

Minors in Musical Theatre/Acting: No

Prominent Alumni: Montego Glover, Kevin Covert, Jessica Patty, Darren Bagert, Tiffany Howard, Amanda Watkins, Trevor Leaderbrand, Christian Delcroix, Mike Everiste, Hardy Weaver, Michael Fatica, D.B. Bonds, Megan Boone, DeLane Matthews, John Papsidera, John Brace

What do you look for in a potential student?

An honest audition . . . one that tells us something about that person as well as something about his or her current level of talent. We want to know the student is trainable and that by the end of four years, we feel comfortable sending him or her out.

What are some of the auditors' pet peeves?

Unfortunate habits displayed by students due to bad coaching.

What are your audition requirements?

For music theatre, everyone attends a dance audition and then individually performs two prepared contrasting songs and a monologue. For acting, two contrasting monologues.

In your eyes, what makes up an excellent college audition monologue? Song?

In both cases, an honest, truthful connection to the material.

If there were one monologue you never wanted to see again, what would it be?

Depends on the year.

If there were one song you never wanted to hear again, what would it be?

Depends on the year.

If you require a pre-screen video audition, what do you look for in those submissions?

We are looking for an honest approach to the material—a nice, clean recording. Don't get too fancy.

Can you walk me through what I can expect at your on-campus auditions?

We have check-in at the College of Music for parents and students at 9 a.m. We have a Q&A about the day, then the auditioners will go over to the dance department and our academic advisor will stay and answer additional questions for the parents. We do the dance audition from about 9:30 until 11 a.m. with everyone together, and then they go and change. They have already signed up for individual time slots (8–10 minutes) for songs and monologues. We will ask them questions or answer any questions they have for us. In the evening, from 4 to 6 p.m., they can attend a show or dance recital. Acting check-in is at 8:30 a.m. Q&A is at 9:30 a.m., followed by a group warm-up. The auditionees will have individual audition slots, and then callbacks will occur in the afternoon.

What is your biggest piece of advice for potential students auditioning?

Be honest and be yourself. Choose material that suits you. Sing songs that you love singing and are comfortable with. Don't go for the big money note if you can't nail it. Treat your songs like a monologue. Choose a monologue you can relate to and one that is as age appropriate as possible. Don't do a classical piece just to impress . . . make sure you understand the language and style. Dance honestly . . . don't "cheese" it up. If you are limited in your dance training, do the very best you can and try to enjoy the experience.

If I audition for your BFA musical theatre program, but don't get accepted, do you still consider me for your BFA acting program or your BA program? Or does each program require its own audition if I'd like to be considered for both?

We always have an acting faculty at our auditions (music theatre). We encourage students to audition for the acting program if they don't quite make the music theatre cut.

After I audition, is there a good way to follow up?

We let students know at the very end of our audition process by letter or phone call. Some students have written thank-you notes after their audition.

Would I get a showcase at the end of senior year?

Yes, if you are in good standing.

Do I have to audition to be accepted into the showcase?

No.

Where are showcases held, and are they successful?

Music theatre is in New York City, and acting is in Los Angeles.

Will I be able to audition/perform as a freshman?

Yes; however, acting students are not allowed to audition their first semester.

If there is a graduate program, will I get the same performance opportunities as an undergraduate?

We do not have a music theatre grad program. The MFA acting program is at the Asolo Theatre in Sarasota, FL; therefore, the undergrads do not compete with grad students.

In what ways can I be involved with the department aside from performing?

BFA students must take tech classes, so they will be working on the other side of performance as well. We have work-study opportunities as well as campus organizations.

Say I get a BA rather than a BFA. Will I actually get to perform?

Possibly.

I love to sing, but I don't consider myself a dancer. Can I still seek a degree in musical theatre at your school?

Our ideal is the triple threat potential, but we look at the potential in two of the three areas as well.

I want to get a BFA in acting, but I also love to sing. Can BFA/BA acting students take voice lessons with top voice faculty?

Acting students have had the opportunity to study with music theatre voice faculty. It isn't always a sure thing depending on the number of majors the voice faculty must accommodate. However, there are voice grad students well qualified to teach.

Do you discourage or encourage students to audition for theatre outside of the department during the academic year?

Students must request our approval in order to audition for and perform in outside activities. This is purely for the protection of the students . . . most of us know the community well enough that we can assess the quality of the past work and decide if the experience would be beneficial or not.

Does your school regularly work in conjunction with any regional theatres?

We have the MFA Acting Conservatory in Sarasota, which works with the Asolo Theatre.

What do students typically do during the summers? Do you actively promote participation in summer theatre auditions?

We strongly encourage students to attend regional auditions for summer employment after their freshman year. A great majority do work professionally.

How many musicals versus straight plays do you do in a season?

We do two musicals, one fund-raiser concert version of a show, and various cabarets and recitals.

What are some of your alumni up to? Do you have an active alumni network?

Our alumni network is extremely strong, especially in New York City. At our annual New York City and Los Angeles showcases, we all get together and there are alum from 20 years ago hanging out with recent graduates. Our graduates are working all over the country—on Broadway, off-Broadway, regional theatre, television, and films.

Anything else I should know?

The BFA in music theatre at Florida State University is a prestigious and competitive degree that began in 1981 and has evolved into one of the top training programs in the nation. Run jointly with the College of Music and with the cooperation of the School of Dance, it is designed to provide comprehensive training in singing, dancing, and acting, thoroughly preparing students to work professionally upon graduation. During the four-year program, students receive a liberal studies education as well as concentrated training in performance (private voice lessons, acting, movement and dance), theory and sightsinging, music and theatre history, repertory, and technical theatre. In addition to the specialized coursework, students have a variety of performance opportunities, which include the musical productions as well as straight plays, films, operas, vocal ensembles, recitals, and dance concerts. Upon graduation, the Music Theatre Senior Showcase in New York City is an opportunity for graduating seniors to perform for an invited audience of agents, casting directors, master teachers, and alumni. Graduates have signed with agents, gained employment, and made important connections in the business as a result of this experience. The FSU New York City alumni network is more than 20 years strong and ever embracing of the newly graduated seniors.

The acting program at FSU is an extremely competitive program designed to prepare highly talented students for work in professional theatre. In addition to the core of required theatre courses, this comprehensive curriculum includes a sequence of courses in acting, voice, movement, and specialized workshops. Acting students are also required to participate in our London Theatre Experience during the summer before their third year. Following the first semester, students audition for a wide variety of performance opportunities, including roles in the Fallon, Lab, and Studio Theatres. This balance of coursework and production experience prepares students to meet the rigors of a demanding professional theatre career. Graduating seniors in the BFA acting program also have the opportunity to participate in the BFA showcase each spring in Los Angeles. Students perform during the showcase for directors, talent agents, and casting directors from all over the United States. The students have the opportunity to meet with the FSU Los Angeles alumni network, which is so beneficial for them in all aspects of their profession.

■ University of Central Florida

Orlando, FL

Compiled by: Christopher Niess, Chair/Artistic Director, Theatre UCF; Mark Brotherton, Associate Professor, Theatre UCF; Earl Weaver, Coordinator of Musical Theatre, Theatre UCF; Bert Scott, Coordinator, Design and Technology, Theatre UCF

Population of School: 68,000+ students; 11,000+ faculty and staff

Conservatory or Liberal Arts: Conservatory-minded program in a liberal arts environment

Degrees Offered:
BA in theatre studies
BFA in acting, musical theatre, design/tech, and stage management
MA in theatre studies
MFA in acting, theatre for young audiences

Degrees on Hiatus: MFA in musical theatre, MFA in design

Population of Department(s): 400 theatre majors (grad and undergrad), 75 theatre minors, 75 dance minors

Theatre Scholarships Available: Department Talent grants, Disney scholarships, Out-of-state Tuition Waiver Scholarship (undergrad), several privately funded scholarships

Audition Required for BFA: All candidates will undergo an audition/interview (all acting/musical theatre tracks), portfolio review (design/tech and stage management tracks), or entrance interview (MA and BA theatre studies).

Pre-screen Video Audition Required: Musical theatre BFA, yes; all other degrees, no (auditions for BFA acting can be submitted through Acceptd, but are not required—see website).

Attends Unifieds: Yes

Location of Unifieds: See website

Number of Students Auditioning Each Year: Approximately 1,000 students interview at auditions in New York, Chicago, Southeastern Theatre Conference, Florida Theatre Conference, Florida Thespians Conference, and at auditions on the Orlando campus

Number of Students Accepted Each Year: Maximum of 20 BFA acting, musical theatre, design/tech, and stage management accepted per year. Maximum number of MA and BA theatre students admitted is open and dependent on interviews. MFA acting and MFA theatre for young audiences programs accept classes every other year—currently six for the acting MFA and four for the MFA theatre for young audiences.

Cut Program or Audition to Remain in Program: MFA and BFA candidates receive oral interviews each semester to monitor progress in the program. There are no scheduled mandated cuts.

Minors in Musical Theatre/Acting: Minors are available in theatre and dance.

Prominent Alumni: David Blue (*Stargate Universe*, *Ugly Betty*, *Moonlight*), Justin Sargent (Broadway: *Rock of Ages*, *Spider-man*), Ben Hope (Broadway: *Once*), James Cleveland (owner/production supervisor, Production Core, New York City; *Peter and the Starcatcher*, *Old Jews Telling Jokes*, *Soul Doctor*), Donte Bonner (*Sydney White*, *Boardwalk Empire*, *Law & Order*), Michael Marinaccio (producer, Orlando Fringe Festival), Natalie Cordone (*The Inbetweeners*), Gary Alexander (DEG Productions, New York), Valery Ortiz (*Date Movie*), Sidonie Weaver (Hamburg, Germany, cast of *Lion King*, *Legally Blonde*), Ginny Parker (Stage Manager, Cirque de Soleil, *La Nouba*), Keston John (*24*, *Lie to Me*), Brian Nolan (*The Lair*, *Beginners*), Chris Brown (Yale University grad school, production manager; Orlando Repertory Theatre), Mike Donohue (master carpenter/assistant technical director, The Studio Theatre, Washington, DC), Merritt Horan (textile artist at Sano Design Services, New York), and many more

What do you look for in a potential student?

Commitment, discipline, and a strong work ethic, as well as a willingness to reach beyond past ideas and an excitement about exploration of new techniques.

What are some of the auditors' pet peeves?

When the audition is not treated professionally in all areas—dress, attitude, poise, and audition preparation. Lack of preparation is probably the most avoidable. One should simply read and follow the audition guidelines set forth by the department. Also, not having music properly prepared for the accompanist, not wearing appropriate dance clothing or the correct shoes for a dance call, or not having audition material memorized can instantly sabotage your audition. Allotting enough time to get to the audition so that you don't arrive late is essential, as well as being fully warmed up and prepared to audition.

If there were one monologue/song/thing you never wanted to see again, what would it be?

An unprepared student. It is worth repeating. Preparation includes much more than memorizing the lines, a series of gestures, and facial expressions. It includes choosing material appropriate for your age and "type." Appropriate material is more important than worrying about whether the material is "overdone." If you choose a popular piece and make it your own, it can be successful. Make sure the material allows your character to be active as opposed to reflective or passive. A character is engaging when he or she is working toward something (an objective) rather than reporting or telling a story about something that has already happened (exposition). Gratuitous emotion can have the same effect. A momentary emotional reaction can be effective, but then it is important to see what the character wants to do next. A monologue that serves only to demonstrate that the actor can cry or be angry for two minutes is not effective.

What's a memorable audition you can remember?

Several in which the actor's choices were truthful, honest, and clear—and yet not safe. By the end of an audition piece, it is much better for the audience (auditors) to be left seeing a character who is not quite sure of what will happen next, which creates a slightly dangerous situation for the character. It also makes the monologue more active. In too many auditions, actors tackle a character as if the character knows everything that has transpired, is transpiring, and will transpire. All that is left to do is herald decisions that have already been made—there is no present action.

Along those lines, some of the best auditions witnessed have been the ones in which the actors have a strong sense of *why* they and their characters are there. For the actor with great potential, there always seems to be an empathy with the character, an enjoyment in playing, and a passion in pursuing the objective that goes far beyond individual ego. The monologue should go well beyond a sense of whether the actor looked good or gave an attractive delivery.

As far as the character is concerned, the best auditions have the clearest sense that the character is fighting for something important (simply put, high stakes, strong objectives, and driven tactics) and leave us with the impression that the character will continue to fight or seek resolution after the monologue is finished. On a more basic level, we witness the best auditions from students who are confident in their dance audition (even if they make mistakes) and have fun; who have prepared quality, age-appropriate audition material (contrasting songs that show a full vocal range/monologue that shows depth of acting technique and stakes). Most important, students who obviously relish the chance to audition and show us who they really are tend to command our attention.

What is your biggest piece of advice for potential students auditioning?

Research the program(s) you are interested in attending. It's important to feel that the program(s) is a good fit. If you are not excited at the possibility of working in this program, it will be evident. Then rehearse, rehearse, rehearse! Get coaching from your instructors and directors before you audition. The auditors want to see the honesty and truthfulness in your monologues. They want to see you breathe freely and enjoy performing and interviewing. It is your chance to let loose and shine for us. The auditors do not want to see the labor or the anxiety or the trauma of auditioning. They honestly want you to be the best person they see all day.

After I audition, is there a good way to follow up?

An email is the simplest way to let the department know you are interested in the program. A simple card or letter expressing this interest is a personable way to follow up as well. Oftentimes, decisions on offers must be delayed, and knowing whether you are serious about the program can help speed the process. If you have not heard from the department by the deadlines for decisions that are given at the auditions, do send an email to check your status.

Would I get a showcase at the end of senior year?

All students are required, after classes on interviewing and auditioning, to obtain a professional internship in order to graduate with a BFA or MFA degree.

Are showcases successful?

The internship requirement (for BFA/MFA) was established in 1998. Placement is consistently 100%.

Will I be able to audition/perform as a freshman?

Casting for the performance season is open to all University of Central Florida students, and all BFA/MFA acting and musical theatre candidates are required to audition each semester. Freshmen have performed in a variety of roles.

If there is a graduate program, will I get the same performance opportunities as an undergraduate?

Theatre UCF has eight productions during the academic year, and two to three during the summer. Academic year productions use primarily a student cast with faculty and guest artists in special circumstances. No roles are reserved for grads/undergrads. Summer shows use a combination of faculty, guests, and student performers.

In what ways can I be involved with the department aside from performing?

Theatre UCF has several active student organizations and various work-study opportunities, and students are encouraged to create material to present at theatre workshops on the regional and national level (SETC, ATHE, USITT, and so on). Independent studies in a student's interest area are encouraged.

Say I get a BA rather than a BFA. Will I actually get to perform?

See the above note on open casting. There is an expectation that if a student is involved in more studio classes, then he or she is more likely to be cast. This tends to hold true, although there are many instances of BA theatre studies majors being cast. Additionally, the student one-act festival provides further performance opportunities that focus on the actor's craft (above technical theatrical elements). The BA program is not intended to be a performance-based major, and students should not enter this program with that expectation.

I love to sing, but don't consider myself a dancer. Can I still seek a degree in musical theatre at your school?

Every instrument (actor) is unique. However, dance and movement are an integral part of the training of a musical theatre artist. Realistically, not everyone will reach the level of a polished Broadway dancer, but can benefit physically from movement/dance training.

I want to get a BFA in acting, but I also love to sing. Can BFA/BA acting students take voice lessons with top voice faculty?

Musical theatre voice class is in the BFA acting curriculum. Musical theatre voice class is available as an elective to BA theatre studies students.

Do you discourage or encourage students to audition for theatre outside of the department during the academic year?

The students' primary responsibility is to their program of study (classes) and performance responsibilities (the laboratory). It is required that students consult their advisor and area coordinator before auditioning/interviewing for an outside job or role to determine if there is any conflict with their studio classes or performance responsibilities. Many students participate in part-time positions, acting jobs with minimal time commitments (such as commercial and film work), and occasionally a role at one of the many area professional venues and entertainment companies, including Walt Disney World, Universal Studios, Sea World, Orlando Shakespeare Theater, Orlando Repertory Theatre, Mad Cow Theatre, and so on.

Does your school regularly work in conjunction with any regional theatres?

Theatre UCF enjoys active partnerships with the Orlando Shakespeare Theater and the Orlando Repertory Theatre that spawn valuable student participation in projects such as Playfest!, Writes of Spring, and so on.

What do students typically do during the summer? Do you actively promote participation in summer theatre auditions?

Theatre UCF produces an active summer season of two or three shows, using a greater concentration of faculty and guest artists. This provides opportunity to work with faculty in a more concentrated fashion in a more professional time frame. Many students also attend Southeastern Theatre Conference and other national auditions and procure work in summer theatres and entertainment venues.

How many musicals versus straight plays do you do in a season?

Two to three musicals, six to eight plays, and one dance concert.

What are some of your alumni up to? Do you have an active alumni network?

To see recent alumni activity, please visit http://theatre.cah.ucf.edu/spotlight.php.

What is the portfolio/interview process for a technical theatre student?

The interview process starts with registering for an interview on the theatre department's website and also applying to the university itself. These are two separate processes. Students must be admitted to the university before they can be admitted to any of the theatre programs. We schedule two Saturdays of interviews in January and February where we interview students and look at their portfolios; give a tour of our facilities; and give the students an opportunity to meet the faculty and current students, and ask questions. In the portfolio, we are looking for work that demonstrates the student's abilities and talents—sketches, photographs of scenic models or costume renderings, scenic drafting, light plots, costume patterning—really anything the student wants to show us that demonstrates his or her skills and talents. We are also happy to see related work—art photography, graphic arts, carpentry projects—again, whatever the student feels best demonstrates his or her skills. We are also very interested in hearing why the student wants to study theatre—what is it about the art form that draws you in? Why costume design and not fashion design? Why set design and not architecture? What is it specifically about theatre that excites you, and what will you specifically bring to the department?

What do you expect to see on a technical theatre résumé?

Ideally we like to see work in a student's chosen area—costume construction or lighting of school plays or set construction for a local theatre, and so on. We also realize, however, that there are vast differences in high school arts programs and that students from magnet theatre programs, for example, have opportunities that students from smaller schools may not have. We are also really looking for curiosity and an entrepreneurial attitude—students who have taken on lighting assignments at their church, who have shadowed a touring Broadway stage manager, or who have in some other way sought out learning opportunities for themselves. These students excite us as much as the ones who have lots of polished work from their large high school theatre programs (we are excited by them too, of course).

I'm interested in lighting, sound design, and stage management. What major should I go for? Can I minor?

Our design program exposes students to all four design areas (scenery, lighting, costumes, and sound) in the academic program and lets them concentrate in one or two areas in the production program. We frequently have students who are interested in multiple design areas, and we encourage students at the undergrad level to explore all of their interests. Our stage management students share classes with the design and technology students, so they are well versed in all of the areas, but their practical assignments are generally only in stage management. We occasionally have very ambitious students who can take on assignments in stage management and a design area, but usually once students see what the actual work process is for these areas in the professional theatre, they pretty quickly decide to choose one. Design and technology and stage management are both tracks in the BFA program (along with acting), so it is not possible to double major in one or the other since, technically, they all lead to the same degree—BFA in theatre. Students certainly can use their elective courses to take classes in other areas, however. So it is entirely possible to major in stage management and also study lighting design and have practical lighting assignments, for example. We do have a minor in theatre, but that is really intended for students who have an interest in theatre as an audience member but do not intend to pursue theatre as a career. The BFA degrees are the pre-professional degrees to prepare a student for entry into the professional theatre world and are very time intensive.

Anything else I should know?

The first line of our mission statement reads: We provide a competitive edge to undergrad and grad students seeking to achieve excellence as professional theatre practitioners and creative intellectual leaders while inspiring them to be aware and enlightened human beings. Our focus is to provide as much as possible to give that "competitive edge" and to produce graduates who work within the industry as well as in related disciplines. Aiding us in that mission are our professional partnerships with the Orlando Shakespeare Theater and the Orlando Repertory Theatre. Grad students receive hands-on training onstage and backstage, through outreach programs, and in management as well. Undergrads benefit from guest lectures, classes, and programs such as the Harriett Lake Festival of New Plays, which uses the skills of many department students. Additionally, Walt Disney World continues to provide a wealth of support through scholarships, visitations, and lectures. A committed professional advisory board brings a wealth of knowledge and mentoring to the student body from a large number of entertainment industry leaders. The high degree of placement of UCF graduates into the area entertainment industry is indicative of their focused support as well as the resultant talent of our graduates.

On campus, students work with a talented faculty and staff in an ample performance season (generally 11 productions including summer). Production work covers a broad range of theatrical material encompassing the contemporary and classical, the cutting edge and the traditional. Productions have included Shakespearean, devised, commedia, farce, historical, and contemporary musical theatre, and many more styles and genres. Theatre UCF is an active participant in the KCACTF, having had productions invited to compete in Region IV for many years. UCF has been fortunate to have a consistent roster of finalists at the regional competition and several finalists at the national level in both the Irene Ryan and Barbizon competitions. Students are also encouraged to participate in regional and national theatre conferences by preparing and presenting workshops and scholastic presentations. This engagement has proven valuable not only for those interested in further work in theatre theory and education, but for developing artists and designers as well.

■ Flagler College
St. Augustine, FL

Compiled by: Phyllis M. Gibbs, Chair of Theatre Arts

Degrees Offered:

BA in theatre arts, with musicals each year as well as music and dance training

Minors Offered:

Theatre arts

Population of Department(s): 75 majors, 30 minors

Audition to Declare a Theatre/Musical Theatre Major? No

Three things you would like our readers to know about your performing arts department:

1. We expect our students to become more marketable by learning all phases of theatre.
2. Talented students can work one on one with supervisors on mainstage productions as designers, choreographers, assistant directors, costumers, and so on.
3. We have one of the most beautiful campuses in the nation—just look at www.flagler.edu.

■ Florida International University
Miami, FL

Compiled by: Marilyn R. Skow, Chair/Artistic Director, Department of Theatre

Degrees Offered:

BA in theatre
BFA in performance
BFA in design/production

Minors Offered:

Theatre

Population of Department(s): 117 students

Audition to Declare a Theatre/Musical Theatre Major? An audition and interview are required for the BA and the BFA in performance; a portfolio review and interview are required for the BFA in design/production; an interview is required for BA stage management students.

Three things you would like our readers to know about your performing arts department:

1. It has an excellent, award-winning faculty.
2. It has a low student–teacher ratio.
3. It provides an integrated program of study, combining classroom learning and practical application in a nurturing environment.

Florida Southern College
Lakeland, FL

Compiled by: Department of Theatre Arts

Degrees Offered:

BFA in musical theatre

BFA in performance

BFA in technical theatre

BA in theatre arts

Minors Offered:

Theatre arts

Population of Department(s): 56 students

Audition to Declare a Theatre/Musical Theatre Major? An audition is not required to declare a BA theatre arts major. All BFA majors require an audition or interview to declare.

Three things you would like our readers to know about your performing arts department:

1. Students have the opportunity to perform major roles right away. There is no substitute for this type of hands-on experience in the theatre.

2. Our program offers a course of study with small, personalized classes in music, theatre, and dance, including private voice study.

3. Our students are accepted into prestigious grad schools such as Harvard, Brandeis, CalArts, and Purdue. Other graduates are working in professional theatres throughout the world in productions such as *Jersey Boys*, *Tarzan*, *Matilda*, *The Little Mermaid*, *Equus*, *Hair*, *The Lion King*, and *Mary Poppins*.

Palm Beach Atlantic University
West Palm Beach, FL

Compiled by: Allen McCoy, Interim Director of Theatre; Don Butler, Associate Professor of Theatre

Degrees Offered:

BA in theatre with tracks in acting, musical theatre, and technology and design

Minors Offered:

Theatre arts

Musical theatre

Technology and design

Population of Department(s): 70 students (44 major/26 minor)

Audition to Declare a Theatre/Musical Theatre Major? Yes, there are eight audition dates throughout the year, and portfolios for design: September 20, October 11, November 22, January 24, February 14, March 28, April 4, and April 25.

Three things you would like our readers to know about your performing arts department:

1. Intimate class sizes at PBA allow for more academic and personal growth, creating more opportunity for hands-on production experience and one-on-one training with our exceptional faculty.

2. Live and study in the heart of downtown West Palm Beach, FL. Our metropolitan environment means we're located adjacent to one of the nation's premiere performing arts centers, world-class ballet and opera, regional theatres, and museums, offering many internships and job opportunities.

3. Training: The faculty has impressive professional, as well as academic, credentials. Individual attention is the hallmark of our department, and because we produce four shows a year, students have many, and early, chances to perform, since freshmen may be cast.

Location: Not only is PBA's Intracoastal Waterway location beautiful, but South Florida also boasts a wide variety of cultural opportunities. We regularly attend workshops and performances at the renowned Kravis Center for the Performing Arts and Palm Beach Dramaworks, both of which are only short walks from campus. In addition, we maintain close relationships with arts organizations from Orlando to Miami.

Spirituality: As a Christian institution, we seek to enlighten minds and enrich souls. We explore redemptive storytelling through the Western theatrical canon and believe our faith and our art are not only compatible but mutually strengthening.

■ Southeastern University
Lakeland, FL

Compiled by: Michael A. Salsbury, MFA, Assistant Professor of Theatre

Degrees Offered:

We currently offer both a BS (designed to transition the graduate directly into the industry) and BA (designed for the student seeking further education) in theatre; however, we are working on a BS and BA in musical theatre to be offered in the near future.

Minors Offered:

Theatre
Musical theatre

Population of Department(s): Currently 28 majors and 22 minors

Audition to Declare a Theatre/Musical Theatre Major? No

Three things you would like our readers to know about your performing arts department:

1. We are a faith-based institution and produce a broad spectrum of the theatrical canon from a Christian worldview, preparing students to serve in both secular and Christian marketplaces.

2. As a relatively small but growing program, we are able to tailor our program to meet the unique calling of the individual theatre artist.

3. Professor Salsbury's own career has covered a broad spectrum of theatrical experiences, uniquely qualifying him to train young theatre artists in numerous theatrical career choices.

Georgia

■ Shorter University
Rome, GA

Compiled by: Kevin Anderton, Director of Theatre

Population of School: 3,000 (total); 1,500 (main campus)

Conservatory or Liberal Arts: Liberal arts

Degrees Offered:
BFA in musical theatre
BFA in theatre
BA in theatre

Minors Offered:
Dance
Theatre
Musical theatre

Population of Department(s): 20 majors

Theatre Scholarships Available: Yes

Audition Required for BFA: Yes

Audition Required for BA/BS/BM: No

Pre-screen Video Audition Required: No

Attends Unifieds: No

Number of Students Auditioning Each Year: 25

Number of Students Accepted Each Year: 12

Cut Program or Audition to Remain in Program: There are reviews every year; cuts are rare

Minors in Musical Theatre/Acting: Yes

Prominent Alumni: Jared Bradshaw (*Jersey Boys*), Justin Murdock (Disney productions), Jeremy Wood (*Grease*, national tour)

What do you look for in a potential student?

Smarts! Do the students know what they are singing or acting? Have they truly thought through what they are saying or singing?

What are some of the auditors' pet peeves?

Songs and monologues that go over the time allotted.

What are your audition requirements?

Musical theatre: 16 measures of a Broadway show tune *and* one art song in its entirety, *and* one contemporary monologue. Limit one minute. Must be age appropriate. Monologue must be extracted from a larger work. In addition to the performance requirement, students will also be evaluated in theory, ear-training, and sight-reading. Vocalists will also be required to demonstrate keyboard sight-reading skills. Musical theatre majors will also have a group movement audition where they will be taught a brief dance combination. Bring a change of comfortable clothing for this part of your audition.

Theatre: One contemporary comedic monologue *and* one contemporary dramatic monologue. Limit one minute for each monologue. Must be age appropriate. Monologues must be extracted from larger works.

If there were one monologue you never wanted to see again, what would it be?

The Foreigner.

If there were one song you never wanted to hear again, what would it be?

"On My Own."

What is your biggest piece of advice for potential students auditioning?

Bring pieces that you can excel in and that show your versatility, and HAVE FUN!

If I audition for your BFA musical theatre program, but don't get accepted, do you still consider me for your BFA acting program or your BA program?

Yes.

After I audition, is there a good way to follow up?

Email.

Would I get a showcase at the end of senior year?

Yes.

Do I have to audition to be accepted into the showcase?

No.

Where are showcases held, and are they successful?

Showcases are held in New York and Atlanta, and yes, they are successful.

Will I be able to audition/perform as a freshman?

Yes.

In what ways can I be involved with the department aside from performing?

Technical theatre labs and work-study with the technical department.

Say I get a BA rather than a BFA. Will I actually get to perform?

It depends.

I love to sing, but I don't consider myself a dancer. Can I still seek a degree in musical theatre at your school?

Yes.

I want to get a BFA in acting, but I also love to sing. Can BFA/BA acting students take voice lessons with top voice faculty?

Yes.

Do you discourage or encourage students to audition for theatre outside of the department during the academic year?

No (though there are exceptions).

Does your school regularly work in conjunction with any regional theatres?

No.

What do students typically do during the summers? Do you actively promote participation in summer theatre auditions?

Yes. We participate in Georgia Theatre Company (GTC) and SETC.

How many musicals versus straight plays do you do in a season?

Two musicals and two straight plays.

What are some of your alumni up to?

Broadway, off-Broadway, regional theatre.

Do you have an active alumni network?

No.

Anything else I should know?

- Master classes with prominent working professionals from Hollywood, Broadway, and The West End.

- Faculty achievement awards in directing, dialect/text coaching, and scenic design.

- Outstanding Achievement award in Direction, Fight Choreography, Musical Direction, and Scenic Design for *Jekyll and Hyde: The Musical.*

- For the past seven years, Shorter University musical theatre and theatre students have represented more than one-third of all college and university students chosen to represent the state of Georgia at SETC; more than 60% of students who audition at GTC are passed on to SETC; a Shorter student has been selected top female performer (2009, 2010).

- Multiple alumni have already completed or are now on national tours (including *The Sound of Music, The Full Monty, Beauty and the Beast, Grease,* and *The Little Mermaid*) or are working on Broadway or off-Broadway (including *Forbidden Broadway* and *Jersey Boys*).

- Nearly 85% of our alumni earn their primary paycheck from working in the theatre within three months of graduation.

- Graduates are currently working in a number of diverse theatre productions at numerous theatres, including Actor's Express (including the artistic director), Dad's Garage Theatre, Atlanta Lyric, Alliance Theatre Company, Orlando Shakespeare Festival, the Wizarding World of Harry Potter, 14th Street Playhouse, Disney, Theatre in the Square, Kudzu Playhouse, and the Village Playhouse.
- Two interns accepted to the prestigious Milwaukee Repertory Theater (2010).

■ Armstrong Atlantic State University
Savannah, GA

Compiled by: Dr. Peter Mellen, Coordinator, Theatre Program, Department of Art, Music, and Theatre

Degrees Offered:

BA in theatre, with tracks in performance, tech theatre, and theatre management
BA in music
BS in music education
BFA in art
BA in art
BS in art education

Minors Offered:

Theatre program offers a minor and is developing minors in musical theatre, acting, tech theatre, and management. The department also offers minors in art and music.

Population of Department(s): 70 theatre majors and some 20 theatre minors (students tend to be traditional college age)

Audition to Declare a Theatre/Musical Theatre Major? No audition is required to declare a theatre major. Auditions are required to be considered for a theatre scholarship.

Three things you would like our readers to know about your performing arts department:

1. Armstrong mounts 12 or more productions per academic year.
2. Many of these productions are student directed and/or designed.
3. We have recently added an improv troupe and are developing a show choir.

■ Clark Atlanta University
Atlanta, GA

Compiled by: John N. Frazier, Assistant Professor of Theatre, Director of CAU Players

Degrees Offered:

Theatre acting

Minors Offered:

Theatre generalist

Population of Department(s): 64 students

Audition to Declare a Theatre/Musical Theatre Major? No.

Three things you would like our readers to know about your performing arts department:

1. Classes are taught by professionals.
2. Integrated curriculum.
3. Performance-based product.

■ Columbus State University
Department of Theatre
Columbus, GA

Compiled by: Dr. Larry Dooley, Chair of Department

Degrees Offered:

BFA in performance
BSEd in theatre education
BA in theatre arts
MSEd in theatre education

Minors Offered:

Theatre

Population of Department(s): Approximately 165 majors

Audition to Declare a Theatre/Musical Theatre Major? Yes—for all degree tracks and the minor

Three things you would like our readers to know about your performing arts department:

1. Student centered.
2. Intensive training in a liberal arts atmosphere.
3. State-of-the-art performance facilities.

■ Georgia College
Milledgeville, GA

Compiled by: Dr. Karen Berman, Theatre Chair

Degrees Offered:

Theatre

Minors Offered:

Theatre
Dance

Population of Department(s): 71 majors, 40 theatre minors, 40 dance minors

Audition to Declare a Theatre/Musical Theatre Major? No

Three things you would like our readers to know about your performing arts department:

1. Freshmen can get lead roles, and student designers design most mainstage shows.

2. Georgia College has taken students to perform off-Broadway with an original script and also taken students to perform in Prague at an international theatre festival, both all expenses paid by the Theatre Department.

3. We are a small liberal arts family atmosphere in a tight community in which everyone supports each other's work, and there are an exceptional amount of shows and opportunities for the size of the program.

■ Georgia Southwestern State University
Americus, GA

Compiled by: Jeffrey Green, Professor and Chair, Department of Theater, Communication & Media Arts

Degrees Offered:

BA in dramatic arts, performance emphasis
BA in dramatic arts, design and technology emphasis
BA in dramatic arts, communication and media arts emphasis

Minors Offered:

Dramatic arts, performance emphasis
Dramatic arts, design and technology emphasis
Dramatic arts, communication and media arts emphasis

Population of Department(s): 30+

Audition to Declare a Theatre/Musical Theatre Major? No

Three things you would like our readers to know about your performing arts department:

1. Truly integrated study of live and mediated (TV and digital cinema) performance. All students receive a basic foundation in both forms.

2. We offer the quality and advantages of a small, private liberal arts institution in a public setting and a public cost.

3. See our endorsements: http://gsw.edu/Academics/Schools-and-Departments/College-of-Art-and-Science/Departments/Theater-Communication-and-Media-Arts/index.

■ Reinhardt University

Waleska, GA

Compiled by: David Nisbet, Theatre Program Coordinator

Degrees Offered:

BA in theatre

BFA in musical theatre

Minors Offered:

Theatre

Population of Department(s): 30

Audition to Declare a Theatre/Musical Theatre Major? Yes, for musical theatre and scholarships

Three things you would like our readers to know about your performing arts department:

1. We have available scholarships.
2. We are young and hungry.
3. We are looking for individuals who want to have a theatre career after graduation.

■ Savannah College of Art and Design

Savannah, GA

Compiled by: Michael Wainstein, Chair of Performing Arts

Degrees Offered:

BFA in performance

BFA in production design

BFA in dramatic writing

MFA in performance

MA in production design

MFA in production design

MFA in dramatic writing

MFA in themed entertainment design

Minors Offered:

Vocal performance

Musical composition

Dance

Population of Department(s): 135 (production design); 185 (performing arts)

Audition to Declare a Theatre/Musical Theatre Major? Yes

Three things you would like our readers to know about your performing arts department:

1. We offer strong training opportunities in musical theatre, acting, and acting for the camera.
2. We have an onsite casting office that casts more than 300 student films and many SAG-AFTRA films throughout the area.
3. We attend URTAs, Unified auditions, and SETC, and auditions are held throughout the year in Savannah. Students can also submit video auditions.

■ University of West Georgia
Department of Theatre
Carrollton, GA

Compiled by: Pauline D. Gagnon, Professor and Chair

Degrees Offered:

BA in theatre with emphasis tracks in performance and design

Minors Offered:

Theatre

Population of Department(s): Approximately 65 students; 8 full-time faculty

Audition to Declare a Theatre/Musical Theatre Major? No

Three things you would like our readers to know about your performing arts department:

1. Individualized attention.
2. Students perform and design beginning freshman year.
3. Guests artist program connects students to professionals.

Illinois

■ DePaul University
The Theatre School
Chicago, IL

Compiled by: Melissa Tropp, Theatre Admissions Counselor

Population of School: DePaul, approximately 25,000 over two campuses; Theatre School, approximately 300

Conservatory or Liberal Arts: Conservatory

Degrees Offered:

BFAs in acting, costume design, costume technology, dramaturgy/criticism, lighting design, playwriting, scenic design, sound design, stage management, theatre arts, theatre management, theatre technology

MFAs in acting, directing, and arts leadership

Population of Department(s): Approximately 300 students (50% performance, 25% theatre studies, 25% design and tech)

Theatre Scholarships Available: Entering first-year BFA and MFA students are automatically considered for talent scholarships. Returning students become eligible for additional merit awards each year.

Audition Required for BFA: The BFA and MFA acting programs require an in-person audition for consideration. All other majors require an interview or portfolio review.

Pre-screen Video Audition Required: Not required or accepted.

Attends Unifieds: We are not technically part of Unifieds, but we hold auditions in many of the same cities at the same time as Unifieds.

Location of Unifieds: The complete list of dates and locations is usually posted on our website by September.

Number of Students Auditioning Each Year: 700–800

Number of Students Accepted Each Year: There are 32 available spots in the first year of the BFA acting program.

Cut Program or Audition to Remain in Program: No. Our cut/reduction that formerly took place at the end of the first year has been eliminated.

Minors in Musical Theatre/Acting: No

Prominent Alumni: Gillian Anderson, John C. Reilly, Judy Greer, Monique Coleman, P.J. Byrne, Elizabeth Perkins, Joe Mantegna

What do you look for in a potential student?

Quite simply, we are looking for fit. Students who are creative, open, and eager to work generally do very well.

What are your audition requirements?

We would like students to prepare one contemporary monologue no longer than two minutes, and to wear or bring basic movement clothes. The full audition and same-day callback process is outlined on our website.

In your eyes, what makes up an excellent college audition monologue? Song?

An excellent audition monologue is the one that shows us *the best you*—a play that you connect with and a character you could actually play professionally.

If there were one monologue you never wanted to see again, what would it be?

Good material is good material, regardless of how many times we've seen it.

Can you walk me through what I can expect at your on-campus auditions?

Our audition focuses on your potential for future growth. We believe that imagination, personal initiative, self-discipline, stamina, seriousness of purpose, commitment to the profession, and trainability are fundamental principles for Theatre School students.

The audition is comprised of two parts: audition and callback. If you are selected for the callback, that session will be held on the same day.

What is your biggest piece of advice for potential students auditioning?

Breathe. We want you to do well, so take the time you need to get the job done. Keep communication open. If something does not make sense, please ask. And most important, have fun! Our audition process is set up to give you a chance to work and play. You should try to get to know us just as much as we're trying to get to know you.

After I audition, is there a good way to follow up?

There's not really any need to follow up, unless we are still missing some of your application materials. You should always feel welcome to contact us if you have any questions, however.

Would I get a showcase at the end of senior year?

All graduating BFA and MFA actors participate in the Graduate Showcase. Our showcase happens in New York City, Chicago, and Los Angeles and is presented to industry professionals in all three of those major markets, along with a networking reception afterward. Other majors are invited to participate in any or all of the showcases in those cities. Many students receive meetings with agents or callbacks to audition for local work while they are still in the showcase city.

Do I have to audition to be accepted into the showcase?

No, the entire graduating class is featured.

Where are showcases held, and are they successful?

Showcases are held in New York City, Chicago, and Los Angeles, and they are well attended by industry professionals.

Will I be able to audition/perform as a freshman?

First-year BFA acting students act in class every day, but not in productions. Instead, those students get to work in other aspects of a production (crew, makeup, PR/publicity, and so on). Starting in the first quarter of second year, BFA acting majors have guaranteed casting each quarter.

If there is a graduate program, will I get the same performance opportunities as an undergraduate?

Yes, all BFA and MFA acting majors receive equal and guaranteed performance opportunities.

What ways can I be involved with the department aside from performing?

Involvement in any aspect of production is limited to full-time theatre majors. Students can work part-time in the scene shop, in the administrative or admissions theatre offices, or as assistants to faculty members.

I love to sing, but I don't consider myself a dancer. Can I still seek a degree in musical theatre at your school?

We do not offer a musical theatre program.

I want to get a BFA in acting, but I also love to sing. Can BFA/BA acting students take voice lessons with top voice faculty?

BFA students can take private voice lessons from faculty or seek opportunities at DePaul's School of Music.

Do you discourage or encourage students to audition for theatre outside of the department during the academic year?

Acting majors are not allowed to audition outside of school during the year. Honestly, they don't have time anyway; they are all already in rehearsals or in production in our own season.

Does your school regularly work in conjunction with any regional theatres?

While we have informal relationships with dozens of the theatres in the Chicago theatre community, there is no one theatre with which we have an established formal connection.

What do students typically do during the summers? Do you actively promote participation in summer theatre auditions?

There is no typical way to spend your summer. Some students stay in Chicago to audition, some go home and work summer jobs, and some look for study abroad or internship opportunities. We consider summer to be students' own time and do not pressure them to participate in theatre if they would like a break.

How many musicals versus straight plays do you do in a season?

We do about 40 productions each year, and many of these will have elements of music and dance. We produce a full mainstage musical at least every other year.

What are some of your alumni up to? Do you have an active alumni network?

We issue a monthly publication on our website called *Theatre School News*. This is generally 20–25 pages of what our alumni are working on, along with what major they were and when they graduated (http://theatre.depaul.edu/alumni/Pages/theatre-school-news.aspx).

What is the portfolio/interview process for a technical theatre student?

Applicants must apply and provide all supplemental materials as well as schedule an interview though our website. For more information, students should refer to the "how to apply" checklist for their major of choice on our website.

What do you expect to see on a technical theatre résumé?

This would vary between all the design and tech majors we offer. We're just hoping to see enough experience to demonstrate a basic understanding of the kind of work associated with the program.

I'm interested in lighting, sound design, and stage management. What major should I go for? Can I minor?

You should go for our lighting design, sound design, or stage management major. We offer seven different specific majors in the design and technical areas of theatre, so it's a good idea to look at them all carefully and select the one you really want. We offer a minor in theatre studies that includes a few classes in design for non-majors, but there is no production work attached.

Anything else I should know?

We are beyond thrilled to announce our new home, a brand-new facility, officially opened September 2013. Designed by the internationally renowned architect César Pelli and his firm Pelli Clarke Pelli Architects, DePaul University's new Theatre School is located at the corner of Fullerton and Racine on the Lincoln Park campus. The design process was informed by its dual function: to be a performance and public space, as well as a private conservatory of all theatrical disciplines.

The school houses two theatre spaces: a 250-seat theatre and a 100-seat flexible theatre. The building also includes our costume, makeup, prop and scene shops, rehearsal studios, lighting laboratories, movement studios, and much more.

This is our new artistic home. Here we rehearse, collaborate, and learn in a facility designed and developed specifically to meet the creative needs of theatre artists and experts, and we perform contemporary and classic plays, as well as bold new work. Please visit us at http://theatre.depaul.edu.

◼ Loyola University Chicago
Chicago, IL

Compiled by: Dr. Mark E. Lococo, Professor, Director of Theatre

Population of School: 15,720

Conservatory or Liberal Arts: Liberal arts

Degrees Offered:

BA in theatre with possible minors in Shakespeare studies and musical theatre

Population of Department(s): 135

Theatre Scholarships Available: Yes (http://luc.edu/dfpa/theatre-scholarships/)

Audition Required for BA/BS/BM: University admission and declaration of major. Audition required for scholarships.

Pre-screen Video Audition Required: No

Attends Unifieds: No

Prominent Alumni: Ian Brennan (creator of *Glee*); Jennifer Morrison (*Once Upon a Time, House*); numerous award-winning actors, directors, and designers in the Chicago theatre community

Would I get a showcase at the end of senior year?
Yes.

Do I have to audition to be accepted into the showcase?
No.

Where are showcases held, and are they successful?
On campus, and yes.

Will I be able to audition/perform as a freshman?
Yes.

In what ways can I be involved with the department aside from performing?
Student opportunities include design, directing, writing, and management.

I love to sing, but I don't consider myself a dancer. Can I still seek a degree in musical theatre at your school?
The musical theatre minor requires a minimum of eight hours of studio dance.

I want to get a BFA in acting, but I also love to sing. Can BFA/BA acting students take voice lessons with top voice faculty?
We do not offer a BFA. BA students may take applied voice lessons with music faculty.

Do you discourage or encourage students to audition for theatre outside of the department during the academic year?
We encourage students to audition for theatre in the city and, on occasion, can offer limited academic credit for professional work.

Does your school regularly work in conjunction with any regional theatres?

As our faculty is comprised of working professionals, we regularly work in most all Chicago theatres.

What do students typically do during the summers? Do you actively promote participation in summer theatre auditions?

We currently do not offer courses during the summer, but we encourage students to work professionally or as interns in theatres in Chicago or elsewhere.

How many musicals versus straight plays do you do in a season?

One musical and four straight plays.

What are some of your alumni up to? Do you have an active alumni network?

Our students work in a wide variety of fields, any of which might take advantage of their work in the Loyola theatre program. Recent graduates are working as actors, directors, designers, stage managers, teachers, and dramaturges in professional theatres in Chicago and elsewhere.

What is the portfolio/interview process for a technical theatre student?

Admission to the university and declaration of the theatre major.

I'm interested in lighting, sound design, and stage management. What major should I go for? Can I minor?

Students can pursue training in any of those areas as a theatre major or minor.

■ Millikin University
Decatur, IL

Compiled by: Sean Morrissey, Interim Chair/Director of Dance

Population of School: 2,300 undergrads, 80 grad students

Conservatory or Liberal Arts: Liberal arts

Degrees Offered:
BFA in musical theatre
BFA in theatre, with acting emphasis, stage management emphasis, design/production emphasis, and theatre administration emphasis
BA in theatre

Population of Department(s): 170

Theatre Scholarships Available: $1,000–$5,000, based on talent and/or academic achievement, renewable annually

Audition Required for BFA: Yes

Audition Required for BA/BS/BM: No, but students seeking a BA must submit the theatre application and essay.

Pre-screen Video Audition Required: No

Attends Unifieds: Yes

Location of Unifieds: North Texas College Unified Auditions, Plano, TX, and Booker T. Washington High School for the Performing Arts, Dallas, TX

Number of Students Auditioning Each Year: 500 (including Unified auditions)

Number of Students Accepted Each Year: A typical freshman class ranges from 60 to 75 students per year in six degree programs

Cut Program or Audition to Remain in Program: A juried advancement program will evaluate students and advance all those who have the skills to move to the next level, regardless of numbers. All students who meet the requirements for advancement move forward.

Minors in Musical Theatre/Acting: Minors in theatre and dance

Prominent Alumni: Sierra Boggess, Jodi Benson, Tim Shew, Joe Machota, Annie Wersching

What do you look for in a potential student?

We seek students who have a passion for learning about the world and about the art of theatre, not just a love of performing, design, and so on. We look for strong academic skills; discipline; an open, collaborative spirit; and substantial potential.

What are some of the auditors' pet peeves?

Lack of confidence, overcoached auditions, and an inability to be flexible if asked to make adjustments to the audition piece. We are also not keen on students who come across as "slick" and/or appear to know everything there is to know about theatre.

What are your audition requirements?

For musical theatre auditions, students must prepare two contrasting songs and a contemporary monologue. A ballet combination will be taught at the audition to assess dance skills.

For acting auditions, students must prepare two contrasting monologues. One should be contemporary. The second may be from the Shakespeare repertoire but is not required to be. For more specifics, see our website at www.millikin.edu/academics/cfa/dtd/prospective/Pages/AuditionInformation.aspx.

If there were one monologue you never wanted to see again, what would it be?

We're open to most anything if it's done well. Avoid monologues found in monologue books. Specifically, we don't want to hear any of Puck's monologues from *A Midsummer Night's Dream.*

If there were one song you never wanted to hear again, what would it be?

We're open to most anything as long as you are connected and it shows off your strengths.

Can you walk me through what I can expect at your on-campus auditions?

For musical theatre, students are warmed up vocally. They will sing their songs first, and then perform their monologue. After songs and monologues are finished, students will then change for the dance audition.

For acting, students will be warmed up physically and then perform their monologues for the audition panel.

After auditions, students will have lunch in our campus dining hall, have opportunities to meet with and talk to current students, and take a campus tour. The day will culminate with an exit interview, at which time students will be given the results of their auditions.

What's a memorable audition you can remember?

We are impressed with auditions that are well (but not overly) prepared, yet genuine and allow the actor to be seen through the character. A combination of honesty, clarity, vulnerability, and accessibility makes for a memorable audition.

What is your biggest piece of advice for potential students auditioning?

Understand what you can and cannot control in an audition. You control your audition material, how you present yourself, and your level of preparation. The rest is out of your hands. Be yourself, live in the moment, and understand that we are rooting for you to succeed. If you can leave the audition knowing you have done your best, you have had a very successful day, regardless of the outcome.

If I audition for your BFA musical theatre program, but don't get accepted, do you still consider me for your BFA acting program or your BA program?

Yes.

After I audition, is there a good way to follow up?

Since we tell students the day of their auditions which degree program they have been accepted into, the best follow-up is to pay the advanced tuition deposit (ATD). ATDs are fully refundable until May 1 and will hold your spot in our program. Once accepted, there will be a lot of information coming your way. We ask that you be prompt with responses to communications from us. We also welcome feedback on your audition and campus visit experiences. Constructive feedback helps us offer a better audition and/or visit experience.

Would I get a showcase at the end of senior year?

We offer a professional development experience for students with plans to enter the New York market. Our approach is a dramatic contrast to the traditional showcase, designed to offer our students an in-depth introduction to the people and places of business frequented by the New York actor. By arranging one-on-one meetings (auditions) with agents and casting directors, our students begin building professional relationships while gaining valuable audition and interview experience. Although we do not currently offer a Chicago showcase, we are exploring ways to offer a similar experience to our students planning to enter that market.

Do I have to audition to be accepted into the showcase?

Yes. Students must audition for the New York professional development experience and must be committed to moving to New York within a few months of graduation to be considered.

Where are showcases held, and are they successful?

Showcases are held in New York City. Many of our students have booked agents and/or jobs and have built valuable relationships with casting directors as a direct result of our "showcase."

Will I be able to audition/perform as a freshman?

Yes. BFA performance majors are required to audition every semester. Non-performance majors are also welcome, and all who audition are seriously considered for casting, regardless of their degree program.

In what ways can I be involved with the department aside from performing?

There are a number of ways to become involved: Alpha Psi Omega (the service-based honorary theatre fraternity); Pipe Dreams Studio Theatre (our student-run theatre company); internships in business management, production management, marketing, and house management; student jobs in the scene shop, prop shop, costume shop, script library, and theatre office; becoming a dramaturg for a mainstage production; or becoming a classroom assistant.

Say I get a BA rather than a BFA. Will I actually get to perform?

Yes, many students in our BA program have had ensemble, supporting, and even leading roles in our mainstage productions.

I love to sing, but I don't consider myself a dancer. Can I still seek a degree in musical theatre at your school?

Yes. While dance is a rigorous, 10-course component to the musical theatre degree, many students with minimal to no dance experience are accepted provided they have excellent acting and singing skills.

I want to get a BFA in acting, but I also love to sing. Can BFA/BA acting students take voice lessons with top voice faculty?

Yes. Students may register for class voice at any point in their eight semesters at no additional charge. Those wishing to study privately may acquire a weekly lesson with a member of the voice faculty through the School of Music Preparatory (Prep) Department (a conservatory open to the public). Students taking Prep voice will study with the same teachers with whom musical theatre and vocal performance majors study. There is a per-semester fee for Prep voice lessons.

Do you discourage or encourage students to audition for theatre outside of the department during the academic year?

If off-campus opportunities do not create conflicts with a student's academic or production obligations, and if a student is in good physical/vocal health and academic standing, we will support off-campus performance opportunities.

Does your school regularly work in conjunction with any regional theatres?

While a number of our faculty members have relationships with various professional theatres, the Department of Theatre and Dance does not have any formal relationships with regional theatres. However, our faculty connections and the strength and reputation of our program has led to many of our students being hired by any number of prestigious theatre companies, including the St. Louis Muny, Stages St. Louis, Illinois Shakespeare Festival, Little Theatre on the Squire, Music Theatre of Wichita, Utah Shakespeare Festival, Santa Fe Opera, and so on. We have also had a number of professional theatre companies, ranging from non-union stock theatres to LORT companies, request to hold auditions on our campus.

What do students typically do during the summers? Do you actively promote participation in summer theatre auditions?

Students in all majors are highly encouraged to seek professional summer opportunities and/or internships in all areas of the industry.

How many musicals versus straight plays do you do in a season?

Our six-show season consists of two musicals, two plays, and a dance concert each year. In alternating years, we either co-produce an opera with the School of Music or produce a third play.

What are some of your alumni up to? Do you have an active alumni network?

The Millikin alumni network is very tightly woven. For those seeking support and connections in the major theatre markets, the alumni network is a powerful resource always ready to lend a hand. Our alumni are working all over the world in all areas of the entertainment industry: Broadway, London's West End, Orlando, Chicago, Washington, DC, Los Angeles, Dallas, Nashville, Las Vegas, cruise ships, national and international tours, and for companies such as Cirque du Soleil, Chicago Shakespeare Theater, the Goodman, the Guthrie, Chicago Lyric Opera, Sacramento Music Circus, and the Goodspeed Opera House. Visit our website for ongoing alumni updates.

Anything else I should know?

Millikin is a student-focused institution where teaching, mentorship, and student development are valued above all else. We offer conservatory-style training within a liberal arts context with a goal of producing well-informed artists who have a comprehensive understanding of the world in which they live and the technical skills to support their artistic voices. We seek committed students who are inquisitive, adventurous risk-takers open to new ideas and experiences.

The Millikin Department of Theatre and Dance puts a high premium on humanity, collegiality, and respect. Therefore, we teach our students to be strong listeners and valued collaborators. As a result, we often hear from companies for whom our students work about how well prepared they are, how respectful they are of their work and their colleagues, and the level of professionalism with which they conduct themselves. We have set high standards for our students, faculty, and degree programs, and we strive to maintain the level of excellence the theatre industry has come to expect from Millikin students and graduates.

■ Roosevelt University
Chicago College of Performing Arts
Chicago, IL

Compiled by: Patrick Zylka, Assistant Dean for Enrollment and Student Services

Population of School: Approximately 280 in the Theatre Conservatory

Conservatory or Liberal Arts: Conservatory within a liberal arts university

Degrees Offered:

BFA in musical theatre, voice emphasis

BFA in musical theatre, dance emphasis

BFA in acting

BM offered by our Music Conservatory

Population of Department(s): Approximately 70 in each of the disciplines listed above

Theatre Scholarships Available: Yes, and approximately 95% of our students receive scholarships from CCPA

Audition Required for BFA: Yes, absolutely required

Pre-screen Video Audition Required: Not currently

Attends Unifieds: Yes

Location of Unifieds: New York City, Chicago, Las Vegas, and Los Angeles

Number of Students Auditioning Each Year: Approximately 700

Number of Students Accepted Each Year: Our freshman cohort is approximately 75 each year

Cut Program or Audition to Remain in Program: No

Minors in Musical Theatre/Acting: No

What do you look for in a potential student?

Above all, we are looking for applicants who present themselves as mature young artists who have the potential to succeed in these disciplines. Being a performing artist requires great commitment and excellent organizational skills.

What are some of the auditors' pet peeves?

One should never perform repertoire he or she is not ready to perform. We would much rather see an applicant perform repertoire that he or she is ready for and hit it out of the park than see an applicant struggle through repertoire that is much too difficult. We know at the point of audition that we have four years to work with a student and prepare him or her for the demands of the more difficult repertoire. Applicants should come to the audition with repertoire that they are ready to perform and feel unbelievably comfortable with. Auditions are stressful enough, and there is no need to add extra stress by performing repertoire that you might not perform very well.

What are your audition requirements?

Applicants to our acting program must perform two contrasting monologues from plays, no more than one of which may be from classical literature. Neither monologue may be longer than two minutes in duration. Applicants to our musical theatre voice emphasis program must perform two contrasting monologues from plays, no more than one of which may be from classical literature. Neither may be longer than two minutes in duration. Applicants must perform 32 bars each of a ballad and an up-tempo song with recorded accompaniment and without recorded lead vocals. A vocal evaluation and dance call is then also required if auditioning live on our campus. Applicants to our musical theatre dance emphasis must perform one monologue from a play that is no more than one minute in duration and 32 bars of a song with recorded accompaniment and without recorded lead vocals. A dance call is then also required.

In your eyes, what makes up an excellent college audition monologue? Song?

Again, we want to see what an applicant is ready to do and feels comfortable with. Never show us unhealthy singing. Never perform a monologue that you do not understand.

If there were one monologue you never wanted to see again, what would it be?

Monologues that applicants are not ready for and/or do not understand.

If there were one song you never wanted to hear again, what would it be?

Same as above. If you are singing a sad song, don't smile during it!

Can you walk me through what I can expect at your on-campus auditions?

Those auditioning will be greeted by smiling admission staff. They are all very friendly and eager to answer questions. We always suggest showing up to your audition location sooner than you think you need to. You never know what traffic or parking obstacles you'll encounter, and you'll need to navigate a building you are not familiar with. The last thing you want to do is show up to your audition late. Regardless of the reasons for being late, it will not leave a favorable impression no matter how well you perform in your audition. Admission staff will then walk you through your individual audition day schedule and show you where you need to go. You will typically not audition in front of more than one faculty member at any given stage of the audition. Pay attention to other events that may be happening on the day of your audition, such as tours, informational sessions, performances, and so on.

What's a memorable audition you can remember?

The auditions we remember for years to come are from the applicants who walk into the room ready to audition *us*. They are comfortable with the repertoire, confident in their abilities, and show us that they absolutely love to perform. Lots of people have beautiful voices or can memorize difficult lines of text. Far fewer are able to do this and show us that they were born to be on the stage.

What is your biggest piece of advice for potential students auditioning?

Stay calm, stay collected, and stay focused. We are not there to find out what you do wrong; we are there to see what you do right and what you shine at.

If I audition for your BFA musical theatre program, but don't get accepted, do you still consider me for your BFA acting program or your BA program? Or does each program require its own audition if I'd like to be considered for both?

Though our programs do have unique audition requirements, we have considered applicants for majors they have not applied to in previous years.

After I audition, is there a good way to follow up?

It never hurts to send the faculty member(s) a handwritten note or email of thanks. We hear so many auditions every year that these professional touches really do go a long way in separating out applicants from one another.

Would I get a showcase at the end of senior year?

Yes.

Do I have to audition to be accepted into the showcase?

Yes.

Where are showcases held, and are they successful?

Showcases are held in Chicago. They are very successful, as many of our students receive opportunities as a result. In recent years, we have received phone calls from other theatre programs around the country asking if we can move our showcase date because they are having difficulty getting scouts out to their showcases.

Will I be able to audition/perform as a freshman?

Yes, though remember you are no longer the big fish in the little sea. There are many talented performers around you, many of whom have been in the conservatory longer than you. You will receive performance opportunities, but you will still have much to learn over your four years. More opportunities will present themselves as you move through the degree sequence.

In what ways can I be involved with the department aside from performing?

There are many opportunities and requirements for students to do stage work, lighting, staging, makeup, costumes, and so on. It is important for students to learn all the different things that need to happen to put on a production, not only for their better understanding of the art but also to expose our students to the very many career paths within the theatrical world.

I love to sing, but I don't consider myself a dancer. Can I still seek a degree in musical theatre at your school?

Yes. Our dance call during the admission process is really to determine if you are comfortable moving in your own body. We have fantastic dance instructors who will help you to develop this skill over your four years.

I want to get a BFA in acting, but I also love to sing. Can BFA/BA acting students take voice lessons with top voice faculty?

Vocal coachings are available. First and foremost is the importance of completing what is required within the four-year BFA degree sequence. However, we always encourage our students to expand upon what is required in order to prepare for the many demands in the professional world.

Do you discourage or encourage students to audition for theatre outside of the department during the academic year?

Yes, we encourage them. All outside performance engagements, however, must be cleared by our faculty in advance. We want to ensure that outside engagements will not interfere with the requirements of being a full-time student. We also want to make sure the opportunities presented to our students are legitimate and worth their time.

Does your school regularly work in conjunction with any regional theatres?

Yes, many of our students enjoy being in the middle of a major metropolitan area and take advantage of the many professional opportunities within the city.

What do students typically do during the summers? Do you actively promote participation in summer theatre auditions?

Yes, summer programs are an excellent way to continue to grow as an artist when classes are not in session and also to work with performers our students do not interact with during the academic year.

How many musicals versus straight plays do you do in a season?

Our season typically offers 16–20 classic and contemporary plays, musicals, and experimental works in mainstage and studio performances.

What are some of your alumni up to? Do you have an active alumni network?

We keep track of our alumni through social media, and they keep track of us. Our alumni know the rigor required to graduate from CCPA's Theatre Conservatory and, therefore, are very helpful in reaching out to our recent graduates, knowing they will make excellent additions to any company. We have alumni active in Los Angeles, Chicago, New York City, and everywhere in between. Courtney Reed, a CCPA musical theatre graduate, was recently cast as Jasmine in the Broadway production of *Aladdin*. Other Broadway credits include *In the Heights* and *Mamma Mia!*

■ Eureka College
Eureka, IL

Compiled by: Holly Rocke, Associate Professor of Theatre Arts and Drama

Degrees Offered:

BA/BS in theatre

Minors Offered:

Theatre

Population of Department(s): 20

Audition to Declare a Theatre/Musical Theatre Major? No

Three things you would like our readers to know about your performing arts department:

1. We encourage students to participate in all areas of theatre.

2. We provide fantastic study abroad opportunities.

3. We have internship connections in Chicago, New York City, and Los Angeles.

■ Illinois State University

School of Theatre and Dance
Normal, IL

Compiled by: Janet M. Wilson, Director

Degrees Offered:

BA/BS in theatre/acting

BA/BS in theatre/design-production

BA/BS in theatre education

BA/BS in theatre studies with concentrations in cinema studies, creative drama, directing, dramaturgy/history, integrated performance, theatre management, dance performance, dance education

Minors Offered:

Theatre

Cinema studies

Dance

Population of Department(s): 320 students

Audition to Declare a Theatre/Musical Theatre Major? Yes. You must audition to become an acting major, dance performance major, or dance education major. You must have an interview and portfolio review to be accepted as a design-production major. You will automatically be considered for a scholarship when you audition or go through a portfolio review. Students may interview for scholarship consideration for theatre education or theatre studies.

Three things you would like our readers to know about your performing arts department:

1. The School of Theatre and Dance is a vibrant, educational environment that combines academic excellence and artistic achievement.

2. We have a strong emphasis on producing a wide variety of plays, musicals, and dance concerts in five different theatres. Students here are very proactive and take a lot of initiative in producing projects they believe in.

3. When you become a student at Illinois State University, you join a community of artists for a lifetime. Our alumni founded Steppenwolf Theatre Company in Chicago and are highly visible in theatre, film, and TV.

■ Knox College

Galesburg, IL

Compiled by: Elizabeth Carlin Metz, Chair

Degrees Offered:

BA in theatre

Minors Offered:

Dramatic literature and history
Playwriting
Performance (acting or directing)
Design
Dramaturgy

Population of Department(s): 4 tenure-track faculty; 1 instructor; 25–30 work-study positions and teaching assistant and post-baccalaureate opportunities. Approximately 25 majors and 20 undeclared with intent to major annually (number of minors is not tracked, but theatre is a very popular minor). Annual cross-disciplinary participation is approximately 200–300, and annual audience served is approximately 3,000.

Audition to Declare a Theatre/Musical Theatre Major? No

Three things you would like our readers to know about your performing arts department:

1. Participation in the Department of Theatre is widely popular across the disciplines—*The Princeton Review* rates the department 12th in the nation in its annual rankings.

2. Students who seek to go to grad school routinely place in top programs, such as University of Washington, University of California, San Diego, Carnegie Mellon, New York University, University of Texas at Austin, and Yale University, and obtain internships/fellowships/apprenticeships at professional theatres such as Steppenwolf, Berkeley Repertory Theatre, New Jersey Shakespeare Theatre, Cleveland Playhouse, Williamstown Theatre Festival, and Vitalist Theatre, the later of which has provided 16 years of Knox theatre graduates with entry to the Chicago theatre scene.

3. The Knox College sense of One Community assures that cliques and divas do not tend to characterize the Knox theatre community. The Mainstage, Studio Theatre, Playwrights' Workshop, Repertory Term, Honor's Projects, and New Plays Festival productions provide more than 250 opportunities to get involved over the course of a student's four years at Knox College.

■ North Central College
Naperville, IL

Compiled by: Carin Silkaitis, Department Chair of Theatre, Theatre Program Coordinator

Degrees Offered:

Theatre
Musical theatre
Technical theatre and design (2014)
Music

Minors Offered:

Theatre
Musical theatre
Technical theatre and design (2014)
Music
Dance

Population of Department(s): Approximately 100 majors and minors in theatre

Audition to Declare a Theatre/Musical Theatre Major? No, auditions required only for scholarships

Three things you would like our readers to know about your performing arts department:

1. We are student centered with a dedicated faculty of working artists.
2. We have an excellent internship program with some of Chicago's best theatres (Goodman Theatre, Chicago Shakespeare on Navy Pier, American Theatre Company).
3. We put on one of the best senior showcases in Chicagoland.

■ Northern Illinois University
School of Theatre and Dance
DeKalb, IL

Compiled by: Alexander Gelman, Director

Degrees Offered:

BFA in acting
BFA in design tech
BFA in dance performance
BA in theatre studies
MFA in acting
MFA in design and technology

Minors Offered:

Theatre studies
Dance performance

Population of Department(s): 220

Audition to Declare a Theatre/Musical Theatre Major? Yes for BFA acting and design tech; no for BA theatre studies and BFA dance performance

Three things you would like our readers to know about your performing arts department:

1. Faculty are working professionals.
2. Strong relationships regionally, in the Chicago theatre community, and internationally with the Moscow Art Theatre.
3. Faculty collaborates closely with each other and the students to ensure personal attention to each individual's journey through the training.

■ Rockford University

Rockford, IL

Compiled by: Timm Adams, Associate Professor of Music, Head of Recruiting for Performing Arts (and Equity actor, professional music director, conductor, vocal coach)

Degrees Offered:

BFA in musical theatre performance

BFA in acting/directing

BFA in design/technical theatre

BFA in theatre management

BA in theatre arts (including strong theatre education program)

BA in music

Minors Offered:

Theatre

Music

Dance (as of fall 2014)

Population of Department(s): We are a small, competitive department with about 40 majors and another 10 minors.

Audition to Declare a Theatre/Musical Theatre Major? Yes, we hold four in-house audition days each year and are able to accommodate individual visits as well. We also recruit at a number of state thespian festivals (Illinois, Missouri, Texas, Kansas, Iowa, and Nevada, to name a few of our annual or recent visits) and the International Thespian Festival each June in Lincoln, NE.

Three things you would like our readers to know about your performing arts department:

1. The Performing Arts Department at Rockford University offers exceptional conservatory-style training in a rich liberal arts setting. A distinguished faculty with many years of professional experience provides classroom teaching and one-on-one mentoring to our students in a practical and experiential learning environment. Rockford's well-established acting curriculum has a proven track record that ensures students reach their fullest potential as actors before they graduate.

2. Students have ample opportunities to perform *beginning freshman year.* (Freshmen do audition and are often cast.)

3. Equity theatre in residence at the university: Artists Ensemble Theater (www .artistsensemble.org/Home.html). Students have the opportunity to audition and perform alongside seasoned professionals and become an EMC. Spring 2013 marked our first full collaboration with AET, and 16 students were a part of the production (onstage) and many joined the EMC program. Many more work backstage, and upperclassmen and recent graduates occasionally receive design credits for working on AET shows. Also, our proximity to Chicago makes us an easy destination for auditions, professional theatre, or a weekend getaway. Many of our graduates settle there after graduation, and our professors have numerous connections in the city.

■ Southern Illinois University Edwardsville

Edwardsville, IL

Compiled by: Chuck Harper, Associate Professor, Head of Performance Area

Degrees Offered:

We currently offer a single major (theater and dance), with specialization in performance, design/tech, theater education, dance, theater history/literature/criticism

Minors Offered:

Theater

Dance

Population of Department(s): 9 tenure/tenure track faculty, 5 full-time instructor/staff, approximately 80 majors

Audition to Declare a Theatre/Musical Theatre Major? No

Three things you would like our readers to know about your performing arts department:

1. There are no class or age restrictions on roles/tech assignments. Students will be cast and assigned based on ability.

2. Student–faculty ratio of approximately 6:1 ensures substantial one-on-one contact with faculty.

3. We produce and host Xfest, an annual festival of experimental and alternative theatre and dance (supported by the University and the College of Arts and Sciences), which brings in performing ensembles from around the United States for a week of performances and student workshops.

■ Southern Illinois University Carbondale

Carbondale, IL

Compiled by: J. Thomas Kidd, Chair, Department of Theater; Timothy J. Fink, Head BFA Program

Degrees Offered:

BA in theater

BFA in musical theater (interdisciplinary degree with the School of Music)

Minors Offered:

Theater

Population of Department(s): 65 undergrad majors, 20 BFA majors, 16 grad majors, 10 full-time faculty members

Audition to Declare a Theatre/Musical Theatre Major? BA in theater, no; BFA in musical theater, yes

Three things you would like our readers to know about your performing arts department:

1. Offer the opportunity to work with the department's professional summer stock company, McLeod Summer Playhouse.
2. Rapidly growing BFA in musical theater program.
3. Strong undergrad and grad programs in playwriting, dramaturgy, theater design, and technology and directing.

■ University of Chicago
Chicago, IL

Compiled by: Heidi Coleman, Director of Undergraduate Studies, Theater and Performance Studies

Degrees Offered:

Theater
Performance studies

Minors Offered:

Theater
Performance studies

Population of Department(s): 100 majors/minors, 500 students involved in productions

Audition to Declare a Theatre/Musical Theatre Major? No

Three things you would like our readers to know about your performing arts department:

1. This is an undergrad program that focuses on the creation of new work in performance.
2. Courses are taught by artistic leaders in Chicago, including artists with Steppenwolf, Lookingglass, Court, and Hypocrites.
3. We produce more than 35 productions a year, including Shakespeare, musicals, new work, and contemporary drama.

■ University of Illinois at Chicago
School of Theatre and Music
Chicago, IL

Compiled by: Neal McCollam, Coordinator of Theatre Operations

Degrees Offered:

BFA in acting
BA in acting
BA in theatre design

Minors Offered:

Theatre

Population of Department(s): 180

Audition to Declare a Theatre/Musical Theatre Major? Yes

Three things you would like our readers to know about your performing arts department:

1. The UIC School of Theatre and Music connects students to Chicago's vibrant theatre culture.

2. Students receive personalized attention from instructors who are working professionals and leaders in their field.

3. UIC provides innovative, rigorous, and comprehensive academic and performance programs as part of its diverse urban context.

■ University of Illinois at Urbana-Champaign
Department of Theatre
Champaign, IL

Compiled by: Tom Mitchell, Associate Head, Director of Undergraduate Studies

Degrees Offered:

BFA in acting

BFA in scene design, scenic technology, lighting design and technology, sound design, costume design and technology, stage management

BFA in theatre studies

MA in theatre studies

MFA in acting, scene design, scenic technology, lighting design and technology, sound design, costume design, costume technology, stage management

PhD in theatre studies

Minors Offered:

Theatre studies

Population of Department(s): 120 BFA; 65 MFA/MA/PhD

Audition to Declare a Theatre/Musical Theatre Major? Auditions required for admission into the program as freshman (or as transfer student)

Three things you would like our readers to know about your performing arts department:

1. We work in the Krannert Center for the Performing Arts, one of the leading performing arts centers in the nation, with outstanding, state-of-the-art facilities as well as a continuous flow of world-class guest artists.

2. We offer professional training led by faculty of working professionals in all areas.

3. Students receive rigorous academic experience in a top-tier research university.

Indiana

■ Ball State University

Muncie, IN

Compiled by: William Jenkins, Associate Professor and Department Chair, Theatre and Dance

Population of School: 20,000

Conservatory or Liberal Arts: BFA/BA/BS program within a liberal arts curriculum

Degrees Offered:

BFA in acting, musical theatre, dance

BA/BS programs in theatre education, design technology, production (which is for directors and stage managers), and theatrical studies

Population of Department(s): 450

Theatre Scholarships Available: Anywhere from $500 all the way up to half tuition waivers

Audition Required for BFA: Yes, for all BFA programs

Audition Required for BA/BS/BM: No, but we have interviews for scholarships

Pre-screen Video Audition Required: No

Attends Unifieds: Yes

Location of Unifieds: Chicago, New York, and now Las Vegas (2014)

Number of Students Auditioning Each Year: 1,150 in all areas, 900 specifically for BFA musical theatre and acting

Number of Students Accepted Each Year: 20 for BFA acting, 20 for BFA musical theatre, 20 for BFA dance. For BA/BS we accept an unlimited amount for theatrical studies, design technology, and theatre education. We accept a total of 10 students for the production major, but you don't deem admittance until you're a sophomore.

Cut Program or Audition to Remain in Program: We are not a cut program, but there is a jury each semester.

Minors in Musical Theatre/Acting: We offer minors in general theatre, musical theatre dance, dance, and design technology.

Prominent Alumni: Joyce DeWitt, Doug Jones, Bryan Woodall, Sutton Foster

What do you look for in a potential student?

We look for directorability and a natural, honest approach to the material. If the student is auditioning for musical theatre, we are looking for someone who is a potential triple threat. We are looking for someone who has a strong artistic vision. We're looking for great human beings as well as great talent.

What are some of the auditors' pet peeves?

Material that does not come from published plays. Material that is presentational and/or show choir-like in its approach. Doing songs that are well out of someone's vocal range. We enjoy confidence, but we don't like egotism.

What are your audition requirements?

For musical theatre, students will be asked to sing two contrasting musical selections, although they should bring a variety of pieces to the auditions so that we can check out other pieces. Usually we ask for 16–32 bars, and the material should be something they can sing on their sickest day. For monologues, we ask for one one-minute monologue from a published contemporary play. The characters should be within their age range, no dialects, and no characters in extremely volatile positions. We are looking for you not to yell and scream but rather to be honest, pure, and simple. For the dance audition, we focus on ballet, jazz, and tap, and it is taught as a dance class.

In your eyes, what makes up an excellent college audition monologue? Song?

Strong connection to material. A clear understanding of the objective, obstacle, and tactics that the character is pursuing. A firm grounding in the reality of the given circumstances of the situation and an honest, genuine approach to the material that is void of emotionally charged, unreal situations.

If there were one monologue you never wanted to see again, what would it be?

Nicky Silver's "Fat Men in Skirts"—the Popo Martin monologue.

If there were one song you never wanted to hear again, what would it be?

Anything from *Wicked*.

Can you walk me through what I can expect at your on-campus auditions?

Auditions start with a meet and greet with current students and faculty, followed by a performance on campus by some of our current students. We then separate amongst the different groups that are auditioning. Parents will have a general meeting where they can ask questions of faculty while the students will begin with interviews in their prospective areas. Acting students do a movement warm-up. Musical theatre students do a dance audition, followed by a vocal and acting audition.

What's a memorable audition you can remember?

A student auditioning this past year in Chicago. She came in and one of the things we were most attracted to was that she was not aware of how talented she was. She was earnest, eager, and interested in getting feedback and wanted to know how she could get better. I think any audition where the person auditioning spends less time worrying about impressing us and more time sharing with us the talents that he or she has is memorable.

What is your biggest piece of advice for potential students auditioning?

If you could do anything else in your life and be happy, I would recommend it.

If I audition for your BFA musical theatre program, but don't get accepted, do you still consider me for your BFA acting program or your BA/BS program?

Yes, for our BFA acting program, and you can always declare a BA/BS in theatrical studies. In addition, several of our theatrical studies students re-audition in November and end up getting into the BFA acting or BFA musical theatre programs.

After I audition, is there a good way to follow up?

Yes, always keeping in touch with us via email is good. In addition, thank-you notes are always appreciated and send a good message to the faculty. If you don't hear from us in a given amount of time, and if Ball State is still of interest even with other offers on the table, keeping in contact with us via the phone is something that we appreciate.

Would I get a showcase at the end of senior year?

Yes, but the showcases are a bit different here. We have faculty members who are casting directors in each of the three major cities, and students are guaranteed three professional auditions with all three casting directors. Then the casting directors select the students for the showcase, not us.

Do I have to audition to be accepted into the showcase?

The casting directors choose who participates—Erica Daniels (casting director for the Steppenwolf Theatre in Chicago), Stephanie Klapper (casting director in New York City for off-Broadway and Broadway shows), and Mark Saks (casting director for *The Good Wife* and *Person of Interest*).

Where are showcases held, and are they successful?

Showcases are held in New York City, Los Angeles, and Chicago. Over the course of the last 10 years, 80% of the students are still working in theatre.

Will I be able to audition/perform as a freshman?

You will be able to audition as a second-semester freshman.

In what ways can I be involved with the department aside from performing?

We have an honorary fraternity/sorority house, Alpha Psi Omega, and tons of other student groups. We also have numerous opportunities for community outreach programs to help the community. A lot of our students will go outside the department and will do outreach projects with the local elementary school kids or kids in the community because we really feel that giving back is a huge part of what artists do.

Say I get a BA rather than a BFA. Will I actually get to perform?

Yes. There are a total of 18 shows we do a year. While we say the first priority goes to the BFA students, as it's part of their curriculum, it is not out of the realm of possibility for BA/BS students to get a chance to audition and perform. Any student on campus can audition, frankly.

I love to sing, but I don't consider myself a dancer. Can I still seek a degree in musical theatre at your school?

It is possible but difficult.

I want to get a BFA in acting, but I also love to sing. Can BFA/BA acting students take voice lessons with top voice faculty?

There are private voice lessons available, and there are also classes that we offer called Singing for the Non-Musical Theatre Major. We do cast acting majors in musical theatre productions on a regular basis.

Do you discourage or encourage students to audition for theatre outside of the department during the academic year?

We don't discourage it, but we also tell students that their first priority is for the department. However, as long as their academic and production work is not affected, we do give them permission to do so.

Does your school regularly work in conjunction with any regional theatres?

We have regular internships with Stephanie Klapper Casting in New York City and Drury Lane in Chicago.

What do students typically do during the summers? Do you actively promote participation in summer theatre auditions?

We do actively promote that. Most of our students attend the MWTA, SETC, or other regional theatre audition opportunities. The vast majority of our students are working professional jobs or internships.

How many musicals versus straight plays do you do in a season?

14 plays and musicals each year.

What are some of your alumni up to? Do you have an active alumni network?

Yes

What is the portfolio/interview process for a technical theatre student?

Students will bring their portfolios in, and usually that is the determination for whether they are eligible for any scholarship money. We have them interview with our faculty and staff members—costume, lighting, scenic, sound, makeup, hair, technical direction. After getting in the program, we'll then go through a portfolio review at the end of each year, which consists of looking at work that has happened in classes, portfolio pictures, and the preparation of the portfolio for the professional world.

What do you expect to see on a technical theatre résumé?

We expect to see that the student has a variety of experiences on his or her résumé and that they are not solely focused on one thing. We want multifaceted applicants and a clear artistic vision for the area that they are most interested in.

I'm interested in lighting, sound design, and stage management. What major should I go for? Can I minor?

We would probably talk to the student about doing a double major between our production option and our design technology option.

Anything else I should know?

Students need to understand that there are lots of very strong programs out there and that any program that tells them they are the only one for them is probably not interested in the student. Students also need to be aware that they should talk to the current students who are at a program—they know firsthand what the experience will be like. Also, as many times as possible, visiting the school and getting an idea of the campus is really important because you are not just choosing a place to study your art, but also you're choosing a place to spend four years of your life that you won't forget. You want a place that will feel like a home. That's important to us.

■ Indiana University
Bloomington, IN

Compiled by: George Pinney, Professor and Head of Musical Theatre, Department of Theatre and Drama

Population of School: More than 43,000 students

Conservatory or Liberal Arts: Liberal arts

Degrees Offered:
BFA in musical theatre
BA in theatre and drama with concentrations in acting/directing, scenic design, lighting design, costume design, sound design, stage management, dramatic literature and history
MFA in acting, directing, playwrighting, scenic design, costume design, lighting design, costume technology, theatre technology
MA
PhD

Population of Department(s): 262 BA/BFA students (42 BFA musical theatre, 221 BA) and 53 grad students (37 MFA, 1 MA, 15 PhD)

Theatre Scholarships Available: The university offers a wide range of scholarships based on academic performance and financial need. To apply for these scholarships, a prospective student must submit an application with all financial forms by November 1. The department does offer scholarships and monetary awards to established students.

Audition Required for BFA: Yes

Audition Required for BA/BS/BM: No

Pre-screen Video Audition Required: Yes

Attends Unifieds: No

Number of Students Auditioning Each Year: More than 200

Number of Students Accepted Each Year: 10–14

Cut Program or Audition to Remain in Program: No

Minors in Musical Theatre/Acting: The department offers a general minor in theatre and drama

Prominent Alumni: Kevin Kline, Colin Donnell, Nicole Parker, Elizabeth Stanley, Rebecca Faulkenberry, Angelique Cabral, Heath Calvert, Ben Livingston, Meg Tolin, Eric Van Tielen, Rob Gallagher, Rob Constantine, Robyn Payne, Roderick Keller, Ben Cohen, Chris Klink, Steve Morgan

What do you look for in a potential student?

We look for students who demonstrate strong potential for a successful professional career. In addition, we look for students who are well centered with a positive outlook on life and team players with the ability to think globally. A student should have strong self-motivation, natural curiosity for discovery, and a passion for art and life.

What are some of the auditors' pet peeves?

Self-centered students who place themselves before anyone else. Not being able to follow instructions. Negative energy. In video submissions, students who employ pitch correction, reverb, or any other sound enhancement.

What are your audition requirements?

Video pre-screen submission with two contrasting songs, a contemporary monologue, and a short discussion on why the student wants to pursue a career in musical theatre. For the on-campus audition, two songs and a contemporary monologue are required. In addition, students participate in morning dance class and acting class.

In your eyes, what makes up an excellent college audition monologue? Song?

The monologue or song should be close to the age range of the student with consideration of cast ability. There should be a strong sense of action wedded with a sense of beginning, middle, and end, the arc of the piece.

If there were one monologue you never wanted to see again, what would it be?

When a monologue is well done, it really doesn't matter. Do stay away from overly offensive language and situation.

If there were one song you never wanted to hear again, what would it be?

Again, if it is well done, we are game for anything.

If you require a pre-screen video audition, what do you look for in those submissions?

We look at potential for a professional career. The student should have a strong sense of self without being self-conscious. We consider choices of material and how appropriate they are for the student. The vocal part of the audition is carefully weighed both for vocal technique and for acting. A successful video audition will give a positive impression. Remember, you are submitting the video for a callback. Demonstrate the positives; it is not a time to take a chance.

Can you walk me through what I can expect at your on-campus auditions?

Students are first greeted and checked in at the Ruth N. Halls Theatre Lobby. The day starts with a dance class and combinations with Professor Liza Gennaro. An acting class with Professor George Pinney follows with emphasis on ensemble building, improvisation, awareness, and musicality. The classes are designed to give the students an opportunity to work with professors in the program to give a better understanding of our department as well as show-case the prospective students' talents and abilities.

During the dance class there is a meeting with parents and musical theatre faculty. This meeting gives an overview of the program as well as what is expected of students. There is also an opportunity to have any questions answered.

The afternoon is devoted to the individual auditions, at which students present their songs and monologues. Short interviews are also given at this time.

What's a memorable audition you can remember?

Many auditions are memorable. What makes them memorable is the students' ability to be themselves with a passion for life and art. An audition is a chance to perform, a chance to share. That is the ultimate goal.

What is your biggest piece of advice for potential students auditioning?

Be yourself and look at the audition as a chance to perform. Bring your love of theatre into the room and leave nerves and doubt outside.

If I audition for your BFA musical theatre program, but don't get accepted, do you still consider me for your BFA acting program or your BA program? Or does each program require its own audition if I'd like to be considered for both?

The BA program does not require an audition. We have had many students who auditioned for the BFA pursue a theatre degree in the BA program.

After I audition, is there a good way to follow up?

A simple postcard or note is best.

Would I get a showcase at the end of senior year?

Yes.

Do I have to audition to be accepted into the showcase?

Yes; however, if a BFA student is not accepted into the showcase after four years of study, something is very wrong somewhere.

Where are showcases held, and are they successful?

Our showcase is presented at the York Theatre, Midtown Manhattan in April. The showcase is highly successful, attracting many agents and casting directors, as well as other professionals in the business. In the spring of 2013, all of our students were called back, with a majority of them being signed. Those who did not sign chose to follow other paths, which included cruise ship contracts, regional theatres, and grad school.

Will I be able to audition/perform as a freshman?

Yes. Departmental policy allows for open casting with the only requirement that a person be an IU student.

If there is a graduate program, will I get the same performance opportunities as an undergraduate?

Yes, the MFA acting studio consists of nine actors. On occasion, an MFA actor has been cast in a musical.

What ways can I be involved with the department aside from performing?

The Department of Theatre, Drama and Contemporary Dance is a full-service department with studies in all areas. A student might assistant direct for a mainstage production, develop an independent project, participate in University Players (an all-student group producing plays and musicals), work in production in the shops, participate in the numerous master classes with visiting guest artists, develop new work, participate in dance-related concerts, or stage manage. The possibilities are quite strong. In addition, IU offers many opportunities as a Big Ten School.

Say I get a BA rather than a BFA. Will I actually get to perform?

Auditions are open to any student. The mainstage is one avenue. Independent projects, directing scenes, graduate directing projects, and University Players are some of the possibilities for performance within the department. The Jacobs School of Music and the Neil Marshall Black Culture Center also offer excellent performance opportunities.

I love to sing, but I don't consider myself a dancer. Can I still seek a degree in musical theatre at your school?

Yes, absolutely. Though we do train in all areas, it is obvious that not all roles require excellent dance ability. To work in the profession, a student must be able to move very well. We bring out the best in the student, and that includes dance. Though a student may not consider him- or herself a dancer, he or she may not have had the right teacher yet.

I want to get a BFA in acting, but I also love to sing. Can BFA/BA acting students take voice lessons with top voice faculty?

The in-house professors who teach voice have a very heavy schedule and focus mainly on the BFA program. All BFA students study with a major professor and not with a grad student. All voice professors are housed in the department and focus on classical technique as a base before focusing on styles. The Jacobs School of Music offers private voice, and many voice professors teach privately.

Do you discourage or encourage students to audition for theatre outside of the department during the academic year?

Yes. Bloomington has a vibrant theatre scene allowing for terrific opportunities.

Does your school regularly work in conjunction with any regional theatres?

There are two regional theatres in Bloomington, Cardinal Stage and Bloomington Playwrights Project. Students are regularly cast in their productions.

What do students typically do during the summers? Do you actively promote participation in summer theatre auditions?

Students are highly encouraged and prepared to audition for summer theatres. The department is very supportive of students seeking outside summer gigs to expand their network, collaborate with other professionals, meet new fellow actors, and build résumés. In addition, our resident Indiana Festival Theatre (IFT) boasts an outstanding summer season of one musical and two plays that are performed in rep. After IFT closes, Premiere Musicals workshops a new work. Two children's musicals round out the summer, making for many opportunities for students to work at IU.

How many musicals versus straight plays do you do in a season?

The winter mainstage season consists of six plays and two musicals. A musical is produced in the fall and in the spring. The summer season consists of one musical, two children's musicals, and one new musical.

What are some of your alumni up to? Do you have an active alumni network?

Our alumni consistently work on Broadway, in regional theatres, on cruise ships, in cabarets, and at theme parks around the world. Our network is quite strong and growing. IU alumni are very loyal and will go out of their way to help those just graduating. In conjunction with the New York City showcase in the spring, we have an alumni gathering at Joe's Pub for the old and new to meet and greet. The showcase performs at the event, and it is a terrific first step.

What is the portfolio/interview process for a technical theatre student?

The BA is liberal arts. There is no portfolio/interview process to enter the design and technology emphasis program. Advanced courses are by instructor permission only, ensuring that the quality and level of challenge is maintained.

What do you expect to see on a technical theatre résumé?

To jump right into a 300-level introduction to costume, scenic, sound, or lighting course, following a first semester of Intro to Production 125, a student needs to demonstrate that he or she can read a play meaningfully for character and dramatic structure, have had some tangible experience in theatre production, and have some familiarity with the subject matter of the 300-level course he or she seeks to take immediately following T125.

I'm interested in lighting, sound design, and stage management. What major should I go for? Can I minor?

A student could take courses in all three areas. There is a limit of how many courses in a major can contribute to graduation, so the student would need to be selective regarding the advanced courses in these areas. The resulting degree would be a BA with emphasis in design and technology. The BA does not specifically designate which design disciplines or stage management.

Anything else I should know?

The BFA in musical theatre provides the rigorous curriculum needed to train students in acting, singing, and dancing. In addition to performance technique classes, students will participate in a rich core of theatre and music classes and professional classes in "careers in professional theatre," as well as enhanced master classes by visiting guest artists. Designed to bring out the best in the individual, the BFA in musical theatre was created within the context of a liberal arts education. Not only will a student receive superior training in performance technique, but also the student will be better prepared for life by fulfilling all requirements of the College of Arts and Sciences.

■ Butler University

Department of Theatre
Indianapolis, IN

Compiled by: Diane Timmerman, Chair of Theatre

Degrees Offered:

BA in theatre
BS in arts administration theatre

Minors Offered:

Theatre

Population of Department(s): 70 theatre majors

Audition to Declare a Theatre/Musical Theatre Major? Yes

Three things you would like our readers to know about your performing arts department:

1. We are a dynamic hybrid of conservatory-quality courses/productions combined with the flexibility of a BA that allows for secondary majors.
2. We have active professional partnerships with three Equity theatres.
3. Butler Theatre has an international theatre program unique in the country.

■ DePauw University

Greencastle, IN

Compiled by: Tim Good, Associate Professor of Communication and Theatre

Degrees Offered:

BA in theatre
BA in communication
BA in English – writing
BA in music
BM in performance

Concentrations: acting, directing, design and technology, dramatic writing, arts administration, musical theatre, theory and criticism

Minors Offered:

Theatre
Media studies
Interpersonal communication
Applied music
Jazz studies

Population of Department(s): 30

Audition to Declare a Theatre/Musical Theatre Major? No

Three things you would like our readers to know about your performing arts department:

1. DePauw Theatre is a family. You are not a number, but an integral, important part of the community. Whether this be the Festival of Shakespeare, ArtsFest, mainstage, or student performances, DePauw Theatre students work with students from other disciplines, families, and artists in Greencastle. You will make friends for life and create a network of future professionals and DePauw alumni who are all willing to support and advise students as they take the next step into the "real world."

2. DePauw Theatre is completely supportive of student-conceived and student-led projects, and you are not limited by studying a particular aspect of theatre. You can act, design, manage, direct, choreograph, write, compose, and more, which makes you a more marketable professional.

3. DePauw's faculty are top notch, and the professors are incredibly accessible. At DePauw, you work alongside the faculty, not underneath them. This faculty includes professors, staff, guest artists, community members, and alumni. They not only teach but also mentor, advise, and support their students, on campus and beyond.

■ Indiana Wesleyan University
Marion, IN

Compiled by: Dr. Katie Wampler, Artistic Professor

Degrees Offered: Theatre

Minors Offered:

Theatre
Shakespeare in performance (in process)

Population of Department(s): 30

Audition to Declare a Theatre/Musical Theatre Major? No

Three things you would like our readers to know about your performing arts department:

1. Acting, directing, designing, playwriting, and managing opportunities available for majors and non-majors.

2. Emphasis on Shakespeare in performance.

3. May term studies in New York and abroad.

■ University of Indianapolis

Indianapolis, IN

Compiled by: Dr. Brad Wright, Director of Theatre

Degrees Offered:

Theatre BA or BS (performance/directing, design/technical, music theatre concentration), theatre teaching

Minors Offered:

Theatre

Population of Department(s): 38 undergrad students

Audition to Declare a Theatre/Musical Theatre Major? No audition to enter program; audition/portfolio review for theatre scholarships

Three things you would like our readers to know about your performing arts department:

1. We offer theatre scholarships up to one-fourth tuition, renewable for eight full-time semesters.

2. We are dedicated to providing personalized attention in a nurturing environment.

3. We are a small- to medium-sized department where students, including freshmen, have many opportunities to perform, design, and work backstage.

■ Clarke University

Dubuque, IA

Compiled by: Ellen Gabrielleschi, Chair of Theatre/Musical Theatre Department

Degrees Offered:

Theatre
Musical Theatre
Music

Minors Offered:

Theatre
Music

Population of Department(s): 18

Audition to Declare a Theatre/Musical Theatre Major? Yes

Three things you would like our readers to know about your performing arts department:

1. Small but very vibrant department that functions as a small acting company.

2. Competitive performing arts scholarships available and renewable.

3. Preparation for future career individualized for each student.

■ Luther College

Decorah, IA

Compiled by: Lisa Lantz, Visual and Performing Arts Department Head

Degrees Offered:

Theatre (performance and technical focus)
Theatre management
Dance

Minors Offered:

Theatre
Theatre management
Dance

Population of Department(s): 100

Audition to Declare a Theatre/Musical Theatre Major? No audition required to declare major.

Three things you would like our readers to know about your performing arts department:

1. Engage in speaking and performance as kinesthetic skills, exploring what it means to be fully human.
2. Illuminate historical and contemporary events and issues through collaboration and performance.
3. Refine imagination through the intentional study and practice of text, movement, and designs in costume, scenery, and lighting.

■ St. Ambrose University
Davenport, IA

Compiled by: Dr. Corinne Johnson, Chair of Department

Degrees Offered:

Theatre

Minors Offered:

Theatre

Population of Department(s): 30 majors, 15 minors

Audition to Declare a Theatre/Musical Theatre Major? No

Three things you would like our readers to know about your performing arts department:

1. Our alumni are working in the field professionally in all aspects of theatre production and performance.
2. We annually perform to more than 9,000 audience members.
3. We have a 50-seat studio theatre that is student run and a 1,200-seat proscenium arch mainstage that houses our fully produced mainstage season.

■ University of Iowa
Theatre Arts Department
Iowa City, IA

Compiled by: Alan MacVey, Director, Division of Performing Arts, and Chair, Theatre Arts Department

Degrees Offered:

BA in theatre arts
Double BA in theatre/music or theatre/dance

Minors Offered:

Theatre Arts

Population of Department(s): About 200 undergrad majors; about 50 grad students (MFA); about 50 minors; about 500 non-majors taking classes each semester

Audition to Declare a Theatre/Musical Theatre Major? No audition for theatre arts major; audition required in music and dance for the double major.

Three things you would like our readers to know about your performing arts department:

1. We offer dozens of courses in every area of theatre, in the context of a liberal arts education, and produce 25 plays a year.

2. We have an outstanding facility with three theatres, classrooms, and shops, all situated beautifully on the Iowa River.

3. Each year more than 20 guest artists join our outstanding faculty to lead courses, workshops, and productions.

■ Waldorf College
Forest City, IA

Compiled by: Dr. Robert E. AuFrance, Director of Theatre/Director of Fine Arts Administration

Degrees Offered:

BA in theatre performance (acting/directing)
BA in playwriting
BA in musical theatre
BA in technical theatre

Minors Offered:

Theatre (performance and technical)
Shakespeare (in collaboration with the English and history departments)

Population of Department(s): 40 total (15 majors, 10 minors, and 15 on additional scholarships to the program)

Audition to Declare a Theatre/Musical Theatre Major? Yes or an interview

Three things you would like our readers to know about your performing arts department:

1. The Waldorf College Theatre Department has generous scholarships for both majors and non-majors interested in studying and participating in theatre.

2. Auditioning and the casting of shows are an open process, meaning that students can be cast regardless of ethnicity or whether the student is a major or not, and class status (year—freshman, sophomore, etc.) is not a determining factor in casting.

3. The Waldorf College Theatre Department prides itself on focusing upon the student and his or her interest(s). Thus, the major intentionally keeps the program to a manageable size so that each student may receive personalized attention.

Kansas

■ Wichita State University
Wichita, KS

Compiled by: Bret Jones, Program Director of Theatre

Population of School: Approximately 15,000

Conservatory or Liberal Arts: Liberal arts

Degrees Offered:

BFA in theatre performance and technical theatre/design
BA/BS/BM in theatre

Population of Department(s): Approximately 60

Theatre Scholarships Available: Yes, many with varied qualifications

Audition Required for BFA: Yes

Audition Required for BA/BS/BM: No, nothing required

Pre-screen Video Audition Required: No

Attends Unifieds: No

Number of Students Auditioning Each Year: 8–12

Number of Students Accepted Each Year: 8–12

Cut Program or Audition to Remain in Program: No

Minors in Musical Theatre/Acting: No

Prominent Alumni: Sai Baig Powers (BA theatre, 2008)—stage manager for Cookie Company at Phoenix Theatre in Phoenix, AZ; box office associate at Phoenix Theatre, Phoenix, AZ; Stephen Barker (BFA musical theatre, 2008)—performer evolution/creation at Quest Theatre Ensemble in Chicago; Brittany Barnes (BA theatre, 2006)—founding member and managing director of the Pavement Group in Chicago, a theatre company dedicated to fostering the next generation of theatre artists, arts managers, and audiences; Richard Baum (BFA musical theatre, 2008)—performer in *Noah the Musical* in Branson, MO; Jen Bechter (BFA musical theatre, 2006)—performer in national tour (2010) of *Beauty and the Beast* (Madame Grande Bouche), prior international tour of *Cinderella* (ugly stepsister) with Lea Salogna.

What do you look for in a potential student?

The ability to be natural, realistic, and not forced in the performance audition.

What are some of the auditors' pet peeves?

Performing funny voices or faces believing that is acting. Performing "outrageous" material believing that showcases good acting.

What are your audition requirements?

Two one-minute contrasting monologues.

In your eyes, what makes up an excellent college audition monologue? Song?

A simple piece with urgency, directed at another person, without any melodramatics believing it shows good acting.

If there were one monologue you never wanted to see again, what would it be?

The Boys Next Door.

Can you walk me through what I can expect at your on-campus auditions?

An interview with the program director, a possible tour, and an audition.

What's a memorable audition you can remember?

It's negative, but a student performed a monologue from The Boys Next Door with the worst "acting" voice I have ever heard.

What is your biggest piece of advice for potential students auditioning?

Don't think you have to have melodramatic material or curse words strung throughout to make an impression. In fact, it does the opposite. Be truthful, not forced—no acting, please!

If I audition for your BFA musical theatre program, but don't get accepted, do you still consider me for your BFA acting program or your BA program? Or does each program require its own audition if I'd like to be considered for both?

Each program requires its own audition.

After I audition, is there a good way to follow up?

By email.

Would I get a showcase at the end of senior year?

A senior jury.

Where are showcases held, and are they successful?

They are juries, and they showcase the student's four years of work.

Will I be able to audition/perform as a freshman?

Yes.

What ways can I be involved with the department aside from performing?

Technical work, writing, promotions.

Say I get a BA rather than a BFA. Will I actually get to perform?

Yes.

I love to sing, but I don't consider myself a dancer. Can I still seek a degree in musical theatre at your school?

You can, but we look for strength in all three, if possible.

I want to get a BFA in acting, but I also love to sing. Can BFA/BA acting students take voice lessons with top voice faculty?

Yes.

Do you discourage or encourage students to audition for theatre outside of the department during the academic year?

We encourage commitment to the university first. We have an off-campus performance agreement.

Does your school regularly work in conjunction with any regional theatres?

No.

What do students typically do during the summers? Do you actively promote participation in summer theatre auditions?

They pursue summer theatre work. Yes, we encourage summer auditions.

How many musicals versus straight plays do you do in a season?

Two musicals and four straight plays.

What is the portfolio/interview process for a technical theatre student?

Faculty take a look at portfolios and the quality of the work—designs, stage manager books, and so on.

What do you expect to see on a technical theatre résumé?

Working on crews, some basic designing, consistent work.

I'm interested in lighting, sound design, and stage management. What major should I go for? Can I minor?

The BFA in technical theatre/design. You can minor if you wish.

Anything else I should know?

Our mission is to teach students to be active participants in the profession. Our shows are considered to be lab space for that mission.

■ Baker University

Baldwin City, KS

Compiled by: Tom Heiman, Associate Chair, Department of Music and Theatre

Degrees Offered:

Theatre
Theatre with a musical theatre emphasis
Theatre education
Music
Music education

Minors Offered:

Theatre
Music

Population of Department(s): 18

Audition to Declare a Theatre/Musical Theatre Major? No

Three things you would like our readers to know about your performing arts department:

1. We offer individualized training. We are small enough to give you stage time even as a freshman and strong enough to find your weaknesses and work on them. From freshman year to senior year, you will be given opportunities and challenges.

2. Our graduates are working, both onstage and backstage, from Chicago to Las Vegas to Argentina.

3. We are a small college in a small town just 15 minutes from Lawrence and 45 minutes from downtown Kansas City. This means lots of opportunity in a small-town setting.

Kentucky

■ Campbellsville University
Campbellsville, KY

Compiled by: Starr Garrett, Theatre Director

Degrees Offered:

Theatre, emphasis in performance or production

Minors Offered:

Theatre

Population of Department(s): 22

Audition to Declare a Theatre/Musical Theatre Major? No

Three things you would like our readers to know about your performing arts department:

1. Our department is centered around a tight-knit, family-like atmosphere, which allows us to tailor the educational experience to the individual student.
2. We seek to expose our students to a wide variety of theatre styles, through mainstage and student productions and field trips.
3. Whether studying performance or production, emphasis is placed on preparing students for employment opportunities.

■ Centre College
Danville, KY

Compiled by: Matthew R. Hallock, Chair of the Dramatic Arts Program

Degrees Offered:

BA in dramatic arts

Minors Offered:

Dramatic arts

Population of Department(s): 35

Audition to Declare a Theatre/Musical Theatre Major? No

Three things you would like our readers to know about your performing arts department:

1. Centre is a small, private liberal arts program dedicated to the idea that our graduates will be able to work at a high level with text, with the actor, and with theatrical space. This, we feel, provides them with a strong foundation to move forward with further study as grad students, apprentices, and interns as they continue to pursue their goals in the theatre.

2. Our small size allows us to provide an intensely personal education. We enter into a four-year negotiation with our students about their goals, their skills, their desires, and the best strategies to achieve them.

3. In addition to our liberal arts approach, we provide our students with professional experiences both on campus, in the college's Norton Center for the Arts (a roadhouse that presents world-class artists, such as Yo-Yo Ma and The Vienna Philharmonic, and Broadway tours of shows, such as *Hair, Ragtime,* and *Rent*), and by connecting them with internships and apprenticeships with leading summer theatres throughout the country (O'Niell Theatre Center, Hangar Theatre, Williamstown Theatre Festival, and so on).

■ Morehead State University
Morehead, KY

Compiled by: Donald R. Grant Chair, Music, Theatre and Dance; Denise Vulhop Watkins, Associate Professor of Theatre

Degrees Offered:

Theatre
Theatre teaching

Minors Offered:

Theatre
Dance

Population of Department(s): Approximately 70 students

Audition to Declare a Theatre/Musical Theatre Major? No

Three things you would like our readers to know about your performing arts department:

1. Tony Award–winning actor Steve Kazee is one of our alumni (2012 Tony for Leading Actor in a Musical for his performance as Guy in the musical *Once*).

2. Students have immediate opportunities to work on productions (musical, contemporary, classic, and dance) in various aspects of theatre, onstage and backstage. One does not have to wait until he or she is an upperclassman or compete with grad students for acting or design opportunities.

3. We offer individualized attention from energetic theatre professors in small class sizes.

■ University of Kentucky

Department of Theatre
Lexington, KY

Compiled by: Nancy C. Jones, Chair

Degrees Offered:

BA in theatre

Minors Offered:

Dance

Theatre

Musical theatre certificate

Population of Department(s): 80 majors, 80 minors

Audition to Declare a Theatre/Musical Theatre Major? Audition for musical theatre certificate in April

Three things you would like our readers to know about your performing arts department:

1. On-stage casting opportunities your first semester.
2. Strong ties to the profession with guest artists and professional networking excursions.
3. One-on-one mentorship with faculty.

■ University of Louisville

Louisville, KY

Compiled by: Dr. Rinda Frye, chairperson

Degrees Offered:

One undergrad major, which can be either a generalist degree or can emphasize either performance or production

MFA in performance

Graduate certificate in African American theatre

Minors Offered:

Theatre arts

African American theatre

Population of Department(s): 65 undergrad majors and minors, 12 grad students in the MFA program

Audition to Declare a Theatre/Musical Theatre Major? No

Three things you would like our readers to know about your performing arts department:

1. We offer the only MFA in theatre in Kentucky. Grad students teach courses in acting and introduction to theatre. Second- and third-year MFA students may be in our Repertory Company, which tours mornings. We currently partner with Stage One Family Theatre and Equity house, and we have partnered on specific projects with Actors Theatre of Louisville.

2. We have an African American theatre program that is fully integrated into our program in terms of curriculum and production.

3. Our graduate certificate in African American theatre is the only one that we know of in the world.

Louisiana

■ Tulane University
Department of Theatre and Dance
New Orleans, LA

Compiled by: Antony Sandoval, Head of Acting

Degrees Offered:

BFA in performance

BA (performance track)

BA (generalist track)

BA (design track)

BFA in design

BFA in stage management

Minors Offered:

Theatre

Population of Department(s): 30–50

Audition to Declare a Theatre/Musical Theatre Major? Yes. Auditions for the BFA performance degree take place at the end of the second-semester freshman year. There are currently no auditions for the other majors, but interested majors much complete an advisor interview for all other BA degrees.

Three things you would like our readers to know about your performing arts department:

1. Our program offers a diverse curriculum with an inclusive methodology, including both psychological and psycho-physical approaches to acting.

2. Our faculty is made up of working theatre professionals in theatre, film, and TV, with both national and international credits.

3. Our department is committed to engaging in and contributing to the deep traditions of the performing arts culture of New Orleans and southern Louisiana.

Maryland

■ Frostburg State University
Department of Theatre and Dance
Frostburg, MD

Compiled by: Nicole Mattis, Chair of Department of Theatre and Dance

Degrees Offered:

Theatre major with three focus areas in acting, design/technology, and theatrical studies

Minors Offered:

Theatre

Dance

Population of Department(s): 60

Audition to Declare a Theatre/Musical Theatre Major? Yes. Auditions are required for entrance into the acting and design/technology tracks of the program. Auditions are held in the spring.

Three things you would like our readers to know about your performing arts department:

1. Housed in a beautiful state-of-the art performance facility, students participate in real-life collaborative experiences during our production season and have opportunities to take on major leadership roles prior to graduation in performance, stage management, and design (costumes, lighting, scenic, sound, properties). We also have student positions for master carpenter, scenic charge artist, and master electrician. Students run two theatre-based student groups: C.A.S.T. is a service organization for theatre, and the Savage Mountain Stage Combat Club trains weekly in the art and safety of stage combat. Students have opportunities to receive certifications through the Society of American Fight Directors (SAFD).

2. Class sizes are small, allowing for one-on-one mentorship with faculty. The average performance class holds 12 students (85% of classes at FSU have 30 students or fewer). The theatre program offers a series of developmental classes focused on preparing résumés, headshots, portfolios, and websites for professional pursuits.

3. Faculty members continue to engage in professional activities as actors, directors, and designers. The department has a Certified Teacher with the SAFD, who is also a theatrical firearms instructor, as well as a Certified Associate Teacher of Fitzmaurice Voicework. Faculty members work with students to prepare them for summer jobs and internships, as well as jobs following graduation.

■ McDaniel College
Westminster, MD

Compiled by: Elizabeth van den Berg, Associate Professor, Chair, Theatre Arts Department

Degrees Offered:

Theatre arts
Music/theatre arts (dual major)
Cinema/theatre arts (dual major)
English/theatre arts (dual major)

Minors Offered:

Theatre arts
Acting
Interactive theatre

Population of Department(s): 30 majors, 20 minors

Audition to Declare a Theatre/Musical Theatre Major? No

Three things you would like our readers to know about your performing arts department:

1. Theatre is a reflection of life, and thus we believe that in order to be well-rounded artists, we must understand the world around us. McDaniel College's Theatre Arts Department focuses on teaching the student in a holistic fashion, so majors are required to take at least one course in every area of emphasis, as well as meeting liberal arts requirements across curriculum.

2. We put on four fully produced productions a year, one of which is a musical. Our 2013–2014 season includes *Pygmalion* by George Bernard Shaw, *Playback* improvised by the company, a student-directed production of *Fat Pig* by Neil LaBute, and *The 25th Annual Putnam County Spelling Bee* by Rebecca Feldman with music and lyrics by William Finn, book by Rachel Sheinkin, and additional material by Jay Reiss.

3. Students who focus in interactive theatre have gone on to careers in drama therapy, psychology, social work, and teaching. Those focused in acting and directing have careers on stage, in film, and in television. Our design and tech students are working professionals in their chosen field. We're proud of our graduates!

■ Washington College

Chestertown, MD

Compiled by: Dr. Michele Volansky, Chair, Department of Drama

Degrees Offered:

BA in drama

Minors Offered:

Drama

Population of Department(s): 40–50 majors plus another 50 or so involved

Audition to Declare a Theatre/Musical Theatre Major? No

Three things you would like our readers to know about your performing arts department:

1. Our production calendar is driven by student work.
2. We are a drama department placed squarely in the liberal arts—you can't represent life on stage unless you know all about it.
3. We are a family that supports and challenges each other, on and off stage.

Massachusetts

■ Boston University
Boston, MA

Compiled By: Paolo S. Difabio, Former Assistant Director

Population of School: Approximately 300 (180 in performance, 120 in design and production, 265 BFAs, 45 MFAs)

Conservatory or Liberal Arts: New conservatory (see additional notes at end)

Degrees Offered:

BFA in acting, design, production, theatre arts, stage management
MFA in design, directing, production, theatre education

Population of Department(s): Approximately 170 students in BFA performance (acting and theatre arts); approximately 80 students in BFA design, production, stage management; approximately 30 MFA students

Theatre Scholarships Available: "Performance Awards" of approximately $5,000–$7,500 offered annually to 10–15 incoming freshmen in all BFA programs (based on artistic review and financial need). For most MFA programs, tuition is either partially or fully funded.

Audition Required for BFA: Yes

Pre-screen Video Audition Required: No

Attends Unifieds: Yes

Location of Unifieds: New York City, Chicago, Los Angeles, Atlanta

Number of Students Auditioning Each Year: 700–800

Number of Students Accepted Each Year: 90–110

Cut Program or Audition to Remain in Program: No

Minors in Musical Theatre/Acting: Non-College of Fine Arts students can minor in theatre (it is a 28-credit course/credit sequence with *no* audition required). There is no minor or major in musical theatre.

Prominent Alumni: Our program prides itself in the fact that all of our alumni are valued, prominent, and celebrated leaders in the arts, education, social and political reform, media, law, entertainment, and of course professional theatre. Our program continues to take pride in a long tradition of storytellers who have an impact on the art and the world.

What do you look for in a potential student?

Cognitive understanding of the text and material; an emotional awareness of the character, the scene, and circumstances; a physical availability necessary to fully engaging the storytelling. We are also looking for students who demonstrate a strong generosity of spirit and a willingness to take directions, make choices, and be unafraid of risks.

What are some of the auditors' pet peeves?

Students who aren't willing to engage in a conversation about themselves.

What are your audition requirements?

Two two-minute contrasting modern monologues:

Modern/contemporary period: theatrical, non-film, 1880 to present.

Classical substitution: If a student wishes, he or she may choose to substitute one of the modern pieces for a classical text. If so, the monologue should be in verse, and preferably Shakespearean. See suggestions below.

- Students are asked to bring a picture and résumé with them to the audition. No additional material is required unless a student wishes to present a portfolio of work representing additional interests in theatre; for example, if a student has written a script and has a writing sample or if a student has a portfolio of directing or design work.

- Auditions are conducted in a workshop style, meaning faculty members reserve the right to ask questions about or give direction to the student for one or both monologues. Such workshop interaction may or may not happen, and it is not guaranteed for all auditions. Students should not view working or not working with faculty during the audition as judgment on the quality of the work itself; for some auditions, time simply does not allow for such a workshop approach.

- A brief interview will follow the audition, providing the faculty member with an opportunity to get to know each student in his or her own words. In total, each audition/interview can take 8–15 minutes.

In your eyes, what makes up an excellent college audition monologue? Song?

Our program does not ask for a song, but in terms of a monologue, when students show a strong cognitive sense of what they are saying and the circumstance of the text. When the work is emotionally aware of the subtleties within the relationship to the target of their speech. And finally, when the performance has become physically available and the entire body is engaged in storytelling.

If there were one monologue you never wanted to see again, what would it be?

Viola, *Twelfth Night*… Never. Ever. Ever… Again.

Can you walk me through what I can expect at your on-campus auditions?

(Note: Times will vary based on city of audition.)

9 a.m.: Check-in, welcome, and information sessions/Q&A.

10 a.m.: Auditions begin. The audition order is initially determined by the order in which applicants reserve appointments online. However, the faculty will work around each student's schedule to make any necessary accommodations for travel or other auditions scheduled for the same day. Students should anticipate "workshop-style" auditions in which the faculty may actively engage them in the work as they might do in a classroom setting.

What's a memorable audition you can remember?

The ones where students picked materials to their strengths, made bold choices, and presented an artistic generosity both in their work and in their willingness to work, which made us want to spend more and more time with them in the audition.

What is your biggest piece of advice for potential students auditioning?

Be yourself, be daring, take risks, choose work that demonstrates your strengths, be willing to fail, and always remain open to the idea of possibilities.

After I audition, is there a good way to follow up?

Students are always welcome to email the faculty for whom they auditioned and follow-up with any questions at all about the program.

Would I get a showcase at the end of senior year?

Yes, in New York City as part of our InCite Arts Festival (www.bu.edu/cfa/incite).

Do I have to audition to be accepted into the showcase?

No. Our senior showcase is an optional student-selected event (both in performance and in design and production. However, students who are in poor academic standing and have been repeatedly contacted by the faculty to improve their standing, but fail to do so, will be denied their option to attend showcase.

Where are showcases held, and are they successful?

Showcases are held at New World Stages on 51st between 8th and 9th. Yes, we continue to see a very successful senior showcase.

Will I be able to audition/perform as a freshman?

No. Because of the rigorous academic workload in our freshman performance core (a seven-course sequence of classes), the average academic workload for our freshmen is about 35–45 hours. We rehearse Tuesday through Friday nights (7 p.m. until 11 p.m.) and on Saturdays (10 a.m. until 6 p.m.), so when students are eligible for casting (starting in the fourth semester), the average workweek is about 75–85 hours. For this reason (in addition to other curricular reasons), students are not eligible for casting in the first three semesters.

If there is a graduate program, will I get the same performance opportunities as an undergraduate?

The MFA programs are very, very small (we only have about five to six grad students in directing and theatre education combined in any given semester); this limited population does not hold great impact on our casting. Additionally, the school has a "guaranteed casting policy," meaning that all undergrads eligible for casting will be cast, even if the school must add shows to its season to meet the needs of a given casting pool.

In what ways can I be involved with the department aside from performing?

The school does offer work-study positions in its office for students who are eligible and awarded such grants as part of their financial aid package.

Say I get a BA rather than a BFA. Will I actually get to perform?

We do not offer a BA program. However, if a student were a theatre minor, then he or she could audition and be considered for casting as part of the School of Theatre production season. However, unlike the BFA majors, theatre minors are not "guaranteed" casting.

I want to get a BFA in acting, but I also love to sing. Can BFA/BA acting students take voice lessons with top voice faculty?

We do offer a four-semester progression of courses in singing for the actor and musical theatre performance. We feel strongly that the approach to performance in songs is the same as it is for monologues and scenes—students must still ask fundamental questions of character, intent, obstacle, and, most important, action.

Do you discourage or encourage students to audition for theatre outside of the department during the academic year?

If students wish to pursue an opportunity with a professional company or film outside of their schoolwork, they must receive faculty approval for time away from classes. This is not done to be difficult or prevent a student from pursuing a valuable opportunity; instead, the faculty wants to ascertain if the opportunity is worth the time missed outside of studio classes. We feel strongly that our students' first commitment is to their college training and experience. If an opportunity will take too much time away from classes, a student should consider a leave of absence in order to commit the necessary time to the outside project. Students taking a leave of absence will be automatically granted return to the program within the first two years from the time they left BU. Returning after two years may require re-auditioning and re-application to the program.

Does your school regularly work in conjunction with any regional theatres?

The School of Theatre has a long tradition of embracing the value of the professional theatre's participation in the education of our students. We have now arrived at a landmark number of professional theatre ventures that embrace the possibilities of building strong bridges between the study and practice of the theatre arts. For more information (including a complete list of our Professional Theatre Initiative affiliates), please visit www.bu.edu/cfa/theatre/professional.

What do students typically do during the summers? Do you actively promote participation in summer theatre auditions?

Summer months can span from internships or apprenticeships with one of our Professional Theatre Initiative affiliates throughout the country, to working with our Boston University Summer Theatre Institute for high school students, to taking liberal arts elective courses toward BFA degree requirements either in Boston or back home, to just taking a summer away from theatre to recharge (in mind, body, spirit, and sometimes wallet).

How many musicals versus straight plays do you do in a season?

Our season (which is broken down into four quarters—fall is Q1 and Q2, spring is Q3 and Q4) is dictated by our directors (faculty, guest artists, grad students, and advanced undergrads in the theatre arts program who have studied directing). If no one is proposing a musical, we will not force one upon the season. Generally, we do about one to two each year, but a number of our productions are plays with music in them (hardly musicals). Because of the guaranteed casting policy and the number of Professional Theatre Initiative casting opportunities that we include, the BU School of Theatre can do anywhere from 25–40 shows each year.

What are some of your alumni up to? Do you have an active alumni network?

We have a very active, professional, and connected alumni network. We are firm believers in the fact that going to BU is more than just a four-year experience. We could run down a list of famous alumni whose names are highly recognizable, but that's not our style. We believe that any alumni actively pursuing artistic opportunities are "working" alumni. And we are just as proud of those alumni who go on to pursue careers outside of theatre as well!

What is the portfolio/interview process for a technical theatre student?

Prior to the portfolio review, each applicant must submit an electronic portfolio, including a résumé and a photograph. Applicants may upload 28 images, in addition to their résumé and photograph, to the school's portfolio submission website. JPEG format is preferred for all work.

Applicants should edit their portfolios so they can discuss each entry and move through the entire collection within 10 minutes. Faculty discussion of the work will likely extend the interview by an additional 10 minutes. Applicants should include a variety of materials. Often, a preliminary quick-study says the most about an artist's intention and native talent. Applicants should expect the interview to be friendly and informative. For an in-person interview, the applicant should provide a hard-copy portfolio containing the same or different images from the online portfolio. The applicant retains the portfolio at the conclusion of the interview.

Design and production portfolios should demonstrate the broadest range of theatrical and artistic expression. Anything that suggests the applicant's ability to communicate using the tools of the visual artist can be included, such as actual theatre renderings, related painting or graphics, working drawings, ground plans, lighting plots, props, masks, photography, and photographs of sculpture, murals, or other non-transportable works.

Stage management portfolios may contain prompt books, programs, director's notes, and examples of creative writing. The interview provides the primary basis for evaluating applicants for the stage management program. Applicants should come prepared to discuss their activities in the theatre.

What do you expect to see on a technical theatre résumé?

More than the quantity of production involvement, the substance and growth of a student's artistic journey is vital. With students in technical theatre opportunities for design/production, leadership can be limited; however, if a student shows significant resourceful development of his or her artistry when chances arose, that will make for a powerful résumé. We also greatly value the exchange of the interview itself, whether in person or via Skype.

Anything else I should know?

The School of Theatre is an energetic place that vales the notion of "the new conservatory." From inside that idea, several core School of Theatre values emerge:

We believe in the artistic possibilities of collaboration that involve faculty, students, alumni, and guest artists in potent explorations of the art form that encourage working together as the best means of achieving artistic growth.

We believe that artists must be provided with a rigorous curriculum that allows mastery of their skill in their particular areas of interest.

We believe that every member of our community is a part of the artistic home that we create together. In that home, we nurture an appreciation of challenge, a conviction for the value of everyone's potential, and a belief in the need for intellectual growth as a core part of developing artistic growth.

We believe that the school can serve the profession by interacting with it and providing a laboratory for the development of new work or new approaches to existing work. Like our colleagues in the sciences, the role of the arts in a university that prizes its excellence as a research institution is no less able to be on the forefront of exploring new possibilities for theatre.

■ Emerson College
Boston, MA

Compiled by: Eric Weiss, Performing Arts Admission Coordinator

Population of School: 3,400 undergrads, 800 grad students

Conservatory or Liberal Arts: A hybrid, "the nation's premiere institution in higher education devoted to communication and the arts in a liberal arts context"

Degrees Offered:

BFA in acting

BFA in musical theatre

BFA in design/technology

BFA in stage and production management

BA in theatre studies (available with concentration in acting)

BA in theatre education (available with concentration in acting)

MA in theatre education

Population of Department(s): Approximately 500 undergrads, approximately 75 grad students

Theatre Scholarships Available: Emerson Stage Awards are given to students accepted to performing arts and are determined by artistic merit. For students entering the college in 2014, the amount of the Emerson Stage Awards was $14,000 annually.

Audition Required for BFA: Yes. A portfolio/interview is required of BFA design technology and stage and production management.

Audition Required for BA/BS/BM: Yes. BA theatre studies and BA theatre education (without the acting concentration) require an additional essay.

Pre-screen Video Audition Required: No

Attends Unifieds: Yes

Location of Unifieds: New York, Chicago, and Los Angeles; regional sites include New Orleans, Atlanta, Houston, and perhaps Miami

Number of Students Auditioning Each Year: BFA acting, approximately 450 auditions; BFA musical theatre, approximately 850 auditions; BA theatre studies and education (combined), approximately 375 auditions

Number of Students Accepted Each Year: BFA acting, 35–40 acceptances, approximately 18 freshmen; BFA musical theatre, approximately 35–40 acceptances, approximately 18 freshmen; BA theatre studies and education, approximately 90 acceptances, approximately 45 freshmen

Cut Program or Audition to Remain in Program: No. Performing arts has moved from a re-audition process requiring 16 students maximum in BFA acting and BFA musical theatre to a probationary system based on conduct, grades, and juries.

Minors in Musical Theatre/Acting: No, but you can minor in dance, performance studies, or music appreciation.

Prominent Alumni: Denis Leary, Henry Winkler, George Watsky, Julie Mattison

What do you look for in a potential student?

Someone who is grounded, passionate, creative, and self-motivated and has potential, a strong work ethic, an interest in collaboration, and a willingness to learn.

What are some of the auditors' pet peeves?

Lack of preparation.

What are your audition requirements?

For BFA and BA acting, please prepare two two- to three-minute contrasting monologues from two contemporary plays. Choose pieces that are important to you; we are looking for honesty and a strong commitment to what you are doing. For BFA musical theatre, please prepare two two- to three-minute contrasting monologues from two contemporary plays, one of which must be comedic. You may not be required to perform both monologues, but be prepared to do so. Choose pieces that are important to you; we are looking for honesty and a strong commitment to what you are doing. For songs, please prepare 32 bars each from two contrasting musical theatre songs of your choice. You may not be required to sing both selections, but be prepared to do so. For the dance portion of the audition, come prepared to perform in a classroom setting and bring practical clothes, including one of the following types of footwear: jazz shoes, jazz sneakers, character shoes, or any lightweight sneakers suitable for dancing.

In your eyes, what makes up an excellent college audition monologue? Song?

When you see the person through what he or she has chosen to do.

If there were one monologue you never wanted to see again, what would it be?

We don't have any and would never want to preclude ourselves from the possibility that someone would bring something new to a well-worn piece.

If there were one song you never wanted to hear again, what would it be?

See above.

Can you walk me through what I can expect at your on-campus auditions?

Sure! We run all of our auditions professionally and warmly because we accept the reality that an applicant is interviewing us just as much as we are auditioning the applicant. We start every audition with a group discussion of our programs. Within their time slot (two hours for all acting majors, four hours for all MT) applicants volunteer when they are ready to audition.

What's a memorable audition you can remember?

We've seen so many it is hard to say, but there is no replacing honesty, simplicity, and connection. It is always a joy to watch an actor make a discovery.

What is your biggest piece of advice for potential students auditioning?

Be yourself; allow us to see who you are through the choice and execution of your material. Breathe.

If I audition for your BFA musical theatre program, but don't get accepted, do you still consider me for your BFA acting program or your BA program?

We consider all performance applicants flexibly for other performance majors automatically. It might be helpful to let your evaluator know that you are interested in other programs as well.

After I audition, is there a good way to follow up?

It's not necessary.

Would I get a showcase at the end of senior year?

We offer showcases for BFA acting and BFA musical theatre, and a portfolio showcase for BFA design/technology. Other majors offer differing types of professional development.

Do I have to audition to be accepted into the showcase?

No.

Where are showcases held, and are they successful?

Showcases are held in New York City in fall and Boston in spring. Yes, they are successful.

Will I be able to audition/perform as a freshman?

Freshmen do not perform in mainstage (Emerson Stage) productions but are allowed to participate in incredibly productive student organizations, student films, classroom projects for directing classes, and so on.

If there is a graduate program, will I get the same performance opportunities as an undergraduate?

Although our grad students participate in Emerson Stage and can audition for productions, the grad program is an MA in theatre education, not a performance training program, so there is typically not competition between grad students and undergrads.

In what ways can I be involved with the department aside from performing?

Students do the bulk of the practical work for Emerson Stage productions—performing, designing, stage managing, technical work, run crews, dramaturgy, and so on. Outside of Emerson Stage, there is an extremely active student life with many opportunities to explore your interests, such as Musical Theatre Society, Shakespeare Society, various comedy troupes, the Evvys, directing projects connected to classes, student films, and so on.

Say I get a BA rather than a BFA. Will I actually get to perform?

Yes! Casting for Emerson Stage shows is blind to major within performing arts.

I love to sing, but I don't consider myself a dancer. Can I still seek a degree in musical theatre at your school?

Yes, we'll train you.

I want to get a BFA in acting, but I also love to sing. Can BFA/BA acting students take voice lessons with top voice faculty?

Yes, private voice is required for musical theatre majors and available to the entire college regardless of major, with the same restrictions of adding any elective class (the instructor has the space in his or her schedule, it fits in the student's schedule, and so on).

Do you discourage or encourage students to audition for theatre outside of the department during the academic year?

With permission from their faculty advisors, students are encouraged to be productive on and off campus but to be responsible with their time so as not to hinder their studies.

Does your school regularly work in conjunction with any regional theatres?

Yes, ArtsEmerson, although it is not a regional theatre. It is not uncommon for regional theatres to contact us with opportunities for our students.

What do students typically do during the summers? Do you actively promote participation in summer theatre auditions?

We encourage and prepare our students to be productive during the summer, whether it be working in the theatre or seeking internships or other opportunities.

How many musicals versus straight plays do you do in a season?

Emerson Stage typically produces two musicals, one Theatre for Young Audiences piece, one evening of student-choreographed dance, one original student-written work culled from a playwriting competition, and three straight plays that round out the yearly eight-production season. Some of our more established student organizations also produce eight productions a season. There is a lot of variety!

What are some of your alumni up to? Do you have an active alumni network?

Our alumni are working in every aspect of film, TV, and theatre, from Hollywood to Broadway and everything in between. They are teachers, designers, directors, producers, technicians, actors, solo performers, performance artists, playwrights, stage managers, and on and on and on. They work in our industry; and they find and forge the connections between our industry and others. They go on to grad school. They start their own companies. They create their own work. They are active, productive, and engaged.

What is the portfolio/interview process for a technical theatre student?

Students wishing to major in design technology or stage and production management will interview with faculty who will discuss their portfolio and résumé with them.

What do you expect to see on a technical theatre résumé?

We expect to see evidence of experience in theatre and an interest in art.

I'm interested in lighting, sound design, and stage management. What major should I go for? Can I minor?

We do not offer minors in theatre. We offer a lighting concentration within design technology and courses in sound design. We offer a degree in stage and production management.

Anything else I should know?

Emerson College is a unique place. It resides comfortably between a liberal arts college and a conservatory. Students here find the connections between their academic classes and the intense focus of their major, connecting ideas and professions in creative ways. Our performing arts students build their lives in the theatre and use the arts as an orienting principle for viewing everything that they do.

It is an incredibly exciting and productive environment. With Emerson Stage, ArtsEmerson, and dozens of highly organized student organizations, there is an overabundance of opportunity to see and do and create. And all of this is framed in a world-class city with a blooming theatre community.

Our campus boasts five mainstage theatres—the brand new Paramount Center, housing the Paramount Theatre and the Paramount Black Box; the 10-year-old Tufte Performance and Production Center, housing the Semel and Greene theatres; and the completely restored Majestic Theatre. However, these spaces are not the strength of the school—the strength of the school is the people. From our industry professional faculty and staff to our passionate students, our training and community foster the growth of professional, industry-leading artists.

■ Amherst College
Amherst, MA

Compiled by: Peter Lobdell, Chair, Department of Theater and Dance

Degrees Offered:

BA in theater

BA in dance

Audition to Declare a Theatre/Musical Theatre Major? No

Three things you would like our readers to know about your performing arts department:

1. It is not a conservatory program.

2. It is part of a liberal arts curriculum.

3. Senior majors create the entire season of performances.

■ Fitchburg State University
Fitchburg, MA

Compiled by: Kelly Morgan, Coordinator of Theater

Degrees Offered:

Theater concentration

Minors Offered:

Theater

Music

Population of Department(s): 70

Audition to Declare a Theatre/Musical Theatre Major? No audition is required. Students are admitted to the university. After successfully completing three courses in the department, they are admitted into the professional program and must maintain a 2.5 GPA in the major in order to perform on the mainstage. Each semester they are evaluated and informed if they should continue in the program.

Three things you would like our readers to know about your performing arts department:

1. All faculty members continue to work professionally as union artists to maintain currency in their field.

2. Our students work on stage and in films for a more viable career path and opportunities.

3. We require a semester of professional internship credit to meet graduation requirements.

■ Regis College
Weston, MA

Compiled by: Dr. Frans Rijnbout, Chair of Department of Art, Music and Theatre

Degrees Offered:

Interdisciplinary arts major with concentrations in visual art, theatre, music, dance, art history, and art administration

Minors Offered:

Visual art

Theatre

Music

Dance

Art history

Population of Department(s): 20

Audition to Declare a Theatre/Musical Theatre Major? No

Three things you would like our readers to know about your performing arts department:

1. We are a small department with personal mentoring. All students will have a chance to perform onstage.
2. Per academic year, we have two mainstage productions by professional directors, plus two productions (often student-written plays) directed by student directors.
3. We offer a 10-day intensive theatre course that takes place in London, England.

■ Salem State University
Salem, MA

Compiled by: Bill Cunningham, Chairperson, Theatre and Speech Communication Department

Degrees Offered:

Theatre
BA in performance or technical theatre
BFA in performance or technical theatre
BFA in theatre design or stage management

Minors Offered:

Theatre
Speech communication

Population of Department(s): Approximately 160 majors

Audition to Declare a Theatre/Musical Theatre Major? There is no audition for entry into the BA program; however, there is an audition/portfolio review and interview for entry in to the BFA performance and BFA design/technical theatre programs.

Three things you would like our readers to know about your performing arts department:

1. Salem State University is an accredited member of the NAST and meets the national standards that are required by NAST in our teaching curriculum and theatre productions.
2. We are a "hands-on" theatre program providing each student with personal interaction with our professionally trained faculty and staff. You will have two degree programs from which to choose: BA or BFA. These programs offer concentrations or options in performance, design, technical theatre, stage management, or secondary education and attract competitive and committed students. Our graduates place exceptionally well in grad schools, conservatories, regional theatres, and the professional world.
3. Salem State Theatre has won numerous national and regional awards with our involvement in the KCACTF. Over the last seven years, a Salem State Theatre student has had his or her work on the stage of the Kennedy Center (three actors, four directors, and one stage manager).

■ Smith College
Northampton, MA

Compiled by: Daniel Elihu Kramer, Chair of Theatre Department

Degrees Offered:

BA in theatre (can be general or with a focus in acting, directing, design, or playwriting)

Minors Offered:

Theatre

Population of Department(s): 30 (junior and senior majors)

Audition to Declare a Theatre/Musical Theatre Major? No

Three things you would like our readers to know about your performing arts department:

1. We value intelligent, passionate students with broad interests in theatre and in the world around them.

2. We work to help women of outstanding promise become leaders among the next generation of theatre artists.

3. Students have opportunities to work with our outstanding faculty of artists and scholars and with guest artists of distinction and to take leadership roles at every level of production.

■ Wellesley College
Wellesley, MA

Compiled by: Nora Hussey, Director of Theatre and Theatre Studies Program

Degrees Offered:

Theatre with emphasis on chosen discipline

Population of Department(s): 50–200 per year

Audition to Declare a Theatre/Musical Theatre Major? No

Three things you would like our readers to know about your performing arts department:

1. Individually designed majors are tailored to each specific student.

2. Professional theatre experience is available as acting, technical, and design paid interns. Often an internship leads to a staff/cast position.

3. All students are mentored by theatre professionals. All faculty are practitioners as well as instructors in their field.

■ Worcester State University
Worcester, MA

Compiled by: Adam Zahler, Chair, Visual and Performing Arts Department

Degrees Offered:

Interdisciplinary visual and performing arts: theatre concentration

Minors Offered:

Theatre

Population of Department(s): 20

Audition to Declare a Theatre/Musical Theatre Major? No

Three things you would like our readers to know about your performing arts department:

1. The Worcester State University Visual and Performing Arts (VPA) Department offers a unique, interdisciplinary, student-centered artistic education that prepares students for professional lives in the arts. Its educational spaces encompass the Fuller Theater, music practice rooms, and art studios at the Worcester Craft Center. VPA students gain in-depth knowledge of their preferred art form—art, music, or theatre—plus an understanding of what the arts have in common and how they are performed and exhibited in the real world.

2. Our theatre faculty and staff work closely with the students, bringing their academic and professional expertise to bear in an immediate way.

3. The VPA major is new and growing rapidly at a university that understands and appreciates the arts. As we grow, our students benefit from increased programming and innovative classes.

Michigan

■ University of Michigan
Ann Arbor, MI

Compiled by: Brent Wagner, Chair of the Musical Theatre Department; Priscilla Lindsay, Chair of Theatre & Drama

Population of School: About 40,000

Conservatory or Liberal Arts: A conservatory-based program within an academic institution

Degrees Offered:

BFA in musical theatre
BFA in performance with concentrations in acting and directing
BFA in design and production
BFA in interarts
BTA in theatre studies

Population of Department(s): 85 in BFA musical theatre, 175 in theatre and drama

Theatre Scholarships Available: Yes. Limited freshman scholarships in the musical theatre department. Merit funding awarded by the Department of Theatre & Drama for sophomores, juniors, and seniors.

Audition Required for BFA: Yes for BFA in musical theatre and for BFA in performance. BFA in interarts requires an audition and interview. For BFA in design and production, there is an interview and a portfolio review.

Audition Required for BA/BS/BM: Not for the BTA

Pre-screen Video Audition Required: Yes for BFA musical theatre, no for all majors in theatre and drama

Attends Unifieds: Yes

Location of Unifieds: For musical theatre, Chicago; for theatre and drama, Chicago, New York City, and Los Angeles

Number of Students Auditioning Each Year: 700 or more audition for musical theatre, 400 for theatre and drama

Number of Students Accepted Each Year: 20–22 for musical theatre, 20 for theatre and drama

Cut Program or Audition to Remain in Program: No

Minors in Musical Theatre/Acting: No minor in musical theatre; minors in African American theatre and arts administration

Prominent Alumni: Gavin Creel, Celia Keenan-Bolger, Hunter Foster, Darren Criss, James Wolk, Zachary Booth, Starkid Productions, James Earl Jones

What do you look for in a potential student?

In the musical theatre department, we look for someone who has intellectual curiosity, imagination, and recognizable talent. Someone who is prepared, confident, sincere, courteous, ambitious, and is clearly a team player. Someone who appreciates and takes pride in the artistic growth of fellow students. Someone who is comfortable physically. Someone who can communicate very specific ideas and choices in dialogue/lyrics, music, and dance. Sings the correct notes, rhythms, and words, with a clear sense of pitch, an understanding of musical line, and a healthy approach that doesn't push the voice higher than is appropriate. In addition, applicants should have music reading skills, especially at the piano. Has interests beyond the arts and a willingness to speak about those interests. Someone who is engaged in the culture of community, ranging from politics to public service, and is excited to find ways in which the arts can enrich American culture. Someone who has a passion for writing and a desire to express personal ideas and points of view. Someone who has done his or her homework about the department and the university by reading official publications and speaking with faculty, students, school officials, and graduates, rather than relying only on Internet opinions or YouTube postings. Someone who is committed to a university environment and has thought carefully about the advantages of pursuing a BFA degree at a university rather than a conservatory.

In the theatre and drama department, we look for someone who can communicate very specific choices in the spoken word and in the body. Someone who has done his or her homework about the department and the university by reading official publications and speaking with faculty, students, school officials, and graduates, rather than relying only on Internet opinions or YouTube postings. Someone who is committed to a university environment and has thought carefully about the advantages of pursuing a BFA degree at a university rather than a conservatory.

What are some of the auditors' pet peeves?

In terms of musical theatre, incorrect notes and rhythms or music that is poorly arranged for the accompanist. Applicants who try to sing too high or loudly. For monologues, ones that are not appropriate for their age and range.

For theatre and drama, we are not fond of pieces that are strictly narratives, without any chance to see the character struggle with a choice, a decision, or an obstacle.

What are your audition requirements?

For musical theatre, two songs (two 16-bar selections, to include at least one song from your video recording; one should be written before 1965), two monologues (neither may exceed 1.5 minutes), and a dance audition (emphasizing ballet technique and including a short combination from a musical).

For theatre and drama, a typed résumé with previous theatrical experience and training, a headshot, a brief personal statement. For monologues, two contrasting monologues from published plays.

In your eyes, what makes up an excellent college audition monologue? Song?

In both cases, one that is in a specific context with clear objectives and tactics.

If there were one monologue you never wanted to see again, what would it be?

I would just rather have students choose one that they can relate to and make their own. If they really just find their own way through it, it doesn't matter to us what they bring.

If you require a pre-screen video audition, what do you look for in those submissions?

(Required for musical theatre, not theatre and drama.) Exactly what we look for in the regular auditions—nothing different. In fact, we ask that students demonstrate some area of dance, since they won't be in a dance class. They can use the same material from their pre-screen video for the in-person audition.

Can you walk me through what I can expect at your on-campus auditions?

For musical theatre, a meeting will start the day with all of the parents and students. Three seniors will speak to them about the department for about 30 minutes, and faculty joins them for about another 45 minutes to talk about the faculty's perspective. We answer any questions and give an overview of the department. Then musical theatre students go to the dance audition, followed by the monologue and song audition in the afternoon. For some people, it can be a full day—it just depends on where they end up on the schedule.

For theatre and drama, a meeting will start the day with all of the parents and students. After the meeting, there is an improvisation workshop/session, followed by auditions in the afternoon. There will be an informational session in the afternoon for the parents while the students are auditioning.

What's a memorable audition you can remember?

Any audition where the student really trusts the material and trusts his or her work to focus on the scene and situation. We're always excited about that.

What is your biggest piece of advice for potential students auditioning?

Don't worry about trying to make an impression—focus on the work. Take your time. You have it within you to do good work.

If I audition for your BFA musical theatre program, but don't get accepted, do you still consider me for your BFA acting program or your BA program?

You can certainly be considered for both. Make your intentions known, and you must go through both sets of auditions. Plenty of people audition for both.

After I audition, is there a good way to follow up?

No need, but nothing wrong with it. You'll get a response generally within about a month.

Would I get a showcase at the end of senior year?

Yes, for musical theatre. No, for theatre and drama. For theatre and drama instead we have a Senior CAPSTONE weekend to showcase our students for invited representatives from agencies and casting offices. Usually a New York agent, a Los Angeles agent and manager, a Chicago agent, and a regional theatre casting director will be in attendance. They spend the entire weekend with the students.

Do I have to audition to be accepted into the showcase?

No.

Where are showcases held, and are they successful?

Showcases are held in New York City only. Yes, they are successful.

Will I be able to audition/perform as a freshman?

There are very limited opportunities for public performance for freshmen because the emphasis is on the class work. For theatre and drama, after the first semester they are required to audition for mainstage shows but not the first semester.

In what ways can I be involved with the department aside from performing?

We require backstage crew work and stage management. We have courses in producing and performing arts management. There are opportunities for students to direct, choreograph, and write. Look at the graduates we have, such as Justin Paul and Benj Pasek, who received a Tony nomination for writing the score of *A Christmas Story*. They were here in the performance program, not in the writing program—but did a lot of writing while they were here. We try to broaden the opportunities depending on interest. Something that is important to us is to allow flexibility in the curriculum, especially in the junior and senior years. That's where students have a variety of opportunities beyond acting, if that is of interest.

Say I get a BTA rather than a BFA. Will I actually get to perform?

Not necessarily. The performance opportunities are tailored for the BFAs.

I love to sing, but I don't consider myself a dancer. Can I still seek a degree in musical theatre at your school?

Absolutely. We cater to everyone.

I want to get a BFA in acting, but I also love to sing. Can BFA/BA acting students take voice lessons with top voice faculty?

Yes, they can. They have to apply for classes with grad students in the school of music.

Do you discourage or encourage students to audition for theatre outside of the department during the academic year?

Anything that is going to take them from school we would discourage. However, we encourage them to study abroad for a semester. They sometimes study in London at the Royal Academy of Dramatic Arts or the Royal Shakespeare Company. We've had numerous students study at the Moscow Art Theatre for a semester. We encourage a semester away, but we don't require it.

Does your school regularly work in conjunction with any regional theatres?

No.

What do students typically do during the summers? Do you actively promote participation in summer theatre auditions?

We don't promote it, no, but we don't discourage it. We let the students make that decision. We'll support it if that's what they want to do, but if they need to get a job and make money for the summer, we encourage that too.

How many musicals versus straight plays do you do in a season?

For the musical theatre department, we do three full musicals and one play in the musical theatre department alone, as well as many studio projects.

For theatre and drama, four or five straight plays a year. There is also an organization called Basement Arts that is a student-run group, and it puts on 7–10 shows a semester. In addition, the senior directing class produces senior thesis productions, and they are open for everyone to audition for.

What are some of your alumni up to? Do you have an active alumni network?

We often bring back graduates to teach here in the department. We have a huge network of graduates. It's really sensational. For theatre and drama, some alumni include Yuri Sardarov, currently in *Chicago Fire*; Jacqueline Toboni, who stars as Trubel in NBC's *Grimm*; Zachary Booth, who opened on Broadway in 2013 in *The Winslow Boy*; James Wolk, who was in *Mad Men* and is with Robin Williams in *The Crazy Ones*; and Margo Martindale, who is in *The Millers*.

What is the portfolio/interview process for a technical theatre student?

Interviews and portfolio reviews are held on campus four times a year.

What do you expect to see on a technical theatre résumé?

Evidence of technical and production work at high school, community theatre, or other such performance venues.

I'm interested in lighting, sound design, and stage management. What major should I go for? Can I minor?

BFA in design and production.

Anything else I should know?

This is the 30th year of the Musical Theatre Department. We're proud of our combination of a wide range of academic opportunities with the focused, carefully structured, and supervised BFA degree program.

This is theatre and drama's 99th year—the 100th anniversary will be in 2015. It's a distinguished department with many famous alums. Because we have no grad degrees, all our focus is on the success of our undergrads.

Grand Valley State
Allendale Charter Township, MI

Compiled by: Dr. Roger Ellis, Professor of Theatre

Degrees Offered:

BA in theatre
BS in theatre

Minors Offered:

Theatre

Population of Department(s): 46 majors, 35 minors

Audition to Declare a Theatre/Musical Theatre Major? No

Three things you would like our readers to know about your performing arts department:

1. Excellent placement record of our alumni across the United States.
2. Opportunity to integrate camera acting studies with theatre.
3. Michigan's oldest and largest Shakespeare festival housed in our program.

Hope College
Holland, MI

Compiled by: Daina Robins, Theatre Department Chair, Resident Director, and Professor of Theatre

Degrees Offered:

Theatre
Music
Students may declare a musical theatre composite major with collaboration between the dance, music, and theatre departments.

Minors Offered:

Theatre
Music

Population of Department(s): 70

Audition to Declare a Theatre/Musical Theatre Major? No

Three things you would like our readers to know about your performing arts department:

1. The Hope College Department of Theatre offers an academic program of recognized excellence, which develops students as practicing theatre artists and engaged audience members.
2. The Hope College Department of Theatre is an accredited member of the National Association of Schools of Theatre.
3. Distinguished Artist Awards (DAA) merit scholarships are awarded each year through an audition process.

■ Michigan State University
East Lansing, MI

Compiled by: Kirk Domer, Chair

Degrees Offered:

BFA in acting
BFA in design
BA

Minors Offered:

Theatre
Dance

Population of Department(s): 125 majors, 60 minors

Audition to Declare a Theatre/Musical Theatre Major? BFA, yes; BA, no

Three things you would like our readers to know about your performing arts department:

1. Focus on individual training.
2. Connection to guest artists.
3. Focus on media acting and design.

■ Oakland University
Rochester, MI

Compiled by: Kerro Knox 3, Program Director

Degrees Offered:

BA in theatre
BFA in musical theatre, theatre design and technology, acting (we are part of a Department of Music, Theatre and Dance, and those two programs offer several degrees)

Minors Offered:

Theatre

Population of Department(s): 120

Audition to Declare a Theatre/Musical Theatre Major? Yes

Three things you would like our readers to know about your performing arts department:

1. Strong, committed faculty.
2. On-stage opportunities for performers and designers.
3. Integration with music and dance with our multidisciplinary department.

■ University of Detroit Mercy
Detroit, MI

Compiled by: Melinda Pacha, Chair of Performing Arts and The Theatre Co.

Degrees Offered:

BA in theatre

Minors Offered:

Theatre

Population of Department(s): 15

Audition to Declare a Theatre/Musical Theatre Major? No

Three things you would like our readers to know about your performing arts department:

1. The Theatre Co. develops creative, articulate, and dynamic artists that become working professionals in many aspects of theatre.
2. Small class size ensures individual attention.
3. Working with professional actors and associate artists encourages rapid growth and development of young actors.

■ Western Michigan University
Kalamazoo, MI

Compiled by: Joan Herrington, Chair

Degrees Offered:

BFA in musical theatre
BFA in theatre performance
BFA in theatre design and technical production
BFA in stage management
BA in theatre studies

Population of Department(s): 200

Audition to Declare a Theatre/Musical Theatre Major? Yes

Three things you would like our readers to know about your performing arts department:

1. Our graduates are very successful in the industry, working on Broadway, in regional theatre, and in film and TV.
2. Low faculty–student ratio with one-on-one instruction.
3. Strong contact with industry professionals through guest artist residencies and student travel.

Minnesota

■ Bethel University
St Paul, MN

Compiled by: Meg Zauner, Chair of Theatre Arts

Degrees Offered:

BA in theatre arts (with three emphasis available: acting/directing emphasis, musical theatre emphasis, technical/design emphasis)

Minors Offered:

Theatre arts

Educational theatre

Population of Department(s): Counting both majors and minors, the department usually has 25–40 students. However, our four productions are open to any student at Bethel, so usually one-third to one-half of the students involved in productions are not majors or minors.

Audition to Declare a Theatre/Musical Theatre Major? No. However, there is an audition required for a theatre scholarship ($2,000 renewable for four years).

Three things you would like our readers to know about your performing arts department:

1. Students apply what they are learning in their classes through involvement in four shows per year, performed in a variety of styles (Greek, realism, musicals, Brecht, and so on) in multiple theatre configurations (proscenium, thrust, arena).

2. Classes are interactive, small enough for individual attention, and allow students to connect with each other.

3. The faculty, all of whom have worked professionally, are highly committed to the students and integrate Christian principles while teaching and modeling excellence in all areas of theatre arts.

College of Saint Benedict/Saint John's University
Collegeville, MN

Compiled by: Leigh Dillard, Chair, Theater Department

Degrees Offered:

Theater

Minors Offered:

Theater, pending

Population of Department(s): 40–50 students

Audition to Declare a Theatre/Musical Theatre Major? No, all students are welcome

Three things you would like our readers to know about your performing arts department:

1. We are an integral part of a private, liberal arts institution and encourage students to explore diverse academic interests as well as other experiential opportunities, such as study abroad. We are not a professional training program but provide a strong foundation in all areas of theater.

2. We offer scholarships to first-year students based on interest in theater, nurture students' creative work, and support students' professional development through their attendance at Kennedy Center American College Theater Festivals, United States Institute for Theatre Technology, and special workshops with guest artists and visiting professionals.

3. We take students to performances at many different professional theaters in the Twin Cities and work with them to find internships and jobs in the cities and across the country.

Hamline University
St. Paul, MN

Compiled by: Bill Wallace, Chair of Department of Theatre Arts

Degrees Offered:

Theatre

Minors Offered:

Theatre

Population of Department(s): 30 majors and 45 students in work-study positions. Auditions for all shows are open to the entire campus.

Audition to Declare a Theatre/Musical Theatre Major? No, but there is a required audition/ portfolio review for the theatre scholarship program.

Three things you would like our readers to know about your performing arts department:

1. Productions are a mix of student and faculty design and director teams. Guest artists are a part of every season.

2. Students have an active role in all aspects of department production, design, and technical work.

3. Hamline theatre training is based in a liberal arts program. Our approach prepares students to use their theatrical training in a number of fields and settings.

■ Saint Mary's University of Minnesota
Winona, MN

Compiled by: Judy Myers, MFA, Associate Professor and Chair

Degrees Offered:

BA in theatre with the following tracks: musical theatre, dance, acting/directing, design/technology, general studies

Minors Offered:

Theatre

Dance

Music

Population of Department(s): 65 theatre majors, 6 theatre minors, 10 dance minors

Audition to Declare a Theatre/Musical Theatre Major? No audition required for entrance, only for scholarship consideration.

Three things you would like our readers to know about your performing arts department:

1. All third-year theatre majors spend their fall semester in London, with a two-week optional workshop at the Gaiety School of Acting in Dublin.

2. Production opportunities are available beginning your first semester on campus and at the Tara Arts Theatre while abroad in London.

3. Lillian Davis Hogan four-year scholarships are available to freshmen (audition required).

■ Winona State University

Winona, MN

Compiled by: Jim Williams, Chair of Department of Theatre & Dance

Degrees Offered:

BA in theatre

Minors Offered:

Theatre

Dance

Population of Department(s): 30 theatre majors, 15 theatre minors, 30 dance minors

Audition to Declare a Theatre/Musical Theatre Major? No

Three things you would like our readers to know about your performing arts department:

1. Auditions and casting are open to freshmen through seniors; we are associated with Great River Shakespeare Festival, a professional Equity company during the summer months.

2. Opportunities are available for students in performance, design, and technical positions, and a charter member of national theatre honorary, Alpha Psi Omega.

3. Every year, our NAST-accredited department produces four mainstage productions, two dance productions, and several student-produced productions.

Mississippi

■ Jackson State University
Jackson, MS

Compiled by: Dr. Mark G. Henderson, Chair

Degrees Offered:

Theatre

Minors Offered:

Theatre

Population of Department(s): 25–50

Audition to Declare a Theatre/Musical Theatre Major? No

Three things you would like our readers to know about your performing arts department:

1. We are a small, intimate unit.
2. 100% of our theatre faculty have their terminal degrees in the area of theatre.
3. More than 85% of our graduates are accepted into grad programs or professional companies.

■ Mississippi University for Women
Columbus, MS

Compiled by: William "Peppy" Biddy, Chair of Theatre

Degrees Offered:

BA in theatre

Minors Offered:

Theatre

Population of Department(s): 20–25 annually

Audition to Declare a Theatre/Musical Theatre Major? No

Three things you would like our readers to know about your performing arts department:

1. We have a great student-to-faculty ratio.
2. Students gain experience in all production elements.
3. Most MUW theatre students receive financial aid.

■ Webster University
Webster Groves, MO

Complied by: Lara Teeter, Associate Professor, Head of Musical Theatre Program; John Wylie, Head of Production Programs

Population of School: 8,500

Conservatory or Liberal Arts: Conservatory

Degrees Offered:
BFA in acting, musical theatre, scene design, costume design, lighting design, sound design, wig and makeup design, concert design, scene painting, costume construction, technical production, stage management
BA/BS/BM in directing, theatre studies, and dramaturgy

Population of Department(s): 225

Theatre Scholarships Available: There are various scholarships that are based in contributions to the program and the community along with GPA.

Audition Required for BFA: Yes

Audition Required for BA/BS/BM: No

Pre-screen Video Audition Required: No. Student can go on Acceptd and send in their videos, but it's just for us to get to know you. It's not used as a pre-screening for us.

Attends Unifieds: Yes

Location of Unifieds: New York, Chicago, Las Vegas, and Los Angeles

Number of Students Auditioning Each Year: 600–700

Number of Students Accepted Each Year: 45, with the hope for a starting class of 25

Cut Program or Audition to Remain in Program: No

Minors in Musical Theatre/Acting: No

Prominent Alumni: Hunter Bell, Norbert Leo Butz, Jerry Mitchell, Michael Scott Gregory, Kevin Worley, Michelle Bossy, Seth Jackson, Frank McCullough, Christine Peters

What do you look for in a potential student?

At Webster, we look for a strong connection to the "other" imaginary partner in both the songs (two contrasting) and the monologues (two contrasting), along with material that is appropriate for the actor/singer. Also a flexible instrument, we like the student to be able to take direction.

What are some of the auditors' pet peeves?

Not being truly prepared. It's a national market, and the competition is too steep not to be fully invested in one of the most defining moments in one's young artistic life.

What are your audition requirements?

Two contrasting monologues for acting. Two contrasting songs and two contrasting monologues for musical theatre.

In your eyes, what makes up an excellent college audition monologue? Song?

Students who are clearly there not merely to "audition" but to take this opportunity to show us their craft. They have done their homework and table work on the script or the song. They have made strong choices within the context while maintaining a strong point of view. They are not playing it "safe" but are making bold choices in their chosen pieces.

If there were one monologue you never wanted to see again, what would it be?

We recommend that the material they choose is close to their age or age range.

Can you walk me through what I can expect at your on-campus auditions?

There is a check-in in the lobby of the theatre where parents and students are required to fill out forms. Then we take the students down to the studio spaces to do a warm-up. It begins with a physical warm-up, and then segues into a vocal warm-up and, if there is time, we try to end with a theatre game of some sort. Important note: This whole time we are viewing the group to see how they work as an ensemble. While the acting students do their two monologues, we take the musical theatre students into another room where they learn a musical theatre dance combination. This dance combination is not a make-or-break situation, as it certainly can be with other programs. It's not a defining moment for the students' auditions on that particular day, but rather it's a chance for us to see them in that situation and it's also an opportunity for them to work with us. The dance combination is treated like a master class more so than an audition. Then we put up a list, and the musical theatre students come in one at a time to do their monologues and songs. When finished, we ask them questions such as "What are you interested in besides musical theatre?" or "What are your dreams?" or "Have you ever had to deal with adversity? Can you give us an example of how you had to cope with adversity in your life?"

What's a memorable audition you can remember?

One in which the personality, the material, the execution, the "vibe" was exactly in line with the type of company member we hope to train. When the walls of the room disappear and I forget I am in an audition and focus on the actor doing his or her craft. When I am able to become an audience member as opposed to an auditor.

What is your biggest piece of advice for potential students auditioning?

Be well prepared and well coached. Do the research! Know who's in the room and what they do. Relax! Have fun! Be yourself, because we are really interested in you. Be the best *you* that you can possibly be!

If I audition for your BFA musical theatre program, but don't get accepted, do you still consider me for your BFA acting program or your BA program?

When you call in to arrange your audition, we will ask if you are auditioning for musical theatre or acting. I suggest that if students are truly interested in attending Webster, they should say both. Our acting and musical theatre programs are completely integrated with each other. If they really love Webster, there are plenty of musical theatre opportunities for acting majors. If both boxes are checked when they walk in the room, we will ask which do they absolutely prefer. There will be times when we really like the person but his or her voice is not competitive, so we consider him or her for the acting program instead. A perfect example is Norbert Leo Butz—he was an acting major.

After I audition, is there a good way to follow up?

Sure! Email, call, and always send a handwritten thank-you card. We look at everything the students send in to us. It all goes into the individual files that we keep on every person who auditions.

Would I get a showcase at the end of senior year?

Yes.

Do I have to audition to be accepted into the showcase?

No.

Where are showcases held, and are they successful?

The New York showcase is at New World Stages. Yes, they are very successful. Many students sign with agents each year. This year, in Los Angeles, we are also doing a master class with a guaranteed number of attending casting directors and agents. They will be put on camera and have the chance to meet with and audition for the attending professionals. We are very excited!

Will I be able to audition/perform as a freshman?

No.

In what ways can I be involved with the department aside from performing?

Like a lot of college programs, we have work-study, which is basically an on-campus job. The students are extremely busy between their class time, crew time, and performance time. We make it very clear that we are a professional theatre training program and that they spend virtually *all* of their time training and prepping for class.

I love to sing, but I don't consider myself a dancer. Can I still seek a degree in musical theatre at your school?

Yes.

I want to get a BFA in acting, but I also love to sing. Can BFA/BA acting students take voice lessons with top voice faculty?

Yes.

Do you discourage or encourage students to audition for theatre outside of the department during the academic year?

Encourage.

Does your school regularly work in conjunction with any regional theatres?

Yes. The St. Louis Repertory Theatre shares our mainstage space with us. Our students do all of the running crew assignments for all of the shows, and they are required to audition and be considered for the Rep's season. We also have a partnership with the MUNY Theatre in St. Louis, the oldest outdoor theatre in the country. For the 2013 season, six of our students received their Equity card! We also have a partnership with Variety Children's Theatre.

What do students typically do during the summers? Do you actively promote participation in summer theatre auditions?

They do summer stock. We have a strong study abroad, as we have 10 international campuses including our London campus. Most of our students who take advantage of this spend six weeks in the summer at RADA (the Royal Academy of Dramatic Art) in London.

How many musicals versus straight plays do you do in a season?

We do four plays and two musicals (one large and one small) a year. This does not include the St. Louis Theatre Repertory casting possibilities along with our senior directing students' "capstone" plays/musicals, which are "small" in terms of cast/production value.

What are some of your alumni up to? Do you have an active alumni network?

Yes. Jerry Mitchell (Broadway, *Hairspray, Legally Blonde, La Cage*) also did *Catch Me If You Can* on Broadway starring another one of our esteemed alums, Norbert Leo Butz. Hunter Bell (Broadway, *Title of Show*) is very involved with our senior showcase and hosts a yearly "get together" for our performance and tech theatre alums.

What is the portfolio/interview process for a technical theatre student?

Applicants in any of the design or technical production areas must present a portfolio, which should indicate the variety and caliber of their work in fine arts or theatre. Such a portfolio might consist of the following:

Design

- Drawings, any subject and media
- Examples of work in color
- Drafting
- Prints
- 3-D projects of any type
- Actual theatrical design work, produced or not
- Figure drawing

Technical Production

- Draftings
- Photographs of projects
- Evidence of work in carpentry, electronics, mechanics, scenic construction
- Any of the items listed for design applicants

What do you expect to see on a technical theatre résumé?

Evidence of key positions held at school. Hopefully, additional work outside of the high school—community theatre, work at roadhouses, other professional work, if possible.

I'm interested in lighting, sound design, and stage management. What major should I go for? Can I minor?

All of our students are encouraged to study multiple areas. Many graduate with two fields of concentration. Most often they major in something and declare a "second area of emphasis."

Anything else I should know?

Our program is an acting-based program. Webster is a Stanislavski-based program. One glance at our curriculum and one can see that the focus is on acting. This is really excellent news for our musical theatre majors as they take the four-year sequence of our core acting classes (acting, voice and speech, movement) right alongside the acting majors. When it comes to casting our conservatory season, our acting majors are cast in our musicals, and our musical theatre majors are cast in our plays, and visa versa. The musical theatre majors also have four years of musical theatre song study (musical theatre styles class) along with their voice lessons, music theory classes, piano, and choir requirements housed in the music school, as well as their dance requirements housed in the dance department. The focus of any young artist should be on self-discovery. We encourage our students to find their "authentic voice," and we hope to train the future visionaries of the theatre arts.

All of our conservatory shows are designed and built by our students. Faculty do not design the student shows, and we have no grad students.

■ Drury University
Springfield, MO

Compiled by: Robert Westenberg, Associate Professor, Chair of Theatre

Degrees Offered:

Theatre

Minors Offered:

Theatre

Dance

Population of Department(s): 75

Audition to Declare a Theatre/Musical Theatre Major? No

Three things you would like our readers to know about your performing arts department:

1. Drury University offers a four-year undergrad program resulting in a BA degree. With an emphasis on excellence and a pre-professional approach to the teaching of theatre, we boast a strong, multifaceted faculty with professional backgrounds and a low student-to-faculty ratio. The Theatre Department is an ideal size, large enough to offer quality productions while providing a substantial opportunity to participate, not only in class, but also in mainstage productions.

2. Freshmen can become immediately active in stage management, production design, acting, and technology. We provide numerous performance, technical, and design opportunities, including five mainstage shows per year, performance touring programs, student-directed one-acts, and original plays.

3. Theatre grants are available for qualifying freshmen. Maximum grants for incoming students are $2,100, plus $700 for theatre minors (minors receiving a total of $2,800), or an additional $1,400 for theatre majors (majors receiving a total of $3,500). Grants may be combined with other scholarships or grants received from other departments. Theatre grants become part of your financial aid package and are renewable from year to year. If a student has worked significantly beyond expectations, students may be offered the opportunity to increase the grant for the next year.

■ Lindenwood University
St Charles, MO

Compiled by: Emily Jones, Department of Theatre Chair

Degrees Offered:

BFA in acting

BFA in musical theatre

BFA in stage management

BFA in technical theatre/design (scenic, costume, lights)

BA in theatre

BA in theatre with secondary teaching certificate

BA in arts management and entertainment production

Minors Offered:

Theatre

Population of Department(s): 125

Audition to Declare a Theatre/Musical Theatre Major? BFA, yes; BA, no

Three things you would like our readers to know about your performing arts department:

1. Abundant opportunities for practical experience.

2. Challenging and supportive environment.

3. Highly competitive financial aid packages.

■ Missouri State University

Springfield, MO

Compiled by: Kurt Heinlein, BFA Acting Coordinator; Michael Casey, Musical Theatre Coordinator

Degrees Offered:

BFA in acting

BFA in musical theatre

BFA in dance

BFA in design/tech/stage management

BA in theatre studies

BS in theatre education

Minors Offered:

Theatre

Music

Population of Department(s): 225—approximately 65 acting, 55 musical theatre (25 in music, 30 in theatre), 35 BA theatre studies, 25 theatre/speech education, 25 dance, 20 design/tech/stage management

Audition to Declare a Theatre/Musical Theatre Major? Yes. Auditions are required for entrance to the BFA acting, BFA musical theatre, and BFA dance programs.

Three things you would like our readers to know about your performing arts department:

1. Missouri State University sponsors successful performance showcases on both coasts, helping students to attain representation, develop alumni networks, and build the bridge from training to profession. Each spring, the BFA acting program hosts a showcase in Los Angeles, and the musical theatre program holds a showcase in New York City. BFA acting and musical theatre students are eligible to perform in both showcase events.

2. Our graduates get right to work and stay working. We have a post-graduation industry employment rate that sets us apart. Older and emerging graduates are both working extensively across the field, including Broadway, off-Broadway, film, TV, and commercials/commercial print. Graduate success is directly linked to the strong professional focus housed within the programs.

3. We are the only program in the region to hold accreditations from NAST, NASM (National Association of Schools of Music), and have a resident professional Equity theatre company, Tent Theatre. Our students regularly work and perform in the Tent company, garnering vital points toward membership in AEA.

■ Northwest Missouri State University
Maryville, MO

Compiled by: Dr. Joe Kreizinger, Coordinator of Speech and Theatre Education

Degrees Offered:

BA in theatre
BS in theatre performance
BS in theatre technical and design
BSEd in comprehensive speech and theatre
BSEd in non-comprehensive speech and theatre

Minors Offered:

Theatre
Speech and theatre education

Population of Department(s): 80 majors, 20 minors

Audition to Declare a Theatre/Musical Theatre Major? No

Three things you would like our readers to know about your theatre department:

1. Constant opportunities for performing for students, freshmen through seniors, in multiple venues, including musical theatre and tour shows (and a special production only for first-year students); also opportunities for students to direct and design productions.

2. Many scholarship opportunities for new students and even more for returning students; also numerous paid positions within the theatre department.

3. Theatre curriculum is up to date (including state-of-the-art technology and facilities), challenging, and emphasizes learning while doing; theatre majors are involved in theatre coursework and in practical experience (production work) from the first week of classes.

■ Stephens College
Columbia, MO

Compiled by: Mimi Hedges, Interim Dean of the School of Performing Arts

Degrees Offered:

BFA in theatre arts
BFA in theatre management
BFA in theatrical costume design
Certificate program

Minors Offered:

Music and voice
Theatre arts

Population of Department(s): 107

Audition to Declare a Theatre/Musical Theatre Major? No

Three things you would like our readers to know about your performing arts department:

1. BFA programs are three-year/two-summer programs.
2. Students have opportunities to perform year-round, including during intensive summer programming.
3. Students work alongside professional faculty and industry professionals who serve as guest artists.

■ Truman State University
Kirksville, MO

Compiled by: Ron Rybkowski, Professor of Theatre

Degrees Offered:

Theatre

Minors Offered:

Theatre

Population of Department(s): 65 majors, 47 minors

Audition to Declare a Theatre/Musical Theatre Major? No

Three things you would like our readers to know about your performing arts department:

1. Our program emphasizes practical experience at every level of production. We offer students transformative experiences; students perform, design, direct, choreograph, construct, circuit, paint, sew, write plays, research, and teach.
2. Our program enforces broad-based learning and practical applications of Truman's liberal arts and science core curriculum. In every area of study and practical training, we demand research, independent analysis, critical thinking, and a high degree of on-the-spot problem solving.
3. Our students are well prepared for the professional theatre world and for life's changing conditions and challenges. Our program emphasizes generalist study and collaboration as it cultivates each individual's talents, temperaments, and potential.

■ University of Missouri—Kansas City
Department of Theatre
Kansas City, MO

Compiled by: Tom Mardikes, Professor and Chair

Degrees Offered:

MFA in acting and directing

MFA in design and technology (costumes, lighting, scenery, sound, stage management, technical direction)

MA in theatre (history, dramaturgy, playwriting)

BA in theatre (tracks in performance, design/technology, general)

Minors Offered:

Theatre

Population of Department(s): 76 MFA, 7 MA, 75 BA majors, 15 BA minors

Audition to Declare a Theatre/Musical Theatre Major? Auditions and campus visits required for MFA and MA programs. BA program requires no auditions.

Three things you would like our readers to know about your performing arts department:

1. UMKC Theatre is one of the elite graduate professional training programs in the United States. The grad program is the highest nationally ranked program in the University of Missouri system. UMKC Theatre is a member of URTA and NAST, and KC Rep is a member of LORT.

2. UMKC Theatre organizes many co-productions with professional theatres in Kansas City, including KC Rep, the Unicorn Theatre, the Coterie Theatre, and Kansas City Actors Theatre.

3. The training focus for actors is stage plays, not musical theatre. The design areas collaborate with the Conservatory of Music and Dance to add productions in opera, dance, and ballet.

Montana

■ Rocky Mountain College
Billings, MT

Compiled by: Sarah Brewer, Associate Professor, Theatre Arts

Degrees Offered:

Theatre, performance or technical emphasis

Minors Offered:

Theatre

Population of Department(s): 20

Audition to Declare a Theatre/Musical Theatre Major? No

Three things you would like our readers to know about your performing arts department:

1. Small department = one-on-one time with faculty.
2. Productions are chosen to highlight strengths of individual students.
3. Students are exposed to a wide variety of genres, from traditional Greek to contemporary musicals.

Nebraska

■ Chadron State College
Chadron, NE

Compiled by: Professor Roger Mays, Head of Theatre Program

Degrees Offered:

Comprehensive BA in theatre with either design/tech or performance/directing emphasis
BSEd (BS in education) with a "subject endorsement" in theatre

Minors Offered:

Theatre

Population of Department(s): 25–30

Audition to Declare a Theatre/Musical Theatre Major? Audition required for eligibility for Theatre Assistantship Waiver, typically worth one-half tuition. No audition required to declare major.

Three things you would like our readers to know about your performing arts department:

1. Students are directly and constantly involved in all aspects of production.
2. Virtually all performance students appear in at least one role in our four-show season, with qualified technicians given major assignments in lighting, sound, and set design.
3. Facilities include 100-seat Black Box Theatre and 650-seat Auditorium with digital lighting and sound.

■ Nebraska Wesleyan University
Lincoln, NE

Compiled by: Jack Parkhurst

Degrees Offered:

Acting
Directing
Musical theatre
Theatre arts
Theatre arts education
Theatre design and technology

Minors Offered:

Theatre arts

Population of Department(s): 107

Audition to Declare a Theatre/Musical Theatre Major? Yes

Three things you would like our readers to know about your performing arts department:

1. Opportunity: 10–14 major shows, 4 musicals, 4 cabarets, 30+ student-directed shows.

2. Students from 16 states.

3. Many working professional guest artists from New York City and Los Angeles every year.

University of Nebraska at Kearney
Department of Music and Performing Arts
Kearney, NE

Compiled by: Darin Himmerich, Assistant Profressor, Director of Theatre/Scene Design/ Technical Director

Degrees Offered:

BA in theatre
BA in education – theatre 7–12
BM in musical theatre comprehensive

Minors Offered:

Theatre
Dance
Music

Population of Department(s): 25–45

Audition to Declare a Theatre/Musical Theatre Major? No

Three things you would like our readers to know about your performing arts department:

1. As an undergrad program, we have plenty of opportunities for each of our students, having a performance, technical, or drama emphasis.

2. We have a strong faculty-to-student ratio, making 1:1 interaction available to all students.

3. We work hard to get our students working in professional summer stock. We usually have more than 50% placement.

Nevada

■ University of Nevada Reno
Department of Theatre and Dance
Reno, NV

Compiled by: Robert Gander, Chair

Degrees Offered:

BA in theatre

Minors Offered:

Theatre

Dance

Population of Department(s): We typically admit 20 majors each academic year; we have an average of 80 majors and 100 minors.

Audition to Declare a Theatre/Musical Theatre Major? Students may declare a theatre major without an audition.

Three things you would like our readers to know about your performing arts department:

1. We are a friendly department at a large university with no grad program, which means undergrad students are performing and designing regularly, allowing them to build impressive résumés and receive in-depth practical experience.

2. Two of our students won the national Irene Ryan Acting Competition sponsored by the Kennedy Center American College Theatre Festival in 2013, direct evidence that our acting program is competitive nationally.

3. We are in the midst of a $3 million renovation of our theatres that will make our learning spaces state-of-the-art training facilities.

New Hampshire

■ University of New Hampshire
Durham, NH

Compiled by: David Kaye, Professor of Theatre and Dance and Chair of the Department of Theatre and Dance (acting/directing)

Population of School: 13,000

Conservatory or Liberal Arts: Liberal arts

Degrees Offered:
BA with emphasis in acting, musical theatre, design and technology, theatre education, dance

Population of Department(s): Average 110 majors, 40 minors

Theatre Scholarships Available: Number of various scholarships ranging from $500 to half in-state tuition

Audition Required for BA/BS/BM: Audition required for performance-based emphasis areas. Interview required for design and technology and theatre education. No audition required to pursue a general theatre major.

Pre-screen Video Audition Required: No

Attends Unifieds: No

Number of Students Auditioning Each Year: Approximately 70

Number of Students Accepted Each Year: We normally have an incoming class of 30

Cut Program or Audition to Remain in Program: No

Minors in Musical Theatre/Acting: Musical theatre, general theatre, and dance

Prominent Alumni: Mike O'Malley (*Glee*), Maryann Plunkett (Tony winner, *House of Cards*), Marcy Carsey (television producer, *Rosanne, Cosby Show, That 70s Show*), Michael Graziadei (*Young and the Restless* regular and film actor), Carl Andress (Charles Busch's collaborator over the last 10 years), David Leon (fight master)

What do you look for in a potential student?
Focus, serious intent, preparation. These are the areas very much in the realm of control of the person auditioning. Beyond that, we are looking for *just* that: potential. Yes, there has to be a

degree of good old-fashioned talent. We need to see that you have a base ability from which we can build a really strong performer.

What are some of the auditors' pet peeves?

When the actor obviously has not put in any real work on the audition. We accept that many students have little real training, but there is no excuse for not having your monologues and songs down.

What are your audition requirements?

All those auditioning spend about three hours with us. Acting must present two contrasting monologues (no more than two minutes each); musical theatre must perform two contrasting solo song selections (one up-tempo and one ballad) of approximately 32 bars each, a monologue, and attend a dance session. All must also take part in an acting class.

If there were one monologue you never wanted to see again, what would it be?

I'll see anything over and over, as long as it is done well.

If there were one song you never wanted to hear again, what would it be?

Same thing.

If you require a pre-screen video audition, what do you look for in those submissions?

Make sure the sound and lighting is good. Don't shoot tight. I want to see detail in your face, but I also need to see how connected you are to your body.

Can you walk me through what I can expect at your on-campus auditions?

Check-in

Meet all faculty

Group warm-up

Group acting class

Individual auditions

Dance class for musical theatre

Brief individual interviews

What's a memorable audition you can remember?

It's been awhile, but one person did an amazing job piecing together the musical pieces and broke up the monologue so the entire audition made contextual sense. It was clever and funny—and very well prepared.

What is your biggest piece of advice for potential students auditioning?

It's tough, but you need to find the fun in all of this. Performing *is* fun, right? If it wasn't, why would you be doing this? Bring that joy to your audition!

After I audition, is there a good way to follow up?

Sending an email is always nice.

Would I get a showcase at the end of senior year?

Presently, we have decided to put our New York City showcase on hold. They have grown out of control. Just too many. We try to bring casting directors and agents to us.

Do I have to audition to be accepted into the showcase?

When we have had them, yes.

Where are showcases held, and are they successful?

Showcases are held in New York City. Good shows. Reasonable turnout.

Will I be able to audition/perform as a freshman?

Yes.

In what ways can I be involved with the department aside from performing?

In *all* areas. We also have an amazing student-producing organization that does three to four major productions a year.

I love to sing, but I don't consider myself a dancer. Can I still seek a degree in musical theatre at your school?

Yes, but you must still fulfill the dance requirements.

I want to get a BFA in acting, but I also love to sing. Can BFA/BA acting students take voice lessons with top voice faculty?

Yes, providing there is space.

Do you discourage or encourage students to audition for theatre outside of the department during the academic year?

We do not encourage it during the academic year.

Does your school regularly work in conjunction with any regional theatres?

One regional and several summer stock.

What do students typically do during the summers? Do you actively promote participation in summer theatre auditions?

Yes.

How many musicals versus straight plays do you do in a season?

One major musical, one studio musical, three straight plays, festival of student-written plays (can be straight or musical), one dance concert.

What are some of your alumni up to? Do you have an active alumni network?

Yes. They are doing so much. Many are performing with national tours and regional theatre; directing theatre and film; and in major administrative positions with BAM, Roundabout Theatre, Manhattan Theatre Club, and the Guthrie. Several are running theatre programs in the United States and United Kingdom. Many have gone on to grad schools in the United States and United Kingdom.

What is the portfolio/interview process for a technical theatre student?

Students meet with the head of design. If they have a portfolio, it is presented, but it can also be based on just the interview.

What do you expect to see on a technical theatre résumé?

Some evidence that the student has had enough exposure to theatre technology and/or design that we can gauge the depth of his or her interest and commitment.

I'm interested in lighting, sound design, and stage management. What major should I go for? Can I minor?

Technology and design. We do not offer a minor.

Anything else I should know?

Our program is designed to cultivate the artist in each and every student, and we approach this with the utmost seriousness. At the same time, we also work to create a department of artists who support each other. In this incredibly competitive profession, building a circle of people who will be your future contacts starts by being a strong, supportive colleague.

We are also training our students in applied theatre techniques, in addition to acting for multimedia platforms. We want to be part of expanding the job market for actors, and we want to train them for these new ways of using their craft. In addition, we have a cutting-edge program in aerial dance that is open to all majors.

■ Dartmouth College
Hanover, NH

Compiled by: Dan Kotlowitz, Professor of Theater, Chair, Department of Theater

Degrees Offered:

BA in theater with concentration in acting, directing, stage managing, playwriting, design, technical theater, dramaturgy, history/lit and criticism, and dance

Minors Offered:

Theater, with a concentration similar to the major

Population of Department(s): 20–30 majors, 10–20 minors

Audition to Declare a Theatre/Musical Theatre Major? No

Three things you would like our readers to know about your performing arts department:

1. Our students get a great deal of one-on-one mentoring in both production and scholarship, from working professionals and established scholars.

2. The Theater Department encourages a broad liberal arts approach to the study of theater—and welcomes both the serious and the casual student of theater.

3. We have numerous production opportunities, including theater, musical theater, dance, and movement-based devised theater.

New Jersey

■ Fairleigh Dickinson University
Hackensack, NJ

Compiled by: Stephen Hollis, Director of the Theater Program

Population of School: 3,000 students

Conservatory or Liberal Arts: Liberal arts

Degrees Offered:

BA in theater arts with concentrations in acting, musical theater, directing, playwriting, design/tech, and theater studies

Population of Department(s): 100 theater majors in all concentrations

Theatre Scholarships Available: Yes, in amounts up to $5,000 annually

Audition Required for BA/BS/BM: Yes

Pre-screen Video Audition Required: No

Attends Unifieds: Yes

Number of Students Auditioning Each Year: Around 150

Number of Students Accepted Each Year: 24

Cut Program or Audition to Remain in Program: No

Minors in Musical Theatre/Acting: Yes

What do you look for in a potential student?

Energy, specificity, focus.

What are some of the auditors' pet peeves?

Speeches from monologue books.

What are your audition requirements?

For acting, two contrasting monologues. For musical theater, one monologue and one up-tempo song.

In your eyes, what makes up an excellent college audition monologue? Song?

A speech with inner conflict. Most monologues are just narrative or storytelling with no conflict.

If there were one monologue you never wanted to see again, what would it be?

Durang's "tuna fish" or Charlie Brown's "she's looking at me."

Can you walk me through what I can expect at your on-campus auditions?

An informal five-minute chat to get to know something about each applicant, followed by the audition. Then a comment on the performance and questions about the program from the applicant. I want to know something that is interesting and original about each student.

What's a memorable audition you can remember?

Listing of the dead soldiers from *Henry VI, Part 3*.

What is your biggest piece of advice for potential students auditioning?

Be yourself.

After I audition, is there a good way to follow up?

We will let you know within two weeks.

Would I get a showcase at the end of senior year?

Yes.

Do I have to audition to be accepted into the showcase?

No.

Where are showcases held, and are they successful?

Showcases are held in Manhattan.

Will I be able to audition/perform as a freshman?

Yes.

What ways can I be involved with the department aside from performing?

Backstage, front of house, publicity, assistant direct.

I love to sing, but I don't consider myself a dancer. Can I still seek a degree in musical theatre at your school?

Yes.

I want to get a BFA in acting, but I also love to sing. Can BFA/BA acting students take voice lessons with top voice faculty?

Yes.

Do you discourage or encourage students to audition for theatre outside of the department during the academic year?

Discourage.

Does your school regularly work in conjunction with any regional theatres?

Yes, Playwrights Theater of New Jersey is our on-campus resident theater company.

What do students typically do during the summers? Do you actively promote participation in summer theatre auditions?

Yes.

How many musicals versus straight plays do you do in a season?

One musical and one straight play each semester.

What are some of your alumni up to? Do you have an active alumni network?

Facebook has one.

What is the portfolio/interview process for a technical theatre student?

A 20-minute interview, looking at portfolio and discussing interests and opportunities.

I'm interested in lighting, sound design, and stage management. What major should I go for? Can I minor?

We have a design/tech concentration and special scholarships for these students.

Anything else I should know?

All our productions are directed and designed by professionals.

Being so close to Manhattan, our students can intern with casting directors, agents, and off-Broadway theater companies.

All theater majors are required to spend a full semester at our campus in England.

■ Montclair State University
Montclair, NJ

Compiled by: Eric Diamond, Deputy Chairperson, Theatre Professor

Population of School: Approximately 18,000

Conservatory or Liberal Arts: We operate as a conservatory program within a larger liberal arts community

Degrees Offered:
BFA in musical theatre
BFA in acting
BFA in dance
BFA in production/design
BA in dance education
BA in theatre studies
MA in theatre studies

Population of Department(s): Approximately 400 in the Department of Theatre and Dance

Theatre Scholarships Available: There are scholarships available in the theatre and dance programs, particularly for out-of-state and need-based students.

Audition Required for BFA: Yes

Audition Required for BA/BS/BM: Yes

Pre-screen Video Audition Required: No

Attends Unifieds: Yes

Location of Unifieds: New York City, Chicago, Las Vegas, and Los Angeles

Number of Students Auditioning Each Year: 450 for BFA musical theatre, 180 for BFA dance, 100 for BFA acting, 45 production design, 100 for BA programs

Number of Students Accepted Each Year: 24 accepted for BFA musical with a target starting class of 18–20 students. The BFA dance and BFA acting accept approximately 20%; BFA production/design, BA theatre studies, and BA dance education accept approximately 50%.

Cut Program or Audition to Remain in Program: No; however, we have juries every year for evaluation.

Minors in Musical Theatre/Acting: Dance, musical theatre, and theatre

Prominent Alumni: Robert McClure, nominated for a Tony Award for *Chaplin* in the title role

What do you look for in a potential student?

The faculty considers all facets of the potential student, including academic excellence and experience in his or her field of study. The promise of professional success is also considered based upon the student's talent.

What are some of the auditors' pet peeves?

A lack of proper preparation and/or training prior to auditions.

What are your audition requirements?

We require two Broadway-type songs (the songs can be the full song), two monologues (no more than 90 seconds each), and a dance audition. Ideally one of the songs should be a pre-1960s musical or traditional Broadway show (Gershwin, Cole Porter, Rogers and Hammerstein, for example).

If there were one monologue you never wanted to see again, what would it be?

While we discourage overdone monologues and songs, we judge each student's audition based on his or her performance.

Can you walk me through what I can expect at your on-campus auditions?

We encourage students to arrive early to sign in. BFA musical theatre auditionees will be assigned a specific arrival time and assigned a singing, acting, and dance time. The BFA acting student auditions will begin at approximately 9 a.m., and each student will have an assigned time followed by a brief interview. For BA theatre majors, their auditions will take the form of group activities followed by an interview. Dancers begin with a warm-up, and then have a ballet class and a modern dance class. Students will then present a short piece of choreography of their own creation followed by an interview. BFA production design students have a portfolio review and interview. All students should be prepared to spend the entire day with us.

What's a memorable audition you can remember?

The best auditions combine talent, originality, and the confidence and poise that come with preparation. We audition so many potential students each year and find that each audition is considered on an individual basis.

What is your biggest piece of advice for potential students auditioning?

Be as prepared as possible and try to enjoy the process.

If I audition for your BFA musical theatre program, but don't get accepted, do you still consider me for your BFA acting program or your BA program?

Yes, but you must audition for those separately. You can schedule those on the same day or another time.

After I audition, is there a good way to follow up?

Potential students are notified by admissions and/or program coordinators once their results have been determined. No follow-up is necessary.

Would I get a showcase at the end of senior year?

We hold a senior showcase for BFA students in New York City in the spring of senior year. Many students receive offers from agents, casting directors, and managers; several students have recently been cast in Broadway shows, national tours, and regional productions.

Do I have to audition to be accepted into the showcase?

No.

Where are showcases held, and are they successful?

Showcases are held in New York City, and they are very successful.

Will I be able to audition/perform as a freshman?

Yes.

If there is a graduate program, will I get the same performance opportunities as an undergraduate?

Students in all programs are welcome to attend auditions for any production.

In what ways can I be involved with the department aside from performing?

We offer many work-study opportunities within the department—students work in the costume and scene shops, in the administrative offices, and assisting faculty.

Say I get a BA rather than a BFA. Will I actually get to perform?

Our BA theatre studies program emphasizes collaboratively created, ensemble-based theatre education that culminates in a senior project created in collaboration with a professional theatre artist and performed as a part of the department's production season. Additional performance opportunities include departmental productions and workshops, directing class scenes, and participation in play-reading series.

I love to sing, but I don't consider myself a dancer. Can I still seek a degree in musical theatre at your school?

Our BFA musical theatre program fuses training in acting, dance, and music. All majors take classes in ballet, musical theatre dance, tap, and jazz. Some previous dance training is recommended, although not required.

I want to get a BFA in acting, but I also love to sing. Can BFA/BA acting students take voice lessons with top voice faculty?

Yes, private lessons are available through the Cali School of Music's preparatory division.

Do you discourage or encourage students to audition for theatre outside of the department during the academic year?

We strongly encourage our students to audition for summer stock and summer intensives related to their respective major. Students who audition for and are cast in outside projects during the academic year are handled on a case-by-case basis.

Does your school regularly work in conjunction with any regional theatres?

We have a state-of-the-art professional theatre on campus, where students are often given opportunities to work with professional artists. We also have ongoing relationships with several regional New York and New Jersey theatres.

What do students typically do during the summers? Do you actively promote participation in summer theatre auditions?

Students actively participate in summer stock productions, summer internships in New York City with agents and casting directors, or summer theatre programs.

How many musicals versus straight plays do you do in a season?

All BFA programs offer at least three fully mounted, mainstage productions per year in any of our six on-campus venues. They also participate in performance workshops, staged readings, operas, off-campus performances, and student-run productions.

What are some of your alumni up to? Do you have an active alumni network?

Our proximity to New York City and our nationally renowned faculty and guest artists provide graduating seniors with unprecedented opportunities to move directly into a professional career in the arts. Our BFA dance alumni are regularly employed by contemporary dance companies such as Urban Bush Women, Nikolais-Louis Dance Company, Pilobolus, and the Martha Graham Dance Company. They perform on Broadway, in music videos, and on television shows such as *Dancing with the Stars*. Our BFA musical theatre and BFA acting alumni have performed nationally and internationally in venues including Broadway, off-Broadway, and regional theatre. Our production/design alumni are working in all facets of production around the country as lighting, set, and costume designers; makeup artists; technical directors; and stage managers. The BA theatre studies alumni are currently working as professional actors, directors, producers, playwrights, and educators. And BA dance education alumni teach in schools and dance studios or begin their own dance-related businesses.

What is the portfolio/interview process for a technical theatre student?

Students participate in a portfolio review in which they are required to provide materials that best represent their area of interest and previous experience. They also participate in a one-on-one interview with faculty from the Department of Production/Design.

What do you expect to see on a technical theatre résumé?

A history of participation in the applicant's field of study.

I'm interested in lighting, sound design, and stage management. What major should I go for? Can I minor?

We offer three concentrations within the BFA production design program. The concentration in design includes the study of scenic design, costume design, lighting, and sound; the management concentration includes stage management and production management. There is also a concentration in technical theatre that encompasses costume, scenery, and lighting.

Anything else I should know?

MSU provides exposure to the professional talent and arts activities found in New York City, which is only 12 miles away and accessible via our on-campus train terminal to Penn Station. Our outstanding facilities include the state-of-the-art 500-seat Kasser Theater, the 900-seat Memorial Auditorium, the 100-seat flexible Fox Studio, a 125-seat dance theatre, and the 275-seat Leshowitz Recital Hall. We provide students with a nationally renowned faculty and guest artists whose credits include film, opera, television, on and off Broadway, throughout the nation and abroad, who mentor our students in every way. *Forbes* magazine recently ranked MSU as the number-one public institution in New Jersey, the third best in the state overall, and among the top 15 best buys in the entire northeast. We are nationally accredited by the NAST, the National Association of Schools of Dance (NASD), and the National Association of Schools of Music (NASM).

■ Centenary College
Hackettstown, NJ

Compiled by: Carl Wallnau, Professor of Theatre Arts, Chair, Fine Arts

Degrees Offered:

BA in theatre (performance studies, dance, management and technical theatre)

Minors Offered:

Theatre

Population of Department(s): 50 majors and minors

Audition to Declare a Theatre/Musical Theatre Major? There is no audition required, although if a student wishes to apply for a scholarship, there is a required interview or audition based on concentration.

Three things you would like our readers to know about your performing arts department:

1. The program is affiliated with the Centenary Stage Company, a not-for-profit Equity theatre located on the Centenary campus. Students work on these productions in all capacities, including as performers. Students may also join the EMC program and earn credits toward their Equity card while working on these productions.

2. Centenary has a "theatre for young audiences" touring program where our students perform in various productions throughout the state. Students receive a stipend for these shows.

3. Students may pursue several concentrations in theatre at the same time. It is not unusual to have students pursuing performance and dance or dance and technical theatre at the same time.

■ Drew University
Madison, NJ

Compiled by: Professor Rosemary McLaughlin, Chair, Department of Theatre and Dance

Degrees Offered:

Theatre

Minors Offered:

Theatre

Dance

Arts administration

Population of Department(s): 85 majors, 15 theatre minors, 16 dance minors, 15 arts administration minors

Audition to Declare a Theatre/Musical Theatre Major? No

Three things you would like our readers to know about your performing arts department:

1. Located close to New York City, Drew University's Theatre and Dance Department is dedicated to a broad-based study of the history, theory, and practice of theatre in the context of a liberal arts education that is integrally connected to a rigorous production program centering on student involvement and leadership.

2. This interaction of the academic and the practical generates an ongoing symbiosis, with each focus actively informing and inspiring the other.

3. Along with growing more knowledgeable and skilled as theatre artists and scholars, our students also develop as critical thinkers and responsible collaborators.

■ Kean University
Union, NJ

Compiled by: Holly Logue, Chair

Degrees Offered:

BA in theatre

BA in theatre with K–12 teacher certification

BFA in performance (musical theatre track and acting track)

BFA in theatre design and technology

Minors Offered:

Theatre

Dance

Population of Department(s): 135 majors

Audition to Declare a Theatre/Musical Theatre Major? Yes

Three things you would like our readers to know about your performing arts department:

1. Four train stops from New York City, allowing our students to audition in New York, allowing us to host our senior showcase on Theatre Row, and allowing us access to countless guest artists to teach master classes for theatre students, some of whom have included Olympia Dukakis, John Lee Beatty, Richard Dreyfuss, Daphne Rubin-Vega, Lee Blessing, William Finn, and the cast of *Rent*.

2. Affordable tuition and numerous scholarship opportunities.

3. Professional theatre in residence that offers internships and EMC credit.

■ Ramapo College
Mahwah, NJ

Compiled by: Beba Shamash, Convener, Theater Program/School of Contemporary Arts

Degrees Offered:

Theater (concentrations: acting, design/tech, directing/stage management, and theater studies)

Minors Offered:

Theater

Population of Department(s): Approximately 60

Audition to Declare a Theatre/Musical Theatre Major? No

Three things you would like our readers to know about your performing arts department:

1. We are a small, very active program with many opportunities for students to act, design, direct, and gain skills in all aspects of production, set, costume, lighting, and sound through hands-on experience.

2. Our students go on to succeed in theater MFA programs, such as Yale, Rutgers, and University of Wisconsin—Madison, as well as in professional theater careers.

3. Our excellent faculty were trained at top theater schools, including NYU and Columbia, and bring professional career experience in TV, theater, dance, opera, and film to Ramapo College. Students are able to take part in professional experiences through the ongoing professional work of the faculty.

■ Rowan University
Glassboro, NJ

Compiled by: Dr. Elisabeth Hostetter, Chair of the Department of Theatre and Dance

Degrees Offered:

BA in theatre (tracks in acting, musical theatre, design/tech, or pre-teaching)
BA in dance

Minors Offered:

Theatre
Dance

Population of Department(s): 120

Audition to Declare a Theatre/Musical Theatre Major? Yes

Three things you would like our readers to know about your performing arts department:

1. Our program is noted for an emphasis on movement-driven theatre that values the integration of the disciplines of theatre and dance in both curriculum and production.

2. We encourage students to view themselves as makers of art for the 21st century and value cutting-edge contemporary theatre and dance that is informed by foundational and traditional coursework.

3. Our faculty members are all practicing artists in Philadelphia and/or New York, and we closely mentor and cast undergrads in our BA program.

■ Rutgers University
Mason Gross School of the Arts
New Brunswick, NJ

Compiled by: Kevin Kittle, Head of BFA Acting

Degrees Offered:

We are a conservatory, so we offer BFAs in acting, design, and production.

Minors Offered:

None

Population of Department(s): 110

Audition to Declare a Theatre/Musical Theatre Major? Audition/interview for acting; interview for design and production

Three things you would like our readers to know about your performing arts department:

1. Company driven with an extremely high standard of technique and professionalism.

2. Entire third year spent studying at Shakespeare's Globe Theatre in London.

3. Close proximity to New York City.

◼ Seton Hall University

South Orange, NJ

Compiled by: Deirdre Yates, MFA Chair of the Department of Communication and The Arts, as well as Professor of performance courses and mainstage director

Degrees Offered:

Theatre
Music performance
Music education

Minors Offered:

Theatre
Musical theatre

Population of Department(s): 525 in the Department of Communication and the Arts, 25 theatre/music majors

Audition to Declare a Theatre/Musical Theatre Major? No audition required for the theatre major or for the musical theatre minor; however, there is a required audition for the music performance major.

Three things you would like our readers to know about your performing arts department:

1. We are a small program, which encourages hands-on experience in your freshman year.

2. We offer a community-oriented, family-like environment (14:1 student–faculty ratio).

3. We run a wonderful theatre in the London study-abroad course.

New Mexico

■ New Mexico State University
Las Cruces, NM

Compiled by: Tom Smith, Department Head

Degrees Offered:

BA in theatre arts

BA in theatre arts with a musical theatre emphasis

Minors Offered:

Theatre arts

Population of Department(s): 90–100 majors

Audition to Declare a Theatre/Musical Theatre Major? No

Three things you would like our readers to know about your performing arts department:

1. We have a guest artist program, so you will work alongside professional actors, directors, playwrights, and designers who can help you find work after graduation.
2. We offer a British studies program, where students go to London for six weeks during the summer to attend class, visit theatres and galleries, and see shows for college credit.
3. Since we don't offer grad degrees, you don't have to compete for roles or directing, stage management, or design opportunities during our mainstage season!

Santa Fe University of Art and Design
Santa Fe, NM

Compiled by: John Weckesser, Chair, Performing Arts Department

Degrees Offered:

BA in theatre design
BA in theatre performance
BFA in theatre, acting specialization
BFA in theatre, music theatre specialization
BFA in theatre, dance specialization
BFA in theatre, design/technical specialization

Minors Offered:

Dance
Theatre design
Theatre performance

Population of Department(s): 121

Audition to Declare a Theatre/Musical Theatre Major? Yes, auditions are a requirement for all majors.

Three things you would like our readers to know about your performing arts department:

1. Students audition for mainstage productions their first year at the university, enabling them to immediately receive hands-on experiences.
2. The Performing Arts Department doesn't just hire pure academics, but practicing professionals who happen to also be really good teachers.
3. In 2012, *Backstage* magazine ranked the theatre program at SFUAD as a Top 5 outside of Los Angeles.

New York

■ Fordham Theatre Program, Fordham University
Lincoln Center, NYC

Compiled by: Carla Jackson, Theatre Program Administrator

Population of School: The Lincoln Center Campus, where the theatre program is located, has 7,603 students enrolled at the entire campus.

Conservatory or Liberal Arts: Liberal arts

Degrees Offered:

BA with concentrations in performance, design and production, playwriting, and directing

Population of Department(s): 116

Theatre Scholarships Available: We have a full Presidential Scholarship and the Denzel Washington Endowed Chair scholarship. There are also smaller packages.

Audition Required for BA/BS/BM: Yes

Pre-screen Video Audition Required: No

Attends Unifieds: Yes, some of them. We go during similar dates, but on our own.

Location of Unifieds: Chicago and Los Angeles and, of course, New York City

Number of Students Auditioning Each Year: More than 600 audition/interview

Number of Students Accepted Each Year: 20 for performance spots, 1–2 directing spots, 1–2 playwriting spots, and 8–12 design/production and stage management spots

Cut Program or Audition to Remain in Program: No

Minors in Musical Theatre/Acting: We have a theatre minor; no audition required.

Prominent Alumni: Denzel Washington, Patricia Clarkson, Taylor Schilling

What do you look for in a potential student?

Imagination, intellectual curiosity, the ability to deeply question, a collaborative and generous spirit, professionalism, someone who takes great joy in the work and process, someone with immense innate talent with great potential for growth who we think has the potential to become a working actor. And yes, we can get a real sense of that during the three minutes.

What are some of the auditors' pet peeves?

Not reading the website carefully and coming in unprepared; going over the monologue time limit; lack of familiarity with our program and school (lack of research).

What are your audition requirements?

Two monologues (one classical, one contemporary, 1.5 minutes each, 3 minutes total)

In your eyes, what makes up an excellent college audition monologue?

Knowledge of the play, your chosen character, your passion for the monologue, commitment, and versatility.

Can you walk me through what I can expect at your on-campus auditions?

The New York City auditions are held at Fordham's Lincoln Center Campus (113 W. 60th Street, New York City) in October, December, January, and February. Each audition day begins at 10 a.m. You will be emailed a confirmation of your audition date/time in advance. (Auditions are scheduled every five minutes throughout the day.) Please be early for your audition. We make every attempt to stay on schedule, but please be prepared to stay if we run late. You can expect to stay between a half hour and three hours, depending on if you participate in the Q&A session and/or take a tour of the campus and dorm.

The Q&A session each day begins at 1 p.m. (and lasts until approximately 1:45 p.m.). This is a time when the theatre faculty will talk with parents and prospective students about the theatre program.

Prospective students also have the opportunity to talk with our Student Theatre Ambassadors about the program while waiting for their appointment times. The Ambassadors periodically give tours of the school and the dorms throughout the day. Sarah Dougan, from the Office of Undergraduate Admission, will be present to answer any questions you have regarding admission, housing, and financial aid.

On the audition day, you will be auditioning for two or more of the following theatre faculty:

- Matthew Maguire, Theatre Program Director
- Tina Benko, Acting Faculty
- George Drance, Artist in Residence, Acting Faculty
- Daniel Alexander Jones, Acting Faculty and Head of the Playwriting Program
- Elizabeth Margid, Acting Faculty and Head of the Directing Program
- Carla Jackson, Theatre Program Administrator
- Dawn Saito, Artist in Residence, Acting Faculty, and Teacher of Movement

What's a memorable audition you can remember?

Once a student was so nervous, he couldn't remember his piece. A faculty member gave him some adjustments, and he was able to take the direction and turn on a dime—again, and again, and again, with just a single line of text. He exhibited great joy in the process and transformed before our very eyes. He was playful and fearless (by taking a risk with each new direction), and in those moments we saw that he had the talent—very raw talent—but a great imagination and physical instrument. We accepted him.

What is your biggest piece of advice for potential students auditioning?

Show us what you love.

After I audition, is there a good way to follow up?

A follow-up isn't necessary, but if students want to write a thank-you note or send a thank-you email to the faculty who auditioned them, that's always a kind gesture.

Would I get a showcase at the end of senior year?

Yes.

Do I have to audition to be accepted into the showcase?

No.

Where are showcases held, and are they successful?

Showcases are held in New York City. They are very well attended by industry professionals.

Will I be able to audition/perform as a freshman?

Yes.

If there is a graduate program, will I get the same performance opportunities as an undergraduate?

We are an undergraduate program, but we have an MFA playwriting program, in association with the off-Broadway theatre Primary Stages. Undergrad actors get to perform in both BA and MFA playwriting students' work.

In what ways can I be involved with the department aside from performing?

Fordham has excellent relationships with the New York City professional theatre world. All Fordham theatre faculty are working professionals, and we introduce our students to the professional world through internships and by inviting guest artists to Fordham, as well as hosting guest directors and designers and so on. There are amazing opportunities in and outside of school. Also, every student has a lab contract—working in an area of the theatre (costume shop, box office, electrics). It's part of our goal in making sure everyone is getting a well-rounded education. If a student is a performance major and wants to design costumes, we encourage that! We believe in experiential learning, and we produce 20 studio and four main-stage shows every year, so there are numerous opportunities in many areas.

Say I get a BA rather than a BFA. Will I actually get to perform?

We are a BA program, and, yes, you will. We produce four mainstage shows and 20 studios each year.

I want to get a BFA in acting, but I also love to sing. Can BFA/BA acting students take voice lessons with top voice faculty?

We have a musical theatre course taught by Alison Fraser, two-time Tony Award nominee, and the class is open to all performance students.

Do you discourage or encourage students to audition for theatre outside of the department during the academic year?

We discourage it, but we don't strictly forbid it. We encourage students to focus on school. Also, so many outside professionals from New York City work with our school that to go outside of it almost doesn't make sense. With that said, a few students in the past have taken a term off to do a play or a movie.

Does your school regularly work in conjunction with any regional theatres?

We've co-produced with several off-Broadway theatres, The Public Theater, Primary Stages, and INTAR, and we will continue to do this in the future. Also, we've workshopped original plays for several theatres such as 13P and Clubbed Thumb.

What do students typically do during the summers? Do you actively promote participation in summer theatre auditions?

Many work at summer theatres; some do internships in New York City, some produce in the New York Fringe Festival, and some study abroad (Fordham offers several programs).

How many musicals versus straight plays do you do in a season?

Even though we're not a musical theatre program, we do a musical every few years, and a lot of our plays have music in them.

What are some of your alumni up to? Do you have an active alumni network?

We have an amazing alumni network! The Fordham Alumni Theatre Company was founded six years ago. Every summer, productions are held, written by Fordham theatre alumni. Some of our recent alums include Taylor Schilling (Netflix, *Orange Is the New Black*), John Johnson (producer, Tony Award–winning *Vanya and Sonia and Masha and Spike*), Jared McNeill (member of touring production of Acclaimed International Producer/Director Peter Brook's *The Suit*), Elizabeth Carena (performer/producer, award-winning Interactive Play, *Then She Fell*), Eljon Wardally (*Docket 32357,* multi-awarded/-screened short film, play, and soon-to-be web series), Aaron Rhyne (nominated for the 2013 Drama Desk award for Outstanding Projection Design for *Wild With Happy*).

Please see www.fordham.edu/academics/programs_at_fordham_/theatre_department/alumni for an extensive list of all that our alumni are doing!

What is the portfolio/interview process for a technical theatre student?

A portfolio with representations of your work (this may include design work, art work, sketches, slides, photos, and so on).

What do you expect to see on a technical theatre résumé?

The résumé is not as important to us as the work and the potential for growth.

I'm interested in lighting, sound design, and stage management. What major should I go for? Can I minor?

Design and production. You can work in some of these areas, and take some classes as a theatre minor.

■ Hofstra University

Hempstead, NY

Compiled by: Jean D. Giebel, Professor of Drama and Dance

Population of School: Approximately 10,000 total full-time undergrads and grad students

Conservatory or Liberal Arts: Liberal arts

Degrees Offered:

BA in drama
BA in dance
BFA in theater arts in performance
BFA in theater arts in production
BS in dance education

Population of Department(s): Approximately 200 in drama and 100 in dance

Theatre Scholarships Available:

- Rosenthal Scholarship for excellence in comedy, $10,000 to a senior
- Kearsley Scholarship for a stage manager or production major, approximately $3,000
- Barnes Scholarship for contributions to the department, approximately $3,000
- Ackerman Scholarship for a senior performance major, approximately $1,000
- Liebson Scholarship for commitment to the department, approximately $1,500
- In addition, we offer approximately $150,000 in activity grants annually that range from $1,000 to $8,000 per year and can be renewed annually.

Audition Required for BFA: Yes

Audition Required for BA/BS: No

Pre-screen Video Audition Required: No

Attends Unifieds: No

Number of Students Auditioning Each Year: Approximately 25–35 students audition for the BFA in performance; approximately 6–8 interview for the BFA in production

Number of Students Accepted Each Year: A maximum of 16 BFA in performance students are accepted. A maximum of two students in each BFA production specialty (for example, two costume design, two set design, two lighting design, two directing, and so on) are accepted per year. Additional stage management students are accepted.

Cut Program or Audition to Remain in Program: Not at this time

Minors in Musical Theatre/Acting: Yes, both

Prominent Alumni: Many graduates have gone on to success in film, TV, and Broadway and off-Broadway productions. They have been recognized with Tony, Oscar, and Emmy awards and nominations. Some prominent alumni include TV and film producers and directors Christopher Albrecht, Francis Ford Coppola, and Phil Rosenthal; theater producers and directors Nick DeGruccio, Jef Hall-Flavin, Irene Lewis, and Susan Schulman; Broadway actors James Barbour, Fred Berman, Felicity Claire, Peter Friedman, and Tom McGowan; TV and film actors Margaret Colin, Lainie Kazan, Joe Morton, Leslie Segrete, and Susan Sullivan; and scores of other entertainment professionals performing in touring companies, regional theaters, and off-off Broadway productions, as well as working behind the scenes.

What do you look for in a potential student?

Talent, of course, but we're not just choosing good actors or technicians; we're looking for people to be part of our community for the next four years. We are looking for students who are passionate, hardworking, ready to learn, and true collaborators.

What are some of the auditors' pet peeves?

Students who arrive late—always come early and be ready to work when your name is called. Students who present themselves in a sloppy or unprofessional way—how you dress communicates your attitude toward the work. Students who want to chat or waste time in the audition room—remember, the auditors are seeing a lot of people in one day, and there's tremendous pressure to stay on schedule and be fair to everyone. If the auditors ask you a question or invite you to ask questions, be concise and to the point. Students who use any kind of dialect or affected voice—the point of the audition is to show off who you are.

What are your audition requirements?

Students interested in performance should prepare an audition consisting of two contrasting pieces, preferably one classical, of no more than two minutes each. Students who wish to sing should prepare one monologue and 32 bars of one song. Bring sheet music. No recorded accompaniment, please. Students interested in design, technical production, stage management, or directing should bring portfolios, prompt books, photographs, or other appropriate supporting material. Candidates who live at a considerable distance may submit an audition DVD or portfolio.

    NOTE: No audition is required to major in drama at Hofstra University. An audition/interview is required for the BFA programs in the sophomore year. While there are no auditions for admission, we do hold scholarship auditions and portfolio reviews each March (usually the third Saturday of the month) for initial grants to first-year students.

In your eyes, what makes up an excellent college audition monologue? Song?

Select a piece that is entertaining and that you enjoy doing. If you love what you are doing, so will we. Know your type and range. The piece should have an arc, or storyline. Look for pieces with realizations, revelations, and surprises. Avoid foul language or rude sexual innuendos. Also avoid using a prop unless it is so essential to the piece that it won't work without one. Also avoid playing someone who whines. Leave the auditors thinking you are passionate and courageous. Finally, avoid recognizable roles played by famous movie stars, because you'll be compared to that star. When singing, choose something with a simple melody that stays well within your range and that you can make sense of in 16 bars. You have to be able to act the song, not just sing it.

If there were one monologue you never wanted to see again, what would it be?

The Star-Spangled Girl by Neil Simon or Boy's Life by Howard Korder.

If there were one song you never wanted to hear again, what would it be?

Any song from a modern sung-through musical. It's almost impossible to get to the point of a 12-minute song in one minute.

Can you walk me through what I can expect at your on-campus auditions?

You will be assigned an audition time in groups. Current students, who can answer your questions about our program from the student perspective, will meet each group in the lobby of the theater. At the appointed time, your group, including parents, will be invited to enter the theater to be met by the entire full-time faculty, rather than a small panel, and have an opportunity to ask questions about the program. After this brief Q&A, you will be asked to return to the lobby, and prospective students will audition one at a time. For students who choose to sing, an accompanist will be provided. Please have your music clearly marked and be prepared to set tempo. There is usually a performance on campus the evening of auditions that you and your family will be invited to attend.

What's a memorable audition you can remember?

The best auditions are ones in which the students have chosen simple, straightforward material that lets them find a strong objective and clear action choices. If singing is involved, students should stay well within their range and do songs that work well within the confines of the audition room.

What is your biggest piece of advice for potential students auditioning?

Remember, your audition begins the minute you enter the room. The most impressive students are composed, focused, and able to display a sense of humor. Also, be flexible enough to roll with whatever happens.

After I audition, is there a good way to follow up?

It's a good idea to send a thank-you note or email. That gives the auditors the opportunity to reply at their convenience. Avoid phone calls unless there is a specific question you need answered.

Would I get a showcase at the end of senior year?

We hold an annual New York City Senior Showcase in April for BFA performance majors.

Do I have to audition to be accepted into the showcase?

All BFA performance majors are required to participate in the showcase. There is no audition.

Where are showcases held, and are they successful?

For the last couple years we have held our showcase at Playwrights Horizons, 416 West 42nd Street in New York City. At our last showcase, every student received interest from industry present.

Will I be able to audition/perform as a freshman?

Yes. First-year students are eligible for casting the second semester of the first year.

If there is a graduate program, will I get the same performance opportunities as an undergraduate?

We do not have a graduate program.

In what ways can I be involved with the department aside from performing?

There are many production opportunities in department shows and positions available to assist faculty and professional guest directors and designers. There are two student clubs on campus, Spectrum Players and Masquerade Musical Theater, that create student-produced work. There are also many department student aide and work-study positions in the scene shop, costume shop, and main office.

Say I get a BA rather than a BFA. Will I actually get to perform?

Yes. Auditions are open to BA and BFA majors, and casting is done without prejudice. Many BA students are cast every semester.

I love to sing, but I don't consider myself a dancer. Can I still seek a degree in musical theatre at your school?

We have a musical theater minor. A vocal audition is required, but no dance audition is required.

I want to get a BFA in acting, but I also love to sing. Can BFA/BA acting students take voice lessons with top voice faculty?

Yes. Private lessons are available through the Music Department and within the musical theater minor.

Do you discourage or encourage students to audition for theatre outside of the department during the academic year?

Students are discouraged to audition off campus during the academic year due to the rigorous production schedule within the department. BFA students are required to get permission for any non-mainstage production for which they wish to audition.

Does your school regularly work in conjunction with any regional theatres?

No.

What do students typically do during the summers? Do you actively promote participation in summer theatre auditions?

We actively assist our students in auditioning or sending production résumés to summer, regional, and New York–area theaters. Our large alumni network in New York City helps students to find summer work and work after graduation.

How many musicals versus straight plays do you do in a season?

Our mainstage season consists of one musical, five plays (including two Shakespeare), and a repertory of student-written, -directed, and/or -acted work for credit. Our student clubs produce two musicals, two plays, and a touring children's show every year.

What are some of your alumni up to? Do you have an active alumni network?

We have a very active alumni network in New York City for recent graduates, helping with everything from entry-level "survival" jobs and housing to auditioning and beginning a career. There are currently multiple off-off Broadway companies created and/or run by Hofstra graduates, including Hyper Aware Theater, Oracle Theatre, Random Access Theatre, The Survivalists, and Variations Theatre Group, as well as many more dance companies and regional theater companies run by Hofstra alumni.

What is the portfolio/interview process for a technical theatre student?

A portfolio review is encouraged for early placement in the BFA program but not required for incoming students. A portfolio of class work and outside work is required for a BFA interview, which can be done in the sophomore year.

What do you expect to see on a technical theatre résumé?

A strong interest and work on high school theater productions. Community or professional theatre work is a plus. Students with a strong background in studio art are also encouraged to apply.

I'm interested in lighting, sound design, and stage management. What major should I go for? Can I minor?

Any student interested in pre-professional production training should go for a BFA in production. Students in the BFA can graduate with a general production degree or focus on technical direction, design, directing, or stage management. We also have a minor in drama that can be focused in production.

Anything else I should know?

Each year, the Hofstra Department of Drama and Dance produces three plays, one musical, two dance concerts, and the nationally renowned Hofstra Shakespeare Festival, the second oldest in the country (produced annually for more than 60 years), which includes both a Shakespeare play and a touring production of a Shakespeare adaptation.

In addition, students in the department produce numerous honors thesis and senior practicum and directing class productions in the Student Rep, with a host of other opportunities to get involved.

In spring 2008, the Drama Department opened the Black Box Theatre. The space is a 50-foot clear square with 20 feet of vertical clearance. The lighting system is replete with a state-of-the-art aircraft cable tension grid, primarily ETC fixtures, and an ETC Emphasis console running on EDMX. Sound is controlled either via a manual 32-channel Yamaha mixing console or via SFX or Cue-Lab playback systems.

Our other producing space is the John Cranford Adams Playhouse, an 1,105-seat proscenium theater with orchestra and balcony. The facility includes a 42-foot-wide by 35-foot-deep stage, an all-ETC Source-4 lighting inventory, computer-controlled synchronized rigging system, in-house scene shop, LightViper optical audio routing system, in-auditorium audio mixing position, and an extensive and expandable video network.

Listed by Backstage.com in the article "Spotlight: 9 Great New York Acting Schools and Universities" (Briana Rodriguez, Sept. 13, 2013) as "a drama program that won't box you in," Hofstra is the place to explore your passion for theater. Whether you are interested in drama, musical theater, directing, designing, or any other aspect of theater, we provide a whole range of exciting opportunities to develop your craft, both onstage and behind the scenes.

New York University

Tisch School of the Arts
New York, NY

Compiled by: Edward Ziter, Chair, Department of Drama

Population of School: More than 50,000 at New York University (relatively even between undergrad and grad students); more than 4,000 at the Tisch School of the Arts (roughly three-fourths are undergrads)

Conservatory or Liberal Arts: The Tisch School of the Arts at New York University combines conservatory training with a curriculum of equally intense liberal arts academics.

Degrees Offered:
BFA in theatre

Population of Department(s): Approximately 1,400 students

Theatre Scholarships Available: NYU offers need-based financial aid. Between 2002 and 2012, the amount of institutional aid to undergrads increased by 138%. All students who submit the Free Application for Federal Student Aid (FAFSA) are considered for need-based aid, and that aid comes from general university funds and endowed scholarship funds. Students do not apply for specific scholarships.

Audition Required for BFA: An artistic review, consisting of a one-one-one audition/portfolio presentation and an interview, is required for admission to the department. The department auditions in several major cities and also accepts video auditions.

Pre-screen Video Audition Required: No

Attends Unifieds: The Department of Drama will hold auditions in New York, Los Angeles, and Chicago during the Unifieds, but will not take part in the Unifieds.

Number of Students Auditioning Each Year: Approximately 2,100 audition

Number of Students Accepted Each Year: Approximately 550 accepted; 400 will attend

Cut Program or Audition to Remain in Program: No

Minors in Musical Theatre/Acting: Minor in applied theatre, but in no other areas

Prominent Alumni: Alec Baldwin, Philip Seymour Hoffman, Matthew Morrison, Chandra Wilson, Nikki James, Ismael Cruz Córdova

What do you look for in a potential student?

We believe that great theatre makers are great theatre thinkers. We look for students who want to combine rigorous professional training with intellectual inquiry so as to move theatre forward.

What are some of the auditors' pet peeves?

Not having read the play from which the monologue is chosen, and thus not being able to converse about the life of the character. Not doing a sufficient amount of research, generally; for instance, why Tisch is a fit for you, specifically.

After I audition, is there a good way to follow up?

Some students choose to send thank-you notes. This is never wrong, but it doesn't necessarily affect your application in any way (positively or negatively).

What's a memorable audition you can remember?

We look for what is special and unique in each student. Great auditions vary as much as the candidates themselves.

If there were one thing you never wanted to see in an audition again, what would it be?

Auditions are most enjoyable when we are able to ascertain what is unique to the applicant. Relax and be yourself.

What is your biggest piece of advice for students auditioning?

Think about why you want to make theatre. Think about why you chose your audition piece. If your auditor directs you, listen carefully and respond fully.

Would I get a showcase at the end of senior year?

The department invites industry to two showcase productions each year. Students are eligible to audition for these showcases after their sophomore year.

Do I have to audition to be accepted into the showcase?

Yes.

Where are showcases held, and are they successful?

Showcases are held in New York, and yes.

Will I be able to audition/perform as a freshman?

Freshmen may not perform in departmental productions.

If there is a graduate program, will I get the same performance opportunities as an undergraduate?

The Graduate Acting Department at Tisch School of the Arts is a separate department from the Department of Drama. All of the performance opportunities in our department are for our students only.

In what ways can I be involved with the department aside from performing?

Students can volunteer to serve as crew on productions. We offer extracurricular workshops and seminars, called "Drama Talks," that students can attend. We have a formal mentorship program that connects students with faculty members for in-depth discussions about mutual areas of interest.

Say I get a BA rather than a BFA. Will I actually get to perform?

We only offer a BFA.

I love to sing, but I don't consider myself a dancer. Can I still seek a degree in musical theatre at your school?

Dance is a key component of our musical theatre training. You do not need to be a trained dancer to be admitted into musical theatre, but you must show aptitude.

I want to get a BFA in acting, but I also love to sing. Can BFA/BA acting students take voice lessons with top voice faculty?

Yes.

Do you discourage or encourage students to audition for theatre outside of the department during the academic year?

We discourage students from auditioning for professional productions while enrolled.

Does your school regularly work in conjunction with any regional theatres?

No.

What do students typically do during the summers? Do you actively promote participation in summer theatre auditions?

We encourage students to return home and relax as much as possible.

How many musicals versus straight plays do you do in a season?

We do roughly 100 productions a year; 12–15 of these are musicals.

What are some of your alumni up to? Do you have an active alumni network?

We have an active alumni network. Here are some examples:

Alec Baldwin: Producer, director, and actor, *Brooklyn Rules, 30 Rock* (Golden Globe 2007, 2009, 2010 Best Performance by an Actor in a Television Series – Musical or Comedy; Screen Actors Guild 2007–2010 Outstanding Performance by a Male Actor in a Comedy Series; Screen Actors Guild 2009 Outstanding Performance by an Ensemble; Emmy 2009 Outstanding Lead Actor in a Comedy Series), *The Departed* (National Board of Review 2006 Best Ensemble), *The Good Shepherd, Running With Scissors, The Cooler* (National Board of Review 2003 Best Supporting Actor), *State and Main* (National Board of Review 2000 Best Acting by an Ensemble); theatre: *Loot* (Theatre World Award 1986)

Kristen Bell: Actress, *Veronica Mars*; theatre: *Tom Sawyer, The Crucible*

Bryce Dallas Howard: Actress, *Spider-Man 3, The Village, Lady in the Water*; theatre: *Tartuffe*

Felicity Huffman: Actress, *Georgia Rule, Desperate Housewives* (Emmy 2005 Outstanding Lead Actress in a Comedy Series; Screen Actors Guild 2006 Outstanding Performance by a Female Actor in a Comedy Series and Outstanding Performance by an Ensemble in a Comedy Series; Screen Actors Guild 2005 Outstanding Performance by an Ensemble in a Comedy Series), *Transamerica* (Golden Globe 2005 Best Performance by an Actress in a Motion Picture – Drama; Independent Spirit Award 2006 Best Female Lead; National Board of Review 2005 Best Actress; Tribeca Film Festival 2005 Best Actress); theatre: *Speed-the-Plow*

Moisés Kaufman: Director, screenwriter, and playwright, *The L Word, The Laramie Project*; theatre: *I Am My Own Wife, The Laramie Project, Gross Indecency*

John Leguizamo: Producer, director, actor, and screenwriter, *The Happening, Righteous Kill, My Name Is Earl, ER, Moulin Rouge, The Babysitters, Land of the Dead*; theatre: *American Buffalo, Sexaholix, Freak* (Drama Desk Award 1998 Outstanding Solo/One-Person Show)

Idina Menzel: Actress, *Rent, Kissing Jessica Stein*; theatre: *Wicked* (Tony Award 2004 Best Actress in a Musical), *Funny Girl, Aida, Rent*

Jesse Metcalfe: Actor, *John Tucker Must Die, Desperate Housewives* (Screen Actors Guild 2005 Outstanding Performance by an Ensemble in a Comedy Series), *Loaded, Smallville*

Anthony Rapp: Actor, *Scaring the Fish, Rent, Six Degrees of Separation, A Beautiful Mind*; theatre: *Rent, Six Degrees of Separation, Precious Sons*

Adam Sandler: Producer, actor, and screenwriter (2008 MTV Generation Award), *Saturday Night Live, Click, The Longest Yard, Spanglish, 50 First Dates* (MTV Music Award 2004 Best On-Screen Team), *Mr. Deeds, Punch-Drunk Love, Little Nicky, Big Daddy* (MTV Music Award 2000 Best Comedic Performance), *The Water Boy* (MTV Music Award 1999 Best Comedic Performance), *The Wedding Singer, Happy Gilmore, Billy Madison*

Molly Shannon: Actress, *Year of the Dog, Saturday Night Live, Phantom of the Opera, Never Been Kissed, How the Grinch Stole Christmas*

Bernie Telsey: Casting director, *Rent, Whoopi, Finding Forrester, Death of a Salesman*; theatre: *Deuce, Legally Blonde, Talk Radio, High Fidelity, Grey Gardens*

What is the portfolio/interview process for a technical theatre student?

The portfolio presentation will include a conversation about your interests, accomplishments, and ideas about your chosen area(s) of specialization. Prospective students are asked to bring a résumé, written statement of purpose, recent photograph, and portfolio of work (designs, drawings, photos, stage manager prompt books). Applicants are interviewed as part of the portfolio presentation discussion. A professional headshot is not necessary.

What is the portfolio/interview process for a technical theatre student?

The portfolio presentation will include a conversation about your interests, accomplishments, and ideas about your chosen area(s) of specialization. Prospective students are asked to bring a résumé, written statement of purpose, recent photograph, and portfolio of work (designs, drawings, photos, stage manager prompt books). Applicants are interviewed as part of the portfolio presentation discussion. A professional headshot is not necessary.

What do you expect to see on a technical theatre résumé?

A production résumé should include your career objective and shows (listed in reverse chronological order) in which you have participated and in what capacity. If you have special skills or have received any awards, those should be listed as well.

I'm interested in lighting, sound design, and stage management. What major should I go for? Can I minor?

All students in our department work toward a BFA in theatre. Only an applied theatre minor is available from our department.

■ Pace University
New York, NY

Compiled by: Wayne Petro, Enrollment Manager, Pace University School of Performing Arts

Population of School: 8,336 undergrads

Conservatory or Liberal Arts: Conservatory-like within a liberal arts environment

Degrees Offered:

BFA in acting, acting for film, television, voice-overs and commercials, commercial dance, musical theater, production and design for stage and screen

BA in acting, directing, stage management

Population of Department(s): 500 majors amongst the eight majors

Theatre Scholarships Available: Yes. A limited amount available in the performing arts department. Most merit aid is given based on the application for admission. Of students, 97% receive aid at Pace, and the vast majority of those do so by review of the application.

Audition Required for BFA: Yes. Separate auditions are required for each major.

Audition Required for BA/BS/BM: Yes. Separate auditions are required for each major.

Pre-screen Video Audition Required: Yes. Every program has its own set of guidelines and requirements that the students will need to follow in order to upload their video auditions to getacceptd.com. Students can refer to the Pace or getacceptd.com websites for those guidelines. They can upload and audition to as many programs as they want. Callbacks are issued within about 36 hours of submitting. When they submit, they request their first- or second-choice audition dates, and hopefully they receive their first choice when they get their callback.

Attends Unifieds: Not officially, although we do audition in the city at the same time as Unifieds. Our acting, design, and musical theater programs coincide with Unifieds; however, our commercial dance does not.

Number of Students Auditioning Each Year: In total, we see about 2,000 auditions per year.

Number of Students Accepted Each Year: About 166, in eight majors

Cut Program or Audition to Remain in Program: No cut. We have an evaluative system every year to make sure the students are on track to graduate in each program.

Minors in Musical Theatre/Acting: No. We do offer a minor in dance for performing arts majors only, and it is by audition only.

Prominent Alumni: Michelle Borth (*Hawaii Five-0, The Forgotten, Combat Hospital*), Rob Hinderliter (Broadway producer, *The Velocity of Autumn, The Realistic Joneses*), Brett Thiele (Broadway, *Spider-Man: Turn off the Dark*), Daniel Quadrino (Broadway: *Newsies*), Britton Smith (Broadway: *After Midnight*), Danielle Bouchard (musician: Oh Honey), and others.

What do you look for in a potential student?

We look for individuals who possess an individualized, unique artistic voice; who are talented, kind, and hardworking; who have an interest in earning a college degree that involves academics; and who are ready to move to New York City to be a part of New York City performing arts.

What are some of the auditors' pet peeves?

Not reading directions. Lack of preparation. Lack of rapport with auditioners or not being kind to pianists. Personal demeanor and behavior comes through on audition day.

What are your audition requirements?

Students should check the website. The requirements are different for each program. In general, there are monologue, song, and dance requirements for musical theatre students. There is a full dance audition for commercial dance and portfolio review for designers and directors. There are elements of the audition that students cannot prepare for. For instance, with acting, the students do scene work that is handed to them at the audition. We also do a movement callback for acting programs. For musical theatre, we might work on some of their material a little bit, so we might ask for additional material and a dance call, which they will not be able to prepare for. For the commercial dance audition, we spend three to four hours in class with faculty.

In your eyes, what makes up an excellent college audition monologue? Song?

A piece that the student can strongly connect to. Students should be able to share their voice in terms of what they like and their interpretation. They should be connected to the material. It is something that maybe takes a risk, but something that isn't hugely exaggerated so that we can't tell who they are. We want to see who they are as an artist in whatever they choose, and the decision of which monologue they choose is a good indicator of that. We like to see that they have prepared, but they haven't necessarily polished and perfected them to such a point that we can't still see if there is some element of "raw" in there. One can be too overly polished to the point where nothing comes across about the individual. It needs to be personalized.

If there were one monologue you never wanted to see again, what would it be?

We don't publish a "do not use," because we would never want to discourage someone from picking a piece because it is popular. If it is something you feel that you love and want to do, and it happens to be very popular, then we want to see that. But, keep in mind that if it is a monologue or song that has been performed by somebody and everyone has heard it, you have to be careful not to mimic what that person is doing. You want to make it your own. If you are doing something that Sutton Foster is playing, you're setting yourself up for a possible comparison, and so then you better really rock it.

If you require a pre-screen video audition, what do you look for in those submissions?

We look for students to bring their best self at all times. The pre-screen video should be prepared to performance quality. It's best to be in a space where we can focus on you, rather than an environment where there is a lot of background and noise. It is best to have an accompanist if you're auditioning for musical theatre. It is best to be in a studio if you are showcasing your dance solo. And it is best to be in a more neutral environment for your monologues. We are looking for them to be at the level that they would be in an in-person audition. Students can use the same material in live auditions, and most do.

Can you walk me through what I can expect at your on-campus auditions?

It varies per major. All auditions take place in our performing arts facility. Student workers and Pace faculty will organize you into a group that you will travel with for the day. All auditions are half-day events, so plan to be there for a large chunk of time rather than just a specific time slot. You will have multiple parts to each audition. Prospective students can expect to meet a lot of current students and faculty who come to audition day to participate.

They can also meet with staff members who can talk them through the logistical information of applying as well as details that they would not normally get on a typical campus visit. We also offer performing arts tours. Prospective students can do multiple auditions, with a maximum of two on one day.

What's a memorable audition you can remember?

For one of his songs, a gentleman prepared a Lady Gaga tune on his guitar. We do ask students to bring in sheet music for our accompanist, which this student had prepared, but he also performed it with guitar separately as something that he felt very strongly about.

What is your biggest piece of advice for potential students auditioning?

Don't try to place yourself in the shoes of the auditioner. Don't do what you think we want to see. Bring your best self to the audition.

If I audition for your BFA musical theatre program, but don't get accepted, do you still consider me for your BFA acting program or your BA program?

No, you must audition separately.

After I audition, is there a good way to follow up?

There is no need to follow-up, per se, except to make sure that you get all of your admissions materials into the Undergraduate Admissions Office and are accepted academically. We convey the results of all auditions after we've seen all candidates. We start sending letters out after the last audition in March. Emails will only be sent out if the applicant is abroad. What is acceptable is a thank-you note to the faculty and staff in performing arts or the person who auditioned you. Additionally, if you still have not heard anything within the first couple weeks of April, it would be a good idea to follow up and make sure nothing was lost in the mail. Students must be admitted academically to Pace before the performing arts department can notify applicants of their status.

Would I get a showcase at the end of senior year?

Yes. All programs have their own type of showcase, even the BAs.

Do I have to audition to be accepted into the showcase?

All musical theatre students are accepted, but for the acting students it is by audition only (varies by program).

Where are showcases held, and are they successful?

Showcases are held in Midtown, New York City, and they regularly lead to students getting agent callbacks. By the time our students are seniors, most already have a professional résumé because we have an open audition policy at the university. The showcase is not the first time that most of them will be seen in front of a casting director. It is something that most students will already have been through. For instance, a current student is already performing in *Spider-Man: Turn off the Dark* on Broadway. We believe that your career starts the day that you begin at Pace, not the day that you leave, and so we are working on honing those audition skills and building that résumé from the start, not just at the showcase.

Will I be able to audition/perform as a freshman?

Yes, but it varies by program as to when this can happen.

If there is a graduate program, will I get the same performance opportunities as an undergraduate?

The graduate program is completely separate from the undergraduate program at Pace. All of our productions involve only undergrad students; we do not mix in the slightest. The graduate program is its own entity and is located in a completely separate area.

In what ways can I be involved with the department aside from performing?

All students do crew assignments and design courses to give some exposure. Students also get to attend tapings of *Inside the Actors Studio* and our masters series, which brings in various masters of the profession. We also have artist-in-residence programs in our musical theatre and commercial dance programs, which expose our students to world-class professionals who work with our students over the course of the academic year. We have Director's Fest for directors to showcase their work on the mainstage. We have Pace New Musicals, which is a commissioned new musical piece—this is a performing/directing opportunity for our students and one that brings in professional writers/composers.

Say I get a BA rather than a BFA. Will I actually get to perform?

Yes. We look at students from all areas for casting. Our mainstage productions are only for performing arts majors. Students from all majors within performing arts will audition, so it does not matter if you are a BA or a BFA. The first year of the BA is a more highly designed program and is called the International Performance Ensemble. This is a really unique training environment. The freshman BA actors and directors are in ensemble-based training in the first year, and so do not participate in mainstage productions in the first year. This is primarily because they are participating in their own work developing pieces, and they take that work abroad in the second year and audition for the mainstage productions with everyone else.

I love to sing, but I don't consider myself a dancer. Can I still seek a degree in musical theatre at your school?

As we know, there are dancer-dancers and movers in the musical theater industry. If you are not a dancer, we're going to want your acting and singing ability to be strong to be competitive. Generally, we say that you need to be strong in at least two of the areas to be competitive with those who audition.

I want to get a BFA in acting, but I also love to sing. Can BFA/BA acting students take voice lessons with top voice faculty?

Not for credit through the program. The lessons would have to be taken outside.

Do you discourage or encourage students to audition for theatre outside of the department during the academic year?

We encourage it.

Does your school regularly work in conjunction with any regional theatres?

We do not.

What do students typically do during the summers? Do you actively promote participation in summer theatre auditions?

Yes, we hold StrawHat auditions for non-Equity summer stock theater on campus, and students are guaranteed an audition, if they wish. Our students in all majors commonly work in summer theatre.

How many musicals versus straight plays do you do in a season?

In the mainstage season, we do at least four musicals and four straight plays.

What are some of your alumni up to? Do you have an active alumni network?

Our students are very active after graduation. We have students working in film and television, on Broadway, off-Broadway, and on national tours. In every field, we have graduates working.

What is the portfolio/interview process for a technical theatre student?

Students upload their portfolio and any other supplemental information to Acceptd.com. We review that information on Acceptd.com, and then contact the student for an interview either in-person or over the phone. The portfolio can be very typical in terms of submitting photos or other design concepts. It can also be more loosely constructed in terms of writing about one's interests, writing stories, or writing down other information that conveys one's connection and interest in the design and production areas. We are very open with that, and the guidelines are on the website. The portfolio can be in whatever format the applicant thinks is appropriate to convey his or her interest in that area.

What do you expect to see on a technical theatre résumé?

A commitment to the production and design realm. It's a brand-new BFA program, and we are looking for students who show a strong commitment and skill in design and production.

I'm interested in lighting, sound design, and stage management. What major should I go for? Can I minor?

There is no minor. You would do production/design. Students are exposed to all main areas within that major—costume design, set design, sound design, lighting design, and media design. In the BFA program, you will begin to take a sequence focused on one or two of those areas. Students interested in stage management are on their own guided track guided by stage management faculty.

■ Syracuse University
Syracuse, NY

Compiled by: Ralph Zito, Department Chair, Professor of Acting

Population of School: Approximately 1,800 in the College of Visual and Performing Arts

Conservatory or Liberal Arts: Conservatory-style training in a university setting in direct partnership with a professional LORT theater (Syracuse Stage)

Degrees Offered:

BFA in musical theater

BFA in acting

BFA in stage management

BFA in theater design and technology

BS in drama with concentration in theater management

Population of Department(s): Approximately 225 majors

Theatre Scholarships Available: Need- and merit-based financial aid distributed through the university financial aid office

Audition Required for BFA: Yes. All performance students must currently enter as BFA candidates. After their first or second year, they may choose to move to a BS in drama, or they may be asked to move to the BS after their second-year evaluation.

Audition Required for BA/BS/BM: No; must currently enter as BFA

Pre-screen Video Audition Required: No

Attends Unifieds: In the same city at the same time, but not with them

Location of Unifieds: Chicago, New York City, and Los Angeles, at the same time as Unifieds

Number of Students Auditioning Each Year: 1,000

Number of Students Accepted Each Year: Accept 130, with the aim of a starting class of 23 BFA musical theater, 23 BFA acting, 5 BFA stage management, 10 BFA theater/design tech, 5 BS theater management

Cut Program or Audition to Remain in Program: For performance students, the second-year evaluation determines whether or not they can continue in the BFA. This is not a quota system; this is a skills assessment. If the student passes the evaluation, he or she moves on to upper-level classes. If the student doesn't pass, he or she may be asked to repeat certain classes and re-evaluate the following term. If the student doesn't pass the second evaluation, he or she will be asked to move to the BS degree.

Minors in Musical Theatre/Acting: Minor in drama but not musical theater

Prominent Alumni: Aaron Sorkin, Vanessa Williams, Julia Murney, Patti Murin, Josh Young

What do you look for in a potential student?

Some combination of accomplishment and potential. We are not looking for a particular type but are interested in helping individuals develop their talents.

What are some of the auditors' pet peeves?

Very high heels, constricting clothing, disorganized sheet music. Lack of knowledge/understanding about the play from which the material is chosen. You must know the context of the piece you are performing.

What are your audition requirements?

For musical theater, one two-minute monologue from a modern play, two 90-second songs (a ballad and an up-tempo); for acting, two contrasting two-minute monologues from a modern play (one comedic/one dramatic).

In your eyes, what makes up an excellent college audition monologue? Song?

A clear beginning, middle, and end to the emotional journey. An opportunity to reveal the individual who is performing it.

If there were one monologue you never wanted to see again, what would it be?

The Laramie Project (more narration than acting).

Can you walk me through what I can expect at your on-campus auditions?

For acting, after an introduction and Q&A session with the chair of the department (Professor Ralph Zito), you will then have the opportunity to go to a vocal warm-up. Then, one-by-one you will go into a room to present your monologue and talk briefly with a panel of one to three faculty members. There is no callback for acting. In musical theater, after the Q&A session, the students get divided into two groups; half go to their dance audition where they will learn a combination for an hour, and the other half will have a brief vocal warm-up and then one-by-one go into the room to present their songs and monologues for one to three faculty members. We have the same on- and off-campus procedures.

What's a memorable audition you can remember?

I remember in this last year of auditions, a student came in who was friendly but a little shy and seemed much younger than his years in his conversation and interview. He then launched into two very different monologues, both of which were much older than he was, and completely transformed in front of me.

What is your biggest piece of advice for potential students auditioning?

Remember, we're looking for people to invite; we're not looking for people to eliminate. Bring yourself, not the person you think we're looking for. "To thine own self be true."

If I audition for your BFA musical theatre program, but don't get accepted, do you still consider me for your BFA acting program or your BA program?

If you indicate that you would like to be, then yes.

After I audition, is there a good way to follow up?

Not necessary. Our admissions department keeps students updated in a timely manner.

Would I get a showcase at the end of senior year?

Our current senior classes are too large for all to attend the showcase. Currently, we select students on the basis of an audition and their record of artistic accomplishment in the department, as well as the faculty's determination that they are ready to enter the profession.

Do I have to audition to be accepted into the showcase?

Yes.

Where are showcases held, and are they successful?

Showcases are held in Syracuse and New York City. Yes, they are successful. Industry attendance increases every year. Representatives of large agencies and casting directors are in attendance.

Will I be able to audition/perform as a freshman?

Freshman year is focused on building foundational skills and self-awareness. It's also a time for students to have a chance to bond with their classmates. For these reasons, freshmen don't perform, design, or stage manage. Since we audition for our productions the semester before they're scheduled, freshman performance students audition in April for the following fall's shows.

In what ways can I be involved with the department aside from performing?

Work-study opportunities at Syracuse Stage (with whom we share a building) include crew assignments as part of Introduction to Theater; Black Box Players, an entirely student-run theater producing organization; freshmen can be production assistants on department shows; community arts practice opportunities through All Star CAST (a class in which students serve as facilitators in a weekly theater workshop for people with developmental disabilities); and opportunities to assist with prospective student auditions and give tours.

Say I get a BA rather than a BFA. Will I actually get to perform?

Students who pursue the BS in drama have the same opportunity to audition and perform in drama department productions.

I love to sing, but I don't consider myself a dancer. Can I still seek a degree in musical theatre at your school?

Not at present. Musical theater students must have potential in acting, singing, and dancing.

I want to get a BFA in acting, but I also love to sing. Can BFA/BA acting students take voice lessons with top voice faculty?

They may on a space-available basis, and there may be an additional cost.

Do you discourage or encourage students to audition for theatre outside of the department during the academic year?

Except for freshmen, students are permitted to participate in outside productions, with the understanding that their commitment to class work is their first priority.

Does your school regularly work in conjunction with any regional theatres?

Yes, our program is in partnership with Syracuse Stage, and students are cast each year in our annual drama/stage co-production and sometimes also in age-appropriate roles in other Syracuse Stage shows. We share a building complex with Syracuse Stage, and several of its professional technical staff teach in our stage management and theater design and technology programs.

What do students typically do during the summers? Do you actively promote participation in summer theatre auditions?

We promote summer theater auditions and internships, and many of our students participate in these activities. We also encourage students to rest, renew, and seek experiences apart from the theater that will help them grow as individuals.

How many musicals versus straight plays do you do in a season?

Two musicals, usually a big book and a small cast musical. Three straight plays. In addition, there is one co-production with Syracuse Stage, which may be either a musical or straight play.

What are some of your alumni up to? Do you have an active alumni network?

We have a very active alumni network, Syracuse University Drama Organization (SUDO), which works with our Alumni Affairs office to share news and opportunities. Very visible people, such as Aaron Sorkin, Arielle Tepper, Jerry Stiller, and the Araca Group, have provided programming support over the years. Others, like Vanessa Williams, Vera Farmiga, and Taye Diggs, stay in contact with former teachers and have returned to work with students. We have active alumni in theater design, production stage management, and casting who return every year to see our senior showcase and provide contacts to graduating students.

What is the portfolio/interview process for a technical theatre student?

An interview appointment with theater design and technology faculty includes a review of the student's portfolio and a conversation about the student's interests and how he or she might intersect with what our program has to offer.

What do you expect to see on a technical theatre résumé?

Some high school and/or community theater experience is always useful.

I'm interested in lighting, sound design, and stage management. What major should I go for? Can I minor?

BFA in theater design and technology or BFA in stage management. The minor is in the more general "drama" offering, but some design classes are open to minors.

◼ Wagner College
Staten Island, NY

Compiled by: Felicia Ruff, Department Chair

Population of School: 1,800

Conservatory or Liberal Arts: Liberal arts

Degrees Offered:
BA in theatre, with three different concentrations in theatre studies, performance, and design technology management
Dual BA major in theatre and education
BS in arts administration, with concentrations in theatre, art, music, and combined arts

Population of Department(s): Total is 300, splits pretty evenly between the BA and BS degrees

Theatre Scholarships Available: Yes

Audition Required for BA/BS/BM: Yes for BA in theatre performance; for the BS, it is an interview.

Pre-screen Video Audition Required: We accept recorded videos from students who can't make it to campus, but no pre-screen is required. 350+ apply for in-person auditions, and 200 are invited to audition on campus based largely on academics.

Attends Unifieds: No

Number of Students Auditioning Each Year: 400 apply, and 200 are invited for on-campus audition.

Number of Students Accepted Each Year: Approximately 50–60 accepted, and we hope for a class of 32.

Cut Program or Audition to Remain in Program: No. Policies are in place that hold students accountable in terms of grades. We usually graduate 26–28 as some students drift to other majors.

Minors in Musical Theatre/Acting: Minors in theatre and dance

Prominent Alumni: Tony Award–winner Randy Graff, Broadway and TV star Kathy Brier, Renee Marino (*Jersey Boys* on Broadway and in the feature film), Drama Desk–winner Janine LaManna, and Broadway director Matt Lenz are among more than 50 others who have worked on Broadway, as one benchmark.

What do you look for in a potential student?

It varies. We are looking to create a class of students who will work and learn well together and fit well with us. Talent matters and ability, of course, but we also look for flexibility and how you respond to feedback/how you present yourself.

What are some of the auditors' pet peeves?

Egotism or rudeness. We are more inclined to work with people who accept feedback and listen openly.

What are your audition requirements?

For monologues, one-minute contemporary. For songs, 16–32 bars, two cuts. For dance, students will take a dance class.

In your eyes, what makes up an excellent college audition monologue? Song?

Something that is close to home. Something that fits the student. Most importantly, material the student understands.

If there were one monologue you never wanted to see again, what would it be?

Nothing specific. If it's good, it's good. If it's bad, it's bad.

Can you walk me through what I can expect at your on-campus auditions?

Students will arrive and be greeted by current Wagner Theatre students. We feel that we are auditioning for the students as much as they are auditioning for us. First thing that happens is an overview of the day. Students will then be taken into three different groups to dance, act, or sing first. While the students are auditioning, the department chair and a panel of students will meet with the parents to answer any questions.

What is your biggest piece of advice for potential students auditioning?

They should be auditioning the school as well as feeling like they are there to audition for the faculty. Make sure to get a sense of the people and the program.

After I audition, is there a good way to follow up?

Applicants don't need to. They certainly can. If they have questions, they can reach out to the faculty. There is no advantage in following up.

Would I get a showcase at the end of senior year?

Yes.

Do I have to audition to be accepted into the showcase?

No. Showcase is a class taken at the end of the senior year to prepare. A showcase is part of the curriculum. If you don't do well in the class, in theory, you could be pulled out.

Where are showcases held, and are they successful?

In New York City at Playwrights Horizons. Everyone is featured, and all students are showcased. We are very in touch with what agents/casting directors are looking for.

Will I be able to audition/perform as a freshman?

Yes.

In what ways can I be involved with the department aside from performing?

Lots of ways. As part of the curriculum, students are required to be part of the production program—wardrobe, lights, box office, designing, stage management, and so on. The entire college is allowed to audition for shows, and non-majors do get cast.

Do you discourage or encourage students to audition for theatre outside of the department during the academic year?

Neither. We let them, and students do get gigs. We just had a student leave for a semester for the international tour of *West Side Story* at the end of his junior year. He did the tour, did a semester here, and then went back on tour.

Does your school regularly work in conjunction with any regional theatres?

We have an affiliation with Surflight Theatre in New Jersey as well as accept many students from the Papermill Playhouse Education Program, but our location in NYC means internships, auditions, and work are available for our students during the school year as well as the summer.

What do students typically do during the summers? Do you actively promote participation in summer theatre auditions?

Yes. Students go to StrawHat and NETC auditions on their own because of our location. We also host several summer stock auditions on campus, including Allenbury Playhouse, Surflight Theatre, and Hope Summer Rep as well as Dorney Park. At least 30%–50% do summer stock. Others go home and live with family, although most work in even community theatre or theatre camps at the very least.

How many musicals versus straight plays do you do in a season?

Our degree is not exclusively a musical theatre degree, although we offer high-level musical theatre performance classes. While it's a BA in theatre, we produce four full-stage musicals. The official department season includes four musicals, three straight plays, and a dance concert. This year we are producing *Hello Dolly, Merrily We Roll Along, Spamalot*, and *Cats* along with Adam Bock's *The Thugs* and Diana Son's *Stop Kiss*.

What are some of your alumni up to? Do you have an active alumni network?

We are celebrating our 46th year, so we have a very active alumni network. Many graduates work on Broadway, regional theatre, national tours, film, and TV. Many keep in contact with Wagner through our alumni network and theatre support group, Friends of the Theatre, as well as social media, especially our WCT Facebook group. This year alone we have had numerous alums performing on Broadway, including *Jersey Boys, The Book of Mormon, Rock of Ages,* and the recently closed *Spider-Man: Turn Off the Dark* and *Nice Work If You Can Get It,* among others. Many are on cruise ships, including starring as Disney princes and princesses. Others are on non-Equity as well as first national tours, including *Mary Poppins, Ghost: The Musical,* and *American Idiot.* And look for WCT alum Renee Marino as Mary Delgado in the Clint Eastwood-directed movie *Jersey Boys.*

What is the portfolio/interview process for a technical theatre student?

Students meet with the faculty on audition day or by appointment for an interview. If they have a résumé and some design work, that's great, but an interview is just fine. We want a good fit and a motivated student.

I'm interested in lighting, sound design, and stage management. What major should I go for? Can I minor?

The department offers a general theatre minor.

Anything else I should know?

Our location on top of a scenic hill overlooking the city skyline, but in one of the boroughs of New York City, allows our students to audition in the city, attend shows, and do internships all while enjoying a traditional college campus with Division I sports, and so on.

Our location also means that students often do several internships at places as far ranging as the Met, MTV, Carnegie Hall, Paul Taylor Dance, the Dramatist Guild, Disney, and so on.

It also means our faculty often work in New York City, including Broadway. Our stage management professor was recently the production stage manager on *First Date* and before that *Memphis*; our resident costumer works regularly on *Mamma Mia!,* our wigs/makeup professor just closed *Nice Work If You Can Get It,* and the professor who teaches our Acting V: The Professional Actor and our Showcase class is Michele Pawk, a Tony Award–winning actress who just starred in *Giant* at the Public Theatre, as well as numerous television credits such as *Law and Order.* We recently hired Theresa McCarthy as a member of the full-time faculty to teach acting; an MFA from the University of California, San Diego (UCSD) and professional actress with Broadway and TV credits, she mirrors the other faculty who are practitioner/educators.

We also have a tradition of success that includes well over four dozen alums who have performed on Broadway, several of whom have won Tony and Drama Desk awards. But because we are a BA program, we often see students become lawyers, teachers, casting agents, talent managers, Air Force pilots, critics, arts administrators, concessions managers, missionaries, ministers, chiropractors, and so on. That is to say, students successfully apply their theatre education from Wagner in pursuit of any number of professional opportunities. Also, many theatre majors study abroad particularly in London but also in Amsterdam, where we offer a class in commedia dell'arte.

Brooklyn College, City University of New York
New York, NY

Compiled by: Victor Marsh, Theater Department Chairperson, Head of Design & Technical Production

Degrees Offered:

BA in theater
BFA in acting
BFA in design and technical theater
MA in theater history and criticism
MFA in acting
MFA in design and technical theater
MFA in performance and interactive media (PIMA)
MFA in performing arts management

Minors Offered:

Theater
Acting
Theater production

Population of Department(s): Around 200

Audition to Declare a Theatre/Musical Theatre Major? Yes for acting programs

Three things you would like our readers to know about your performing arts department:

1. It provides a hands-on, fully immersive learning experience that includes all aspects of production.
2. The undergraduate and graduate communities intertwine throughout the season, making it possible to learn from peers as well as from the excellent faculty and staff.
3. The cost of tuition makes it possible to go out and experience theatre in the city.

City College of New York
New York, NY

Compiled by: Rob Barron, Chair of Department of Theatre and Speech

Degrees Offered:

Theatre and speech (as well as the opportunity to pursue a track in performance, playwriting, directing, and technical theatre and design)

Minors Offered:

Theatre and speech

Population of Department(s): 130 majors and 50 minors

Audition to Declare a Theatre/Musical Theatre Major? No

Three things you would like our readers to know about your performing arts department:

1. Our faculty members are working professionals, in addition to being fabulous teachers in the classroom.

2. Students may perform in up to five productions per academic year, in addition to summer and off-campus productions that are connected to the theatre department. There are multiple backstage and design possibilities available as well.

3. There is *a lot* of financial aid available from the university!

■ Hunter College
New York, NY

Compiled by: Joel Bassin, Chair of Department of Theatre

Degrees Offered:

BA in theatre
MA in theatre
MFA in playwriting

Minors Offered:

Theatre

Population of Department(s): 90

Audition to Declare a Theatre/Musical Theatre Major? No

Three things you would like our readers to know about your performing arts department:

1. We encourage and support student-generated work with project grants and awards.
2. We offer internships with theatre institutions throughout New York City.
3. Our majors receive training and experience in all aspects of theatre.

■ Niagara University
Niagara University, NY

Compiled by: Sharon Watkinson, PhD, Professor and Chair, Department of Theatre and Fine Arts

Degrees Offered:

BFA in theatre performance
BFA in theatre design/tech
BFA in theatre general

Minors Offered:

Theatre studies
Design/tech
Dance

Population of Department(s): 92 students for 2013–2014 academic year (77 performance, 10 design/tech, 5 general)

Audition to Declare a Theatre/Musical Theatre Major? Yes

Three things you would like our readers to know about your performing arts department:

1. We offer a genuine conservatory approach to actor training set within a liberal arts curriculum; we offer a theatre design/tech sequence blending studio/classroom training and hands-on experience.

2. We produce eight major productions a year, ranging from Shakespeare, to American and British realism, to musical theatre, for which all performance students must audition, including freshmen through seniors, and all design/tech students must crew.

3. We frequently bring in nationally recognized guest artists such as composers John Kander and Charles Strouse; playwright Tina Howe; and actors Debra Monk and David Hyde Pierce.

■ Skidmore College
Saratoga Springs, NY

Compiled by: Lary Opitz, Professor and Theater Department Chair

Degrees Offered:

BS in theater with concentrations in acting, directing, design, technical theater, stage management, dramaturgy, playwriting, and theater administration

Minors Offered:

Theater

Population of Department(s): Approximately 150 majors

Audition to Declare a Theatre/Musical Theatre Major? No

Three things you would like our readers to know about your performing arts department:

1. Theater students at Skidmore can take half of their academic credits in theater and still have a rich, well-rounded liberal arts education at a small school with an excellent student–faculty ratio.

2. Most of our students go on to professional careers in theater or a related field. Those who choose to go to grad school are admitted to the top MFA programs in the country.

3. Our students are encouraged to study abroad and to work and train in professional programs during the summers, and most do. We place interns in our own summer Equity company (the Saratoga Shakespeare Co.).

■ St. Lawrence University
Canton, NY

Compiled by: Ann Marie Gardinier Halstead, Associate Professor and Co-chair

Degrees Offered:

Performance and communication arts (students choose either theatre/performance studies or rhetoric/communication studies as their primary track and the other area as their secondary track)

Minors Offered:

Performance and communication arts (students choose either theatre/performance studies or rhetoric/communication studies as their primary track and the other area as their secondary track)

Population of Department(s): 85

Audition to Declare a Theatre/Musical Theatre Major? No

Three things you would like our readers to know about your performing arts department:

1. Our program is unique in that not only do students study performance, but also they study communication. Our courses emphasize that all performances are communicative, and all acts of communication are performative. This approach, coupled with St. Lawrence's liberal arts setting, aids our majors in becoming well-rounded students, artists, and citizens.

2. Our class sizes are small, so therefore students benefit from individualized attention. In addition, we are a faculty that prides itself on excellence in teaching.

3. St. Lawrence offers a host of off-campus programs, including some that are of particular interest to students who major in performance and communication arts, namely our London and New York City programs.

■ St. Bonaventure University
St. Bonaventure, NY

Compiled by: Ed. Simone, Professor of Theater and Director of the Theater Program

Degrees Offered:

BA in theater

Minors Offered:

Theater

Population of Department(s): 12–20

Audition to Declare a Theatre/Musical Theatre Major? No, but majors and minors are required to audition or tech interview for all productions.

Three things you would like our readers to know about your performing arts department:

1. We are small and happy to be so—small classes, lots of individual attention, and significant performance/tech opportunity from the beginning.

2. Our faculty are working professionals in theater and related media, and our students participate in KCACTF, USITT, and other academic and professional programs.

3. We foster a welcoming, supportive program that stresses creative ensemble and artistic collaboration in a diverse liberal arts environment.

■ State University of New York at Binghamton
Binghamton, NY

Compiled by: Barbara Wolfe, Chair of Theater

Degrees Offered:
Theater with an emphasis in acting/directing, design/technical, dance
5-year joint BA/MPA in any of the above
MPA
We are applying for a stage management emphasis and should have that soon.

Minors Offered:

Theater

Population of Department(s): 72 majors, 69 minors

Audition to Declare a Theatre/Musical Theatre Major? No audition, except to get in shows

Three things you would like our readers to know about your performing arts department:

1. The theater department offers a theater major with three emphases: acting/directing, dance, and design/tech. The program provides specific training sequences to prepare students to be accepted into excellent master's/MFA programs or to begin educational internships to start their careers. The production program is a core component of all majors, and the five mainstage and student-directed studio productions provide plenty of opportunities for actors, directors, dancers, designers, stage managers, and all the others. Teachers work closely with students, providing focused individual training, unique among undergrad liberal arts theater programs. Our students graduate with produced shows on their résumé and in their portfolios. They also get a superb basis for graduate study, based on responses from graduates.

2. Students from BU's theater department work in all areas of entertainment. In the past year, former students have been on TV in *Beauty and the Beast* and *Cold Case* and on Broadway in *Chinglish* and *Tribes*. As well as having actors working in the field, alumni are stage managers, producers, and agents on Broadway and for national tours. In fact, BU theater alumni are well represented in a wide variety of working theater/entertainment professions.

3. The theater department has a relationship with the National Academy of Chinese Theater Arts (NACTA) in Beijing, in which we have jointly produced *All My Sons* to be performed both in Binghamton and in Beijing, and mounted a Chinese-inspired version of *Romeo and Juliet,* directed by a highly respected director from NACTA, as well as exchanging teachers and students. This semester, the design faculty and students of NACTA have an exhibit of their design works at the University Art Museum.

■ State University of New York at Potsdam
Potsdam, NY

Compiled by: Jay Pecora, Associate Professor, Director of Theatre Education Program and Chair of Department

Degrees Offered:

Theatre
Dance
Theatre education

Minors Offered:

Acting
Dance
Design and production
Theatre studies
Arts management

Population of Department(s): 133 majors, 84 minors

Audition to Declare a Theatre/Musical Theatre Major? No

Three things you would like our readers to know about your performing arts department:

1. We value diversity of all kinds. This commitment is manifest in our interdisciplinary approach to providing students with real-world skill sets, our production choices, and course offerings.

2. We produce student-directed and choreographed work each semester, including a 10-minute play festival and choreographer concert in the fall and one-act play festival and senior choreographer concert in the spring. All seniors create a department-sponsored individualized capstone project their final year.

3. We have just opened a new Performing Arts Center with professional theatre and dance venues, audio/visual lab, aerial arts grid, and education lab. This facility is home to the newly established annual Lougheed Festival of the Arts.

■ East Carolina University

Greenville, NC

Compiled by: John Shearin, Director, School of Theatre and Dance

Population of University: 27,000

Conservatory or Liberal Arts: Liberal arts

Degrees Offered:
BFA in theatre arts, concentrations in professional acting, musical theatre, design/production, stage management, theatre for youth
BFA in theatre education
BFA in dance performance
BFA in dance education
BA in theatre arts

Population of Department(s): 190

Theatre Scholarships Available: 30–40

Audition Required for BFA: Yes

Audition Required for BA/BS/BM: No

Pre-screen Video Audition Required: For musical theatre only

Attends Unifieds: No

Number of Students Auditioning Each Year: Varies

Number of Students Accepted Each Year: 14 professional acting; 14 musical theatre; varies in other concentrations

Cut Program or Audition to Remain in Program: Annual juries

Minors in Musical Theatre/Acting: No

Prominent Alumni: Sandra Bullock, Beth Grant, Howell Binkley, Jeremy Woodard, Marisha Wallace, BJ Britt, Alicia Hillis, Chuck Giles, Kevin Williamson

What do you look for in a potential student?
Talent, work ethic, humility.

What are some of the auditors' pet peeves?

Arrogance, self-centeredness.

What are your audition requirements?

Monologues (acting); monologue, songs, movement (musical theatre).

If you require a pre-screen video audition, what do you look for in those submissions?

The same—talent, work ethic, humility.

What is your biggest piece of advice for potential students auditioning?

Prepare *thoroughly*.

If I audition for your BFA musical theatre program, but don't get accepted, do you still consider me for your BFA acting program or your BA program? Or does each program require its own audition if I'd like to be considered for both?

Each requires an audition.

After I audition, is there a good way to follow up?

Email.

Would I get a showcase at the end of senior year?

Yes, as part of the curriculum.

Do I have to audition to be accepted into the showcase?

No.

Where are showcases held, and are they successful?

Showcases are held on campus as the "capstone" experience.

Will I be able to audition/perform as a freshman?

Yes.

In what ways can I be involved with the department aside from performing?

You will be required to take several crew courses.

Say I get a BA rather than a BFA. Will I actually get to perform?

Yes.

I love to sing, but I don't consider myself a dancer. Can I still seek a degree in musical theatre at your school?

You will learn to dance as part of the curriculum.

I want to get a BFA in acting, but I also love to sing. Can BFA/BA acting students take voice lessons with top voice faculty?

Yes, if they qualify.

Do you discourage or encourage students to audition for theatre outside of the department during the academic year?

Encourage.

Does your school regularly work in conjunction with any regional theatres?

No.

What do students typically do during the summers? Do you actively promote participation in summer theatre auditions?

Most students work in summer theatres.

How many musicals versus straight plays do you do in a season?

One to two musicals, two to three plays.

What are some of your alumni up to? Do you have an active alumni network?

Yes, we have an active network both in New York and in Los Angeles, and developing in Chicago.

What is the portfolio/interview process for a design/production student?

See our website at www.ecu.edu/cs-cfac/theatredance/programs/designproduction.cfm.

Anything else I should know?

Although some students choose to pursue graduate training, we focus on preparing our students to go to work immediately upon graduation in professional theatre, film, and TV (or in teaching). Students have our guarantee that, if they work diligently with careful attention to the details of curriculum and instruction, they will be ready to work professionally by the time they graduate.

■ Elon University
Elon, NC

Compiled by: Kimberly Rippy, Auditions Coordinator, Program Assistant

Population of School: 5,357

Conservatory or Liberal Arts: Liberal arts

Degrees Offered:

BFA in acting
BFA in dance performance and choreography
BFA in music theatre
BA in theatrical design and production
BA in theatre studies and arts administration
BS in dance science

Population of Department(s): 250

Theatre Scholarships Available: Yes

Audition Required for BFA: Yes

Audition Required for BA/BS/BM: Interview for theatrical design and production

Pre-screen Video Audition Required: Yes

Attends Unifieds: No

Number of Students Auditioning Each Year: 750

Number of Students Accepted Each Year: Aim for 16–18 in each BFA program

Cut Program or Audition to Remain in Program: No

Minors in Musical Theatre/Acting: No

What do you look for in a potential student?

Instinct, talent, passion, commitment.

What are some of the auditors' pet peeves?

Not following instructions, not being prepared, and being late.

What are your audition requirements?

Varies by degree program, please see www.elon.edu/perarts.

In your eyes, what makes up an excellent college audition monologue? Song?

Material that the student loves that is very well prepared and fits the audition requirements.

If there were one monologue you never wanted to see again, what would it be?
"I'm Popo Martin."

If there were one song you never wanted to hear again, what would it be?
"Astonishing."

Can you walk me through what I can expect at your on-campus auditions?

Please see the audition FAQ sheet listed under the "apply now" link at www.elon.edu/perarts.

What is your biggest piece of advice for potential students auditioning?
Be prepared.

If I audition for your BFA musical theatre program, but don't get accepted, do you still consider me for your BFA acting program or your BA program?

No. A separate audition is required for each program you wish to be considered for. The BA in theatre studies is open enrollment.

After I audition, is there a good way to follow up?

No. Decisions are released in December for fall auditions and in March for the remainder.

Would I get a showcase at the end of senior year?
No.

Will I be able to audition/perform as a freshman?

It is required of our BFA majors to audition their first year.

In what ways can I be involved with the department aside from performing?

Costume, sets, lights, sound, front of house, and so on.

Say I get a BA rather than a BFA. Will I actually get to perform?

All of our productions are open auditions.

I love to sing, but I don't consider myself a dancer. Can I still seek a degree in musical theatre at your school?

You may audition, but dance is an integral part of our program.

I want to get a BFA in acting, but I also love to sing. Can BFA/BA acting students take voice lessons with top voice faculty?

Yes.

Do you discourage or encourage students to audition for theatre outside of the department during the academic year?

It is fine so long as they meet their department obligations first.

Does your school regularly work in conjunction with any regional theatres?

No.

What do students typically do during the summers? Do you actively promote participation in summer theatre auditions?

Yes. We encourage students to work during summer. More than 60% of our students have professional summer work.

How many musicals versus straight plays do you do in a season?

Three musicals and three straight plays

What are some of your alumni up to? Do you have an active alumni network?

Our alumni are on Broadway, national tours, regional theatre, TV commercials, and top grad programs around the country.

What is the portfolio/interview process for a technical theatre student?

Please see the audition/interview requirements under the "apply now" link at www.elon.edu/perarts.

What do you expect to see on a technical theatre résumé?

A summary of all of your theatrical and art experience.

I'm interested in lighting, sound design, and stage management. What major should I go for? Can I minor?

BA in theatrical design and production. We do not offer a minor in that area.

Anything else I should know?

Please visit www.elon.edu/perarts.

■ Appalachian State University
Department of Theatre and Dance
Boone, NC

Compiled by: Joel Williams, Professor of Theatre

Degrees Offered:

BA in theatre studies with concentrations in general theatre, performance, design and technology, teaching theatre arts K–12

BA in dance studies

Minors Offered:

Theatre arts
Dance studies

Population of Department(s): 120

Audition to Declare a Theatre/Musical Theatre Major? Theatre arts – performance requires an interview and audition following the freshman year; theatre arts – design and technology requires an interview and portfolio review after the freshman year; teaching theatre arts requires acceptance into the College of Education.

Three things you would like our readers to know about your performing arts department:

1. Detailed information can be found online at www.theatre.appstate.edu. Prospects are encouraged to review alumni biographies listed on this site.

2. The department is committed to providing opportunities for students to participate both onstage and backstage beginning with an annual fall-semester First Year Showcase featuring all new theatre and dance students.

3. The department strives to maintain a rigorous schedule of curricular and co-curricular learning that encourages students to become successful lifelong learners. Lessons learned in creativity, collaboration, and character building are applicable to whatever endeavors our graduates choose to pursue.

■ Fayetteville State University
Fayetteville, NC

Compiled by: Jeremy Fiebig, Assistant Professor of Theatre and Area Coordinator

Degrees Offered:

Theatre

Minors Offered:

Theatre
Dance

Population of Department(s): 30–40 students in theatre program; more than 150 in the entire department including other arts programs

Audition to Declare a Theatre/Musical Theatre Major? Audition for scholarships

Three things you would like our readers to know about your performing arts department:

1. One-on-one faculty contact from day one.

2. Significant performance and technical opportunities from day one.

3. Meaningful partnerships with local professional and semi-professional theatres.

Gardner-Webb University
Boiling Springs, NC

Compiled by: Sue Fair, Theatre Arts Instructor, Designer and Managing Director

Degrees Offered:

Theatre

Minors Offered:

Theatre

Population of Department(s): 20

Audition to Declare a Theatre/Musical Theatre Major? No, just an interview

Three things you would like our readers to know about your performing arts department:

1. To provide the necessary information, skills, and experiences for theatre majors to pursue successful careers in professional, educational, and community theatre.
2. To provide meaningful cultural experiences for the university family as well as the community at large.
3. To offer opportunities for students, staff, faculty, and community members to participate in professionally mounted theatre productions, fulfilling in part the mission of a liberal arts institution.

Greensboro College
Department of Theatre
Greensboro, NC

Compiled by: Wm. Perry Morgan-Hall, Head of Musical Theatre Program

Degrees Offered:

Performance
Directing
Stage management
Musical theatre
Theatre education
Design/tech
Arts administration
Costuming

Minors Offered:

Theatre
Dance

Population of Department(s): 40

Audition to Declare a Theatre/Musical Theatre Major? Yes

Three things you would like our readers to know about your performing arts department:

1. Our professors, teaching full-time, also stay very busy in the professional theatre world, which means important contacts for you!

2. Our class sizes are small, offering one-on-one experiences with your professors, and immediate performing, directing, and design opportunities for you.

3. Even though we are a "private school," we are affordable!

■ Guilford College
Greensboro, NC

Compiled by: David Hammond, Chair, Department of Theatre Studies

Degrees Offered:

Theatre studies, with specialized tracks in performance, design/tech, and history/literature, as well as theatre studies generalist

Minors Offered:

Theatre arts
Musical theatre
Film and video

Population of Department(s): 35–40

Audition to Declare a Theatre/Musical Theatre Major? No

Three things you would like our readers to know about your performing arts department:

1. Guilford's Department of Theatre Studies is unique in providing rigorous professionally oriented undergraduate theatre training within the context of a well-rounded liberal arts education that can prepare students for a broad range of future careers. An interested undergraduate at Guilford can pursue theatre training in classes as challenging as those offered in any conservatory in the nation, while simultaneously obtaining a solid undergraduate education that keeps other options open as the developing student explores the work of a professional artist. The department seeks to produce creative individuals with intellectual acuity and the analytical and problem-solving skills of the theatre worker. Many alumni have gone on to prestigious graduate theatre programs; professional internships; and employment in theatre, film, and television, while others have pursued graduate work and careers in fields as diverse as law, medicine, psychology, and social work. Guilford believes that theatre training develops skills and thought processes applicable to problem solving in all areas of life.

2. The program offers both majors and non-majors the chance to experience the collaborative process by which actors, designers, directors, scholars, and technicians interpret a playscript and translate a shared vision of its meaning into the medium of theatrical production. Classes develop the skills essential to this process: critical thinking, research methods, intuitive reasoning, communication, project planning and time management, problem solving, teamwork, and leadership. The school strives also

to instill in students awareness of the transformative power of theatre as an instrument of social change and the corresponding ethical responsibility of the artist for the integrity of the transaction between actor and audience.

3. Faculty members and staff have worked as practicing theatre artists in the professional theatre as actors, directors, designers, or technicians. Recognizing that guest artists are essential to the vitality of any theatre program, the department also brings practicing theatre artists of high caliber to the campus to work with students.

■ Meredith College
Raleigh, NC

Compiled by: Catherine Rodgers, Professor of Theatre

Degrees Offered:

BA in theatre with a focus in performance, production, or musical theatre; K–12 theatre licensure is also offered; a professional performance certificate is available by audition or portfolio review

Minors Offered:

Theatre

Population of Department(s): 25 majors, 5 minors

Audition to Declare a Theatre/Musical Theatre Major? No

Three things you would like our readers to know about your performing arts department:

1. The theatre program at Meredith College is student centered and challenges women to strive, struggle, and achieve in the art of theatre.

2. We have dedicated professional faculty and guest artists who guide each individual in an in-depth program of academically rigorous study in performance, production, and design.

3. Stillwater Theatre is our professional, in-house theatre company and provides our students with experiential learning experiences that focus on promoting women's issues in theatre.

■ University of North Carolina—Asheville
Asheville, NC

Compiled by: Laura Bond, Department Chair

Degrees Offered:

BA in drama
BA in drama teacher licensure

Minors Offered:

Drama

Population of Department(s): 42

Audition to Declare a Theatre/Musical Theatre Major? No

Three things you would like our readers to know about your performing arts department:

1. We are a drama department within North Carolina's Public Liberal Arts University, and so we offer a holistic approach to theatre education. Our students receive a well-rounded education in all aspects of theatre production and history, while also having the chance to select one or two areas of personal focus and experience thorough development in this area while at UNC Asheville.

2. We are an open and student-centered department where students can get involved in our classes and productions from their first semester on campus. We offer many opportunities for students to produce their own theatre productions as well as hold leadership positions within our mainstage productions.

3. Our theatre is an arena-style experimental theatre space that we adapt to many different configurations, from full theatre-in-the-round, to thrust configuration, to proscenium, for varying experiences in theatre production.

■ Western Carolina University

School of Stage & Screen
Cullowhee, NC

Compiled by: Thomas Salzman, Director

Degrees Offered:

BFA in theatre with concentrations in acting and musical theatre
BA in stage and screen, with concentrations in design/technical and general

Minors Offered:

Dance
Music

Population of Department(s): Total population including our film students is 150 (20 acting, 35 music theatre, 30 BA)

Audition to Declare a Theatre/Musical Theatre Major? Yes, audition and a separate application to the school directly

Three things you would like our readers to know about your performing arts department:

1. You will not only get excellent training for theatre, but also you will learn to act for the camera. We do four mainstage theatre productions and two major films per year.

2. We are an undergraduate training program, so all of our classes are taught by our faculty of working professionals, not grad students.

3. Our programs are designed for the student who is firmly committed to a professional career in the entertainment industry. We teach the art, craft, and business of show business.

North Dakota

■ Dickinson State University
Dickinson, ND

Compiled by: Ron Gingerich, Professor of Theatre, Chair, Department of Fine and Performing Arts

Degrees Offered:
BA in theatre
BS in theatre education

Minors Offered:
Dance, theatre (BA)
Theatre education (BS)

Population of Department(s): 20

Audition to Declare a Theatre/Musical Theatre Major? No

Three things you would like our readers to know about your performing arts department:

1. Lots of performance opportunities.
2. Individual attention.
3. Small class sizes.

■ Minot State University
Minot, ND

Compiled by: Kevin R. Neuharth, Director of Theatre and Coordinator of Communication Arts

Degrees Offered:
BA in theatre
BS in education: theatre

Minors Offered:
Theatre management
Creative dramatics and movement

Population of Department(s): 25 majors, 20 very active non-majors

Audition to Declare a Theatre/Musical Theatre Major? No

Three things you would like our readers to know about your performing arts department:

1. Students expected to be involved in all areas of theatre production. Scholarships offered.
2. Energetic production schedule on three different stages.
3. Just completed our 48th Summer Theatre season where we produce three musicals and one farce each summer in an outdoor amphitheatre setting.

■ Baldwin Wallace University
Berea, OH

Compiled by: Victoria Bussert, Director of the Music Theatre Program; Adam Heffernan, Chair, Department of Theatre & Dance

Population of School: Total enrollment of 4,177; 2,985 day students, 476 evening/weekend students, 504 MBA, 212 graduate education

Conservatory or Liberal Arts: Conservatory for music, liberal arts for rest of school

Degrees Offered:

BM in music theatre
BA in theatre with tracks in acting/directing, design, and stage management

Population of Department(s): 60–65 in music theatre, 90 in theatre (65 acting/directing, 15 design, 10 stage management)

Theatre Scholarships Available: Yes, five total (two in technical theatre, three in a variety). For Department of Theatre & Dance, six total (two in tech, four given to any discipline, split among 12–15 recipients)

Audition Required for BFA: No

Audition Required for BA/BS/BM: Yes for BM in music theatre, no for the BA in theatre

Pre-screen Video Audition Required: No

Attends Unifieds: No

Number of Students Auditioning Each Year: 400 in musical theatre

Number of Students Accepted Each Year: Musical theatre accepts 20–22, to yield 16–18

Cut Program or Audition to Remain in Program: No

Minors in Musical Theatre/Acting: Minor in music without audition, minor in dance without audition

Prominent Alumni: Jill Paice, Kate Rockwell, Steel Burkhardt, Kyle Post

What do you look for in a potential student?

For musical theatre, we really look for somebody who has a connection with communicating through music theatre material as opposed to just a great voice. We feel that we can train students vocally, dance-wise, and acting-wise, but what you can't train is that connection and passion for this specific art from.

What are some of the auditors' pet peeves?

People singing or acting material that they are not connecting with, that was obviously assigned to them, and that they have no personal point of view on. We don't have an over-done list. We want to see who that person is and how he or she interprets that material from his or her life experiences. Material that is inappropriate either life experience-wise or age-wise would be a primary pet peeve. Not reading the requirements for this specific audition is another. For example, we ask students to prepare three songs, and some will come in with only two prepared. That said, we are a fairly easygoing group. We want to make auditions as comfortable as possible. We know that students are putting in a lot of work for these auditions, and it is important that they come prepared. A final pet peeve would be doing a monologue from a play when you haven't read the play or singing a song when you don't know the story of a musical. How a student interprets the piece given the circumstances of the broader work is really revealing in terms of his or her work ethic and love of the actual art form.

What are your audition requirements?

Three 32-bar cuts. We will choose two of those three in the audition room. We do that so that students do not come in on auto-pilot. We don't want students to know exactly what it will be so it will be spontaneous and we can get a sense of who they are as a person. Material can be anything that they are comfortable with and connect with. We just ask that it be in English. All of the selections should show us something about who they are. It should be a short monologue—a minute or less—of age-appropriate material that they connect with. There is a group dance call at the end of the day that is conducted like a normal, professional dance call with all of them together. We ask that the students spend the day with us. There will be theory testing and piano testing for those who have taken piano before, simply to find out where a student will be placed. Admission is not based on those tests at all. Students also get to attend a master class with a New York agent or New York casting director that we have in on every audition day.

In your eyes, what makes up an excellent college audition monologue? Song?

We do not have an overdone list, because it will never have been done by *that* person. It is only overdone when people are replicating the same things, either that they've heard on a recording or otherwise.

Can you walk me through what I can expect at your on-campus auditions?

Students arrive at the conservatory at 8:30 a.m. for a welcome session and will be assigned a current music theatre major who will see them through the entire day. They will be escorted everywhere they need to go. They will be given a practice room before their singing auditions. They will come into the room with Victoria, Scott (chair), Nancy Myer (musical theatre music director), and Greg Daniels (head of dance). We will ask what three songs they have prepared, and then we will choose two of those. They will sing those two songs in any order they'd like and then do their monologue. Then, they will attend the master class. Following that, we have a session with two senior students attended by only the applicants where they can ask any questions they want. After that, students will have lunch, and from there will head to the dance hall, which will be the last thing they do for the day. Following the dance hall, there will be an open Q&A session. Applicants will really get to know the school, the environment, the students, and what life might be like here. Oftentimes, there are student performances occurring on audition days, and applicants are able to see our students actually working in a production. That is an important thing to check if the applicant would like to see a performance.

What's a memorable audition you can remember?

We are always rooting for students to be fantastic. Last year, a young man came in from West Virginia in jeans—which is fine, but not looking like somebody who was going to be on top of his material—and he blew us away! Not only was he brilliant with his musical theatre material, but also on his résumé you could see that he had already won an opera competition. You just live for those moments, where somebody completely surprises you! He will be one of our incoming freshmen.

What is your biggest piece of advice for potential students auditioning?

Be yourself on a good day. It's important to present your best possible self as opposed to the self that is hanging out at home.

If I audition for your BFA musical theatre program, but don't get accepted, do you still consider me for your BFA acting program or your BA program?

We do have a number of students who are not accepted into the musical theatre program who decide to go to Baldwin Wallace as a theatre BA major. We also offer two music theatre classes for non-majors, so it is still possible to get music theatre training, just not the concentrated training of a musical theatre major.

After I audition, is there a good way to follow up?

It's really not necessary. We don't give feedback on auditions because of the number of students we have. If they do early admittance, they will audition in November and will be notified by the end of December if they have been admitted or not. If they wait and audition in January or February, then they will be notified by the end of March.

Would I get a showcase at the end of senior year?

Yes, for musical theatre. No, for BA theatre. There is financial assistance for travel to theatre conferences and grad school auditions.

Do I have to audition to be accepted into the showcase?

No. When you are accepted as a freshman, we are seeing you through all the way.

Where are showcases held, and are they successful?

Showcases are held at the York Theatre in New York City for four performances. For the past five years, all seniors have signed with agents.

Will I be able to audition/perform as a freshman?

Yes, for music theatre. We do not have any rules in terms of auditioning and performing, and students can audition for everything, not just for the musicals. They can audition for and are cast in operas, straight plays, Shakespeare, and so on—all of it is available. Yes, for BA acting, and students can audition for the musicals. Auditions for all shows are open to any student attending BW.

In what ways can I be involved with the department aside from performing?

Stage managing, production managing, directing, building costumes, dramaturgy, playwriting, publicity, assistant directing, producing, and so on.

I want to get a BFA in acting, but I also love to sing. Can BFA/BA acting students take voice lessons with top voice faculty?

Yes. They have to pay extra, but they are allowed to do that.

Do you discourage or encourage students to audition for theatre outside of the department during the academic year?

For musical theatre, we ask the students to discuss off-campus projects with us on a project-by-project basis. Our students tend to be very popular in town, and we always want to make sure that it is worth their time to do the project.

For BA in theatre, we encourage outside work. Cleveland has one of the largest and best-funded theatre communities in the country, with several internationally recognized arts organizations, including Playhouse Square, Great Lakes Theater, Cleveland Play House, and Cleveland Public Theatre.

Does your school regularly work in conjunction with any regional theatres?

For musical theatre, yes. Victoria is the resident director at the Great Lakes Theater, Downtown Cleveland. We also do a co-production, a spring musical, with Playhouse Square, which is the top-producing organization downtown. We also do a co-production every winter with the Beck Center for the Arts. So, we have a lot of professional interaction for our students. There are several students a year who get their Equity cards, and almost every student in musical theatre graduates with an Equity card.

For BA in theatre, yes, see above list. Many students work as interns, understudies, and staff members at a large number of area theatres.

What do students typically do during the summers? Do you actively promote participation in summer theatre auditions?

For musical theatre, we do. Our sophomores all attend the Unifieds summer stock auditions, either Midwest or StrawHat. Currently, all of our sophomores have been hired for the summer. After their sophomore year, we really encourage them to branch out to different theatres and start putting their skill sets to work in a practical environment.

For BA in theatre, we provide financial aid for students to attend audition conferences (SETC, NETC, StrawHat, and so on). Students work locally and out of state as staff, company members, or interns at summer stock, Shakespeare festivals, and other arts organizations. See a list of current student summer activities at www.bw.edu/academics/theatre/student-success.

How many musicals versus straight plays do you do in a season?

For musical theatre, we do three musicals, two operas, and five or six straight plays including evenings of one-acts. We also have a dance concert every year that our students are able to petition to choreograph.

What are some of your alumni up to? Do you have an active alumni network?

Working at major regional theatres as designers, actors, technicians, stage managers, literary managers, and so on. We currently have six musical theatre alums working on Broadway this season, as well as many doing international and national tours, regional theatre, and off-Broadway.

What is the portfolio/interview process for a technical theatre student?

To get into the program, there is no interview process.

What do you expect to see on a technical theatre résumé?

By the time they graduate, students should work during the summer at summer stock.

I'm interested in lighting, sound design, and stage management. What major should I go for? Can I minor?

Technical students are required to minor in art. Stage management majors have a minor in business and arts management.

Anything else I should know?

We are a program that is taught by working professionals. Our acting program has a heavy emphasis on classical works and new play development. We produce one play by Shakespeare each year and offer a diverse training experience. We have a large number of adjunct faculty who are working professionals in the local industry. The training is focused on the individual's needs and goals, and no two students have the same experience. Techniques used in acting courses include Alexander, Meisner, Folio, Linklater, and many others.

■ University of Cincinnati—College-Conservatory of Music
Cincinnati, OH

Compiled by: Richard Hess, Drama Department Chair; Aubrey Berg, Musical Theatre Chair

Population of School: The Conservatory of Music (CCM) has approximately 1,500 students, with 780 undergrads and 710 grad students. It is set within a large state school, the University of Cincinnati, with a population of around 33,000 students.

Conservatory or Liberal Arts: Conservatory

Degrees Offered:

BFA in musical theatre
BFA in acting
There are no BA or BS programs at CCM. There is an entire music division offering every BM imaginable.

Population of Department(s): There are generally around 70 majors in the musical theatre program. CCM Drama holds a population of 50–55.

Theatre Scholarships Available: Yes

Audition Required for BFA: Yes

Audition Required for BA/BS/BM: Auditions are required for all BM programs.

Pre-screen Video Audition Required: The BFA musical theatre and BFA drama program do not offer pre-screen video auditions. All auditions are seen live.

Attends Unifieds: Yes

Location of Unifieds: New York and Chicago for drama; New York, Chicago, and Los Angeles for musical theatre

Number of Students Auditioning Each Year: 750–800 for musical theatre, 200 for drama

Number of Students Accepted Each Year: For musical theatre, we accept incoming freshman class of approximately 20. For drama, we will take in a first-year class of 15–18.

Cut Program or Audition to Remain in Program: No for musical theatre. Majors perform for the faculty twice a year to satisfy the NAST requirement of "periodic review" for all students. There is no cut system, but students are expected to meet long- and short-term goals set by the faculty and to demonstrate continued improvement in voice, dance, and acting. CCM drama does not have a cut program, but it does have a retention policy. Students are evaluated twice a year during their first and second years. Grades, performance, and overall academic/artistic health are measured.

Minors in Musical Theatre/Acting: Drama students do not have room in their schedules to minor unless the choice is made to do summer school for extra coursework. No minors are offered to University of Cincinnati students in musical theatre/acting.

Prominent Alumni: Many musical theatre alumni are appearing in Broadway and off-Broadway shows, in national and international touring productions, at regional theatres, in stock, on TV, and in almost every entertainment-related field. They also forge careers as writers, composers, directors, musical directors, choreographers, agents and managers, producers, conductors, and teachers of the craft. Graduates have been nominated for and won the Tony, Drama Desk, Outer Critics Circle, Astaire, and other major industry awards.

CCM drama celebrates 32 years of training actors by highlighting the careers and accomplishments of 32 notable CCM Drama Alumni: http://ccm.uc.edu/theatre/drama/alumni/ccm-dramaalumni.html.

What do you look for in a potential student?

AT CCM, the audition for the musical theatre program is as much to see *who* you are as *how* you perform. It is an opportunity for you to show your personality, the strengths and traits that make you a unique performer, and your accomplishments in the three component areas of the program—voice, dance, and acting. For drama, a great deal of our evaluation concerns who you are. Therefore, be proud of who you are, share with us honestly, and work hard on your preparation. We look for students who have big hearts, who feel passionately about their lives and life around them. We look for their acting to be organic and seemingly natural, unbound, and free of being too planned. We look for students who sincerely connect with their characters' hearts and issues.

What are some of the auditors' pet peeves?

The musical theatre website contains a page called "Dos and Don'ts," which outlines our approach to auditioning. In his excellent book, *Acting Professionally*, Robert Cohen suggests that an actor needs a strong personality. For him, the most undesirable quality for an actor is to be bland—a "good little boy or girl"— nice, dull, and unmarketable. So, too, at CCM we look for a magnetic stage presence, a confident air, and a unique personality. Our applicants can transform a routine audition into a memorable one, and make us eager to enroll them as students. On the CCM drama website, we offer advice and guidelines for our audition process. A pet peeve would be evidence that the auditionee did not do his or her homework and follow directions, such as going over the allotted time or choosing monologues from the banned monologue list or not from a high-quality, full-length play. It is never helpful to choose weak material: good playwriting produces good acting.

What are your audition requirements?

For musical theatre, the dance call is the most direct part of the audition. It takes no immediate preparation, though several years at the barre are certainly beneficial. It consists of a warm-up (stretching exercises, floor work, and so on) and a combination from a Broadway musical. The combination is taught to applicants as a group by students in the musical theatre program and is then performed in groups of five. Applicants should learn the combination quickly and accurately and dance it with verve. Enthusiasm occasionally substitutes for lack of specific training. The vocal audition requires the preparation of two selections chosen from the standard musical theatre repertoire. One selection should have a sustained legato line; the second should be up-tempo and provide a contrast in rhythm, mood, characterization, style, and approach. It may show special skills such as comic timing, dramatic flair, ability with patter, or, for women, the "belt" voice. By selecting songs that are similar in every way, inexperienced auditionees often miss the opportunity to show a range of abilities. Selections should be no longer than 32 measures each. Long verses or repeated choruses are not recommended. For the acting audition, auditionees should prepare a comic or dramatic monologue from a contemporary or classical play. The monologue should be suited to the age of the auditionee and should not be in dialect. The monologue should be no longer than one minute. Longer selections will be cut off by the timekeepers. Adjudicators may engage applicants in a short question and answer session. Auditionees must provide a headshot or recent photograph and a résumé listing theatre training and roles played. Scrapbooks, press clipping, and videotapes are not accepted. For drama, two monologues, not to exceed five minutes in length, contrasting in both type and style, one classic and the other contemporary, plus an interview. See our website at http://ccm.uc.edu/theatre/drama/apply.html.

In your eyes, what makes up an excellent college audition monologue? Song?

No one can succeed in musical theatre without skills in its three component areas. These are the areas we assess during your audition. We try to gauge your level of accomplishment in each, and in all three as a whole. But we are also looking for more than mere accomplishment. Your skills must be complemented by drive, commitment, confidence, and likability. Your performance can be greatly enhanced by the way you present yourself; in fact, the "packaging" can transform a pleasant audition into a striking one. Your aim is simple: to convince the auditors that you are the student we most need for the success of our program. The personality you project is the basis for your audition. It includes the clothes you wear, the way you introduce your material, and your ability to answer questions. Even the materials you choose to perform can be revealing. But remember, please, personality is not an alien persona affected for the occasion—it is just the simple use of the characteristics that make you distinctive as a performer and a human being. An excellent college audition reveals an interesting and interested self, ready for the challenges and joys of four years of BFA training.

If there were one monologue you never wanted to see again, what would it be?

Do not select pieces that attempt to shock with their use of bad language or obscene physical action. Auditors are seldom shocked, but often bored! Present the material naturally, and remember that you are using the words of others in order to sell yourself. Through your choice of material and your performance behavior, show yourself to be a person of taste, confidence, sincerity, and sensitivity. We ask you to avoid climactic material that requires great depth or intensity of emotion; it is too difficult to be truthful and can lead to overacting. I never need to hear the "tuna fish" monologue from *Laughing Wild* ever again.

If there were one song you never wanted to hear again, what would it be?

Select material suitable for youthful performers. Many students hide behind phony elderly voices and mannerisms, the characterizations that won them acclaim in the high school play. Remember, we want to see who *you* are. Do not attempt songs obviously created for mature characters, songs such as "I'm Still Here," "Send in the Clowns," "Fifty Percent," "Rose's Turn," or any Sondheim song written for an older character.

Can you walk me through what I can expect at your on-campus auditions?

For musical theatre, the day begins with the dance audition. This consists of a warm-up and a combination from a recent Broadway musical, usually in the jazz idiom. Generally, this is followed by a short performance by students in the program, demonstrating some of the pieces currently in rehearsal. Thereafter, students perform songs and monologues at pre-assigned time. Throughout the day, there are tours of the campus, the performing arts center, and various amenities on campus. Demonstrations by programs within the conservatory continue throughout the day.

In Cincinnati for BFA drama, the first portion of the audition consists of a group warm-up. (There are no group warm-ups at the regional audition sites.) The purpose of this is two-fold. The first goal is to loosen you up mentally, physically, and vocally. One of the current drama students will lead the audition group through a series of exercises for 20–30 minutes. The second goal of the warm-up is to help you relax and breathe. Tension is one of the biggest enemies of a good audition. There is no preparation necessary for this part of the audition. The warm-up is not overly rigorous; no special clothes are needed.

The performance of two contrasting monologues is the centerpiece of the audition. It is also the portion over which you have the most control. Auditionees have a total of five minutes to present both pieces. We require two contrasting pieces: the first should be a classical piece, which for the purposes of this audition we will define as anything from roughly 1910 backwards. The second piece should be contemporary, that is, anything from 1910 to the present. Be brave and bold in your choices, and look hard for pieces that speak to you strongly, to which you deeply connect, on which you just love working, and that you can't wait to perform. Do not present a monologue by a character that you have played in a high school or community production. We love fresh pieces that you choose for yourself. In fact, during the interview later, we often ask you why you chose your pieces. Also, be sure the pieces chosen show characters in contrasting situations and emotions (one comic, one serious). By selecting monologues that are similar, you are missing the opportunity to show us the range of your abilities.

After you perform your two well-rehearsed monologues, we may ask you to do the piece again with an "adjustment." An adjustment is merely a new direction, a different outlook, or a different set of circumstances given to you by one of the faculty members to apply to your monologue as you present it again. This does not mean that you performed incorrectly the first time. To the contrary, it means that we were excited by your work and are eager to try working the piece again in a new way. We then get a chance to see how well you take direction, how open you are to new ideas, and how much you are willing to play. Often an adjustment leads to a new discovery in your performance, and sometimes it doesn't. If one of the panel members asks you to try your monologue again in a new way, don't be surprised. The results may excite both you and us.

The last portion of the audition may include a very short informal mini interview. We are very interested in our auditionees, and usually we just want to know a little more about your background, your high school drama experience, your ideas about CCM, and your needs and desires for college training. We are interested in getting to know you as a person, however briefly, so that we can make our choices based on the whole you.

What's a memorable audition you can remember?

From the musical theatre department: A professional training program such as the one at CCM is designed to help singers, dancers, and actors become "triple threats"—imaginative, creative, and capable of bringing their talent and intellect to bear on a popular art form—vocally, physically, intellectually, and emotionally. A memorable audition at CCM is one that shows the applicant has *potential* in the areas listed above. We are not in the business of recruiting "stars." Rather, we are looking for students who want to learn how to work in a way that contributes positively to the art of musical theatre, to free their own creativity, and to build a lasting appreciation for the performing arts.

From the drama department: A good audition is when I fall in love. Time stands still, and I know I want to spend the next four years with this young person watching him or her grow into a professional artist and global citizen. It happens all the time.

What is your biggest piece of advice for potential students auditioning?

Many things are special about the musical theatre at CCM. Perhaps the most special are the performers who graduate from our program: men and women well grounded in the demanding techniques of musical theatre—imaginative and creative, and capable of bringing their intellectual and artistic gifts to bear on the problems of the art. In an audition, show that you can think and do, can explore a piece in depth, and can communicate your intentions in fluid and expressive ways. Musical theatre demands a high level of commitment from our students. Discipline and professionalism are the essential components of this program. Show your passion—the commitment that led you to pursue theatre in the first place. Of course, today, a performer wishing to pursue a career in musical theatre should be able to sing and dance and act with technical mastery and craft—but show us more. Show us that our program would be poorer for not accepting *you*.

Look your best. Dress casually but neatly in clothes that allow freedom of movement. Present yourself as a prospective student who will be fun to teach and highly employable after graduation. Consider your deportment. That means the way you behave (and are seen to behave) from the moment you arrive at the audition to the moment you leave. Show that you are well prepared and have done your research about the school and the program. Ask intelligent questions, exude confidence as you enter the room, say your name with authority, answer questions in a provocative way, look your best, thank the faculty for their attention, and leave with the air of a job well done. And if you are really interested in pursuing the program, write a note to the faculty on your return home. Be confident. Like yourself. Be proud of who you are. In short, make the faculty want to teach you. Arouse their interest through the sheer force of your personality. Dare to be different—in other words, true to yourself.

Check out our website www.ccm.uc.edu/drama; do your homework; be proud of who you are, your work, your dreams, and your future; and have fun!

If I audition for your BFA musical theatre program, but don't get accepted, do you still consider me for your BFA acting program or your BA program? Or does each program require its own audition if I'd like to be considered for both?

At CCM, a student must apply for and audition for each BFA program separately. (There is no BA program.)

After I audition, is there a good way to follow up?

From the musical theatre department: You may wish to send a note with commentary about the audition experience. We often use excerpts from unsolicited mail on our web pages.
From the drama department: Always feel free to write/email the head of recruiting for CCM Drama, Professor K. Jenny Jones. Links can be found on our website at www.ccm.uc.edu/drama.

Would I get a showcase at the end of senior year?

For musical theatre, yes, two performances in New York City. For drama, yes (two!), in Los Angeles and New York.

Do I have to audition to be accepted into the showcase?

No, all seniors are given a place in the showcase.

Where are showcases held, and are they successful?

For musical theatre, showcases are held at the Ailey Theatre on 9th Avenue at West 55th Street. Showcases are very well attended by agents, casting directors, and members of the industry. For drama, more than 150 agents, casting directors, managers, and industry personnel attend our Los Angeles and New York showcases each year.

Will I be able to audition/perform as a freshman?

From the musical theatre department: All years of the program perform in mainstage and studio productions. In addition, freshmen create an original revue of songs and monologues performed for the public at the end of the year.

From the drama department: Yes, all freshmen perform in *Transmigration: A Festival of Student Created New Works*. In addition, every student performs every day in each of the core classes.

In what ways can I be involved with the department aside from performing?

From the musical theatre department: We have an extensive series of master classes for all majors. Some of our students perform professionally at area theatres, with the Cincinnati Pops, and at galas, industrials, and fund-raisers within the greater Cincinnati community.

From the drama department: We have an Ambassador program, where our students meet with prospective students, take them on tours, answer financial aid questions, and overall be our number-one recruitment tool. Their joy and enthusiasm for where they study and train is something our students love to share. CCM drama offers a series of master classes. Past invitees are Anne Bogart (SITI Company), Geoff Soffer (ABC Casting), Brian Crowe (New Jersey Shakespeare), Bill Lengfelder (Kitchen Dog Theater), Sandy Logan (ABC Casting), Gary Krasny (The Krasny Office), and Cindi Rush (Cindi Rush Casting). Our students founded a university club called The Theater Project, which devotes its resources to securing even more master classes. Invitees include Theater Mitu, the SITI Co., André Gregory, and Studio 6.

I love to sing, but I don't consider myself a dancer. Can I still seek a degree in musical theatre at your school?

The musical theatre program at CCM is widely recognized for its "triple-threat" approach to training, and many of its graduates are following careers as performers and creative artists in every facet of the entertainment industry. Because of the "triple threat" nature of the program, all majors take classes in voice, acting, and dance. Training in dance includes requirements in ballet, jazz, tap, and modern, as well as pilates classes.

I want to get a BFA in acting, but I also love to sing. Can BFA/BA acting students take voice lessons with top voice faculty?

CCM has one of the highest regarded voice faculties in the United States. CCM drama majors are required to take group voice lesson classes in the sophomore year; those with a keen interest can then pursue private lessons.

Do you discourage or encourage students to audition for theatre outside of the department during the academic year?

From the musical theatre department: We encourage musical theatre majors to audition for and accept summer work, especially at theatres offering Equity cards or membership points. Although seniors may audition for outside work, for undergrads the degree workload precludes the management of a professional career during term time.

From the drama department: Encourage. We not only support our students' work outside the department, we require it. Professional experiences are expected. We also encourage our students' success beyond theatre. Many have working relationships with local talent agencies and unions doing film and TV, voice-over, and industrials. (Currently, a senior serves as the Cincinnati/Columbus representative on the Ohio-Pittsburgh SAG-AFTRA Board.)

Does your school regularly work in conjunction with any regional theatres?

Locally, musical theatre students have performed with the Cincinnati Playhouse in the Park, Ensemble Theater of Cincinnati, Cincinnati Shakespeare Festival, the Human Race Theatre, the Know Theatre, New Stage Collective, New Edgecliff Theater, Covedale Center for the Performing Arts, the Showboat Majestic, the Carnegie Theater, and the Cincinnati Fringe Festival.

Though CCM drama does not have any contractual relationships with regional professional theaters, our students have performed with the Cincinnati Playhouse in the Park, Ensemble Theater of Cincinnati, Cincinnati Shakespeare Festival, the Human Race Theatre, the Know Theatre, New Stage Collective, New Edgecliff Theater, Covedale Center for the

Performing Arts, the Showboat Majestic, the Carnegie Theater, and the Cincinnati Fringe Festival.

What do students typically do during the summers? Do you actively promote participation in summer theatre auditions?

From the musical theatre department: We encourage our students to train and perform during the summer months. Many go to New York, Chicago, or Los Angeles for internships, training intensives, and performance opportunities. Musical theatre students often perform during the summer at reputable summer theatres (The Muny, West Virginia Public, Music Theatre of Wichita, Sacramento Music Theatre, Pittsburgh Civic Light Opera, and so on). We also encourage summer study abroad.

From the drama department: We encourage our students to train and perform during the summer months. Many go to New York or Los Angeles (and around the world) for internships, training intensives, and performance opportunities. We encourage summer study abroad. Several join summer acting conservatories, take classes, or intern with the following: the SITI Company, the Society of American Fight Directors, Royal Academy of Dramatic Art, London, Second City, Steppenwolf, the Atlantic Theatre, the Groundlings, The Dell' Arte International School of Physical Theater, the Hangar Theatre, DC Improv Comedy School, the Shakespeare Festival of St. Louis, and the Edinburgh International Festival. See our website at http://ccm.uc.edu/theatre/drama/studyabroad.html.

How many musicals versus straight plays do you do in a season?

An equal amount: four plays, four musicals, and a festival of student-created new works. The musical theatre program is part of a division of performing arts that mounts four plays, four musicals, and four operas each year, as well as lab productions of student-generated work.

What are some of your alumni up to? Do you have an active alumni network?

From the musical theatre department: Many of our alumni are appearing in Broadway and off-Broadway shows, in national touring productions, at regional theatres, in stock, on TV, and in almost every entertainment-related field. They also forge careers as writers, directors, musical directors, choreographers, agents and managers, producers, conductors, and teachers of the craft.

From the drama department: We have a very strong community of alumni, all over the country, who support and encourage our young graduates. We have actors, producers, directors, writers, musical directors, visual artists, musicians and singers, voice-over artists, models, stuntpeople, magicians, clowns, and comediennes amongst our alums. From Broadway to motion pictures, from TV to Las Vegas and the White House lawn, CCM drama is there. Our alums regularly return to campus to share stories, news, and advice with the entire department. For more specific information on the professional activities of our graduates, we encourage you to peruse the website at www.ccm.uc.edu/drama.

What is the portfolio/interview process for a technical theatre student?

Please visit www.ccm.uc.edu/tdp for more information about technical and design degrees and opportunities at CCM.

Anything else I should know?

The musical theatre program at CCM is the oldest in the country and was the first of its kind. It was used by the National Association of Schools of Theatre in formulating the guidelines for accreditation of musical theatre programs nationwide. It is widely recognized for its "triple-threat" approach to training, and many of its graduates are following careers as performers and creative artists in every facet of the entertainment industry.

Musical theatre training at CCM includes:

- A two-fold approach to vocal training with private voice lessons that focus on technique and "vocal coaching," which integrates voice and acting skills in the interpretation of the musical theatre song
- A rigorous acting curriculum, which includes the work of Anne Bogart, Michael Chekhov, Sanford Meisner, and Robert Cohen, as well as Suzuki actor training, cabaret techniques, audition skills, and acting for the camera
- Extensive dance training in ballet, jazz, tap, modern, and pilates, and the opportunity to explore choreography for the musical stage
- Showcases that bookend the training experience: a freshman showcase presented in Cincinnati and a senior showcase presented for agents and casting directors in Chicago and New York City
- Comprehensive production schedule with five musicals presented in three dynamically different state-of-the-art theatre spaces each season

"CCM's program consistently produces some of the most talented and well-trained collegians in the nation." —Scott Cain, *Talkin' Broadway*

■ Capital University
Bexley, OH

Compiled by: Bill Kennedy, Director of Theatre

Degrees Offered:
Communication, focus on theatre studies
Vocal performance, emphasis in musical theatre/opera (conservatory)

Minors Offered:
Theatre studies
Entertainment technology

Population of Department(s): Currently 6 students in the program

Audition to Declare a Theatre/Musical Theatre Major? No, for theatre studies. Yes, for conservatory.

Three things you would like our readers to know about your performing arts department:

1. We are a small but very active program.
2. We produce a wide range of shows—from classics to musicals to original scripts.
3. We encourage internships, double majoring, and minoring.

■ Franciscan University of Steubenville
Steubenville, OH

Compiled by: Shawn Dougherty, Professor of Drama; Dr. Monica Fay Anderson, Professor of Drama, Chair of Department of Fine Arts

Degrees Offered:

Drama (two tracks, one in performance and one in dramatic literature)

Minors Offered:

Drama

Population of Department(s): 20

Audition to Declare a Theatre/Musical Theatre Major? No

Three things you would like our readers to know about your performing arts department:

1. While we produce a range of plays, from classical to contemporary, we focus on the classics with special attention to Shakespeare.
2. We strongly support the Catholic Mission of the university, and our classes and play selection reflect that mission.
3. We are a liberal arts theatre program, and our goal is to prepare our students for graduate school or an internship or apprenticeship in a major regional theatre.

■ Heidelberg University
Tiffin, OH

Compiled by: Chris Tucci, Director of Theatre

Degrees Offered:

Theatre
Music

Minors Offered:

Theatre
Music

Population of Department(s): 25

Audition to Declare a Theatre/Musical Theatre Major? No

Three things you would like our readers to know about your performing arts department:

1. Scholarships are available for majors, minors, and participants.
2. Each year we travel around the world to see great theatre and workshop with artists.
3. Our graduates work.

■ Kenyon College
Gambier, OH

Compiled by: Jonathan E. Tazewell, Chair of the Department of Dance, Drama, and Film; Thomas S. Turgeon, Endowed Professor

Degrees Offered:

Dance

Drama

Film

Minors Offered:

Dance

Population of Department(s): Currently 8 dance, 30 drama, and 30 film majors and minors; current course enrollments: 117

Audition to Declare a Theatre/Musical Theatre Major? No

Three things you would like our readers to know about your performing arts department:

1. Kenyon College is the alma mater of Paul Newman, Allison Janney, Josh Radnor, Chris Eigeman, and many others in the theatre, film, and TV industry, including writers, directors, producers, and designers.
2. All classes and productions are open to all Kenyon students, regardless of major, and many of our most involved students are non-majors.
3. Kenyon is a rigorous academic liberal arts college, and all students are expected to develop a broad background within the department and throughout the college's curriculum, including the completion of a capstone senior thesis project.

■ Marietta College
Marietta, OH

Compiled by: Renee M. Bell, Assistant Professor/Costumer

Degrees Offered:

BFA in theatre

BA in theatre

Minors Offered:

Theatre

Population of Department(s): 50

Audition to Declare a Theatre/Musical Theatre Major? No

Three things you would like our readers to know about your performing arts department:

1. Marietta College is a small liberal arts college in Marietta, OH.

2. We provide students with excellent opportunities to engage in all areas of the theatre arts.

3. The Department of Theatre provides training both for students who wish to pursue careers in professional theatre and for students who wish to complete a theatre minor as part of a liberal arts education.

■ University of Findlay
Findlay, OH

Compiled by: Christopher Matsos, Assistant Professor of Theatre, Director of the Theatre Program

Degrees Offered:

BA in theatre, with emphases in either performance or theatre design/technology

Minors Offered:

Theatre

Population of Department(s): Approximately 30 in the theatre program

Audition to Declare a Theatre/Musical Theatre Major? No. We attend auditions at the Ohio, Michigan, and Indiana thespian festivals for scholarship purposes, but auditioning for our program is not required.

Three things you would like our readers to know about your performing arts department:

1. Our approach is like that of a small, professional theatre company, where our ensemble of student actors and designers fully commits to the collaborative production process to create exciting, challenging theatre while developing practical skills. The theatre program at The University of Findlay offers four mainstage productions each academic year, including a musical.

2. We offer generous scholarships to *all* theatre students willing to commit to working onstage or backstage for each production.

3. Through our Donnell Broadway Concert Series, we host a renowned Broadway musical theatre artist every semester. These performers offer public concerts and work exclusively with our theatre students.

■ Wittenberg University
Springfield, OH

Compiled by: Corwin Georges, Professor and Chairperson

Degrees Offered:

BA in theatre
BA in dance

Minors Offered:

Technical theatre

Theatre performance

Dance

Population of Department(s): 31 majors, 20 minors

Audition to Declare a Theatre/Musical Theatre Major? No

Three things you would like our readers to know about your performing arts department:

1. Students study all aspects of theatre and dance in an intimate liberal arts learning environment that fosters scholarship, creativity, self-discovery, and artistic expression.

2. Numerous performance opportunities and individualized attention from faculty.

3. Nationally recognized program.

■ Wright State University
Department of Theatre, Dance, and Motion Pictures
Dayton, OH

Compiled by: Victoria Oleen, Managing Director

Degrees Offered:

BFA in acting

BFA in acting/musical theatre

BFA in design/technology

BA in theatre studies

Minors Offered:

None

Population of Department(s): 83 acting/musical theatre, 40 design/technology, 20 theatre studies

Audition to Declare a Theatre/Musical Theatre Major? Auditions are required for the BFA acting and musical theatre programs. Scholarship interviews are available for the BFA design/technology program.

Three things you would like our readers to know about your performing arts department:

1. Wright State University offers first-class conservatory training at state university prices.

2. We have no graduate program, so our students do not have to compete with graduate students for theatre experience. In addition, students are taught by nationally and internationally recognized faculty who work professionally.

3. Our graduates start work immediately. Over the course of four years at Wright State, students will be prepared for working in all parts of the industry.

Oregon

■ George Fox University
Newberg, OR

Compiled by: Rhett Luedtke, Professor of Theatre (Acting/Directing)

Degrees Offered:

Theatre

Interdisciplinary major (theatre with another academic degree of your choice)

Minors Offered:

Theatre

Music

Population of Department(s): 35 majors, 15 minors

Audition to Declare a Theatre/Musical Theatre Major? Scholarship auditions take place in February, but students don't need to audition to get into the program.

Three things you would like our readers to know about your performing arts department:

1. Become a servant storyteller dedicated to integrating faith and artistic excellence in order to make an impact in our local and global communities.

2. Learn from theatre professors who have been nationally recognized by the Kennedy Center American College Theatre Festival. Learn from working professionals who are currently engaged as directing, acting, design, and theatre management professionals on the West Coast.

3. Experience the academic rigor, creative expertise, and emotional and spiritual stamina required to be a professional theatre artist.

■ Pacific University
Forest Grove, OR

Compiled by: Dr. Ellen Margolis, Chair of Theatre and Dance

Degrees Offered:

Theatre
Applied theatre
Dance

Minors Offered:

Theatre
Applied theatre
Dance

Population of Department(s): Approximately 40

Audition to Declare a Theatre/Musical Theatre Major? No

Three things you would like our readers to know about your performing arts department:

1. Our degree tracks are challenging and well rounded, integrating theory and history with rigorous practice.

2. Our applied theatre track is unique in the country. In this program, students train not only in traditional theatre skills, but also in the use of performance to serve individual and community wellness (working with senior citizens, at-risk youth, special-needs children, and so on).

3. All of our faculty are working professionals who continue to gain recognition in their fields. Our relationships with the regional and national theatre profession help position our students for top internships, graduate programs, and jobs!

■ Southern Oregon University
Ashland, OR

Compiled by: Jackie Apodaca, Associate Professor, Head of Performance

Degrees Offered:

BA or BS in theatre arts
BFA in performance, stage management, lighting design, costume design, costume construction, scene design, sound design, technical direction

Minors Offered:

Shakespeare studies

Population of Department(s): 240

Audition to Declare a Theatre/Musical Theatre Major? No.

Three things you would like our readers to know about your performing arts department:

1. Designated a Center of Excellence in the Fine and Performing Arts by the Oregon University System (OUS), Southern Oregon University is the longest-standing OUS institution to offer the pre-professional BFA degree in theatre.

2. The theatre arts program is unique on the West Coast because it is focused entirely on undergraduate students. As a result, students experience close working relationships with faculty who are specialists and practitioners in every aspect of theatrical study. The process of gaining skills and building portfolios comes from hands-on experience staging productions in two theatres every term.

3. The program includes a rigorous and competitive BFA in acting degree, which culminates in the opportunity to audition for a spot in the actor-trainee program at the world-renowned Oregon Shakespeare Festival. The OSF trainee program is open only to students at SOU. The BFA acting program blends traditional conservatory training with audition and business preparation in a uniquely intensive way, preparing students to work on stage and screen, while also managing their vital careers in the arts.

■ Muhlenberg College
Department of Theatre and Dance
Allentown, PA

Compiled by: Charles Richter, Director of Theatre

Population of School: 2,200 full-time students

Conservatory or Liberal Arts: Liberal arts

Degrees Offered:
BA with concentrations in performance (acting/musical theatre), directing, stage management, design and technical theatre (lighting, costume, scenery, sound), performance studies (theatre history and criticism)
BA in dance
Students can double major in dance and theatre—musical theatre students often do

Population of Department(s): 250 theatre students, 100 dance students

Theatre Scholarships Available: Yes, audition is required.

Audition Required for BA/BS/BM: No audition is required for admission to the theatre or dance major program. There is an optional audition program for students who want their talent to be considered as part of their application process. Auditions are required for talent scholarship consideration.

Pre-screen Video Audition Required: No

Attends Unifieds: No

Number of Students Auditioning Each Year: 400

Number of Students Accepted Each Year: Students are not accepted by major. Muhlenberg is a competitive liberal arts college that admits about 40% of the applicants.

Cut Program or Audition to Remain in Program: No

Minors in Musical Theatre/Acting: We offer complete musical theatre training at Muhlenberg. Students have the option to do a theatre performance (acting) major and minor programs in music and dance. They can also do double majors in theatre and dance and take voice lessons or double major in theatre and music and take dance classes. Students have had major professional success with a variety of training sequences. We offer students the ability to customize their training programs to fit their specific needs. It isn't a lock-step program.

Prominent Alumni: David Masenheimer (*Les Mis*, *Scarlet Pimpernel*, *Side Show*, and others on Broadway), Frankie Grande (*Mamma Mia!* on Broadway), Allison Levy (*Scarlet Pimpernel* on Broadway), George Psomas (*South Pacific* at Lincoln Center), Kam Chang (*Miss Saigon* on Broadway), Michael Biren (*Billy Elliot* national tour), also several in film and TV

What do you look for in a potential student?

Intelligence, ability to pursue clear objectives in the acting audition, integration of physical life into the audition, high-quality audition material from good plays or films, and for singers, a natural vocal quality.

What are some of the auditors' pet peeves?

Audition pieces that are narrative rather than active. Bad song choices—75% of musical theatre auditionees come in with songs that are of terrible quality, out of their vocal range, and too difficult to sing.

What are your audition requirements?

Two contrasting monologues (no more than four minutes total) for actors. Two contrasting monologues (no more than four minutes total) and one musical theatre song (32 bars) for musical theatre performers. Optional dance auditions consist of taking an accelerated intermediate ballet class and presenting a 90-second prepared piece in any dance idiom. The dance audition is recommended for students with a strong ballet background.

In your eyes, what makes up an excellent college audition monologue? Song?

The monologue should show a character making active choices rather than narrating a past event or events. I want to see the ability to pursue objective. A song written before 1970 that is in the vocal range of the student. The song should show off the voice well.

If there were one monologue you never wanted to see again, what would it be?

Anything from Durang or Phoebe from *As You Like It*.

If there were one song you never wanted to hear again, what would it be?

"Astonishing" from *Little Women*.

Can you walk me through what I can expect at your on-campus auditions?

You would come to Muhlenberg on a weekday. You would attend an acting class, have a tour and information session about the theatre and dance program, and do your audition pieces for the director of theatre, who will interview you before and after the audition. There is only one person in the room, and it is a very relaxed process. The process in the audition room takes about 20 minutes. The tour and information session takes about 40 minutes.

What's a memorable audition you can remember?

I've done thousands of auditions over the past 30 years. A highlight last year was a girl who sang a little known Irving Berlin tune with great intelligence and period style.

What is your biggest piece of advice for potential students auditioning?

Choose quality material that is in your range. Don't pick difficult material because you think it will impress. Do material you can do well with. Be overprepared. Nerves can make you forget your lines.

After I audition, is there a good way to follow up?

An email or note is fine.

Would I get a showcase at the end of senior year?

Yes.

Do I have to audition to be accepted into the showcase?

No.

Where are showcases held, and are they successful?

Showcase is in New York. It is a three-day experience that includes workshops with casting directors, managers, and agents. On the final day, there is a showcase for the industry. About 20%–30% of students get management/agent offers. All students who go to the showcase find it valuable even if they don't get management. We view it as a career development workshop.

Will I be able to audition/perform as a freshman?

Any student in the college, including freshmen, can audition for any production. Casting is competitive for our mainstage series (six productions), but not as competitive for workshop productions (20–40 productions). Freshmen are often cast. Casting in productions is not guaranteed.

In what ways can I be involved with the department aside from performing?

Any student at Muhlenberg can work on production crews and can volunteer in any area of production.

Say I get a BA rather than a BFA. Will I actually get to perform?

All of our students are BA students, and anyone can audition for any production. There is no guarantee that you will be cast.

I love to sing, but I don't consider myself a dancer. Can I still seek a degree in musical theatre at your school?

Any student can structure a program that includes complete training in voice, dance, and acting.

I want to get a BFA in acting, but I also love to sing. Can BFA/BA acting students take voice lessons with top voice faculty?

We have nine top-quality voice teachers on the staff, and any student in the college can study with any of the voice teachers. Voice training is on an individual basis, and students are assigned a voice teacher to start, but they are free to change voice teachers at the end of any semester.

Do you discourage or encourage students to audition for theatre outside of the department during the academic year?

Theatre students are allowed to work outside of the department. We don't encourage or discourage them. Students have been given leaves of absence to do professional work on Broadway and in regional theatre.

Does your school regularly work in conjunction with any regional theatres?

We have a strong relationship with the Enchantment Theatre Company, a top-quality national children's touring theatre. The entire company is made up of Muhlenberg theatre and dance alumni.

What do students typically do during the summers? Do you actively promote participation in summer theatre auditions?

We have a major in-house summer theatre, the Muhlenberg Summer Music Theatre Festival. All members of the company are paid and given housing—80% of the performing company and technical staff are made up of Muhlenberg students. We often use alumni Equity guest artists. Many students also audition and work in a variety of other summer theatres.

How many musicals versus straight plays do you do in a season?

We do six mainstage productions during the year, and one or two of those is always a musical. We do two major musical productions and a children's musical in the Muhlenberg Summer Music Theatre. There are also 20–40 student-directed workshop productions. Three or four of those are usually musicals.

What are some of your alumni up to? Do you have an active alumni network?

See above—many are working as directors, administrators, and actors in theatres across the country and in film and TV. We have a very active alumni network in New York called the Fishbowl Collective. They produce work, do workshops on and off campus, and serve as an excellent resource for our students and working alumni. Check out alumni pages of our website for more information: www.muhlenberg.edu/main/academics/theatre-dance/meetOurAlumni/updates.html and www.muhlenberg.edu/main/academics/theatre-dance/meetOurAlumni/alumniprofiles.html.

What is the portfolio/interview process for a technical theatre student?

Prospective technical theatre students do a portfolio/interview with the head of our design/technical theatre area, Curtis Dretsch.

What do you expect to see on a technical theatre résumé?

A good deal of high school experience. For scene and costume designers, some training in drawing.

I'm interested in lighting, sound design, and stage management. What major should I go for? Can I minor?

You can do a theatre major with concentrations in lighting, sound design, or stage management—we have programs in all three. Theatre students at Muhlenberg are free to double major or minor in any discipline.

Anything else I should know?

At Muhlenberg, we have state-of-the art facilities—three theatres, well-equipped shops, and studios in ultra-modern buildings. The theatre and dance department is the third largest on campus and a real focus of college life at Muhlenberg. Students take major leadership roles in the production program, including directing and designing mainstage productions as well as all studio productions.

We have 23 full-time faculty/staff and numerous guest artists coming from New York (less than two hours away). Our acting, directing, design, and dance faculty all have major professional experience and are highly respected in the profession. Several of our faculty have taught at top conservatory and MFA programs.

All Muhlenberg theatre and dance students receive top-quality, professional-level studio training and a strong liberal arts education. Our four-year graduation rate is well over 80%, and we have a strong retention rate in the theatre and dance department.

Prospective students should contact Charles Richter, director of theatre (richter@ muhlenberg.edu) for further information.

■ Temple University
Department of Theater
Philadelphia, PA

Compiled by: Peter Reynolds, Head of Musical Theater, Director of Student Affairs – Theater/ Assistant Chair

Population of School: 35,000

Conservatory or Liberal Arts: Liberal arts

Degrees Offered:

BA in theater with concentrations in acting, design/tech, directing, musical theater, theater studies
MFA in acting
MFA in directing
MFA in design
MFA in playwriting

Population of Department(s): 300

Theatre Scholarships Available: Limited, see www.temple.edu/theater/resources/ scholarships.html

Audition Required for BA/BS/BM: For undergraduates, an audition is required for entrance into musical theater concentration. Acting concentration auditions occur prior to Acting I, II, III, IV, and V. There is rolling acceptance to the acting concentration.

Pre-screen Video Audition Required: No

Attends Unifieds: No

Number of Students Auditioning Each Year: 200 (musical theater and acting)

Number of Students Accepted Each Year: 15–18 (musical theater), 75 (theater)

Cut Program or Audition to Remain in Program: No

Minors in Musical Theatre/Acting: No, but a minor in theater

Prominent Alumni: Kunal Nayyar (television, *Big Bang Theory*), Da'Vine Joy Randolph (Broadway, *Ghost*), Kevin Del Aguila (Broadway, *Peter and the Starcatcher*; writer, *Altar Boyz*), Michael Rady (film, *Sisterhood of the Traveling Pants*; television, *Melrose Place, The Mentalist*), Austin Durant (Broadway, *War Horse, Macbeth*), Evan Jonigkeit (film, *X Men*; Broadway, *High,* off-Broadway, *Really, Really*), Lawrence Stallings (Broadway, *Book of Mormon, Hair, Passing Strange*), Amina Robinson (Broadway, *Mamma Mia!, Godspell*; film, *Precious*), Josh Tower (Broadway, *The Lion King*), Jason Winston George (television, *Grey's Anatomy, Mistresses*), Johnny Gill (television, *Rectify, Harry's Law*), Bryan Terrell Clark (Broadway, *Motown*), Jamyl Dobson (Bill T. Jones/Arnie Zane Dance Co.), Nikiya Mathis (public theater, *The Brother/Sister Plays*)

See www.temple.edu/theater/alumni/notablealumni.html.

These answers refer to the musical theatre concentration audition.

What do you look for in a potential student?

A curious, talented actor/singer/dancer interested in being a citizen artist.

What are your audition requirements?

Musical theater: two 16-bar selections, a short monologue, dance call led by head of dance.

In your eyes, what makes up an excellent college audition monologue?

A story the young person *needs* to tell that is age appropriate and from a play that is good literature. Song? Tell us a story; don't show off notes.

If there were one monologue you never wanted to see again, what would it be?

If it is done compellingly and with passionate intention, we can listen to any monologue.

If there were one song you never wanted to hear again, what would it be?

Likewise, if it is sung compellingly, with needful intention, we can listen to any song.

Can you walk me through what I can expect at your on-campus auditions?

The day begins with the dance call, followed by individual song and monologue auditions. The entire process is less than three hours.

What's a memorable audition you can remember?

A young woman who told a complete story in her monologue, and then told two more stories with her two 16-bar cuts.

What is your biggest piece of advice for potential students auditioning?

As you can never ascertain what an auditor or a school "wants," all your focus should instead be on presenting *you* and what you do in the most prepared and professional manner.

If I audition for your BA musical theatre concentration, but don't get accepted, do you still consider me for your BA program?

Yes.

After I audition, is there a good way to follow up?

You will be contacted via email or letter.

Would I get a showcase at the end of senior year?

Philadelphia Annual College Senior Showcase for Philadelphia theater community.

Do I have to audition to be accepted into the showcase?

Yes.

Where are showcases held, and are they successful?

Showcases are held in Philadelphia. Temple alumni can be found on every professional stage in Philadelphia.

Will I be able to audition/perform as a freshman?

Yes.

If there is a graduate program, will I get the same performance opportunities as an undergraduate?

Yes.

What ways can I be involved with the department aside from performing?

Our undergraduates also study design, production, directing, and stage management. Top undergraduate designers get to design mainstage shows in their senior year; all shows have undergraduate stage managers.

I love to sing, but I don't consider myself a dancer. Can I still seek a degree in musical theatre at your school?

Yes, but a dance audition is required.

I want to get a BFA in acting, but I also love to sing. Can BFA/BA acting students take voice lessons with top voice faculty?

Voice lessons through the Boyer College of Music and Dance are assured for musical theater concentration students only. Limited voice lessons are available for students in other majors.

Do you discourage or encourage students to audition for theatre outside of the department during the academic year?

Philadelphia is one of the biggest theater centers in the country, with lots of performance opportunities on stage, in film, and in new media, and our students are often cast. We neither encourage nor discourage you to audition. If you do work outside the university, you are responsible for keeping up your scholastic responsibilities and maintaining your GPA.

Does your school regularly work in conjunction with any regional theatres?

Unofficially, Temple alumni are a part of every major regional theater company in the area, and Temple students find employment in these companies as well.

What do students typically do during the summers? Do you actively promote participation in summer theatre auditions?

Yes.

How many musicals versus straight plays do you do in a season?

At least one large musical per year and six mainstage productions annually, with myriad other performance opportunities.

I'm interested in lighting, sound design, and stage management. What major should I go for? Can I minor?

BA with a design/tech concentration.

Anything else I should know?

Entering its 46th active year of operation, the Department of Theater is now a proud part of the new Division of Theater, Film and Media Arts/Center for the Arts at Temple and was recently ranked by *U.S. News & World Report* among the top 25 theater programs in the nation. The faculty and staff of the department represent highly trained scholars and professionals with theater credits in Philadelphia, in New York City, nationally, and internationally. Our BA program features strong professional concentrations in theater studies, musical theater, acting, directing, and design/tech. In addition, graduate MFA programs are offered in acting, directing, design, and playwriting, engendering countless opportunities for interdisciplinary creative and scholarly synergy between all levels.

■ University of the Arts
Philadelphia, PA

Compiled by: David Howey, Head, Acting Program; Nick Embree, Head, Theater Design and Technology Program, Ira Brind School of Theater Arts

Population of School: Roughly 300

Conservatory or Liberal Arts: Liberal arts

Degrees Offered:
BFA in acting
BFA in musical theater
BFA in directing, playwriting, and production (DPP)
BFA in theater design and technology

Population of Department(s): 120 in musical theater, 100 in acting, 50 in DPP, 25 in design/tech

Theatre Scholarships Available: There are various grants and scholarships available to those interested and accepted into the University of the Arts. Scholarships and grants are determined from your initial audition, financial need, and merit within respective programs.

Audition Required for BFA: Yes

Pre-screen Video Audition Required: No, although video audition submissions are acceptable if you are unable to attend university-hosted auditions or Unifieds. You can use getacceptd.com as a preliminary audition. Details can be found at https://app.getacceptd.com/uarts.

Attends Unifieds: Yes

Location of Unifieds: New York, Los Angeles, and Chicago, as well as other major cities around the nation

Number of Students Auditioning Each Year: Roughly 700

Number of Students Accepted Each Year: 90

Cut Program or Audition to Remain in Program: We do not have a cut program or a system of annual auditions for accepted students to determine their readmission into the program.

Minors in Musical Theatre/Acting: We have a musical theater minor program open to acting; design, playwriting, and production; dance; and voice majors. Check our website for more information on this minor.

Prominent Alumni: KaDee Strickland (BFA '98, *Private Practice*), Kate Flannery (BFA '89, *The Office*), Ana Ortiz (BFA '93, *Ugly Betty*), Sarah Bolt ('02, *Sister Act*), Jackson Gay ('99, prominent New York director), Kelli Barrett (*Rock of Ages*)

Check out our alumni webpage for more names: www.uarts.edu/audiences/alumni.

What do you look for in a potential student?

Preparedness, honesty, authenticity, approachability.

What are some of the auditors' pet peeves?

Getting too close to the table. Apologizing for themselves. Overselling in an interview.

What are your audition requirements?

Acting: two contrasting monologues totaling three minutes. Musical theater: two contrasting songs and two monologues. Design/tech: Details are available at http://www.uarts.edu/admissions/college-performing-arts-audition-requirements#theater.

In your eyes, what makes up an excellent college audition monologue? Song?

Choice of material, song, or monologue that the auditioner is interested in and not merely using to show off. Material that helps to reveal something about the auditioner, but doesn't overwhelm the room or the auditioner.

If there were one monologue you never wanted to see again, what would it be?

Phoebe from *As You Like It,* Viola from *Twelfth Night,* or anything from Christopher Durang.

If you require a pre-screen video audition, what do you look for in those submissions?

Shot in front of a simple background with material that bears the same hallmarks as above.

Can you walk me through what I can expect at your on-campus auditions?

The on-campus acting audition will be conducted in two rounds. In the first round, you will present your monologues to a member of the Brind School acting faculty. Your performance will be evaluated on the basis of honesty, expressiveness, vocal strength, and conviction, as well as the professionalism and preparation of your presentation. After this initial presentation, selected applicants will be invited for a second callback audition. Students who have submitted a video for pre-screening will skip this first round and proceed directly to the callback. At the callback, you will present your pieces again, and you may be asked to make an adjustment in your presentation, undertake a brief improvisation, or discuss your interpretation of the pieces you've chosen. This callback will include a personal interview with a faculty member who will explore your training, your aspirations, and the suitability of the University of the Arts as a venue to pursue your studies.

What is your biggest piece of advice for potential students auditioning?
Be thoroughly prepared and relax. We want you to succeed.

If I audition for your BFA musical theatre program, but don't get accepted, do you still consider me for your BFA acting program or your BA program?
Most definitely.

After I audition, is there a good way to follow up?
Just wait with fingers crossed.

Would I get a showcase at the end of senior year?
Yes.

Do I have to audition to be accepted into the showcase?
No.

Where are showcases held, and are they successful?
Showcases are held in New York and Philadelphia, with many of our students getting work and viable connections directly from both showcases.

Will I be able to audition/perform as a freshman?
Second semester.

If there is a graduate program, will I get the same performance opportunities as an undergraduate?
There is no graduate program.

In what ways can I be involved with the department aside from performing?
We have a very active chapter of the theater fraternity, Alpha Phi Omega, that is involved in both university and community projects centered around the performing arts. Also, there are work-study opportunities.

I love to sing, but I don't consider myself a dancer. Can I still seek a degree in musical theatre at your school?
Yes.

I want to get a BFA in acting, but I also love to sing. Can BFA/BA acting students take voice lessons with top voice faculty?
Yes, and they can participate in the musical theater minor that offers classes in vocal techniques and musical theater performance techniques.

Do you discourage or encourage students to audition for theatre outside of the department during the academic year?
Upperclassmen are encouraged.

Does your school regularly work in conjunction with any regional theatres?
We have strong affiliations with prominent regional theaters such as the Arden, Wilma, Walnut, and others in Philadelphia.

What do students typically do during the summers? Do you actively promote participation in summer theatre auditions?

Yes. They seek internships, work in our summer programs, and so on.

How many musicals versus straight plays do you do in a season?

50/50.

What are some of your alumni up to? Do you have an active alumni network?

Yes, we have an active alumni network. Many of our alumni are pillars of the Philadelphia theatre scene. Also, we have a national theater school alumni association that publishes a newsletter that serves as a gathering of information for our alums. The university also regularly sponsors alumni events both on campus and throughout the United States.

What is the portfolio/interview process for a technical theatre student?

We have portfolio auditions rather than performance auditions. The interview typically lasts 30–45 minutes, and most of that time is spent looking at the student's portfolio and résumé and discussing the student's experiences, skills, interests, and goals.

The portfolio serves to illustrate and document the student's work and to present it in an organized and accessible format. Ideally, a portfolio contains examples of all of the elements used in a designer or technician's process, from samples of research and early "what-if" doodles all the way to finished drawings/drafting/renderings and photographs of the finished results. A portfolio can also present other non-theater skills and talents, especially in the fine arts. Examples might include photography, sculpture, computer rendering, graphic arts, woodworking, charcoal figure sketching, jewelry making, fashion drawing, oil painting, welding, garment construction, ceramics, and so on.

The student should be familiar with and comfortable with both portfolio and résumé and should be able to present them confidently without resorting to a memorized pitch.

What do you expect to see on a technical theatre résumé?

There is no one thing we require on a résumé. We actually prefer to assemble a group of students with very different skills and backgrounds rather than a set of students with all the same experiences. While the very strongest applicants we interview have scores of production credits plus extensive training and many useful skills, we do accept students whose strength in one area may be offset by a limited experience in another. Generally speaking, the most useful credits are those that demonstrate strength in the area the student intends to pursue, such as lighting design credits for a lighting student, for example. However, fine arts skills can be very valuable even if they are not applied to theater work. An average student applicant has 10–12 shows on his or her résumé, with lead responsibilities for three or four of those as a designer, technical director, charge scenic artist, and so on.

I'm interested in lighting, sound design, and stage management. What major should I go for? Can I minor?

A student with these interests should probably apply to the theater design and technology program (DT, for short) at UARTS. While stage management as a focus belongs to the directing, playwrighting, and production program (DPP, for short), it is a relatively smaller part of that major than lighting and sound are in the DT major. DT students can and do stage manage for shows on our stages, and they take a stage management course as part of our major. Advanced stage management is available to DT students as an elective.

If stage management is the primary of these three interests, the student might consider majoring in the DPP program and using electives to take lighting and sound design from the DT offerings.

There are no official minors in DT or DPP, but some students take electives that could be considered equivalent to such a minor. DT and DPP courses are generally open to the other's majors.

■ Alvernia University
Reading, PA

Compiled by: Nathan Thomas, PhD, Director of Theatre

Degrees Offered:

BA in theatre
BA in communication with focus area in theatre

Minors Offered:

Theatre

Population of Department(s): Approximately 15

Audition to Declare a Theatre/Musical Theatre Major? No

Three things you would like our readers to know about your performing arts department:

1. We are a Franciscan institution. Inclusiveness is very important to the theatre program. We regularly practice color-blind and gender-neutral casting.
2. Students have the opportunity to learn practical, real-world approaches to theatre. The program includes doing world-premiere and American-premiere plays. Students work with professional guest artists. Our faculty are working professionals.
3. We're currently celebrating our 10th season. We're a "young" program, and students can help shape the nature of what they do.

■ Cedar Crest College
Allentown, PA

Compiled by: Kevin Gallagher, Associate Professor of Performing Arts, Technical Director

Degrees Offered:

Theatre with concentrations in performance, design/technology, arts administration
Dance with concentrations in performance, arts management

Minors Offered:

Theatre
Dance

Population of Department(s): 40

Audition to Declare a Theatre/Musical Theatre Major? No

Three things you would like our readers to know about your performing arts department:

1. Cedar Crest is an all-women's college dedicated to the development and advancement of women leaders through the arts.

2. We encourage our young artists to create passionately inspired works, and we educate them with the skills to excel in the competitive global environment.

3. We have a nationally recognized forensic speech team consisting of students from every academic discipline.

■ DeSales University
Center Valley, PA

Compiled by: Dennis Razze, Chair of Theatre

Degrees Offered:

BA in theatre with specialized programs in acting, directing, musical theatre performance, design, technical theatre, stage management, and secondary education

Minors Offered:

Dramatic literature
Design/technical theatre

Population of Department(s): 140

Audition to Declare a Theatre/Musical Theatre Major? Yes

Three things you would like our readers to know about your performing arts department:

1. Paid professional internships available each summer with the Pennsylvania Shakespeare Festival in residence on campus.

2. Study abroad and professional internships available in England, London, and Rome.

3. New York senior showcase held each spring in off-Broadway theatre, seen by more than 50 agents, casting directors, managers, and industry professionals.

■ Dickinson College
Carlisle, PA

Compiled by: Todd Wronski, Professor of Theatre and Chair, Department of Theatre and Dance

Degrees Offered:

Theatre arts (focus areas offered in acting/directing, design/technical theatre, dramatic literature, dance)

Minors Offered:

Theatre

Dance

Population of Department(s): Typical graduating class will have 5–10 majors; 15–20 declared majors spread out over three years; 5–10 minors annually

Audition to Declare a Theatre/Musical Theatre Major? No

Three things you would like our readers to know about your performing arts department:

1. Notable international experiences in both performance and study.
2. Professionally active faculty who regularly employ students as professional interns.
3. A program that serves intensely committed students, whether they are majors, minors, or majoring in another field.

■ Elizabethtown College
Elizabethtown, PA

Compiled by: Michael Swanson, Director of Theatre and Dance

Degrees Offered:

Theatre performance

Theatre technology – two majors

Minors Offered:

Theatre performance

Theatre technology – two minors

Population of Department(s): We are not a separate department, but Theatre and Dance is a division of the Fine and Performing Arts Department. About 50 students are involved annually in theatre productions at E-town.

Audition to Declare a Theatre/Musical Theatre Major? No

Three things you would like our readers to know about your performing arts department:

1. Students will have close contact with faculty members, with theatre class size averaging 7–10 students.
2. Every theatre major is required to direct a play for the college audience by completing the required class in directing.
3. Students can also design productions and take part in many other real-world experiences, including interning at local theatres.

Gettysburg College
Gettysburg, PA

Compiled by: Chris Kauffman, Chair of Theatre Arts

Degrees Offered:

Theatre

Minors Offered:

Theatre

Population of Department(s): Typically 25 majors; 100 involved per year in co-curricular way

Audition to Declare a Theatre/Musical Theatre Major? No

Three things you would like our readers to know about your performing arts department:

1. We are a small but vibrant program that offers academically rigorous courses in the acting, directing, and design disciplines, dramatic literature, theatre history, and world drama. Our size allows us to pay close attention to our majors and minors and advise them appropriately on the myriad career options.

2. We allow for production experience through three mainstage productions per year from the classical and contemporary repertoire in our 220-seat thrust stage. We do a musical every other year in conjunction with the Conservatory, using the 800-seat roadhouse with full pit orchestra.

3. We prepare students for lives as artists, scholars, and technicians in the theatre, but also use theatre for learning experiences regardless of major. Everyone is welcome to participate. There are many student-run performance opportunities throughout the year, including a student-run chamber musical theatre group.

Indiana University of Pennsylvania
Indiana, PA

Compiled by: Brian Jones, Chair, Department of Theater and Dance

Degrees Offered:

BA in theater with concentrations in performance, design/technology/management, theory and criticism
BA in interdisciplinary fine arts, musical theater track
BA in interdisciplinary fine arts—dance arts track

Minors Offered:

Dance
Theater

Population of Department(s): Approximately 100

Audition to Declare a Theatre/Musical Theatre Major? Yes

Three things you would like our readers to know about your performing arts department:

1. You will participate in our main theater and/or dance season beginning your very first semester and every semester, to apply what you're learning in the classroom under the personal attention of a caring, accomplished faculty.

2. We provide great breadth and depth with more than 50 courses by 10 professional faculty whose primary focus is to teach and train undergraduate students.

3. You will be able to produce, direct, design, and write your own productions in our studio theater. Our objective is to get you ready to create your own work by the time you graduate.

■ Lycoming College
Williamsport, PA

Compiled by: Dr. N. J. Stanley, Chair of the Theatre Department

Degrees Offered:

BA in theatre with three concentrations from which to choose: acting, directing, and design/ tech

Minors Offered:

Three different minors in theatre: performance, technical theatre, and theatre history and literature

Population of Department(s): 25

Audition to Declare a Theatre/Musical Theatre Major? No audition required, but you can audition for a theatre talent scholarship.

Three things you would like our readers to know about your performing arts department:

1. We produce 7–10 shows a year in our two theatres.
2. Concentrations allow students to specialize in their areas of interest.
3. Our theatre program focuses on production and hands-on experiences.

■ Messiah College
Mechanicsburg, PA

Compiled by: Tymberley A. Whitesel, Associate Professor of Theatre Design, Chair of Theatre and Dance

Degrees Offered:

BA in theatre with emphases in acting, directing, technical theatre and design
BA in dance
BFA in musical theatre
BA in theatre (business)
BA in digital media, church media concentration

Minors Offered:

Theatre

Dance

Population of Department(s): 40

Audition to Declare a Theatre/Musical Theatre Major? Theatre, yes; dance, yes; musical theatre, yes; theatre (business), no; digital media, no

Three things you would like our readers to know about your performing arts department:

1. Each year, majors apply classroom knowledge by participating in one or more of the six to eight productions within the season.

2. A new dance studio and black box theatre have been added to the existing proscenium theatre and shop spaces to create a state-of-the-art training facility.

3. Students will explore the intersections between Christian faith and their art as they use their talents and gifts to interpret the world in creative ways.

■ University of Pittsburgh
Pittsburgh, PA

Compiled by: Annmarie Duggan, Chair, Theatre Arts

Degrees Offered:

BA in theatre arts with emphasis in performance or design tech

We also have a musical theatre component to our performance area MFA and performance pedagogy PhD

Minors Offered:

Theatre arts with emphasis in performance or design tech

Population of Department(s): 56 major, 84 minors, 2 MFA

Audition to Declare a Theatre/Musical Theatre Major? No

Three things you would like our readers to know about your performing arts department:

1. Our students are receiving professional training in their area of interest.

2. We have a high rate of after-graduation placement.

3. Undergraduates contribute in every way to our productions both on and off stage.

Rhode Island

■ Providence College
Providence, RI

Compiled by: Dr. Wendy Oliver, Chair

Degrees Offered:

Theatre

Minors Offered:

Theatre

Dance

Film

Population of Department(s): 18 majors, approximately 38 minors

Audition to Declare a Theatre/Musical Theatre Major? No

Three things you would like our readers to know about your performing arts department:

1. We have a small, personalized program with many performing opportunities. Students are extremely proud to be a part of our performance series, which boasts three mainstage plays, two dance concerts, and a film festival.

2. We have a well-rounded theatre major curriculum that culminates in a capstone project during the senior year. Students learn about theatre as a historical and cultural force, as well as studying its hands-on components.

3. We have a lovely facility that is about seven years old, with two beautiful theatres and a dance studio. Our production values are very high; we use both resident faculty directors and guest artists from New York City and the New England area. We have top-notch guest designers from around the region.

■ Roger Williams University
Bristol, RI

Compiled by: Dr. Jeffrey B. Martin, Chair, Department of Performing Arts

Degrees Offered:
Theatre, performing arts, dance, music with concentrations in acting, musical theatre, directing, design, and production

Minors Offered:
Theatre
London theatre

Population of Department(s): 60

Audition to Declare a Theatre/Musical Theatre Major? No. We are a liberal arts theatre program open to all. Students from all majors participate in the program, both classes and productions.

Three things you would like our readers to know about your performing arts department:

1. The theatre department has a very active production program (four major productions a year including a musical and a number of smaller offerings). Students are involved from their first day in the department and encouraged to participate in every capacity. Our theatre productions take place in a remodeled 150-year-old barn that encourages flexibility, creativity, and intimacy.

2. The liberal arts academic program and the active production program are intertwined so that students apply in the studio, in the shop, and on stage what they are learning in the classroom. The liberal arts approach provides a strong background that goes beyond theatre, while the production program promotes hands-on skill and creativity. We have many internship opportunities, and graduates go on to further study or careers in the theatre, but many also use their liberal arts background to follow their own path into other areas.

3. London theatre program: All majors/minors spend the fall of their junior year in London in a program the department has operated since 1970. Located in the heart of London, students see more than 40 plays in a wide range of styles and venues while studying theatre, art, history, and culture. In London, students tour theatres, meets theatre artists, and participate in workshops. Courses include daily site visits throughout London but also field trips to York, Cambridge, Stratford-upon-Avon, Oxford, Bath, Dover, Stonehenge, and a number of other sites.

South Carolina

■ College of Charleston
Charleston, SC

Compiled by: Todd McNerney, Associate Professor and Chair

Degrees Offered:

BA in theatre with concentrations in costume design and technology, scenic/lighting design and technology, theatre for youth, performance, and general theatre studies
BA in dance with concentrations in general dance studies and performance/choreography
MAT in performing arts with a concentration in theatre

Minors Offered:

Theatre
Dance

Population of Department(s): 130 theatre majors, 60 theatre minors, 40 dance majors, 70 dance minors

Audition to Declare a Theatre/Musical Theatre Major? No

Three things you would like our readers to know about your performing arts department:

1. Our department is grounded in our liberal arts and sciences traditions. Any student may declare a major in theatre or dance and may take any classes, so long as they fulfill the prerequisite requirements. Many of our students double major or participate in the Honors College.

2. We produce an annual season of six or seven plays and a dance concert. Our student theatre organization produces another four to six plays per year. All productions are fully mounted in one of our three theatres. Our Dance Alliance presents student choreography and guest artist classes.

3. We have three theatres, two acting studios, two dance studios, a lighting design laboratory, a design studio, a costume shop, and scene shop, along with 14 full-time faculty and 10 adjunct faculty.

Limestone College

Gaffney, SC

Compiled by: Dr. Timothy Baxter-Ferguson, Chair of Theatre

Degrees Offered:

BFA in theatre (with concentrations in acting, playwriting, tech)

BFA in musical theatre

BA in theatre

BA in English/theatre

Minors Offered:

Theatre

Population of Department(s): 25

Audition to Declare a Theatre/Musical Theatre Major? Yes (for BFA)

Three things you would like our readers to know about your performing arts department:

1. Our small college environment allows multiple casting opportunities and individual attention.
2. We have active and lasting relationships with several theatres in the Charlotte, NC, area, and encourage our students to augment their training with outside professional work.
3. We are one of the few institutions in our area to offer the BFA, which allows young artists to more fully immerse themselves in their craft in preparation for their future careers in the arts.

Newberry College

Newberry, SC

Compiled by: Pat Gagliano, Professor of Theatre and Speech/Chair, Department of Arts and Communications

Degrees Offered:

BA in theatre

Minors Offered:

Theatre

Speech

Population of Department(s): 15 majors and minors; 25 involved each semester

Audition to Declare a Theatre/Musical Theatre Major? Not to declare major, but to earn scholarship, yes

Three things you would like our readers to know about your performing arts department:

1. We have many opportunities for theatre work in performance and technical theatre.
2. We perform our shows on campus and at out beautiful, restored Newberry Opera House, a professional touring house just a mile from campus.
3. We belong to three professional organizations and subsidize student travel for auditions, networking, and performances.

■ North Greenville University
Tigerville, SC

Compiled by: Jessica Snyder, Theatre Department Administrator

Degrees Offered:

BA in theatre with three tracks: performance, design/tech, and applied theatre
BA in interdisciplinary studies for musical theatre

Minors Offered:

Theatre

Population of Department(s): 40 majors

Audition to Declare a Theatre/Musical Theatre Major? No

Three things you would like our readers to know about your performing arts department:

1. The NGU theatre faculty consists of five full-time faculty in history/theory, performance, design, and technical direction; and one adjunct faculty in playwriting. All faculty have terminal degrees in their fields and work professionally in the upstate South Carolina theatre community.

2. Each year the department mounts four major productions and a number of other student-directed shows. All production cast and crew positions are filled by students.

3. Scholarships are offered to theatre majors as well as work-study positions in the theatre box office and scene shop.

■ Winthrop University
Rock Hill, SC

Compiled by: Daniel Gordon, Chair of the Department of Theatre and Dance

Degrees Offered:

BA in dance
BA in dance education/teacher certification
BA in theatre, with concentrations in performance, technology and design, musical theatre, theatre education/teacher certification

Minors Offered:

Theatre
Dance

Population of Department(s): About 140

Audition to Declare a Theatre/Musical Theatre Major? No, but merit scholarships are awarded through audition.

Three things you would like our readers to know about your performing arts department:

1. The department presents four mainstage productions (three in theatre, one in dance), two student choreography showcases, five studio dance/theatre productions, and other informal performances each year.

2. Very few undergraduate programs offer the amount of opportunities for students to perform, design, direct, choreograph, stage manage, and run productions that Winthrop does.

3. Winthrop University was named to *U.S. News & World Report's* top 10 regional public universities in the South in the magazine's "America's Best Colleges" 2014 edition.

■ Wofford College
Spartanburg, SC

Compiled by: Mark Ferguson, Professor of Theatre and Chair

Degrees Offered:

BA in theatre

Minors Offered:

Theatre

Population of Department(s): 25

Audition to Declare a Theatre/Musical Theatre Major? No

Three things you would like our readers to know about your performing arts department:

1. Theatre inspires empathy, self-examination, and compassion in the audience and the artist. At Wofford, we believe the study of theatre will open your eyes, mind, and heart, so that your work will have the same impact on the audience.

2. In addition to our three faculty-directed mainstage productions, Wofford Theatre also hosts Pulp Theatre, the all-student theatre group that produces a crazy and/or provocative musical each year with zero faculty involvement.

3. What you will acquire as a Wofford theatre major will prepare you well for many careers—you might pursue a career as an actor, director, lawyer, physician, secondary school teacher, or entrepreneur; you might pursue an MFA in acting, directing, or design; you might pursue an MA or PhD in dramatic literature, English, or philosophy; or you might found your own theatre company.

South Dakota

■ Mount Marty College
Yankton, SD

Compiled by: Andy Henrickson, Division Chair, Arts and Humanities

Degrees Offered:

Theatre

Music education

Music performance

Creative writing

Graphic design + media arts

Minors Offered:

Theatre

Music

Art

Graphic design + media arts

Population of Department(s): New theatre major–seeking students looking for a department with Catholic identity, double-major opportunities in liberal arts setting; up to 15% of student body participates in performing arts.

Audition to Declare a Theatre/Musical Theatre Major? No. Auditions are required for scholarships in theatre and music.

Three things you would like our readers to know about your performing arts department:

1. Presents a musical theatre production each fall; strong cooperation among theatre and music departments.

2. Growing choral activities program with three ensembles.

3. 602-seat proscenium mainstage space; 100-seat flexible black box.

■ Northern State University

Aberdeen, SD

Compiled by: Daniel Yurgaitis, Director of Theatre

Degrees Offered:

BA in musical theatre

Minors Offered:

Theatre

Arts management certificate

Population of Department(s): 30

Audition to Declare a Theatre/Musical Theatre Major? No, but auditions are necessary for incoming scholarship consideration.

Three things you would like our readers to know about your performing arts department:

1. Produce four productions a year, including two mainstage musicals in a 1,000-seat auditorium, a 350-seat auditorium, and a 200-seat black box.
2. Smaller class size means enhanced student–teacher ratio.
3. NSU offers a professional summer theater experience for its students at its Northern Fort Playhouse at Fort Sisseton Historic State Park.

■ South Dakota State University

Brookings, SD

Compiled by: J.D. Ackman, Professor and Director of Theatre

Degrees Offered:

BS in theatre

Minors Offered:

Theatre

Population of Department(s): Approximately 40 majors in theatre

Audition to Declare a Theatre/Musical Theatre Major? No

Three things you would like our readers to know about your performing arts department:

1. The theatre program at South Dakota State University places an emphasis on breadth of knowledge and production experience. Students are encouraged to gain experience in areas beyond their primary interest. Our alumni have been very successful in admission to graduate programs and work in theatres across the country.
2. Our summer company, Prairie Repertory Theatre (www.prairierep.org), offers excellent production opportunities for SDSU students, as well as a significant number of students from regional schools.
3. Scholarships are available for incoming students, as well as second-, third-, and fourth-year students.

Tennessee

■ Bryan College
Dayton, TN

Compiled by: Bernie Belisle, Theatre Department Head

Degrees Offered:

Theatre

Musical theatre

Minors Offered:

Theatre

Music

Population of Department(s): 13+

Audition to Declare a Theatre/Musical Theatre Major? Yes

Three things you would like our readers to know about your performing arts department:

1. Small department with low student–teacher ratio and excellent track record for admission to MFA programs (for those wishing to advance their acting degree).

2. Three major productions per year with excellent opportunities to be involved at varying capacities.

3. Distinctive Christian worldview focus in a liberal arts model.

■ Cumberland University
Lebanon, TN

Compiled by: Christopher Byrd, Technical Director of Theatre

Degrees Offered:

BA in theatre

BA in fine arts with emphasis in music theatre

MA in fine arts with emphasis in theatre and the dramatic arts

Minors Offered:

Theatre

Population of Department(s): Approximately 15–20 full-time majors and minors

Audition to Declare a Theatre/Musical Theatre Major? No

Three things you would like our readers to know about your performing arts department:

1. We are a small program where professors are able to spend time "one on one" with the student.

2. Due to our size, students are offered more opportunities to work in our stage productions than at larger universities, starting from their first year.

3. The plays we choose to perform and the techniques we use to produce them prepare our students for their beginning experience in professional theatre.

■ Lipscomb University
Nashville, TN

Compiled by: Mike Fernandez, Department Head

Degrees Offered:

Theatre
Acting
Directing
Musical theatre
Design

Minors Offered:

Acting
Directing
Musical theatre
Design
Dance
Playwriting

Population of Department(s): 75

Audition to Declare a Theatre/Musical Theatre Major? Yes

Three things you would like our readers to know about your performing arts department:

1. Three stage venues on campus.

2. Associated with semi-professional theatre companies that perform on our campus.

3. Lipscomb is a Christian private university affiliated with Churches of Christ.

■ Middle Tennessee State University
Murfreesboro, TN

Compiled by: Jeff Gibson, Chair of Speech and Theatre

Degrees Offered:

BA and BS in speech and theatre, with concentrations in theatre and in theatre with teacher licensure

Minors Offered:

Theatre

Entertainment arts design

Population of Department(s): 140 majors

Audition to Declare a Theatre/Musical Theatre Major? No

Three things you would like our readers to know about your performing arts department:

1. The program offers a diverse array and depth of coursework in all areas of theatre studies.
2. The program offers many study-abroad opportunities, including annual trips to London as well as locations such as Honduras, Ireland, and many others.
3. The program regularly brings national guest artists to campus for workshops and artistic residencies to work alongside students.

■ Sewanee: The University of the South
Sewanee, TN

Compiled by: Dr. Peter Smith, Artistic Director/Chair

Degrees Offered:

BA in theatre

Minors Offered:

Theatre

Shakespeare

Population of Department(s): 22 majors

Audition to Declare a Theatre/Musical Theatre Major? No

Three things you would like our readers to know about your performing arts department:

1. We are the recipients of the estate of Tennessee Williams.
2. We have a full-time faculty/staff of nine.
3. We offer a comprehensive major—students study acting, directing, design, scriptwriting, history, and performance theory.

■ Trevecca Nazarene University

Nashville, TN

Compiled by: Jeffrey D. Frame, PhD, Professor of Dramatic Arts

Degrees Offered:

Dramatic arts

Theatre education (7–12 licensure)

Minors Offered:

Dramatic arts

Applied theatre

Musical theatre

Population of Department(s): 20 dramatic arts and theatre education majors in the Department of Communication Studies, which runs approximately 60+ students overall

Audition to Declare a Theatre/Musical Theatre Major? No

Three things you would like our readers to know about your performing arts department:

1. Trevecca specializes in equipping students in a distinctly Christian community with the needed skills for professional jobs in the industry, for jobs in theatre education, and for positions in Christian ministry with the career-building vision that graduates should be creators of new work, forms, and ideas, not merely imitators of existing work, forms, and ideas.

2. In its unique location in the booming arts town of Nashville, TN, Trevecca provides outstanding opportunities for students to work alongside professionals in the field, from local artists and guest directors, such as Nat McIntyre (actor, *Warhorse* at the Lincoln Center, New York City), Tony Morton (actor, Tennessee Repertory Theatre and Playhouse, Nashville), to professional internships, both local (Nashville Children's Theatre, Tennessee Repertory Theatre, PK Productions, and so on) and abroad (Points New York City and in Los Angeles at the Los Angeles Film Studies Center).

3. Trevecca's premiere minor in applied theatre is the only one of its kind in the central United States.

Texas

■ Baylor University
Waco, TX

Compiled by: Stan Denman, Department Chairman

Degrees Offered:

BA in theatre
BFA in theatre performance (option for concentration in musical theatre)
BFA in theatre design and technology
BFA in theatre studies

Minors Offered:

None

Population of Department(s): 125 capped enrollment

Audition to Declare a Theatre/Musical Theatre Major? Yes

Three things you would like our readers to know about your performing arts department:

1. Baylor Theatre is a nationally ranked undergraduate theatre program and a member of the National Association of Schools of Theatre.
2. Baylor Theatre fosters a sense of support and community that branches out beyond the university to the Baylor Theatre network nationwide.
3. Baylor Theatre is a faith-based institution that does not shy away from edgy and provocative work that challenges both audience and performer alike.

■ Hardin Simmons University
Abilene, TX

Compiled by: Larry Wheeler, Associate Professor of Theatre, Theatre Department Chair, Theatre Technical Director

Degrees Offered:

BA in theatre
BFA in theatre with tracks in acting, musical theatre, design/theatre technology, stage management, and theatre education

Minors Offered:

Theatre

Population of Department(s): 30

Audition to Declare a Theatre/Musical Theatre Major? No audition for BA, audition required for BFA.

Three things you would like our readers to know about your performing arts department:

1. Small Christian university that allows for great student–teacher ratio.
2. Five full-length productions, one evening-of-one-acts production slot, allowing for many acting and designing opportunities.
3. Three performance spaces as well as travel study opportunities.

■ Lamar University
Beaumont, TX

Compiled by: Dr. Deena Conley, Chair of Theatre and Dance

Degrees Offered:

Emphasis areas in:

1. Acting
2. Technical theatre
3. Musical theatre (new as of fall 2014)
4. Dance

Minors Offered:

Theatre
Dance

Population of Department(s): Approximately 45, but that number is expected to increase dramatically with the addition of the musical theatre emphasis

Audition to Declare a Theatre/Musical Theatre Major? Audition for scholarships

Three things you would like our readers to know about your performing arts department:

1. We don't have a "bench system"; first-year students audition for productions.
2. We offer scholarships for outstanding students.
3. The department is large enough for competition, but small enough for one-on-one instruction.

■ McMurry University
Abilene, TX

Compiled by: Charlie Hukill, Professor of Theatre

Degrees Offered:

BA in theatre: acting/directing focus
BA in theatre: design/technology focus
BA in theatre: theatre arts education focus
BFA in theatre: acting/directing focus
BFA in theatre: design/technology focus

Minors Offered:

Theatre
Musical theatre
Theatre graphic design and promotion
Creative writing

Population of Department(s): 25

Audition to Declare a Theatre/Musical Theatre Major? Only for paid work positions

Three things you would like our readers to know about your performing arts department:

1. McMurry Theatre is a very active, production-oriented program, despite our relatively small size, staging six to eight full-length productions and as many as 10 one-acts per year.

2. We place great importance on playwriting and promoting works by new authors. Since 1999, the Texas Educational Theatre Association has recognized 28 outstanding college-/university-level playwrights, and 11 of those have been McMurry students. Since 1997, we have fully staged 30 original scripts (29 student written and 1 faculty written) and have had staged readings of 10 student-written scripts.

3. We have many students working successfully in various aspects of the field, from professional theatre to community theatre, and from public school to college/university theatre education programs, and to radio and TV. We train theatre generalists with a broad-based knowledge of all aspects of theatre to fully prepare our graduates for careers in the profession.

■ Midwestern State University
Wichita Falls, TX

Compiled by: Laura Jefferson, Interim Dean of Fine Arts

Degrees Offered:

BFA in theatre performance
BFA in theatre tech/design
BFA in theatre with teacher certification

Minors Offered:

Theatre

Population of Department(s): 48–50

Audition to Declare a Theatre/Musical Theatre Major? No

Three things you would like our readers to know about your performing arts department:

1. We are accredited with National Association of Schools of Theatre.
2. We have only an undergraduate program; consequently, more performance and tech/ design opportunities are available.
3. Students receive private school education at public school prices and facilities beyond compare.

■ Rice University
Houston, TX

Compiled by: Christina Keefe, Professor in the Practice and Director of Theatre

Degrees Offered:

BA in visual and dramatic arts

Population of Department(s): 20–25 in theatre track; 70 in entire department

Audition to Declare a Theatre/Musical Theatre Major? No

Three things you would like our readers to know about your performing arts department:

1. Small but growing.
2. Lots of opportunities in both acting and tech.
3. Strong mentors.

■ Stephen F. Austin State University
School of Theatre
Nacogdoches, TX

Compiled by: Scott Shattuck, Director, School of Theatre

Degrees Offered:

BA in theatre (liberal arts, with a minor in another subject)
BA in theatre education (with K–12 teacher certification)
BFA in theatre (acting and directing concentration)
BFA in theatre (technical theatre and design concentration)
BFA in theatre (stage management concentration)

Minors Offered:

Theatre
Film studies (interdisciplinary)

Population of Department(s): Approximately 175 theatre majors

Audition to Declare a Theatre/Musical Theatre Major? Yes (or portfolio presentation or interview)

Three things you would like our readers to know about your performing arts department:

1. We do 25–30 shows a year, and new students are urged to audition or get involved backstage from day one.

2. We have outstanding international programs with excellent scholarship support.

3. When you audition to become a theatre major, you will also be considered for a scholarship automatically.

■ Texas A&M University
Department of Performance Studies
College Station, TX

Compiled by: Donnalee Dox, Interim Head, Department of Performance Studies

Degrees Offered:

BA in theatre arts with concentrations in acting/directing, theatre and culture, design/technical theatre

Minors Offered:

Theatre arts
Performance technology

Population of Department(s): 78 in Department of Performance Studies (combined music and theatre arts)

Audition to Declare a Theatre/Musical Theatre Major? No

Three things you would like our readers to know about your performing arts department:

1. Texas A&M's theatre arts program encourages generalization, which creates adaptive artists with a wide variety of skills. Texas A&M's theatre productions are hands-on laboratories that involve the students in every aspect from start to finish. We connect our students to the world at large through national and regional experiences, environmental stewardship, and visiting artists and scholars.

2. Texas A&M's strength as a program is in its small size. Students are not anonymous. The collaboration between our dedicated students and working-professional faculty in music and theatre make us truly excellent at what we do. Students have access to a wide array of scholarly and performance opportunities, residencies with world-class visiting artists, and state-of-the-art resources.

3. Texas A&M's Department of Performance Studies is an excellent place to develop and exercise leadership skills applicable anywhere—in theatre, in business, or life in general. This program's coursework helps students develop the skills for pursuing a career in theatre and related fields, as well as advanced degrees. A mentoring program helps students focus on how they want to apply their skills and knowledge beyond graduation.

■ Tarleton State University
Stephenville, TX

Compiled by: Mark Holtorf, Theatre Area Coordinator

Degrees Offered:

BFA in theatre (theatre generalist)

Minors Offered:

Theatre

Music

Population of Department(s): Approximately 250 students in the Department of Fine Arts, with 40 theatre majors

Audition to Declare a Theatre/Musical Theatre Major? No

Three things you would like our readers to know about your performing arts department:

1. Excellent facilities with four performance spaces, a costume shop, a scene shop, and eight dressing rooms.
2. The emphasis is on technical theatre.
3. Numerous theatre internship opportunities, including study abroad.

■ Texas Christian University
Fort Worth, TX

Compiled by: Dr. Harry B. Parker, Professor and Chair, Department of Theatre

Degrees Offered:

BA in theatre

BFA in theatre, emphasis in acting

BFA in theatre, emphasis in design

BFA in theatre, emphasis in musical theatre

BFA in theatre, emphasis in production

BFA in theatre, emphasis in theatre studies

Minors Offered:

None

Population of Department(s): Approximately 40 BA and 90 BFA (all emphases); approximately 130 total

Audition to Declare a Theatre/Musical Theatre Major? BA is open to all TCU students without an audition/portfolio review. All BFA emphases require an audition (acting, musical theatre) or portfolio review (design, production, theatre studies) and interview for admission.

Three things you would like our readers to know about your performing arts department:

1. TCU is home of the Trinity Shakespeare Festival, an award-winning, professional Equity summer company that annually employs 12–15 TCU students to work side-by-side with five to six Equity actors and professional directors, designers, and stage managers to create acclaimed, indoor Shakespeare productions in true repertory.

2. TCU is located in one of the nation's largest professional theatre markets, Dallas-Fort Worth, and TCU theatre students regularly participate in professional internships at excellent professional theatres, including Dallas Theatre Center, Circle Theatre, Amphibian Stage Productions, Hip Pocket Theatre, Jubilee Theatre, Stage West, Theatre Arlington, Water Tower Theatre, Bass Performance Hall, AT&T Performing Arts Center, and many others. We also frequently produce co-productions with local professional theatres, including recent ones with Casa Manana, Circle Theatre, and Amphibian Stage Productions.

3. TCU offers a BFA showcase (alternating between New York and Los Angeles) for senior students to showcase their work for professional agents and casting directors.

■ Texas Woman's University
Denton, TX

Compiled by: Dr. Patrick Bynane, Program Director and Associate Professor of Drama

Degrees Offered:

BA in drama
BA in drama with Texas teacher's certification
MA in drama

Minors Offered:

Drama

Population of Department(s): Approximately 65

Audition to Declare a Theatre/Musical Theatre Major? No

Three things you would like our readers to know about your performing arts department:

1. We offer a liberal arts, private school atmosphere in a public school setting with public university value.

2. We pride ourselves on giving our students individualized attention and a student-centered curriculum.

3. Located in the Dallas-Fort Worth metro area, our program is close to a wealth of cultural and artistic opportunities that we happily incorporate into our program of study.

University of St. Thomas
Houston, TX

Compiled by: Claire M. McDonald, MFA, Fine Arts and Drama Chair

Degrees Offered:

BA in drama

Minors Offered:

Drama

Population of Department(s): 60 (15 majors)

Audition to Declare a Theatre/Musical Theatre Major? No (Yes for scholarship consideration)

Three things you would like our readers to know about your performing arts department:

1. We provide outstanding attention to each individual's artistic development.
2. We offer extraordinary onstage performance and backstage technical opportunities for majors and non-majors.
3. Our liberal arts core curriculum supports and encourages the drama student's other interests and opens avenues for many future career directions.

University of Texas at Austin
Department of Theatre and Dance
Austin, TX

Compiled by: Lucien Douglas, Associate Professor, Director of Performance Division and Head of Acting Program

Degrees Offered:

BFA in theatre studies (this is for students wanting to be high school theatre teachers and directors)
BFA in dance (including BFA in dance plus teacher certification)
BA in theatre and dance
Actor training program (undergraduate pre-professional actor training)

Minors Offered:

Concentration offered (at undergraduate level): musical theatre, technical theatre, stage management

Population of Department(s): 350 undergraduate students, 77 grad students (includes master's and doctoral programs in performance as public practice and master's programs in design and design technology, drama and theatre for youth and communities, dance, directing, playwriting)

Audition to Declare a Theatre/Musical Theatre Major? Yes, auditions are required for actor training program and musical theatre emphasis; interview required for BFA in theatre studies (teacher training).

Three things you would like our readers to know about your performing arts department:

1. The Department of Theatre and Dance at the University of Texas at Austin has a highly distinguished faculty of approximately 45 scholars and working professional theatre artists. The department presents numerous productions annually, including three major dance concerts, on its mainstage and laboratory theatre spaces. It has a special dedication to devised and original work, producing three to four new scripts per year in a laboratory setting, as well as presenting its nationally recognized New Works Festival bi-annually.

2. Alumni of our program have distinguished themselves with great success in all areas of theatre, film, and TV; among those actively working in the profession are Robert Schenkkan (Pulitzer Prize for *Kentucky Cycle,* 2013 production of *All The Way* starring Bryan Cranston); Marcia Gay Harden (Oscar for *Pollock,* Tony Award for *God of Carnage*); Kevin Alejandro (*Golden Boy* on ABC-TV); Todd Lowe (*True Blood* on HBO-TV); Kevin Adams (Tony Award–winning lighting designer); in addition to many alumni working as artists and/or scholars in both the academic and professional worlds of theatre and dance.

3. Our undergraduate actor training program endeavors to prepare students with the foundational training and education necessary for tackling their future theatrical interests, whether these lie in advanced training at the graduate level or the pursuit of a professional acting career. In so doing, courses taught by a professional faculty of working artists will address past, present, and anticipated trends in a professional actor's career.

   Curriculum, guest artist workshops, and performance experiences will reflect the uniqueness of the University of Texas at Austin Department of Theatre and Dance by offering classes and practical experiences in work for the stage, film, and TV; devised work; and new media. Attentive to acting for the camera, the undergraduate actor training program also offers collaborations with such programs as the UT Department of Radio-Television-Film; under the tutelage of professional guest artists working in the industry (as well as an option to participate in the UT Semester in Los Angeles program), students will have the opportunity for learning skills in managing the business aspects of a professional acting career.

■ University of Texas at El Paso
El Paso, TX

Compiled by: Joel Murray, Chair of Theatre and Dance and Head of Acting

Degrees Offered:

BFAs in performance, musical theatre, stage management, design/technical, and dance
BAs in performance, design/technical, theatre education, dance education, and a generalist in theatre

Minors Offered:

Performance

Design/technical

Generalist

Population of Department(s): Approximately 170

Audition to Declare a Theatre/Musical Theatre Major? No. Students wishing to be BFAs are accepted on a probationary status. If they meet standards, they remain in their chosen degree program.

Three things you would like our readers to know about your performing arts department:

1. Faculty have a rich, professional background.
2. We offer an uncommon amount of performance opportunities, including four to five musicals a year.
3. We have a new relationship with a professional theatre company, Frontera Repertory.

Utah

■ Brigham Young University
Provo, UT

Compiled by: Tim Threlfall, Chair of Music, Dance, Theatre Program

Population of School: 34,000

Conservatory or Liberal Arts: Conservatory-style pre-professional in a liberal arts setting

Degrees Offered:

BFA in music, dance, theatre (MDT)
BFA in acting
BA in theatre studies
BA in theatre education

Population of Department(s): Approximately 400; 65 major in the BFA MDT program and 40 in the BFA acting program

Theatre Scholarships Available: Half tuition. Very limited due to the extremely low cost of tuition for members of the Church of Jesus Christ of Latter-day Saints, which owns and operates the university.

Audition Required for BFA: Yes for MDT prior to admission to the university. BFA acting auditions following admission to the university.

Audition Required for BA/BS/BM: No

Pre-screen Video Audition Required: Yes, MDT auditions are conducted via a pre-screen audition due November 15, followed by an invitation-only live audition the first weekend of January in Provo. The initial video (DVD) auditions are open to any interested individual. BFA acting auditions are open only to those already accepted to the university. A minimum of two auditions are required for admission to the BFA acting program. Admission to the MDT program does not include acceptance to the university. Admission to BYU is highly competitive and involves a process separate from the MDT program audition.

Attends Unifieds: No

Number of Students Auditioning Each Year: Varies

Number of Students Accepted Each Year: MDT admits 16, BFA acting accepts 10, BA is open enrollment

Cut Program or Audition to Remain in Program: No. We are committed to the success of each student we accept into the program.

Minors in Musical Theatre/Acting: No

Prominent Alumni: Neil LaBute, Aaron Eckhart, Mireille Enos, Will Swenson

What do you look for in a potential student?

A commitment to personal excellence as a performer, a learner, and an individual.

What are some of the auditors' pet peeves?

A lack of preparation. The MDT website is particular and specific in regards to the taped audition presentation. Auditions that follow the format are always at a distinct advantage.

What are your audition requirements?

For audition DVD for MDT: For music, two musical theatre excerpts that demonstrate classical theatre and belt styles. One ballad and one up-tempo selection are recommended. For dance, prepare and perform a one- to two-minute solo that demonstrates your skill in one or more of the following dance forms: ballet, jazz (various styles), and/or modern dance. The solo should showcase your technical skill and performance ability. For theatre, two contrasting monologues from established play, musical, or film scripts. One selection should be comedic; one should be serious/dramatic. Both selections should allow the student to reveal basic honesty and clarity of objectives.

In your eyes, what makes up an excellent college audition monologue? Song?

Any material, no matter how "overdone," is still engaging if it is spectacularly performed. Finding something fresh is always advisable, but if you do an old standard wonderfully and it is your best work, don't hesitate to use it. Stay within your age range and type. It is difficult to adjudicate the work of a 19-year-old if he or she has chosen to play a 70-year-old with an accent!

If you require a pre-screen video audition, what do you look for in those submissions?

Material that reveals the individual.

Can you walk me through what I can expect at your on-campus auditions?

It's much more of a group audition. Students will be taught a dance audition, and they will be given an opportunity to do a dance solo if they choose. They should be prepared with the same monologues/songs as the pre-screen and be prepared to work on the monologues as well as the songs. We do individual coaching with them to see how we might work with them.

What's a memorable audition you can remember?

We are always looking for auditions that reveal the personality and soul of the performer. Each person is an individual and unique. That individuality revealed in the work, whether while dancing, singing, or acting, is the "edge" we look for. We're looking for someone who seems as if he or she is really communicating with another human being in his or her monologues and songs.

What is your biggest piece of advice for potential students auditioning?

BYU operates under a dual mandate to educate students both in their field of study and spiritually. This unique blend of the sacred and secular is what makes BYU unique. Many find this duality of purpose exactly what they are seeking. For others not interested in a spiritual education, BYU would not be the right choice.

BYU is owned and operated by the Church of Jesus Christ of Latter-day Saints. All who attend the university are required to take religion courses and adhere to a very strong "Honor Code." This code includes complete abstinence from alcohol and tobacco, as well as sexual activity outside the bonds of legal marriage. Dress and grooming standards that include modest clothing, hair above the ears and collar for men, no facial hair for men beyond a moustache, no excessive hair colors or styles, and no tattoos are also enforced.

If I audition for your BFA musical theatre program, but don't get accepted, do you still consider me for your BFA acting program or your BA program?

Yes. It is a separate audition. For BFA acting, you have to be accepted first to the university and then audition once you are there to get in.

After I audition, is there a good way to follow up?

November 15 is the last date for submission of an audition DVD. Students selected for the live audition in January are notified before the end of the fall term. Those invited to the live audition usually number about 30. Slightly more than one-half of those invited to the live audition will be admitted to the program for the following fall. Notification of acceptance into the program generally is completed within three weeks of the live audition. Very little follow-up on the part of student applicants is necessary.

Would I get a showcase at the end of senior year?

Yes. BYU graduating BFA seniors travel to New York for a showcase each April. Generally, 12–18 students attend the senior showcase each year.

Do I have to audition to be accepted into the showcase?

The showcase is by audition and open to both BFA performance program majors.

Where are showcases held, and are they successful?

Showcases are held in New York City. This will be year 12, and yes, they are successful.

Will I be able to audition/perform as a freshman?

Freshmen are required to play "as cast" in the mainstage musical(s) in their freshman year. All MDT students must perform in the ensemble of a production once while in the program.

What ways can I be involved with the department aside from performing?

BYU Theatre and Media Arts Department has an extensive film program. BFA performance majors are encouraged to work in the numerous student films produced on campus. In addition, the LDS Church operates a fully functioning film studio minutes from the BYU campus. The Utah film market is very active with recent films, such as *127 Hours,* shot in the state, and film properties, such as *Napoleon Dynamite,* which began as a BYU student film, provide additional opportunities.

As of 2013, nearly half of the entire BYU student body was also employed by BYU. With fewer graduate programs than most universities of its size, BYU has more work-study and research opportunities for undergraduates than many similar institutions.

An unprecedented 77% of all BYU students speak a second language due to LDS Church missionary service. Opportunities for cultural exchanges and study abroad at BYU are exceptional.

Say I get a BA rather than a BFA. Will I actually get to perform?

Most BYU campus productions are open to anyone who auditions.

I love to sing, but I don't consider myself a dancer. Can I still seek a degree in musical theatre at your school?

The MDT degree is granted one-third from music, one-third from dance, and one-third from theatre. Equal emphasis is given to all three disciplines. However, exceptional talent in two of the three areas will qualify an applicant for the program. There are also 7.5 elective hours that allow MDT students to focus on an area of particular interest or special need. The program truly is interdisciplinary.

I want to get a BFA in acting, but I also love to sing. Can BFA/BA acting students take voice lessons with top voice faculty?

Yes. BFA acting and BFA MDT students take many classes together, and BFA acting students are required to take private vocal instruction.

Do you discourage or encourage students to audition for theatre outside of the department during the academic year?

About 75% of all MDT students work in at least one summer stock company during their time in the program. There is also a requirement within the MDT program to work in one show outside the university prior to graduation.

Does your school regularly work in conjunction with any regional theatres?

The BYU MDT program works with Tuacahn Center for the Arts in St. George, UT. Tuacahn is a LORT-contracted theatre with an annual budget of about $12 million per year and is housed in a $23 million state-of-the-art outdoor amphitheatre.

What do students typically do during the summers? Do you actively promote participation in summer theatre auditions?

BYU has unofficial connections with at least three professional theatre companies. While no roles in these companies are guaranteed to BYU students, traditionally many BYU students and alumni work regularly with these professional venues. At least one is a LORT theatre that offers a six-month season and EMC points. Many BYU students have joined AEA from work with this organization. Sundance Summer Theatre, the Jackson Hole Playhouse, and Coeur d'Alene Summer Theatre typically employ BYU students.

How many musicals versus straight plays do you do in a season?

MDT produces one mainstage musical in a 1,400-seat venue every other year. On the opposite years, two musicals are presented; one in a 500-seat proscenium and one "new" musical in a flexible black box. BYU is a member of the National Alliance for Music Theatre (NAMT) and attends the NAMT conference each year in New York looking for new musicals to mount. BYU recently produced the made-for-television new musical *Berlin,* which garnered an Emmy and a CINE Golden Eagle Award. The show was broadcast on the satellite network owned by the LDS Church and was available to more than 50 million homes worldwide. The MDT program was one of the first collegiate programs to mount Andrew Lloyd Webber's *Phantom of the Opera* in 2013.

What are some of your alumni up to? Do you have an active alumni network?

BYU carefully tracks its alumni and their work. The BYU MDT website offers a document with the names of the numerous Broadway shows, Broadway national tours, regional theatres, films, TV shows, and other entertainment projects our alumni are involved with. The list is too extensive for this format. Google BYU MDT and the first reference will take you directly to the website. Then look under the heading "alumni."

What is the portfolio/interview process for a technical theatre student?

We interview technical theatre students on campus in Provo and at regional high school theatre conferences as well as KCACTF regional gatherings.

What do you expect to see on a technical theatre résumé?

The theatre studies major with an emphasis in specific technical areas.

I'm interested in lighting, sound design, and stage management. What major should I go for? Can I minor?

The theatre studies major with an emphasis in specific technical areas.

■ Middlebury College
Middlebury, VT

Compiled by: Cheryl Faraone, Professor of Theatre, Department of Theatre & Dance, Professor of Gender, Sexuality & Feminist Studies Program

Degrees Offered:

Theatre

Dance

Minors Offered:

Theatre

Dance

Population of Department(s): 30–40 in the theatre program, 25 in the dance program

Audition to Declare a Theatre/Musical Theatre Major? No

Three things you would like our readers to know about your performing arts department:

1. Students in theatre study all aspects of the art form and may elect senior work in acting, directing, playwriting, design for the theatre, theatre and social change, and so on. Most graduates of the department continue in professional or academic theatre or work in film and TV.

2. The theatre program is affiliated with PTP/NYC, a New York–based, 28-year-old, award-winning professional off-Broadway theatre company that does an annual summer season. Students may audition for roles in the company or work in the areas of design and stage management. For more information about PTP, go to www.potomactheatreproject.org.

3. Our alum network is extensive, particularly in New York; Los Angeles; Washington, DC; and Chicago.

Virginia

■ Eastern Mennonite University
Harrisonburg, VA

Compiled by: Heidi Winters Vogel, Associate Professor of Theater

Degrees Offered:
Theater with concentrations in acting, directing, devised and applied theater, design and stage management

Minors Offered:
Theater

Population of Department(s): 25

Audition to Declare a Theatre/Musical Theatre Major? No

Three things you would like our readers to know about your performing arts department:

1. EMU theater emphasizes devised performance and applied theater to foster justice and model peace to develop intelligent, faithful, and compassionate artists.
2. We produce ambitious seasons of canonical works and plays by underrepresented voices.
3. We integrate performance, history, and theory in the classroom, on the stage, and in the studio.

■ George Mason University
School of Theater
Fairfax, VA

Compiled by: Ken Elston, Director

Degrees Offered:

Bachelor:
Design and technical theater
Performance (acting and directing)
Playwriting and dramaturgy

Teaching theater arts PK–12

BA/accelerated masters of arts management

BFA concentrations:

Design for stage and screen

Performance for stage and screen (acting and directing)

Writing and dramaturgy for stage and screen

Certificate in musical theater, BA or BFA

Certification for musical theater

Graduate studies:

BA/accelerated masters of arts management

Teaching theater arts PK–12 graduate certificate

Minors Offered:

Theater

Population of Department(s): 150

Audition to Declare a Theatre/Musical Theatre Major? Yes

Three things you would like our readers to know about your performing arts department:

1. Taught by working professionals from the vibrant DC arts region.
2. Offers a liberal arts education in all facets of stage and screen.
3. Six productions each season offer opportunities for all Mason students, freshmen through seniors, onstage and off stage, including networking and master class opportunities with professionals from across the United States.

■ Hollins University
Roanoke, VA

Compiled by: Ernie Zulia, Theatre Department Chair

Degrees Offered:

Theatre

Minors Offered:

Theatre

Arts management

Population of Department(s): 30

Audition to Declare a Theatre/Musical Theatre Major: No

Three things you would like our readers to know about your performing arts department:

1. Hollins Theatre was recently named one of the top 20 Best College Theatres by the 2014 Princeton Review and is the winner of eight awards from the 2013 KCACTF. Hollins University was also the host of the Region IV KCACTF in February 2014.

2. The intimate program at Hollins Theatre allows for tremendous individual attention and focus for each student in whichever areas interest him or her. Different areas include acting, directing, technical direction, design and playwriting, history, and literature.

3. Hollins Theatre also provides a recently renovated state-of-the-art theatre facility, which includes a student-run studio theatre.

■ University of Mary Washington
Fredericksburg, VA

Compiled by: Gregg Stull, Chair, Department of Theatre & Dance and Chair, Department of Music

Degrees Offered:

Theatre

Minors Offered:

Musical theatre

Population of Department(s): 45 majors, 200 active students

Audition to Declare a Theatre/Musical Theatre Major? No

Three things you would like our readers to know about your performing arts department:

1. We are a student-centered department that values strong interaction and mentoring between faculty and students.

2. We offer a strong career focus that enhances our liberal arts perspective.

3. Our proximity to Washington, DC, and New York, NY, provides relevant professional connections for our students.

Washington

■ Central Washington University
Ellensburg, WA

Compiled by: Scott Robinson, Department Chair

Degrees Offered:

BFA in performance

BFA in design and production with options in scenic design and technology, costume design and technology, lighting design and technology, sound design and technology, stage and production management

BFA in musical theatre

BA in theatre studies

MA in theatre studies

Minors Offered:

Theatre generalist

Apparel design

Dance performance

Non-profit organization management

Theatre management specialization

Population of Department(s): 120 majors, 49 pre-majors, 29 minors

Audition to Declare a Theatre/Musical Theatre Major? Yes, audition into the BFA program is required. The initial screening is done through getacceptd.com. Pre-admission courses required for BA program.

Three things you would like our readers to know about your performing arts department:

1. Small, vibrant, and growing program with 85%–100% of graduates each year placed in skill-specific jobs, or grad programs, within six months of graduation.

2. Small classes of 12 give students the personal connection with faculty that leads to effective education and learning, in a liberal art environment.

3. Our alumni continue to LEARN. DO. LIVE. in professional settings, which include New York City; Los Angeles; Portland, OR; Orlando, FL; and Seattle, WA; among others.

■ Saint Martin's University
Lacey, WA

Compiled by: David Hlavsa, Chair, Theatre Arts

Degrees Offered:

Theatre

Minors Offered:

Theatre

Population of Department(s): 12

Audition to Declare a Theatre/Musical Theatre Major? No

Three things you would like our readers to know about your performing arts department:

1. If you're passionate about theatre, the great advantage of coming to a small school like Saint Martin's is that you get to do it all: acting, directing, playwriting, design, and tech.

2. It's a hands-on program—before you graduate, you're expected to act a major role, direct a play, write a play, and undertake a major design/technical project—opportunities you may not get at a larger school.

3. If you find that you really do want to be an actor, a director, a costume designer, or a playwright, Saint Martin's offers intense mentorship and training.

■ Seattle University
Seattle, WA

Compiled by: Ki Gottberg, Professor of Theatre/Fine Arts

Degrees Offered:

Theatre: performance track, technical track

Minors Offered:

Theatre

Population of Department(s): 45 majors

Audition to Declare a Theatre/Musical Theatre Major? Yes, entrance review required

Three things you would like our readers to know about your performing arts department:

1. Our students are nimble—they do everything related to theatre, not just their main interest. They have small classes with one-on-one learning with working theater professionals throughout the school year.

2. Our students are well educated—they are required to take the CORE curriculum in this Jesuit University. They have much to draw from that informs their art.

3. Our students get work—we have interns at all the major and many smaller theatres in Seattle. Our students write, act, design, dramaturge, and work backstage around town, and they also are confident and knowledgeable self-producers in this vibrant theatre city of Seattle.

University of Puget Sound
Tacoma, WA

Compiled by: Jess K. Smith, Assistant Professor of Theatre Arts

Degrees Offered:

BA in theatre arts

Minors Offered:

Theatre arts

Population of Department(s): 50–70

Audition to Declare a Theatre/Musical Theatre Major? No

Three things you would like our readers to know about your performing arts department:

1. Students in theatre arts come to the University of Puget Sound for the chance to make connections across disciplines through an exceptional liberal arts education, the unique location in the beautiful Pacific Northwest near the thriving artistic community of Seattle, a campus environment that celebrates and supports student initiative, and the opportunity to explore all aspects of making theatre, starting with a strong dramaturgical foundation with deep applications in acting, directing, design, and history.

2. Students have a chance to participate in theatre in a plethora of ways on campus. From the two faculty-directed mainstage productions each year; the festival of student-directed one-acts; the improv and sketch comedy troupe (Ubiquitous They); a festival of student-written, -directed, -acted, and -produced one-acts (Towne Crier); a festival of full-length, student-initiated work (Infinite Monkeys); to the culminating Senior Theatre Festival (a festival of four full-length plays selected, directed, and produced by the senior class of theatre majors and presented throughout the month of April). It's easy to get involved in theatre as an actor, director, designer, dramaturg, stage manager, and producer.

3. "The University of Puget Sound is a bright spot on the map of American higher education. Students searching for thoughtful professors, a lively interdisciplinary vibe, friendly classmates, and a beautiful setting ought to add the university to their short list." —Colleges That Change Lives

University of Washington
School of Drama
Seattle, WA

Compiled by: Andrew Tsao, Associate Professor, Head, Undergraduate Drama Program

Degrees Offered:

BA in drama, areas of emphasis include performance, design, and general drama

Minors Offered:

None

Population of Department(s): 65 majors, more than 100 non-majors, and more than 300 students enrolled in introductory courses

Audition to Declare a Theatre/Musical Theatre Major? No audition required.

Three things you would like our readers to know about your performing arts department:

1. Comprehensive BA education aligned with the College of Arts and Sciences mission of teaching critical thinking, creativity, collaboration, entrepreneurship, and scholarship.

2. Our student-run theatre company, the Undergraduate Theatre Society, provides a fully functioning theatre space for students to apply classroom learning in a professional environment. Students administer, plan, produce, direct, design, and perform a full season of shows each year.

3. Our faculty teaches both graduate and undergraduate classes. Students in the BA program have access to master teachers, workshops, guests, and more because our department believes in providing the best undergraduate theatre education possible.

■ Carthage College

Kenosha, WI

Compiled by: Professor Martin McClendon, Department Chair

Degrees Offered:

BA in theatre

BA in theatre performance

BA in theatre technical production and design (scene design emphasis, costume design emphasis, stage management emphasis)

Our music theatre major is an interdisciplinary major shared with the music department. Teacher licensure is also available.

Population of Department(s): 82 theatre majors and minors, 36 dance minors, 28 music theatre majors

Audition to Declare a Theatre/Musical Theatre Major? Yes

Three things you would like our readers to know about your performing arts department:

1. Carthage Theatre offers intensive theatre training within a liberal arts environment. Small class sizes and individual attention, coupled with our senior thesis capstone requirement, make for a unique academic theatre experience.

2. Carthage Theatre commissions new plays by prominent playwrights every year. Our students have premiered works by Eric Simonson, Laura Jacqmin, and Jeffrey Hatcher, among others.

3. Our ideal location, situated between Milwaukee and Chicago, and two thriving arts communities, coupled with extensive J-term travel opportunities, mean that Carthage theatre students can explore the wider world of theatre and dance.

■ Marquette University
Milwaukee, WI

Compiled by: Stephen Hudson-Mairet, Department Chair

Degrees Offered:

BA in theatre arts

Minors Offered:

Theatre

Population of Department(s): 55

Audition to Declare a Theatre/Musical Theatre Major? No

Three things you would like our readers to know about your performing arts department:

1. Our nationally accredited (NAST), professionally oriented theatre arts program is taught in small classes in a strong liberal arts environment. We provide intensive personalized instruction from our expert faculty.

2. Students are active from the first day in our mainstage program, which produces five shows each season: a musical, a classic, theatre for young audiences, and a theatre and social justice play—a mix of traditional comedies, dramas, and new works.

3. We look for interested and interesting students seeking to use their art form to create change in the world.

■ University of Wisconsin—Parkside
Kenosha, WI

Compiled by: Lisa Kornetsky, Chair, Theatre Arts Department

Degrees Offered:

Theatre with concentrations in acting, design/technology, directing/management

Minors Offered:

Theatre

Population of Department(s): We are capped at 65 students

Audition to Declare a Theatre/Musical Theatre Major? Yes

Three things you would like our readers to know about your performing arts department:

1. We have a company model with students, faculty, and staff working closely together, focused on high production values and students first.

2. Located between Milwaukee and Chicago, we have strong connections with professional theatres throughout the region.

3. Our program won a statewide teaching excellence award given by the University System's Board of Regents in 2009.

■ University of Wisconsin—Stevens Point

Department of Theatre and Dance
Stevens Point, WI

Compiled by: Gary Olsen, Chair

Degrees Offered:

BA in dance

BA in drama

BFA in acting

BFA in design and technology

BFA in musical theatre

Minors Offered:

Drama

Dance

Population of Department(s): 170 majors and minors

Audition to Declare a Theatre/Musical Theatre Major? Yes

Three things you would like our readers to know about your performing arts department:

1. Selective admission leading to small class size and personal attention.

2. Exceptional faculty and renowned guest artists.

3. Excellent training at a public school cost.

■ University of Wisconsin—Whitewater

Whitewater, WI

Compiled by: Marshall Anderson, Professor and Chair of Department

Degrees Offered:

BA in theatre

BSE in theatre, theatre education

BFA in theatre, performance

BFA in theatre, design/technology

BFA in theatre, stage management

BFA in theatre, management/promotions

Minors Offered:

Theatre

Dance

Arts management

Population of Department(s): Approximately 80 majors, 55 dance minors, 20 arts management minors, 15 theatre minors

Audition to Declare a Theatre/Musical Theatre Major? No audition to declare any of the majors or minors. For the BFA program, there is an official application process after one year, with entrance based on talent and GPA.

Three things you would like our readers to know about your performing arts department:

1. Our academic year season consists of six productions, including one musical/opera, one touring children's theatre production, and our annual dance concert. These productions are performed in either our 400-seat proscenium Barnett Theatre or our Hicklin Studio Theatre.

2. We also offer a two-show summer season in our Hicklin Studio Theatre; this season normally features one small musical as well as one other production.

3. We are a "hands-on, learning-by-doing" department, offering students a wide range of experiences, including several guest and visiting artists every year.

27691044R00176

Made in the USA
Middletown, DE
19 December 2015